Walter Benjamin and the Critique of Political Economy

Critical Theory and the Critique of Society Series

In a time marked by crises and the rise of right-wing authoritarian populism, **Critical Theory and the Critique of Society** intends to renew the critical theory of capitalist society exemplified by the Frankfurt School and critical Marxism's critiques of social domination, authoritarianism, and social regression by expounding the development of such a notion of critical theory, from its founding thinkers, through its subterranean and parallel strands of development, to its contemporary formulations.

Series editors: **Werner Bonefield**, University of York, UK and **Chris O'Kane**, University of Texas Rio Grande Valley, USA

Editorial Board:
Bev Best, Sociology, Concordia University
John Abromeit, History, SUNY, Buffalo State, USA
Samir Gandesha, Humanities, Simon Fraser University
Christian Lotz, Philosophy, Michigan State University
Patrick Murray, Philosophy, Creighton University
José Antonio Zamora Zaragoza, Philosophy, Spain
Dirk Braunstein, Institute of Social Research, Frankfurt
Matthias Rothe, German, University of Minnesota
Marina Vishmidt, Cultural Studies, Goldsmiths University
Verena Erlenbusch, Philosophy, University of Memphis
Elena Louisa Lange, Japanese Studies/Philology and Philosophy, University of Zurich
Marcel Stoetzler, Sociology, University of Bangor
Moishe Postone†, History, University of Chicago
Mathias Nilges, Literature, St Xavier University
Charlotte Baumann, Philosophy, Sussex/TU Berlin
Amy De'ath, Contemporary Literature and Culture, King's College London
Rochelle Duford, Philosophy, University of Hartford
Edith Gonzalez, Humanities, Universidad Intercultural del Estado de Puebla, México
Sami Khatib, Art, Leuphana University
Dimitra Kotouza, Education, University of Lincoln
Claudia Leeb, Political Science, Washington State University
Jordi Maiso, Philosophy, Complutense University of Madrid
Cat Moir, Germanic Studies, University of Sydney
Kirstin Munro, Political Science, University of Texas, Rio Grande
Duy Lap Nguyen, Modern and Classical Languages, University of Houston

Available titles:
Right-wing Culture in Contemporary Capitalism, Mathias Nilges
Adorno and Neoliberalism, Charles Andrew Prusik
Toward a Critical Theory of Nature, Carl Cassegård
Spectacular Logic in Hegel and Debord, Eric-John Russell

Walter Benjamin and the Critique of Political Economy

A New Historical Materialism

Duy Lap Nguyen

BLOOMSBURY ACADEMIC
LONDON • NEW YORK • OXFORD • NEW DELHI • SYDNEY

BLOOMSBURY ACADEMIC
Bloomsbury Publishing Plc
50 Bedford Square, London, WC1B 3DP, UK
1385 Broadway, New York, NY 10018, USA
29 Earlsfort Terrace, Dublin 2, Ireland

BLOOMSBURY, BLOOMSBURY ACADEMIC and the Diana logo
are trademarks of Bloomsbury Publishing Plc

First published in Great Britain 2022
This paperback edition published in 2024

Copyright © Duy Lap Nguyen, 2022

Duy Lap Nguyen has asserted his right under the Copyright, Designs
and Patents Act, 1988, to be identified as Author of this work.

For legal purposes the Acknowledgments on pp. viii–ix constitute
an extension of this copyright page.

Series design by Ben Anslow

All rights reserved. No part of this publication may be reproduced or transmitted
in any form or by any means, electronic or mechanical, including photocopying,
recording, or any information storage or retrieval system, without prior
permission in writing from the publishers.

Bloomsbury Publishing Plc does not have any control over, or responsibility for,
any third-party websites referred to or in this book. All internet addresses given
in this book were correct at the time of going to press. The author and publisher
regret any inconvenience caused if addresses have changed or sites have
ceased to exist, but can accept no responsibility for any such changes.

A catalogue record for this book is available from the British Library.

A catalog record for this book is available from the Library of Congress.

ISBN: HB: 978-1-3501-8042-0
PB: 978-1-3503-3105-1
ePDF: 978-1-3501-8043-7
eBook: 978-1-3501-8044-4

Series: Critical Theory and the Critique of Society

Typeset by Integra Software Services Pvt. Ltd.

To find out more about our authors and books visit www.bloomsbury.com
and sign up for our newsletters.

For Giovanni

Contents

Acknowledgments		viii
Preface: Historical Materialism and Profane Messianism		x
Introduction: Capitalism and Eternity		1
1	Knowledge and Ephemeral Experience in the Coming Philosophy	21
2	The Doctrine of Right and the Critique of Violence: Benjamin's Anarchist Revision of Kant's Moral Philosophy	41
3	The Aesthetic Extreme and the Dialectic of Allegory: Schmitt, Lukács, and the Origin of the *Trauerspiel* Book	63
4	Mechanical and Historical Time in Benjamin and Heidegger	107
5	Neo-Kantianism and the Critique of Political Economy	123
6	Fourier or the Arcades: The Liberation of Work and Desire or an Eternity of the New	151
7	Benjamin and Bataille: The General Economy of the Arcades or Expenditure in the Age of Mechanical Reproduction	193
Conclusion: The Angel of History, the Owl of Minerva, and the Eternal Return		225
Notes		232
Selected Bibliography		277
Index		280

Acknowledgments

For their inspiration, support, and encouragement, I thank, most of all, my wife, my son, and my daughter. I also thank Marco and Massimo for picking us up in Milan, and the *nonne gemelle*, Cari and Stefi, for the trip to the Alps where we passed two sunny weeks of the global pandemic, eating pizzoccheri and shopping for shoes. By now, hopefully no one remembers the priest who almost screwed up the wedding by double-booking us with a funeral. I thank Julie and Cedric for their parenting tips, toys, and hand-me-down clothes, Keith E. McNeal, Ivan and Na-Rae, Professor Hue-Tam Ho Tai for Thanksgiving in Cambridge and for putting Giovanni to work picking apples in the post-peak Fall foliage at sunset. I thank the Asia Center at Harvard for loaning me the desk where I finished the manuscript, Howard Eiland for the translated volumes of Benjamin's work upon which this study depends and for sharing his profound expertise over cookies and tea, Mathew Charles for his help with the "Coming Philosophy," Neil Larsen, Christopher Connery, Gabriel Rockhill, Chris O'Kane, and Werner Bonefeld. Of course, all the mistakes in this book are my fault.

I conceived of this project while reading the esoteric Heideggerian-Situationist version of the end-of-politics thesis. At the time, it seemed like a plausible way of weaving a professorial robe in the anteroom where I wanted to wake sleeping beauty by boxing the scullery boy in the ear, believing the shock would resound through the halls of academe. But in the substratum, there was always the dull humming emitted by the endless podcasts and newsfeeds about the ever-greater disasters that capitalism, determined to destroy the natural world before dying a natural death, still had in store for the angel of history.

The almost calculable moment in economic and technical development when we could have dissolved existing society, when the lit fuse could have been severed, elapsed ages ago. The system would not be undone by terrorist violence, the refusal of work, or even class conflict. "History," however, which "knows nothing of the evil infinity contained in the image of ... two wrestlers locked in eternal combat," is not only the history of class struggle, but also of the contradictory movement of capital. Its owners, therefore, remain "doomed by the inner contradictions that in the course of development will become deadly," but as it turns out, not only for capitalism but also for the wrestlers who thought they could go on fighting forever.[1] Confronting the unimaginable catastrophe is a hapless humanity that Giorgio Agamben described as a parody of the classless society, a global petite bourgeoisie, governed by a "spectacular-democratic world organization" with the "task of managing the survival of *humanity in an uninhabitable world*."[2]

But the slogan "human extinction or classless society" was mass reproduced and repeated so often that it became a banality. Like Benjamin's view of mechanical warfare, whose "most disastrous aspects ... [result from] the gaping discrepancy between the gigantic power of technology and the minuscule moral illumination it affords," the looming planetary disaster is one from which no pathos arises.[3] It is as though we were trapped in a vulgar new version of the hallucinatory projection that paralyzed Louis Auguste Blanqui at the end of his life, re-watching the history of humanity in time-lapse photography. The "most brilliant civilizations disappear without leaving a trace," and their highest achievements are only a testament to our eternal transience.[4] "So much meaning, so much forfeiture to death."[5] All that remains, I suppose, is hope in the hopelessness of salvation itself, hope in a messianism whose method is nihilism.

Preface: Historical Materialism and Profane Messianism

It is typical today in the scholarship to reject the idea that Benjamin's writings can be neatly divided into an early theological-metaphysical phase and a later historical materialist one. There seems to be no such consensus, however, on how to define the two different stages of Benjamin's work. If the two phases, therefore, are continuous, what this continuity consists of is still a subject of controversy. Nevertheless, the tendency that seems to be prevalent today rejects the decisively non-religious reading of Benjamin proposed by Giorgio Agamben, adopting a perspective resembling what Agamben described as the "scientific mythologeme" of the originary ambivalence of the sacred.[6]

Thus, Peter Gordon, for example, challenges a "narrative [that] would confirm Benjamin's reputation as a resolute secularist," arguing that from beginning to end Benjamin's thinking is "poised in indecision between a theological and a nontheological understanding of modernity."[7] Benjamin's work is defined by an "ambivalent secularization," expressed in figures like the mechanical chess-playing Turk, operated in secret by a dwarf called theology.[8] According to Gordon, this ambivalence defines Benjamin's philosophy of history as well as the history of philosophy that operates in the background of his theory. According to this theory, modernity is not characterized by the "disappearance of religion but only its *concealment*."[9] Like Carl Schmitt, then, Benjamin believed that the secularism of modern society is only an appearance that disguises the persistence of theology.

Against such religious readings of Benjamin's work, *A New Historical Materialism* proposes a strictly profane interpretation of both his early philosophy and his later historical materialism. Contrary to what critics have argued, the secular idea of redemption that appears in Benjamin's later writings was not the result of his turn toward Marxism, of his conversion to "the profane cause of the class struggle."[10] This view assumes a theological opposition between religious salvation and creaturely life, an opposition that Benjamin rejected in favor of a completely secular idea of redemption, the idea of a bare life redeemed in all of its transience.

For Benjamin, the messianic does not refer to a salvific moment when mere creaturely life is transcended, and all past mortal suffering receives its divine reparation. Nor is it a concluding event within history in which the moral ends of humanity are finally actualized—the Kantian "crossover" point in which the ethical realm of moral autonomy meets the natural realm of necessity.[11] Rather, redemption is identified paradoxically with the return to an original state of *irredeemable imperfection*, a state that humanity, as a result of its history, will no longer need to transcend: "My definition of politics: the fulfillment of an unimproved humanity."[12] The paradise from which mankind is expelled is not that of a morally innocent historical infancy, but a primordial condition that preceded the "Fall" into conceptual and ethical judgment, morality, and mechanical reason.

As the neo-Kantian philosophers who were Benjamin's teachers understood, the attempt to make judgment conform with the objects of knowledge, and to make reality correspond to our moral imperatives, is an infinite task. For Benjamin, who criticized this concept of history throughout his career, this meant that a return to paradise is impossible so long as redemption is regarded as the restoration of an original state of perfection, which never existed. Redemption is not, as Hermann Cohen conceived it, "the dominion of the good on earth."[13] The "Messiah's coming" does not "consists in … the ultimate end of injustice," achieved through continual progress toward the actualization of ethical principles.[14] Rather, in Benjamin's philosophy of history, the messianic is identified with the irresolvable contradictions that lead to the inevitable failure of ethical laws, and with "the curious and at first discouraging discovery of the ultimate insolubility of all legal problems."[15]

Thus, in Benjamin's critique of Kant's doctrine of right, "justice" is associated with an original condition of anarchy in which everyone has a claim upon everything while things have the right to be free from possession, a condition that must be denied by every legal order of property. Justice, therefore, is precisely what must be excluded by every relation of property as a presupposition of right. Justice is what cannot be presented as a moral and legal demand.

In Benjamin's materialist phase, this messianic idea takes the form of "the revolutionary energies that appear in the 'outmoded,'" commodities which, stripped of their newness or novelty, are restored to the state of being possessor-less things that anyone can appropriate.[16] In the later stage of Benjamin's research on the *Arcades*, the revolutionary possibility of the abolition of law would be redefined in terms of Charles Fourier's conception of socialism and Marx's critique of political economy. Liberated from the capitalist mode of exchange and from the "antinomies of industrial capitalist society," machinery, as Benjamin suggests, could create the conditions for a hedonistic utopia in which progress toward moral perfection is not finally realized, but is at last made unnecessary.[17]

This profane idea of redemption, which is a defining characteristic of both the theological and materialist phases of Benjamin's work, suggests a view of the Enlightenment and of the role of science and technology in capitalist modernity that differs from that of many of Benjamin's contemporaries. Contrary to Jacques Derrida, Benjamin's work, "at once Marxist and messianic," does not belong "to the great antiparliamentary and anti-'*Aufklärung*' wave on which Nazism … surfaced … in the 1920s,"[18] a tendency that believed in the "theory of the fall and of originary authenticity."[19] This interpretation is based on a theological understanding of Benjamin's messianism, which purportedly seeks to redeem the "perversion" in modern society of an original state of perfection. For Benjamin, however, the paradise from which humanity is expelled is that of an original *pre-ethical* state that will receive a profane form of redemption in the messianic "fulfillment of an unimproved humanity."[20]

This humanity, moreover, is not one whose spirit is denied or concealed by the mechanical reason, reification, or calculative rationality that appears to prevail in modernity. Benjamin's profane Marxist messianism does not oppose the technical to the spiritual. On the contrary, he attributes this opposition to fascism, which celebrates the triumph of the will in exploiting technology in order to dominate nature, and views sacrifice as a pure assertion of spirit against the mechanical character of modern society. For fascism, which searches for a meaning in the meaningless horror of industrial war, "the new warfare of technology … appears … as the highest revelation of existence."[21] For Benjamin, therefore, revolution entails the liberation of labor as well as the emancipation of machinery from the fetters imposed upon it in bourgeois society, which produces "enslaved and enslaving objects."[22]

This affirmative view of technology was not, as some have alleged, the result of Benjamin's turn toward an undialectical and deterministic version of Marxism. Rather, it is consistent with his early pre-Marxist philosophy, which adopted a view of the relationship between modernity, science, and secularization that departed from that of many of his contemporaries. For Benjamin, the distinguishing feature of modern bourgeois society is not its mechanical character, but the fact that it "cannot help insulating everything technological as much as possible from the so-called spiritual."[23] Capitalism, moreover, according to Benjamin, is not characterized by the concealment of religion, as Gordon contends. Rather, it is an "essentially religious phenomenon" that only appears to be secular.[24]

In his later writings, Benjamin will draw upon Marx's critique of political economy, his critical theory of capitalism as a historically specific and transitory form of society that appears as an immutable fact, in order to analyze the cultic religion underlying modern society. For Marx, as well as for Fourier—the great precursor to Marx's critique, whose utopian socialism informed the *Arcades*—what defines capitalism is not its dependence on technology. Rather, capitalism is characterized by the contradiction between technology and the value relation that arises from the exchange of commodities, or what Fourier described as the conflict between the means of production and the mode of exchange in bourgeois society, which leads to crises of overproduction. These crises—which Benjamin characterized as slave revolts of technology against capitalist relations of property—are created by the antagonism between the fetishism of commodities, as the cultic religion of capitalism, and scientific and technological progress. As a result of this conflict, "the progress in mastering nature" is accompanied by the "retrogression of society."[25]

This contradiction is covered over in theories of capitalism that identify it with the process of secularization and the increasing predominance of science and mechanical reason. In *Capital*, on the other hand, Marx defines the value relation, underlying the capitalist economy, as a "supernatural" substance that resembles the natural properties that science uncovers through the process of abstraction.[26] The abstraction of value, which distinguishes capitalism as an historically specific and transitory form of society, appears as an immutable fact of science. In political economy, this scientific appearance serves as a cover for a modernity that is essentially religious in character.

This critique of political economy is one that Benjamin develops in the *Arcades*, in his account of the "phantasmagoria" of a modernity that eternalizes itself by projecting its image "across the heavens."[27] In the fatalistic version of this phantasmagoria presented in Louis-Auguste Blanqui's *Eternity by the Stars*, analyzed in the *Arcades*, a rationalistic worldview provides the basis, paradoxically, for a modern mythology that immortalizes the capitalist mode of production. This mythology, based on "mechanistic natural science," is one in which the struggles in nineteenth-century

France to overturn bourgeois society must be repeated for all of eternity.[28] In an effort to shatter this myth, Benjamin, drawing on Marx's "secularized ... idea of messianic time," sought to develop a new historical materialism with which to unmask the religion of capitalism in a manner consistent with the profane idea of redemption presented in his earlier work.[29]

Introduction: Capitalism and Eternity

In a letter to Max Horkheimer in 1938, Walter Benjamin reports a "rare find" that would "decisively influence" the direction of the manuscript on which he had labored for over a decade, a project which would ultimately remain incomplete at the time of his suicide two years later. The fortuitous discovery was *Eternity by the Stars* by the French revolutionary Louis-Auguste Blanqui, written at the end of his life while imprisoned on the island fortress of Taureau. The chance encounter with a text which had been largely "ignored to the present day" would provide Benjamin with the conceptual framework for his own final work[1]—the "Paris Arcades ... the theater of all my struggles and all my ideas,"[2] "the great philosophical work that has no end in view but itself, that makes no concessions to anybody, and that, in its significance, will compensate [me] ... for so much that has happened."[3] In this "*chef d'oeuvre* like no other," a "wide-eyed presentation" of empirical facts retrieved from nineteenth-century France would be elucidated with reference to Blanqui's unsettling view of modernity as a particular historical moment that must be repeated forever.[4] "As for 'modernity' ... [its] philosophical reconnoitering ... is reserved for the third part [of the *Arcades*], where the subject will be ... brought to a conclusion in the dialectic of the new and the ever-same."[5]

As Benjamin describes in the letter, the text that would serve as a frame for the *Arcades Project* was the "last thing Blanqui wrote in his final prison,"[6] a final testament to a "career covering all of the ... periods of insurgency" in nineteenth-century France, from the July Revolution to the Paris Commune.[7] For Blanqui, the most revered revolutionary of the period, these attempts to overturn bourgeois society were repetitions of the French Revolution, struggles seeking to finally actualize the eternal ideals of freedom, fraternity, and equality. Blanqui, therefore, considered himself to be the "political manifestation of the French Revolution in the nineteenth century."[8]

The insurrections in nineteenth-century France would fail, however, to accomplish their aim, a failure repeated in what Benjamin called "the experience of our generation: that capitalism will not die a natural death."[9] In Blanqui's final work, this defeat is portrayed as a scientific certainty. The text, which was entirely "unexpected coming from this great revolutionary than it would be from anyone else," presents what appears to be a cosmological proof of the impossibility of abolishing capitalism,[10] a proof that gives "the lie to the author's revolutionary élan."[11] The *Arcades Project*, then—which, for Benjamin, was "the true, if not the only, reason not to lose courage in the struggle for existence"—would be framed by a figure who, at the end of his life, had relinquished all hope in the struggle to transform existing society.[12] Adopting the standpoint of an idle theorist (a perspective that Blanqui had ridiculed throughout his career as an activist committed to the violent overthrow of bourgeois society), *Eternity by the Stars* records a "private contemplation on the meaning of fate."[13] Having participated in "four narrowly failed revolutions, countless foiled conspiracies," Blanqui, at the end of his life, assumed the role of a dispassionate spectator.[14] The text surveys the tragi-comic cycle of incomplete revolutions in nineteenth-century France, which had failed to create a more just and equal society in accordance with the ideals of the French Revolution. *Eternity*, therefore, is a melancholic reflection on "a life of missed opportunities and for a world that shall never come to be what it ought to," a reflection on the "gap between ought and is ... that three revolutions had failed to bridge."[15]

In these reflections, the struggle to abolish bourgeois society is portrayed as an interminable task in an infinite labyrinth, like the ones that populate the parables of Jorge Luis Borges, many of which were inspired by Blanqui's final work.[16] Since the universe is eternal, everything that occurs in the present, and everything that will ever occur in the future, must have already happened innumerable times in the past. But as such, the novelty of the present is only an appearance that conceals the return of occurrences that are immeasurably old. Because of this eternal return, the new, disclosed in all its uniqueness in the here-and-now, can only reveal what has already happened repeatedly in countless other places and times. What *is* has *already been*. In Benjamin's words: "Everything new [that humanity] could hope for turns out," for Blanqui, "to be a reality that has always been present; and this newness will be ... [in]capable of rejuvenating society."[17]

While the future, in an infinite universe, only reveals what has already happened, the past becomes a facsimile of itself without an original: every origin or beginning is an imitation of an earlier present that repeats a previous one *ad infinitum*. Consequently, "there is no progress. Alas! no, these are vulgar reissues, repetitions. So too are the copies of past worlds, so too are those of future worlds."[18]

From this standpoint, the revolutionary struggles in nineteenth-century France to realize a communist society of the future appear as repetitions of a meaningless drama that has been performed from time immemorial: "There's nothing new under the sun. All that's done is done, and will be done. ... Men of the nineteenth century, the hour of our appearances is forever fixed, and it will always bring us back the same." What appeared to the revolutionaries of that century, then, as historical progress toward a future which would constitute a complete break with the past was, in fact, precisely the opposite—the eternal return of the same. "What we call 'progress' is ... everywhere ... the same drama, the same setting, on the same narrow stage ... a noisy humanity infatuated with its own grandeur ... living in its prison as though in some immense realm ... repeats itself endlessly."[19]

In *Eternity*, then, two opposing conceptions of history come into conflict. Blanqui appears to repudiate his earlier "faith in progress,"[20] his belief in the concept of history as a "progression through empty, homogeneous time," which the nineteenth century inherited from the Enlightenment and the French Revolution. In the exposé on the *Arcades*, Benjamin characterizes this concept as the "phantasmagoria" that "dominates the period 1831–1871," "holding sway over the early years of the proletariat," the "illusion that the task of the proletarian revolution is to complete the work of 1789 hand in hand with the bourgeoisie."[21]

This rationalist view is rejected in favor of an irrational vision of history, one that anticipated (and informed) the Nietzschean doctrine of eternal return, which affirmed an "existence … without meaning or aim … recurring inevitably without any finale of nothingness."[22] The Enlightenment faith in the "indefinite perfectibility of humankind" is confronted with the nihilistic conception of history as a meaningless chain of events, occurring and recurring in a linear succession of time, which becomes circular as it extends to infinity.[23]

As Benjamin argues in the *Arcades*, these opposing concepts of time constitute "indissoluble antinomies."[24] Viewed dialectically, each is identical to its opposite. These dialectical complements belong to a specific form of society, one that Blanqui had unsuccessfully tried to destroy. In the *Communist Manifesto*, Marx and Engels define the particular period of which Blanqui regarded himself as a later manifestation in terms of the unprecedented political and technological change that accompanied the rise of the capitalist class:

> The bourgeoisie, during its rule of scarce one hundred years, has created more massive and more colossal productive forces than have all preceding generations together. Subjection of Nature's forces to man, machinery, application of chemistry to industry and agriculture, steam-navigation, railways, electric telegraphs … what earlier century had even a presentiment that such productive forces slumbered in the lap of social labour?[25]

In this context, thinkers like Pierre-Simon Laplace, whose celestial mechanics informed the infernal vision of the cosmos in *Eternity by the Stars*, assumed that the dissemination of a worldview based upon natural science would help to create a new social order. "Let us apply to the political and moral sciences the method … which has served us so well in the natural sciences. Let us not offer … resistance to the inevitable benefits derived from the progress of enlightenment."[26] "In the early period of the … bourgeoisie, the exact sciences," therefore, as Benjamin noted, "had combined to form a worldview whose vanishing point lay in the realm of freedom and perpetual peace. This offered a perspective on the plane of history which was in no way inferior to the one sketched by Kant and Laplace on the plane of cosmology."[27] In accordance with the program proposed by Laplace, Blanqui, then, in his earlier writings, had advocated "the teaching of cosmography based on a deterministic use of probabilities … as an antidote to all superstitions and religions."[28]

This rational vision of history would persist into the twentieth century in the ideology of groups like the Social Democratic Party, for which "furthering technological progress constituted a political achievement."[29] Already in the nineteenth century, however, the repeated failure of revolutions to establish a new social order led many to doubt the ideal of endless perfectibility. At the same time, for many thinkers, moreover, the empirical sciences, as Benjamin noted, "ceased to be a tool for human liberation," and appeared increasingly as an "instrument of control."[30]

It was in this context, as Stéphane Mosès describes, that Nietzsche developed the doctrine of eternal recurrence in part as a criticism of the "reigning mechanism," of the mechanical view of the universe associated with modern natural science, and, specifically, with Newtonian physics. For Nietzsche, the "mechanical interpretation which now seems to be victorious" posits an infinite universe devoid of human significance.[31] It is the "stupidest of all possible interpretations ... Mr Mechanic ... insists that mechanics is the doctrine of the first and final laws on which existence may be built ... But an essentially mechanistic world would be an essentially meaningless world!"[32]

As Benjamin suggests in an early philosophical fragment, this meaninglessness was the product of "mechanical time." In natural science, time is "merely the measure that records the duration of a mechanical change." This empty, homogeneous time, which is "infinite in every direction and unfulfilled at every moment," is indifferent to the phenomena that it measures: "we cannot conceive of a single empirical event that bears a necessary relation to the time of its occurrence."[33]

For Benjamin, this problem is one that also defines the philosophy of Immanuel Kant, as well as the work of the Marburg School of neo-Kantianism, which adopted a "mechanical concept of experience" "whose quintessence, was Newtonian physics."[34] Like natural science, the Kantian and neo-Kantian theories of knowledge presuppose a concept of mechanical time that excludes all "singularly temporal" experience.[35] In these theories, the immediate experience of the ephemeral moment, or the now, is effaced by the empty, homogeneous time that is used as its measure. As Benjamin explains in "On the Concept of History," repeating an argument developed in his earlier writings, the "substitution of homogeneous configurations [of time] for changes in the physical world ... [is] the basis of the natural sciences."[36]

As Mosès points out, this was precisely the problem to which Nietzsche responded in the thought of eternal recurrence. In "depriving the moment of its uniqueness, of its irreducible specificity, [natural science] neutralizes the very substance of life which it transforms into a purely mechanical system."[37] From the standpoint of mechanism, the "ephemeral character" of the "present minute ... will always prevent it from being given absolute value. On the linear time axis, the present instant will always be defined as a point of passage between the instant which precedes it and the one which follows it ... as a simple transition, or as a limit ideal, devoid of its own reality."[38] The now, then, is conceived either as a transition to some other condition or as a vanishing moment (always not yet or no longer) that disappears or dissolves upon closer inspection.

Against the mechanical conception of time, Nietzsche proposed the thought of eternal return, in which every ephemeral instant, "each fragment of time," undergoes a "projection into the absolute."[39] In an infinite universe, every moment must be repeated interminably, and, as a result, every fleeting experience becomes an eternity. "What disappears here would only be the transitory character of the moment, its transient and provisional nature."[40] The now must be reproduced in all its uniqueness again and again for all of eternity. The "Nietzschean idea of the eternal return must then be understood as a figure of thought intended to free the moment from the transience which is inherent to it so as to elevate it to a sort of eternity."[41] Like Marcel Proust's experiments with involuntary memory, the thought of eternal recurrence achieves "the monstrous feat of letting the whole world age a lifetime in an instant."[42]

However, by turning every transient moment into an eternity, this infinite repetition also deprives every event of its singular (or unrepeatable) character, just as mass reproduction, by proliferating identical copies, "substitutes a mass existence for a unique existence."[43] "The idea of eternal recurrence transforms the historical event itself into a mass-produced article."[44] In a dialectical reversal, therefore, the thought of eternal return—which accords every ephemeral experience an absolute value from the vantage point of eternity—also divests time itself of all meaning. The infinite repetition of every event in all of its irreducible difference, the "stylization of existence down to the tiniest fractions of its temporal process," amounts, therefore, to an eternal return of the same.[45]

But in that case, the idea of eternal recurrence, as Benjamin explains in the *Arcades*, is identical to the "stupid" and meaningless mechanical view of the universe to which it opposes itself, a view in which every segment of time is exactly identical to every other. The "eternal return appears precisely as that 'shallow rationalism' which the belief in progress is accused of being."[46] In Benjamin's writings, therefore, "[q]ualitative time" is not, as Michael Löwy has argued, "radically opposed to the empty flow of the purely quantitative time of historicism and 'progressism.'" Rather, the two conceptions of time are portrayed as dialectical complements.[47]

The twofold critique of the concepts of progress and eternal return presented in the *Arcades* would appear to conform to the requirements for the "coming philosophy," outlined in Benjamin's early writings. This philosophy would acknowledge the limits of both the mechanical notion of time and "vitalist" forms of philosophy, such as those of Henri Bergson, Edmund Husserl and Ludwig Klages, which claim to grant access to an unmediated experience of the vanishing present. In Benjamin's words, the coming philosophy would be "directed toward both the timeless validity of knowledge and the certainty of a temporal experience … regarded as the immediate."[48]

In the *Arcades*, this theory of time is adapted to a criticism of ideology: the opposition between progress and eternal recurrence covers over the fact that both conceptions of history perform an identical function in disguising the historical character of bourgeois society. In the account of eternal return that appears in *Eternity by the Stars*, the shallow rationalism of mechanistic natural science, which Blanqui had conceived as an "antidote to all superstitions and religions," provides the pseudo-scientific foundation for a capitalist "theology." In a representation derived from the "secularization of time … hidden in the 'worldview of the natural sciences,'" the revolutions in nineteenth-century France are portrayed as a mythical hell in which humanity is doomed to repeat the progress of bourgeois society for all of eternity.[49]

Beginning, therefore, with a linear mechanical conception of time, derived from the natural sciences, Blanqui arrives as a mythological view of modernity as a moment in history repeating events from an immemorial past in which the fate of humanity was already decided. The world exists now as it "already was, and so it will always be, without an atom or second of variation. There's nothing new under the sun. All that's done is done, and will be done."[50] In Blanqui's cosmology, "the vision of a deterministic world that dominated the nineteenth century is elevated to the status of myth."[51]

In this myth, the "worldview of the natural sciences," which had provided a historical justification for the rise of the capitalist class, serves as a new kind of theology that naturalizes the society that Blanqui had devoted his life to destroying. "While deriving his data from mechanistic natural science, the worldview that Blanqui outlines is in fact an infernal view, and is at the same time, in the form of a natural view, the complement to a social order that Blanqui had to recognize as victorious over him in the last years of his life." *Eternity by the Stars*, then, "represents," in Benjamin's words, an "unconditional submission, but at the same time the most terrible accusation against a society that has reflected this image of the cosmos as a projection of itself onto the heavens."[52] As Mosès describes, "Blanqui's text … interprets this scientific theory in the light of the archaic idea of cyclical time, and projects the regularity and immutability of natural rhythms onto human development."[53]

In *Eternity*, then, a rationalist and irrationalist vision of history—progress and eternal recurrence—appear as dialectical "complements," opposing perspectives on science that provide a theological justification for capitalism, conferring upon it the appearance of fate. In Blanqui's mechanistic cosmology of the mythological origins of the capitalist mode of production, the bourgeois revolution of 1789 is portrayed as a struggle that has and will be repeated for all of eternity.

In the 1939 *exposé*, which contains "Benjamin's most lucid remarks concerning the theoretical goals of the *Passagenwerk*,"[54] this "phantasmagoria"—in which historic events in present-day bourgeois society appear immeasurably old—is identified with modernity itself. Modernity, then, in Blanqui's infernal mechanical vision, is a condition in which capitalism appears to encompass the universe in its entirety.

> This resignation without hope is the last word of the great revolutionary. The century was incapable of responding to the new technological possibilities with a new social order. That is why the last word was left to the errant negotiators between old and new who are at the heart of these phantasmagorias. The world dominated by its phantasmagorias—this, to make use of Baudelaire's term, is 'modernity.' Blanqui's vision has the entire universe entering the modernity …
> In the end, Blanqui views novelty as an attribute of all that is under sentence of damnation.[55]

Blanqui's resignation, therefore, his total capitulation to the phantasmagoria of a capitalist modernity that exists throughout time and space, was tied to his inability to imagine a new social order adequate to the rapid technological development spurred by industrial capitalism.

In the *Arcades*, this "failure … characteristic of the [nineteenth] century … the bungled reception of technology" is attributed to the "fact that technology serves [bourgeois] society only by producing commodities."[56] This account relies on another important resource that Benjamin discovered during the last stage of his research on the manuscript, a text which, like *Eternity by the Stars*, would also decisively influence the project: Karl Korsch's interpretation of *Capital* in *Karl Marx*.

As Korsch explains in the study, the key to Marx' critical theory is the concept of commodity fetishism. The "fetish character of the commodity" is the "kernel of the *Marxian Critique of Political Economy*" and the "quintessence of the ... theory of *Capital* and the most explicit and most exact definition of the theoretical and historical standpoint of the whole [of Marx's] materialis[m]."[57] In *Capital*, Marx identifies commodity fetishism with the concept of "value," a social relation that assumes the form of a super-sensible property which, congealed in commodities, makes them equivalent and therefore exchangeable. The latter, according to Marx, is not a "geometrical, physical, chemical or other natural property," but rather a "super-natural" substance that no natural science could ever discover.[58] To the "bourgeois consciousness of political economists," however, this fictional property, which underlies the bourgeois economy, appears "to be ... a self-evident and nature-imposed necessity."[59] Because of this naturalization, the foundation of a specific mode of production, based on commodity exchange, appears as an "eternal necessity ordained by nature," just as the revolutions in nineteenth-century France appear, in Blanqui's scientific deduction, as a fate that must be repeated forever.[60]

As Marx argued, however, the ideals for which these revolutions were waged are rooted in the fetishism of commodities. The "equality-idea resulting from the epoch of bourgeois commodity-production and expressed in the economic 'law of value' is ... bourgeois in its character."[61] Just as the value-relation, as the basis of capitalism, is fetishized as a natural fact, as the "eternal natural form of social production,"[62] so the notion of human equality acquires "the permanence of a fixed popular opinion."[63] Marx, therefore, derided the "foolishness of those socialists ... who want to depict socialism as the realization of the ideals of bourgeois society articulated by the French revolution," thereby affirming political principles which belonged to the very society they proposed to abolish. Because these socialists failed to perceive "that exchange value ... is in fact the system of equality and freedom," mistaking the latter for universal ideals, their criticism of capitalism was based upon principles that were inextricably tied to the very society they wished to dismantle.[64] In this way, they unwittingly demonstrated, "to the consolation of all good petty bourgeois, that the production of commodities is a form as eternal as justice."[65]

While the spread of these seemingly eternal ideals in the era of bourgeois ascendency was accompanied by unprecedented scientific and technological change, these principles, based on the value relation, would later serve, as Korsch pointed out, to block the emergence of a new social order.

> Such high ideals of bourgeois society as ... freedom and equality of all citizens in the exercise of their political rights, and equality of all in the eyes of the law, are ... nothing but *correlative concepts to the Fetishism of the Commodity*, drawn from the existing system of exchange. All these far-flung additions to the basic form of the commodity-fetish which for a time had served as stimulators of material progress are to-day but ideological expressions of a particular type of production-relations that have degenerated into mere fetters of the further development of the productive forces of society.[66]

Fettered by the fetishism of commodities (or the mode of exchange in bourgeois society), the development of the forces of production, rather than creating the conditions for a more equal society, becomes the cause of catastrophe in crises of overproduction. In "all earlier epochs," the latter "would have seemed an absurdity … Society suddenly finds itself … cut off [from] the supply of every means of subsistence … [b]ecause there is … too much means of subsistence."[67]

For Marx, as Korsch pointed out, it was precisely the absence of an historical analysis of the value-relation that constituted the primary weakness of Blanqui's criticism of capitalism. Unlike Marx's critique of political economy, this criticism identified the ideals of the French Revolution with justice itself, denouncing bourgeois society by appealing to its own moral precepts. "Political economy without morality: its moral indifference strips it of any critical power. Justice is the only true criterion that applies to human things."[68] Instead of developing a critique of capitalism as a society founded on a commodity fetish that blocks the creation of a new social order, Blanqui espoused a moral condemnation of bourgeois society, based on concepts, correlative to this fetishism, which are taken to be eternal ideals.

This criticism, however, does not provide a sufficient account of the contradictions that arise from the value-relation. In crises of overproduction, as Blanqui himself recognized, technological progress, which multiplied goods that could be consumed by society, paradoxically increased the misery of both workers and capitalists. "The more things of *useful value* abound, the less money can be made from them." The "resulting abundance of goods for sale, are taken to be a calamity that is ruinous for producers and that puts industry and business in dire straits. Political economy openly consecrates this blasphemy."[69] For Blanqui, the inexplicable coincidence of poverty and prosperity in capitalist crises could only be explained as the result of "some radical vice in a system which … seems to multiply the embarrassments of producers at the same time that it forces them to multiply their products."[70] Because of some extreme immorality, machinery, which earlier socialist thinkers like Fourier had frivolously assumed would create the conditions for a "burlesque [future] utopia,"[71] precipitated instead the "madness" of crises of material abundance in the midst of mass human poverty.[72]

Condemning bourgeois society for committing this blasphemy, Blanqui called for a "revolutionary conspiracy," using violence to establish a "dictatorship of a revolutionary elite," which would then "throw down [social order] to rebuild on the basis of equality."[73] This moral demand for revolution corresponds to what Benjamin, in his early anarchist theory of politics, described as the notion that violence can be justified according to its ends, a view "for which the terrorism in the French Revolution provided an ideological foundation."[74] This tradition was based on the "naive belief that 'after the bourgeois regime had been consolidated, justice would depend on a return to virtue,'" a belief that, according to Benjamin, "cannot be divorced from the institution of terror."[75] "The Blanquists," as Georges Sorel described in *Reflections on Violence*, "who look upon themselves as the legitimate owners of the Terrorist tradition, consider that for this very reason they are called upon to direct the proletarian movement."[76]

In this bourgeois tradition, violence, as Benjamin explains in the "Critique of Violence," is viewed as "a product of nature … in no way problematical, unless force is misused for unjust ends."[77] Since Robespierre regarded liberty and equality as natural rights (rather than correlative concepts to the fetishism of commodities), he understood insurrection as a natural response to oppression, "determined by the law of nature."[78] Subject to the "boundless tyranny" of the capitalist class, the revolutionary dictatorship, representing the laboring class, had the legal prerogative to exercise an extra-juridical violence on behalf of the people:[79] "Political action cannot meet the expectations of the people if it respects the rules laid down by its enemies ... The revolutionary government needs no other legitimacy, no other limit than that of the control of the people of Paris."[80]

In Blanqui's ideology, therefore, revolutionary violence is justified as a means toward the end of creating a future society based on equality, a "principle ... which slowly works to destroy all forms of exploitation of man by man." "Blanqui understood that bourgeois society is incapable of realizing the universalist principles of *'liberté, égalité, fraternité'* and that their fulfillment requires the establishment of communism."[81] Since these ideals, however, according to Marx, are "bourgeois right[s]" (incompatible with the communist principle, "From each according to his ability ... "),[82] such violence would only result in a futile repetition of the French Revolution, which attempted to realize ideals that are unrealizable. Indeed, during the French Revolution, as Max Horkheimer observed in a text cited by Benjamin, the masses who were "mobilized under the watchwords of liberty and justice ... were to be incorporated [by Robespierre] into a new society that would be anything but classless."[83] Against those socialists, therefore, who "desire[d] to undertake the superfluous business of realizing the ideal expression," Marx declared that the "realization of equality and freedom ... prove to be inequality and unfreedom."[84]

As Korsch argued, therefore, Marx's critique of Blanqui (which is developed in the *Arcades*) was not simply directed at its volunterism, at the disregard for economic conditions that characterized his conspiratorial program of revolutionary violence. Marx and Engels, in fact, maintained that a temporary dictatorship of the oppressed was necessary in order to overturn the institutions of the legalized violence, or law-preserving authority, imposed by the "bourgeois dictatorship ... of ... united exploiters." The "proletariat rallies ... around revolutionary socialism ... for which the bourgeoisie has ... invented the name of Blanqui. This ... dictatorship of the proletariat [is] ... the necessary transit point to the abolition of class distinctions."[85]

For Marx, then, Blanqui's theory of revolution was "unscientific" not because it relies on subjective moral criteria, instead of recognizing objective economic realities. Rather, its weakness was that it failed to perceive that its moral ideals were correlative concepts to the value-relation, as the naturalized fetish or fiction that constituted the basis of the bourgeois economy. "While Marx and Engels," therefore, according to Korsch, "had no quarrel with such practical exponents of revolutionary force as Blanqui, they pointed at every possible opportunity to the scientific emptiness of ... 'theories of violence.'" Promoted by "'socialistically-minded' people who [are] ... candidly unconscious of the real motive force of historical development ... deliberately ignoring all economics," these theories "endeavoured to trace the existing forms of production, of class relationship ... to pure force, politics, etc., in order to appeal from such 'brute' forms of violence to the organizing power of reason, of justice, of humanity, or similar classless immaterialities." Against "such ... despisers of economics," "Marx and Engels ... always affirmed their allegiance to the deeper ... historical knowledge of bourgeois society which is contained in the economic concept of 'value.'"[86]

Unable to unmask what Benjamin called the "semblance of 'value,'"[87] Blanqui, and the century that he symbolized, proved "incapable of responding to the new technological possibilities with a new social order."[88] As a result, the nineteenth century remained trapped in "modernity," trying to awaken from the phantasmagoria of a "society that has reflected this image of the cosmos as a projection of itself onto the heavens."[89] Although the vision of eternal recurrence is opposed to a rationalist "view of history that puts its faith in the infinite," like the neo-Kantian idea of the classless society, Blanqui's infernal vision condemns humanity to the pursuit of a bourgeois ideal, eternalized as an infinite task.[90] Against these "indissoluble antinomies," Benjamin, therefore, proposed a "dialectical conception of historical time," which would suspend the dialectic of history while bringing the cycle of eternal return to a standstill.[91]

This dialectical critique of *Eternity by the Stars* encapsulates an important component of a new historical materialism, which Benjamin was in the process of developing in his later body of work. Like Benjamin's style of thinking in general, which stood "apart from all tendencies,"[92] this materialism, developed by the "most peculiar Marxist ever produced," departs from many, if not virtually all the main currents of Marxist philosophy in the twentieth century.[93] At a time when his contacts among the Surrealists looked to the young Hegelian Marx for an alternative to Soviet orthodoxy, Benjamin turned his attention to Marx's later "critique of the capitalistic mode of production," as a theory that "would make it possible for capitalism to abolish itself."[94] This scientific criticism of capitalism, moreover, is one that Benjamin would attempt to reconcile with the "pre-scientific" utopian socialism of Charles Fourier, developing an "erotic and artisanal" conception of communism, in a "personal version of a 'phalansterial' renewal."[95] In this future utopia, the fetishism of commodities would be abolished in an "unfolding of work in play,"[96] which would liberate both desire and labor by emancipating machinery or "second technology."

This affirmative view of technology distinguished Benjamin's Marxism from that of Adorno and Lukács, who accused him of falling victim to reification (to an "uncritically affirmed fetishization"), and to an uncritical celebration of technological progress, contrary to Marxism.[97] This seemingly un-Marxist position, however, was rooted in part in a particular interpretation of Marx, which claim that Marxism had fundamentally misunderstood him, and that the "most important point made in Marx's historical materialism was later missed ... by ... 'orthodox' Marx[ists]."[98] As Korsch explained, this important point is that the theory developed in *Capital* is not an all-encompassing worldview, but a reflexive critique of a specific form of society that assumes an eternal appearance, an appearance which is reenforced by orthodox interpretations of Marx. Because of the fetishism that underlies capitalism, as an historically determinate mode of production, the continual social and technological progress generated by bourgeois society results in catastrophe, crisis, and conflict. If Benjamin's "new heretical Marxism,"[99] therefore, was one of the "most peculiar ... ever produced by the movement," its peculiarity was partly derived from a reading of *Capital* that claimed to use "Marx's own Marxism" against his own orthodox followers.

In the late stage of his research on the *Arcades*, Benjamin would begin to coordinate this particular reading of Marx with key elements of his early philosophy. At the core of this philosophy is a dialectical theory of time, a theory which, in the *Arcades*, is aligned with Marx's critical theory of capitalism as a "historical and transitory" mode of production that assumes an eternal appearance. This "phantasmagoria"—which Benjamin identifies with modernity itself as an historically specific condition that appears as a cosmological fate—is a defining ideological feature of both rational and irrationalist conceptions of history: "[F]aith in progress seems no less to belong to the mythic mode of thought than does the idea of eternal return."[100] What distinguishes the historical materialism that Benjamin develops in his later writings, therefore, is the insistence on the need to historicize conceptions of history—rational or irrational, Marxist or non-Marxist—that claim to be universal in character. Thus, for example, the concept of "historicity," which Heidegger develops in *Being and Time*, is criticized for its lack of an "historical index," indicating that it "belong[s] to a particular time."[101]

One of the main arguments in this book is that this new historical materialism was not a departure from the early "metaphysical phase" of Benjamin's work. Rather, it was an extension and reorientation of the "metaphysical anarchism," outlined in his early essays and fragments. This philosophy consists of an epistemology, an anarchist "politics," and a critique of aesthetic and teleological judgment presented in the form of a "revision" of Kant, directed against what Benjamin later described as the "bourgeois trinity of the true, the beautiful, and the good."[102] Because Benjamin, however, believed that the "dignity of a philosophical view ... appear[s] most clearly in [its] philosophy of history," these elements of Benjamin's early "theoretical anarchism" were intended to serve as the basis on which to develop a new conception of history.[103] To risk the use of broad formulations which are not Benjamin's own, this concept of history is a cumulative one in which a historical movement, arising from an irreconcilable contradiction, creates the condition, not for its resolution, but for a messianic arrest of the movement itself. Thus, in a fragment written in 1919, Benjamin presents the following account of his anarchist political philosophy: "My definition of politics: the fulfillment of an unimproved humanity."[104] For Benjamin, then, history is not, as in the Enlightenment notion of progress, a teleological movement of illimitable moral perfectibility, but a process in which an irredeemably imperfect humanity finally achieves its fulfillment precisely as such.

This messianic conception of history is one that Benjamin will later attribute to Marx. "Marx ... set himself the task of showing how the revolution could arise from its complete opposite, capitalism, without the need for any ethical change." In his later writings, Benjamin, adapting this definition of politics in order to develop an "historical materialism which has annihilated within itself the idea of progress," identifies the moment of fulfillment with the revolutionary event.[105] The latter is defined as a product of historical progress that, instead of achieving its end, suspends its momentum. Revolutions, therefore, are not the "locomotive of world history," but "an attempt by the passengers on this train—namely, the human race—to activate the emergency brake."[106] "Progress has its seat not in the continuity of elapsing time but in its interferences—where the truly new makes itself felt for the first time."[107]

In Benjamin's writings, this philosophy of history was developed together with a history of philosophy, one that departs from the conventional periodization of modernity and the process of secularization, underlying the work of many of Benjamin's contemporaries. This history (which will be described in more detail in the outline of the chapters presented below) can be briefly stated as follows: in the seventeenth century, a "total secularization" of history occurs as a result of a "general 'mechanization of the world view' of that time," a period when natural science became increasingly dominant.[108] This process of secularization, however, was reversed by the rise of bourgeois society. In "modernity," the secularized conception of nature and history that emerged in the seventeenth century comes to appear as a mythological image of bourgeois society, just as value is fetishized as a real physical property. In a paradoxical form of re-enchantment that appears as its opposite, as the disenchantment of the world (a theologization that Benjamin identifies with modernity), capitalism "projects this image of the cosmos—understood as an image of itself—across the heavens."[109] As a result, the "shallow rationalism" of mechanical reason becomes the eternal appearance of a particular mode of production. The alienation of abstract labor time, as the historically specific foundation of capitalism, is disguised as the reified time of natural science.

Outline

A New Historical Materialism presents an interpretation of Benjamin's historical materialism and its relation to his early philosophical writings. As Benjamin explained to Gershom Scholem in 1938, the materialist method developed in later texts like the work of art essay and the *Arcades Project* was a "transposition into Marxist perspectives of [my earlier] metaphysical and even theological ideas."[110] The book contends that these later writings can be seen as an attempt to establish a constellation between ideas from Benjamin's early work in philosophy and a specific reading of Marx, one that emphasizes Marx's critique of political economy, and that is inflected by the utopian socialism of Charles Fourier.

In his early essays and fragments, Benjamin develops an anarchist critique of both rationalist and irrationalist forms of philosophy, including that of the Marburg and Baden schools of neo-Kantianism and the "vitalism" of Friedrich Nietzsche, Henri Bergson, and Edmund Husserl. Benjamin expressed this early "metaphysical anarchism" in Kantian terms, although usually against Kant himself, in the belief that its intelligibility and "historical continuity [would be] ... ensured by following the Kantian system."[111] The result was a strikingly un-Kantian philosophy defined in relation to Kant's critique of pure reason, moral philosophy, theory of judgment, and philosophy of history.

Chapter 1 examines the "coming philosophy" or theory of knowledge that Benjamin develops in his early philosophical fragments. For Benjamin, Kant's theoretical philosophy failed to fully confront the consequences of the Enlightenment and its rejection of dogma. The historic result of the absence of authority was a condition of epistemological anarchy in which knowledge was compelled to justify itself on the basis of a bare, "naked" form of existence, stripped of its proximity to God.

As Benjamin argues, however, Kant fails to provide this justification. Instead of developing an epistemological theory founded on experience itself, the *Critique of Pure Reason* attempts to justify the timeless validity of knowledge using a concept of experience derived from the sciences. Because this concept of experience, which Benjamin identifies with mechanical reason, is timeless and universal in character, it necessarily excludes experience itself, which is "singularly temporal." By taking the principles of experience from natural science, Kant, therefore, "managed to give a valid explanation [as to] … the certainty of knowledge that is lasting," while failing to establish "the integrity of an experience that is ephemeral."[112] Kant's theory, in other words, provides an undogmatic demonstration of the "timeless validity of knowledge," but fails to account for how this knowledge can apply to experience. The *Critique of Pure Reason*, then, justifies the mechanical reason employed in natural science without appealing to God, while "abandoning the deduction of that 'empty, godless experience,'" the bare form of existence exposed by the disappearance of all higher authority.

Because this mechanical knowledge excludes the immediate experience that is its object, the progress of science becomes an infinite task. In the neo-Kantianism of the Marburg School, this concept of science is developed into a quasi-theological justification for the bourgeois conception of progress. In his early "revision" of Kant's theory of knowledge, Benjamin, therefore, insists on the need for a "coming philosophy," "directed toward both the timeless validity of knowledge and the certainty of a temporal experience … regarded as the immediate … object of that knowledge."

To accomplish this task, Benjamin will turn to phenomenology as a method for ascertaining the certainty of immediate experience. In the works that Benjamin read as part of his "entrance exam" into the school of phenomenology, Husserl adapts the Cartesian method of doubt to establish the necessity of an immediate intuition.[113] Through a suspension of judgment that brackets conceptual knowledge, the phenomenologist achieves certainty of the act of perception itself, a certainty that needs no guarantee from a higher authority, and which is distinct from the timeless validity of the laws of natural science.

But precisely because the certainty of experience is different from the universal necessity of mechanical reason, the phenomenological method, according to Benjamin, cannot account for the origin of scientific abstractions. The latter cannot be derived from immediate experience any more than experience can be reduced to conceptual knowledge. Just as the categories of natural science, therefore, exclude experience as such, so "vitalist" theories like Husserl's that attempt to ground knowledge in bare life risk-reducing reason to mere intuition. Against both phenomenology and the neo-Kantianism of the Marburg School, Benjamin, then, proposes a dialectical synthesis and critique of the two theories of knowledge. The synthesis will take the form of a coming epistemological theory that would realize the "philosophical interest … directed toward both the timeless validity of knowledge and the certainty of a temporal experience … regarded as the immediate … object of that knowledge."

Moving from epistemology to political philosophy, Chapter 2 examines three early texts that were intended as part of a treatise on anarchism that Benjamin never completed: "Notes Toward a Work on the Category of Justice," the "Critique of Violence," and the "Theological-Political Fragment." Written during a period marked by a wave of revolutionary and counter-revolutionary violence, this anarchist politics (expressed in terms of a Kantian moral philosophy that it is also directed against) follows a program that broadly resembles that of the "Coming Philosophy."

In "Notes toward a Work on the Category of Justice," Benjamin identifies a missing component in Kant's moral justification for property. Unable to derive legal possession from the universal moral imperative that one should always act in a way that coheres with the freedom of others, Kant argues instead that this principle must be suspended since, in the absence of ownership, no one would be able to use anything. This justification of property excludes what Benjamin describes as an original condition of anarchy in which everyone has a claim upon everything, and yet every good has the right not to be owned. The institution of property, then, is based on a subjugation of things that denies the "good-right of the good," while simultaneously depriving other people of the claim they have to dispose of them as they will. In that sense, property is founded upon an original violence, one which, because of its irrational and contingent character, is contrary to right, which must be necessary and rational.

For Benjamin, this implies that Kant's moral philosophy lacks an independent criterion with which to evaluate violence itself as a means employed to achieve a particular end. In the "Critique of Violence," Benjamin attempts to identify this criterion, which necessarily differs from the universal criterion of the categorical imperative since the latter applies only to ends. Just as the coming philosophy, then, will be an epistemology directed at "both the timeless validity of knowledge and the certainty of [immediate] … experience," so Benjamin's political theory will be oriented toward both the "absoluteness of ends" and the "contingency of means." In that way, the theory provides the missing criterion in Kant's doctrine of right.[114]

In the "Critique of Violence," this criterion is defined in the following manner: Just as ends are moral if they can be universally willed, so an act of historical violence is either illegal or lawmaking depending on whether it can overturn the whole legal structure and establish itself in its place. As the foundation of law, this lawmaking violence serves to confer the appearance of fate upon a contingent event within history, thereby creating a new legal order.

In terms of Benjamin's revision of Kant's doctrine of right, the function of this critique of violence, which provides the doctrine with its missing criterion, is to unmask the basic mechanism allowing the universal constructions of law to apply to both people and things. The purportedly rational deduction of right performs the *theological* function of transforming contingency into fate, making ownership, for example, over "possessor-less" things (which are under no moral obligation to be owned) seem like a logical necessity. In this way, exceptions to law in the form of particular instances of contingent historical violence are mythologized as its legitimate origins.

By defining separate criteria of both just means and ends, Benjamin's theory, moreover, lays the groundwork for a critique of both rationalist and irrationalist theories of law. These theories attempt to either exclude violence from right, as in Kant's deduction of property, or ground the legal order in violence, as in Carl Schmitt's theory of the state of exception. By conflating the criteria for means and ends, these opposite views perpetuate what Benjamin calls the "dialectical rising and falling in the lawmaking and law-preserving formations of violence," just as the conflation of reason and experience results in the notion of science as an infinite task.[115]

Against these theories, the "Critique of Violence" attempts to delineate the possibility of a pure revolutionary violence that does not conform to the criteria of either just ends or justified means, a violence that is neither lawful nor lawmaking in character. Chapter 2 argues that this possibility can be understood in terms of the project, proposed by anarchists like Gustav Landauer, of constructing a stateless society based on cooperative labor that could allow for a permanent withdrawal from capitalism as well as state power.

Chapter 3 presents a reading of *Origin of the German* Trauerspiel and argues that the text can be considered the culmination of Benjamin's early metaphysical anarchism, encapsulating much of his "revision" of Kant's epistemology, politics, and aesthetics. In the "Epistemo-Critical Prologue," Benjamin outlines a theory of knowledge that realizes the program of the coming philosophy in its orientation toward the universal as well as the singular. Against a nominalism that rejects all historical classification in the name of the uniqueness of art and inductive theories that subsume diverse works under general categories, Benjamin proposes the "constellation" as a dialectical unity of incomparably singular artworks. From this vantage point, the history of the *Trauerspiel* play appears neither as a necessary progression toward a specific aesthetic ideal nor as a profusion of incommensurable works that cannot be identified as belonging to a particular genre or a common historical epoch. In the habilitation, this approach is used to criticize Kant's identification of the aesthetic with the excellent or exemplary. Drawing on both Husserl's phenomenology and Carl Schmitt's political theory, Benjamin analyzes the *Trauerspiel* as an aesthetic "extreme" that is unique precisely because it fails, in unexemplary ways, to conform to earlier artistic ideals.

In the habilitation, this approach succeeds in disclosing a "virtual history" of the seventeenth century that Benjamin will use to challenge the principal thesis of *Political Theology*, the work from which the concept of the extreme was derived. In the text, Schmitt argues that the modern theory of the state is a secularized theology, and that this theology was taken from seventeenth-century political thought, which regarded the sovereign as the "Cartesian god transposed to the political world." As Benjamin argues, however, this analogy is not, in fact, the expression of a political theology, but rather of a natural science of God, one which Descartes developed in order to prove the validity of his mechanical account of the universe. As Benjamin points out in the habilitation, mechanical causality presupposes the reduction of singular temporal experience into a homogeneous time that is identical in all of its moments. For Cartesians in the seventeenth century, this homogeneous time depended upon an analogy or "psychophysical parallelism" in which time is represented as space, as in the movement of the hands of a clock. But because temporal experience cannot be reduced to spatialized time, Descartes postulated a God whose continuous movement guaranteed the analogy between space and time that ensured the operation of the mechanical laws, revealed by natural science. Whereas Kant's epistemology secures the timeless validity of knowledge without demonstrating the certainty of singular temporal experience, in Descartes' physics, knowledge and experience are both grounded in God, who is conceived in a secular manner as the only true mechanical cause in the universe.

For Benjamin, then, the analogy between the Cartesian conception of God and the seventeenth-century sovereign implies that the purportedly theological notions that informed the modern conception of politics were *already secularized*. In this analogy, God guarantees the psychophysical parallelism that underlies all causal laws, just as the sovereign ensures the regular operation of a juridical order whose laws can never conform to reality. And just as God guarantees the analogy that constitutes time as an infinite homogeneous quantity, so the sovereign decision on the state of exception ensures the progression of history as a causal chain of events in empty, homogeneous time.

In the habilitation, moreover, the spatialization of time, which Benjamin defines as a distinguishing secular characteristic of the *Trauerspiel* plays, is implicitly opposed to Schmitt's account of the miraculous instant of the sovereign decision upon the exception. Whereas classical drama is defined by the irreversible character of the tragic event, in the *Trauerspiel*, the temporal succession of actions receives a spatial representation in the machinations of the schemer for whom all the parts of the plot are conceived simultaneously.

The analysis of this particular aspect of the *Trauerspiel* play not only provides the occasion for a confrontation with Schmitt's theory of sovereignty. It also implicitly criticizes the concept of reification, which György Lukács defined as the degradation of "time to the dimension of space," or the reduction of time to "an exactly delimited, quantifiable continuum filled with quantifiable 'things.'" Against this view of spatialized time, Benjamin presents the following argument: If the analogy between space and time, thematized in the *Trauerspiel* plays, represents the irreducibility of singular temporal experience to the homogeneous time of natural science, it also expresses the fact that time cannot appear in itself, but only in its reified representation as space.

In the habilitation, however, this critique of the concept of reification is not directed at Lukács' *History and Class Consciousness*. Rather, it is presented in a theory of allegorical representation that challenges Lukács' account in the "Metaphysics of Tragedy" of the ideal of timelessness in classical drama. For Lukács, tragic representation depends on a successive arrangement of action in time that must transcend the "plane of temporal experience" itself. This concept of tragedy corresponds to the idea of the symbol as an immediate unity of content and form that overcomes temporal succession to express its meaning in a total and instantaneous manner. As Benjamin argues, however, the instantaneity of the symbol and its unity with its content conceal the irreducible difference between time and its spatial representation. The symbol, in other words, sublimates precisely what allegory expresses—the fact that the psychophysical parallelism is impossible.

In the seventeenth century, this function of allegory, which Lukács' ignored, was related to a particular representation of nature. For the Baroque, nature not only appeared as a harmonious unity, revealed in its totality in the mystical instant, but also as the infinite extension of time, condemning everything to impermanence. The *Trauerspiel* book, therefore, proposes a dialectical theory that grasps both the transcendence of time within tragedy and the allegorical representation of transience, in a manner resembling the dual orientation of the coming philosophy toward both the eternal and the ephemeral.

According to Benjamin, this secularized representation of nature underlies a Baroque eschatology. In contrast to the religious idea of salvation, this eschatology was not directed at the ideal of eternal life, which transcends the "creaturely plane of existence" that is confined to spatialized time. Rather, the secularized eschatology of the Baroque is oriented toward the paradise of a mere creaturely life that exists in a transient present that is no longer conceived as the transition toward an eternity that the creature can never attain.

Chapter 4 considers the relationship between this Baroque eschatology, the Enlightenment notion of progress, and the profane idea of redemption that defines Benjamin's work, both early and late. The chapter argues that this idea succeeds in reconciling what Jürgen Habermas characterized as the irreconcilable tension in Benjamin's thinking between the concept of revolution as a product of history and the notion of the messianic event as a rupture with the historical continuum. Synthesizing the two opposing perspectives, Benjamin argues that progress toward an unachievable goal acts in the "opposite direction" to create the conditions for a messianic suspension of progress itself. In this contradictory movement—a movement in which history is consummated by running "counter to the Messianic direction"—humanity arrives at an end that was also its original condition. In contrast to the Christian scheme of salvation, however, this condition is not a state of moral purity preceding the original sin and the expulsion from Eden. Rather, it is the paradise of a profane creaturely life prior to all ethical judgment. In Benjamin's profane idea of redemption, progress toward the impossible goal of achieving moral perfection allows for a messianic return to an original state of moral indifference.

The profane character of Benjamin's messianism is also apparent in his positive view of the concept of "now-time" or *Jetztzeit*, which, in Heidegger's account of the constitution of history, is used to refer to the vulgar notion of time as a "now" that lacks a futural orientation. This orientation distinguishes the vacuous *Jetztzeit* from the "instant" or *Augenblick* in which the subject projects possibilities into the future, possibilities which realize a potential that was already there in a "heritage" or a past that is posited in the act of projection itself. Rejecting the opposition between authentic and mechanical time in Heidegger's work, Benjamin's messianism accords a positive role to the *Jetztzeit* as a now that is not just a moment through which the past is retrieved by the future. Instead of recuperating the memory of the oppressed by reinserting it into the official record of history, this profane messianism seeks, paradoxically, to redeem the past by interrupting its very transmission in the form of tradition, thereby revealing "a present which is not a transition." In "On the Concept of History," this messianic task is compared to mechanical reproduction, "history in time lapse mode." By capturing the passage of empty, homogeneous time at a slower frame-rate, the time lapse technique provides a messianic representation of nature as an empty eternity that seizes the truth of every tradition in recognizing its transience.

As context for the discussion of Benjamin's historical materialism, Chapter 5 examines the historical relationship between neo-Kantianism, which provided Benjamin with the terminology he used to articulate his early metaphysical anarchism, and Marx's critique of political economy. In the late nineteenth and early twentieth centuries, the predominance of neo-Kantianism, which rejected German Idealism, would promote a misreading of the materialist application of the dialectical method in *Capital*, among both its defenders and critics. During this period, neo-Kantian thinkers popularized the caricature of "historical materialism" as the reduction of history to natural or mechanical causality, while providing social democracy with its "school philosophy" in the concept of socialism as an infinite task. Against the revisionism of figures like Eduard Bernstein, who viewed neo-Kantianism as a scientific foundation for socialism and an alternative to Marx's Hegelianism, Marxists like Georgi Plekhanov affirmed the theory in *Capital* as an all-encompassing materialist worldview.

Like neo-Kantian socialism, however, this vindication of Marxism would also obscure the defining feature of the critique of political economy, which Benjamin referred to as the "restriction of the materialist conception of history."[116] While neo-Kantianism hypostatized political principles that arise from the social relations that constitute bourgeois society, elevating them to the status of eternal ideals, the orthodox Marxist critiques of the latter ignored the historically restricted character of Marx's analysis. This analysis is one that Benjamin will incorporate into the *Arcades Project* during the second stage of its development from 1935 to 1939. Drawing on Karl Korsch's reading of *Capital*, which emphasizes "the principle of historical specification," Benjamin applied Marx's historically specific analysis to criticize the ahistorical conception of capitalism and socialism in Georg Simmel's *Philosophy of Money*.[117]

Chapter 6 interprets the *Arcades Project* as a synthesis of Benjamin's early anarchist philosophy and Marx's critique of political economy. If the *Trauerspiel* book is the culmination of Benjamin's early work, the *Arcades* is the theater of all his ideas. The historical materialism that Benjamin develops in this project, however, also draws upon an important precursor to Marx's critique: Charles Fourier's utopian socialism. Like *Capital*, the latter presents a dialectical analysis of crises in capitalism, which are defined as the product of a contradiction, specific to bourgeois society, between the mode of production and the mode of exchange, between technology and the exchange of commodities. In these crises, "poverty," according to Fourier, "is born of superabundance." Bound by bourgeois relations of property, the ability of technology to increase production and make labor irrelevant causes catastrophe.

This analysis informed what critics have characterized as Benjamin's uncritical infatuation with the purportedly progressive tendencies of technology, an infatuation which he supposedly shared with vulgar materialism. According to Richard Wolin, Benjamin espoused a "version of Marxism ... that was extremely undialectical and simplistic; a problem which anyone sincerely interested in Benjamin's relevance for the legacy of historical materialism today is obligated to confront fully."[118] The chapter contends that this criticism of Benjamin, as articulated by Adorno and others, is rooted in a generalizing misinterpretation of the concept of commodity fetishism, a misinterpretation informed by neo-Kantianism. Against this critique, the chapter argues that this view of technology is fully consistent with Marx's critique of political economy as well as with Benjamin's early anarchist theory of justice, based on the right of the thing to be without a possessor. In Benjamin's later historical materialism, the "good-right of the good" assumes the form of "technology's right of co-determination in the social order," an order based on relations of property that create poverty out of the superabundance produced by machinery.

This Fourierist account of capitalist "crises of plethora" underlies the peculiar conception of revolution proposed in the work of art essay and the *Arcades Project*—revolution as a collective attempt to realize the right of "second technology" to transform work into play. For Benjamin, the socialism that such a revolution seeks to establish is not that of an ethically perfect society conforming to the categorical imperative, but rather what Fourier described as a hedonistic utopia in which morality is abolished along with wage labor and capital.

In the nineteenth century, however, the revolutionary impulse, aroused by technology, to liberate desire and labor would be redirected by bourgeois society toward the consumption of new forms of industrial leisure. For Benjamin, the products for sale in the Parisian arcades commodified the utopian will for a "better arrangement for the union of the sexes and the exchange of industrial products," or what Fourier described as an amorous regime of impassioned labor and unfettered affects.[119] In these products, of which fashion is a privileged example, the wish for a utopian society of erotic freedom and unalienated labor is both expressed and excluded in the form of new industrial commodities. By stimulating sexual fetishism and the desire to belong to the upper classes, these commodities diverted the collective demand to create a classless society, free from both class exploitation and the bonds of a bourgeois morality that continually provoke their transgression.

In the nineteenth century, these products, which were based on the principle of "newness," would provide industrial capitalism with a means of overcoming its "crises of plethora," perpetuating the interminable cycle of production and overproduction. As a result, the reproduction of novelty—new habits, manners, and styles—becomes an unchanging condition of bourgeois society, as obligatory as the transmission of tradition had been for the reproduction of earlier social formations.

This phenomenon is identified in the *Arcades* as the historical condition for the critique of the concept of progress in the writings of Friedrich Nietzsche and Louis Auguste Blanqui. In an era in which tradition was dissolved by the endless production of novelty, which emerged as an unchanging condition of bourgeois society, Blanqui and Nietzsche conceived the idea of an eternal return in which progress, repeated *ad infinitum*, appears utterly meaningless. Benjamin characterizes this doctrine as a critique of the bourgeois conception of history that also affirms the latter as fate. In Blanqui and Nietzsche, the unending drama of progress in bourgeois society must be repeated forever even though this movement belongs to a particular mode of production. In that sense, the concept of eternal return is a dialectical complement to the notion of progress. Both serve to conceal the transitory nature of bourgeois society.

Against these opposing notions of history, Benjamin called for a "dialectical conception of historical time" that could bring progress as well as its eternal return to a standstill. This dialectical conception of historical time conjoins Benjamin's early critique of vitalism and rationalism with a critical theory of capitalism that seeks to unmask the latter's eternal appearance—its "modernity"—by exposing its historically determinant character. In this way, Benjamin's historical materialism continues and consummates his early philosophical anarchism.

In the concepts of progress and eternal return, the secularized notion of nature and history, resulting from the "mechanization of the world view," becomes a mythological image of bourgeois society, just as value is fetishized as a real physical property. In a paradoxical form of re-enchantment (which appears as its opposite, as the disenchantment of the world), capitalism "projects this image of the cosmos—understood as an image of itself—across the heavens."[120] As a result, the "shallow rationalism" of mechanical reason becomes the eternal appearance of a particular mode of production. The alienation of abstract labor time, as the historically determinate foundation of capitalism, is disguised as the reified time of the natural sciences. In the nineteenth century, the emergence of this second nature, disguised as the mechanical time of the cosmos, was accompanied by the commodification of bodily life and desire, by the fetishization of a "first nature," masking the bare creaturely condition, uncovered by the Baroque.

Chapter 7 examines the influence of Benjamin's historical materialism on Pierre Klossowski, whose work informed the attempts by postwar French philosophers, including Gilles Deleuze and Michel Foucault, to rethink the relation between political economy and psychoanalysis. The chapter contends that Klossowski's writings can be understood as a critical appropriation of the *Arcades* and the work of art essay (which Klossowski translated into French), one that sought to refute the Fourierism that inflected Benjamin's Marxism. The aim of the chapter is to confirm, negatively as it were, the book's central argument on the relationship between Benjamin and Marx by considering a post-structuralist critique of the historically determinate analysis of capitalism that Benjamin adopted from Marx and Fourier. This refutation—which was a response to Benjamin's criticism of the ideology of the Acéphale group as a form of "pre-fascist aestheticism"—challenges the critical apparatus of the *Arcades* from the standpoint of the concepts of "expenditure," "transgression," and "general economy," developed by Georges Bataille. According to Klossowski, the perversions that Fourier wanted to liberate for his hedonistic utopia are inextricably bound to the bourgeois institutions he proposed to abolish. Freed from the repression from which it arises, the desire that Fourier wanted to use as the foundation for his future utopia would no longer exist. Thus, despite its critique of bourgeois civilization as a historically specific form of society, Fourier's socialism universalizes a libidinal economy that is specific to nineteenth-century capitalism. From the perspective of general economy, moreover, Fourier's proposal to transform work into passionate play erases the difference between labor and "unproductive expenditure," depriving work of the calculative character that defines it as such, while dissolving all sensual pleasure.

The chapter ends with a reading of the work of art essay as a preemptive rejoinder to Klossowski's refutation of Fourier. From the perspective of Benjamin's historical materialism, Bataille's account of transgression, and of the co-implication of perversion and moral repression, is a dialectical complement to the neo-Kantian conception of socialism as an infinite task. Like the idea of eternal return, transgression affirms the infinite task of ethical progress as an inescapable fate for the sake of preserving desire. In this way, it denies technology's right to abolish bourgeois society by transforming work into play and making morality irrelevant.

1

Knowledge and Ephemeral Experience in the Coming Philosophy

Enlightenment, Experience, and Mechanical Reason

In a curriculum vitae composed in 1928, Benjamin describes his early philosophical studies as follows: "during my time as a student, I concerned myself with Plato and Kant, in connection with Husserl's philosophy and the Marburg school."[1] In the courses Benjamin attended in Freiburg from 1912 to 1915, the reading focused on three thinkers in particular: Kant, Husserl, and Heinrich Rickert, the most prominent member of the Baden or Southwestern school of neo-Kantianism.[2]

In his writings, Rickert distinguished the rationalism of neo-Kantianism from the "contemporary trend" of philosophies of "lived-experience," from a philosophy of life or *Lebensphilosophie* which held that reason could be reduced to existence or "bare life." This trend was one that Rickert identified in particular with Nietzsche, Schopenhauer, Henri Bergson, and Husserl.[3] In "Some Motifs in Baudelaire," Benjamin describes this philosophical current in the following manner:

> Since the end of the nineteenth century, philosophy has made a series of attempts to grasp 'true' experience ... These efforts are usually classified under the rubric of 'vitalism.' ... [Wilhelm] Dilthey's book *Das Erlebnis und die Dichtung* represents one of the earliest of these efforts, which culminate with Klages and Jung, who made common cause with fascism. Towering above this literature is Bergson's early monumental work, *Matière et mémoire*.[4]

The ambivalence toward vitalist theories of "true" experience expressed in this passage was already a feature of Benjamin's early philosophy. His account of the latter in the curriculum vitae, as defined by a concern for "Kant, in connection with Husserl ... and the Marburg school," suggests what Fabrizio Desideri described as an interpretation of Kant that departs from both neo-Kantianism and vitalist criticisms of Kant: "Benjamin distances himself explicitly both from the Neo-Kantianism of his era and from the phenomenological program of Husserl."[5]

This interpretation is partially outlined in "On the Program of the Coming Philosophy" (1918). In the text, Benjamin criticizes the "extreme extension" of "mechanical reason" resulting from the attempt by Hermann Cohen and the Marburg School to "rectify" Kant's theory of knowledge.[6] As Benjamin explains in the "Coming Philosophy," Kant's philosophy is unique in that it recognizes the need to justify knowledge, and in its attempt to arrive at "epistemologically secured principles" that do not extend beyond the limits of reason.[7]

This unique characteristic was a product of the particular historical period in which Kant devised his philosophy. As a result of the European Enlightenment, neither knowledge nor experience could rely any longer on dogmatic authority to ensure their validity. "For the Enlightenment there were no authorities, in the sense not only of authorities to whom one would have to submit unconditionally, but also of intellectual forces who might have managed to give a higher context to experience."[8]

As "a man who ... shared the horizon of his times," Kant recognized that knowledge required justification since its certainty could no longer be grounded in God.[9] This justification, moreover, could only be found in experience, an experience which, because of the absence of any higher authority, was defined "by an extraordinary superficiality and godlessness." As a consequence of the Enlightenment, "experience," which had previously "been ... exalted ... [as] close to ... divine," "was increasingly stripped of its proximity to God." Rejecting God's authority, the Enlightenment conceived of experience as "godless" and "empty."[10]

This empty experience, which "pertain[s] to the entire modern era," is the same as the one that, according to Scholem, the Russian nihilist movement would later confront in the nineteenth century.[11] During this period, the "withering of meaning of the authority structures ... engulfed" revolutionaries in Russia, who became "fundamental opponent[s] to every form of authority," refusing to "accept any principles based on belief."[12] As Benjamin noted in a later essay, the impoverishment of experience would also define the twentieth century, which witnessed the meaningless death and destruction of industrial warfare: "experience has fallen in value, amid a generation which from 1914 to 1918 had to experience some of the most monstrous events in the history of the world. ... Wasn't it noticed ... how many people returned from the front in silence? Not richer but poorer in communicable experience?"[13]

It was within this specific horizon of history, that of a sort of epistemological anarchy, that Kant attempted to produce a philosophy that could justify knowledge based on a form of experience that could no longer recognize any authority outside of itself. Kant "undertook his work on the basis of an experience virtually reduced to a nadir, to a minimum of significance ... an experience which had almost no intrinsic value and which could have attained its ... sad significance only through its certainty."[14]

Because of the anarchic absence of authority, this certainty had to be predicated upon an empty experience defined by the "utter groundlessness of modern existence."[15] For Kant, this meant that knowledge could not "surpass the bounds of all experience."[16] Putting "a stop to empty flights of fancy," Kant argued that objects that exceeded experience, such as the idea of the soul and the notion of God as the unconditioned ground of all things, were only transcendental illusions created by the attempt to extend human cognition beyond sensibility.[17] Stripped of the proximity to God that had once granted it certainty, experience, which could now only be sure of itself, could no longer guarantee the existence of God.

Against theology, then, as well as the speculative rationalism of thinkers like Plato who "abandoned the world of the senses ... [for] the empty space of pure understanding,"[18] Kant proposed a "finitist" theory of knowledge, restricting the latter to the realm of experience.[19] In order to justify knowledge—that is, in order to demonstrate that knowledge is capable by itself of cognizing truths that are universal and timeless—such a theory would require an account of the validity of knowledge that is consistent with its fundamental finitude. Since knowledge cannot "take refuge in principles that overstep all ... experience,"[20] its ideas must be shown to be universally true on the basis of the sensible world upon which they depend, a world which, unlike the objects of theology, exists within space and time. As Benjamin noted: "It is well known that Kant ... made the validity of the categories [of the understanding] for the experience of nature dependent on time and space. It is in this declaration of dependence that Kant's opposition to metaphysics is grounded."[21]

But as such, the task imposed upon the critique of pure reason and its justification of knowledge is a paradoxical one. The critique must demonstrate the validity of human cognition, showing that it is capable of a knowledge that is universal and timeless (and therefore "entirely *a priori*, independent ... of experience"), even while acknowledging its finitude, its dependence upon experience. Kant, in other words, must demonstrate the possibility of a knowledge that transcends the experience from which it arises and to which it is bound.

According to Benjamin, this task is one that Kant could only succeed in accomplishing by reducing experience to the "best aspect" of the "relatively empty Enlightenment concept of experience," namely, the concept employed in the godless domain of the sciences.[22] "Like most men of his age, Kant," as Wolin describes, "naturally considered the only possible legitimate idea of experience to be one based on the proven foundations of Newtonian physics."[23] In Benjamin's words, Kant, in his attempt to justify knowledge on the basis of experience alone, took "the principles of experience from the sciences—in particular, mathematical physics." In the latter's "mechanical concept of experience," "whose quintessence, was Newtonian physics," space and time are understood as measurable forms. Time, conceived as "mechanical time," serves as "the measure that records the duration of a mechanical change" within space.[24]

In his theory of knowledge, therefore, Kant comes close to "conflating" experience with the concept of space and time in Euclidean geometry and Newtonian physics, a conflation that will come to define the philosophical program of the Marburg school of neo-Kantianism.[25] As Benjamin argues, however, this "mechanical experience" does not correspond to the concept of "'experience' in ordinary use." In contrast to the latter, the concepts of space and time employed in the sciences are intuitions that are already rationalized or mediated by knowledge.[26] As such, they constitute a "knowledge of experience" distinct from the "immediate and natural concept of experience." Thus, insofar as Kant's theory of knowledge identifies the "ordinary meaning of experience" with mechanical experience, it risks reducing experience to reason.[27]

But in that case, Kant's justification for science fails to conform to the critical principle that knowledge cannot exceed the bounds of experience. Despite his insistence on finitude, Kant, then, does not justify knowledge within the bounds of experience since experience "was never identical with the object realm of ... science." Instead, in the *Critique of Pure Reason*, the eternal validity of knowledge is derived from "mechanical reason," which is a form of knowledge itself. "Kant ... proceeds not from experience but simply from reason *a priori*."[28]

But as such, the Kantian theory depends upon an account of experience that paradoxically *excludes experience itself*. "Paradoxical though it sounds, experience does not occur as such in the knowledge of experience."[29] In Kant's attempt to develop a finitist theory in which knowledge is independent of the experience upon which it depends, experience itself is excluded by its reduction to mechanical reason. While the theory succeeds in justifying knowledge on the basis of the concept of experience employed in the godless domain of the sciences, it fails to confront the finitude of experience as such, which is exposed in the Enlightenment by the anarchic absence of all authority. Benjamin's critique of Kant's theory of knowledge, then, is not that it "proffer[s] a concept of a hollow experience, 'virtually reduced to a nadir', and that the "Kantian categories ... constitute experience but also diminish it to its rudiments."[30] On the contrary, Benjamin argues that the theory fails to confront the emptiness of experience in the Enlightenment, relying on categories derived from the sciences that do not constitute experience, but rather exclude the bare form of the latter revealed by the absence of a higher authority. As a result of this failure, Kant's critique of pure reason does not provide an account of "experience, in its total structure."[31] By taking the principles of experience from natural science, "Kant managed to give a valid explanation [as to] ... the certainty of knowledge that is lasting," but, in doing so, he overlooked the need to establish "the integrity of an experience that is ephemeral," or "singularly temporal."[32]

Contrary to what many commentators have argued, then, the critique of Kant presented in the "Coming Philosophy" is not that his theory of knowledge is based on an impoverished idea of experience. For Benjamin, it was not Kant's "selection of this inferior object domain," that of the natural sciences, that "proved his undoing." Rather, the issue is that his theory focuses only on the "best side" of the empty Enlightenment idea of experience, justifying mechanical reason while "abandoning the deduction of ... 'empty, godless experience.'" The oversight is understandable, according to Benjamin, since "in an age in which experience was characterized by an extraordinary superficiality and godlessness, philosophy, if it was honest, could have no interest in salvaging this experience for its concept of knowledge."

What this implies, however, is that already in his early theological phase, Benjamin took an affirmative view of the impoverishment and profanation of experience that characterizes modernity, proposing to salvage it for his coming theory of knowledge. In Benjamin's early anarchist politics (see Chapter 2), the practical correlate to the concept of "empty, godless experience" is that of an original pre-ethical state of humanity, a humanity that will be redeemed without any moral improvement. In his habilitation on the German *Trauerspiel*, the messianic "fulfillment of an unimproved humanity" assumes the form of a worldly redemption of mere creaturely life, a life that no longer conceives of the transient present as a transition toward an otherworldly salvation (see Chapter 3).[33]

This affirmative view of bare life reappears in various forms in Benjamin's materialist writings, including that of a "positive concept of barbarism" in which the "poverty of experience" provides the condition for complete demystification, the "total absence of illusion about the age." In the *Arcades*, it appears as a "cracking open" of Kant's teleology, in which progress toward the impossible ideal of moral perfection and the rise of a "second technology" create a "different" kind of utopia, a hedonistic utopia of creaturely pleasure in which morality is irrelevant (see Chapter 7).

Singular Experience and the Problem of Identity

The critique of Kant and the Marburg School in the "Coming Philosophy" draws on the work of the Baden school of neo-Kantianism, specifically, that of Heinrich Rickert,[34] who developed a nominalistic philosophy arguing that "natural scientific knowledge is not knowledge of reality." In Rickert's philosophy, "only the singular, the unique, the individual exists," "only the particular actually occurs." "Today," therefore, "we no longer recognize any general realities, but for us everything real is contained in the visual and individual, consequently, in the particular."[35]

Since "the unique and individual character of empirical reality cannot … be subsumed under the concepts of natural science," Rickert concluded that natural science is not "a science of reality." "If in the content of natural scientific concepts nothing Individual and visual enters, then from this it follows that in it nothing real enters." The progress of science, therefore, can never arrive at a true knowledge of reality, which is excluded by its very conceptual nature ("Once the natural scientific concept is formed, everything real disappears from its content"). On the contrary: "The goal and meaning of natural science is to ever more sharply elaborate the opposition between the content of concepts and the given 'visible reality,'"[36] the opposition between the abstractions of science and immediate experience.

This critique of Kant's theory of knowledge is reiterated in Benjamin's early writings. In several philosophical fragments, Benjamin examines how the principles of identity and non-contradiction that underlie mechanical reason exclude "experience itself and unto itself," which is "singularly temporal" in nature.[37] In "Theses on the Problem of Identity," written roughly at the same time as the "Coming Philosophy," Benjamin argues that the problem with the identity principle is that it can never establish a relationship of certainty with respect to immediate temporal and spatial experience. "The formula of identity … 'A = A' … does not assert the equality of two spatially or temporally distinct stages of A. But neither can it express the identity of any A existing in space or time," since the "identity-relation … exist[s] beyond time and space."[38] The formula of identity, then, equates objects (or stages of the movement of objects) that are not identical by excluding their spatially and temporally singular character.

In another fragment, "The Paradox of the Cretan," Benjamin pursues the same argument from a different perspective, that of the law of non-contradiction, a law from which Kant derives the identity principle in the *Critique of Pure Reason*. The paradox is as follows: Epimenides declares that "All Cretans are liars," but since Epimenides is a

Cretan, the statement must therefore be untrue. But if Cretans, in fact, all tell the truth, then the statement that "All Cretans are liars" is true. "And with this ... the vicious circle must begin."[39]

Benjamin describes the paradox as a logical version of Descartes's evil demon, "transposed from the sphere of perception to that of logic." Just as the supposition of the demon, in Descartes's *Meditations*, threatens to reduce all our perceptions to the "illusions of dreams," so the paradox of the Cretan suggests that knowledge, trapped in an "insoluble chain of contradictions," can never achieve certainty.[40]

According to Benjamin, this paradox, which is "insoluble within logic itself," is, in fact, "easily resolved."[41] And he does so by distinguishing, once again, between the timeless validity of logical forms and "truth" about a specific temporal experience. The paradox is only insoluble if we assume that the statement, "All Cretans are liars," is true of all places and times. As Benjamin points out, however, there is no reason that a liar's words should carry the weight of a logical proposition. Nor does a liar necessarily lie on each and every occasion. "The concept of the liar does not mean that a liar departs from the truth every time he opens his mouth, nor, even if he did so, that what he says would be the absolute contrary of the truth."[42] The contradictions that arise from the paradox of the Cretan, therefore, exist only "in the realm of logic, without being in any way ... nonsensical in itself ... on the ontological plane," that is, on the plane of the truth of temporally specific experience.[43] Like the identity principle, then, the law of non-contradiction exists in a realm beyond time and space that excludes ephemeral experience, which Benjamin identifies with being itself.

Experience and Speculative Rationalism in Kant's Theory of Knowledge

Thus, in establishing the validity of knowledge based on the principles of mechanical reason, Kant inadvertently abandons the world of the senses, making knowledge independent of the realm upon which it is supposed to depend. But in that way, Kant's theory of knowledge "risks turning into the very speculative rationalism that it positioned itself against," a rationalism in which reality is deduced *a priori* from knowledge.[44] The result is what Benjamin calls a "*metaphysics* of nature [that] could be described as the *a priori* constituents of natural objects on the basis of the determinants of the knowledge of nature in general."[45]

This problem, however, was one of which Kant himself was acutely aware. As Benjamin explains in a fragment titled "Perception," "Kant feared nothing so much as this abyss," which he himself had created by attempting to justify knowledge through natural science. Kant feared the abyss of an "exaggerated concept of reason and of the excesses of a concept of understanding that had ceased to be based on an actual intuition."[46] By limiting knowledge to a mechanical form of experience, Kant's finitist epistemology lapses into speculative rationalism, which denies experience, rather than knowledge.

In order to avoid the reduction of intuition to thought (or, in Benjamin's words, in order to keep knowledge from "suck[ing] all experience into itself"), Kant, in his architectonic, would impose a strict separation between the categories of the understanding and the forms of pure sensibility. "His method," as Benjamin writes, "was not only to relate all knowledge ... to space and time as constitutive concepts, but to distinguish these concepts absolutely from the categories."[47]

In Kant's architectonic, therefore, the categories of the understanding are separated from the *a priori* forms of pure space and time by virtue of the latter's proximity to an uncognizable "material of sensation," the cause of which is an unknowable thing-in-itself. As Benjamin describes in the "Coming Philosophy," this material of sensation is passively given within intuition, providing the content that is schematized by the categories:

> Kant postulated the so-called material of sensation to express the separation of the forms of intuition from the categories. This "material of sensation" was artificially distanced from the animating center of the categories by the forms of intuition by which it was only imperfectly absorbed. In this way Kant achieved the separation ... between pure knowledge and experience.[48]

By separating knowledge and experience in this manner, Kant, as Matthew Charles describes, was "able to introduce a check or critical limit with which to resist speculative deduction: the requirement that the 'flights of fancy' of the understanding be grounded upon intuitability."[49] This critical limit—which had to be imposed "artificially" because of the abyss created by the conflation of experience and mechanical reason—restricts human knowledge from both the objects of religion and immediate ephemeral experience.[50]

Natural Science and the Exclusion of God and Bare Life

Paradoxically, then, the emphasis placed upon the mechanical form of experience excludes both religion and the empty and irreligious experience that characterizes modernity. By identifying experience with the secular domain of the sciences, Kant denies theology and its metaphysical flights of fancy as well as the "empty, godless experience" of the Enlightenment.[51] His theory of knowledge excludes a "naked, primitive" form of experience, which constitutes "a reality of ... the lowest ... order," while failing to "systematically incorporate this 'highest' region of knowledge into the schema of philosophy ... the absolute."[52] In the *Critique of Pure Reason*, then, both God and bare life are placed beyond the limits of knowledge.

To address this exclusion, the "coming philosophy" that Benjamin announced in his early philosophical writings will require a twofold revision of Kant's theory of knowledge. On the one hand, Benjamin, as Howard Caygill describes, attempts to "introduce ... the 'absolute' ... into Kant's deliberately finitist concept of experience"[53] and his "rigid epistemological ban on thinking the absolute."[54] Against this finitist theory, Benjamin argues that a "philosophy that does not include the possibility of soothsaying ... and cannot explicate it cannot be a true philosophy."[55] Confronted with what Julia Ng has described as a "critical project [that] places 'religion' firmly out of grasp," Benjamin will propose a "concept of experience which will also encompass realms that Kant failed to truly systematize," the "foremost" of which is the "realm of religion."[56]

Whereas Kant believed that he had to "deny knowledge in order to make room for faith," Benjamin would seek to revise the former's theory of knowledge in order to make room for religion. Kant had excluded this region because of the mechanical concept of experience that he uses in order to justify knowledge. As such, a revision of Kant will require a theory of knowledge that can justify religion as well as the timeless validity of natural science: "Thus, the task of the coming philosophy can be conceived as the discovery ... of that concept of knowledge which .... makes not only mechanical but also religious experience logically possible."[57]

But in that case, Benjamin was not an esoteric or mystic who was constitutively averse to "binding, generally valid statements" and to analyzing "rationally explainable process[es]."[58] Rather, his coming philosophy was concerned with the project of establishing, in a rigorous manner, the logical possibility of mystical experience as well as the universal validity of the mechanical laws of mathematical physics.

The project is directly opposed to Kant's attempt to rescue both religion and Newtonian physics. Kant makes room for religion by situating it beyond all experience, while conflating experience with mechanical reason. Theology thereby is saved in a negative form through a critique of pure reason that makes its objects unknowable, and therefore irrefutable. In that way, Kant's "finitist concept of experience" allows for the existence of an absolute being. In the coming philosophy, on the other hand, an expanded account of experience allows for a secularized view of religion as logically possible.

Contrary to Wolin, Benjamin does not characterize Kant's theory of knowledge as "mythological in essence" because it is based upon a "profane concept ... of experience ... removed from contact with the absolute."[59] Rather, it is mythological because, by identifying mechanical reason with experience unto itself, it preserves the religious authority on which it can no longer depend in its attempt to justify knowledge. Against this modern mythology, based on a narrowly mechanistic idea of experience, Benjamin proposed a coming epistemology that could allow for a completely profane understanding of the absolute.

As Benjamin suggests in his later writings, this theory was partially realized in the practice of surrealism, which, as Wolin points out, sought the "redemption of everyday reality" through the "method of profane illumination." The later constitutes a purely secular form of religious experience, "a materialistic, anthropological inspiration, to which hashish, opium or whatever else can give an introductory lesson." "Like religious illumination, profane illumination," as Wolin describes:

> ... captures the powers of spiritual intoxication in order to produce a 'revelation'
> ... which transcends the prosaic state of empirical reality; yet it produces this vision in an immanent manner, while remaining within the bounds of possible experience, and without recourse to otherworldly dogmas.[60]

Likewise, in the coming philosophy, religion would be included within the bounds of possible experience by correcting the conflation of experience unto itself and mechanical reason, which allowed Kant to preserve the illusion of God. In the coming philosophy, on the other hand, an expanded theory of knowledge would allow one to experience religion as an illusion, one that serves a set of logical functions that are not merely mechanical, such as the function of God as the "circumference" of the "realm of Ideas."[61] Like surrealism, such a profane understanding of God would make possible a "creative overcoming of religious illumination," as well as what Ricardo Ibarlucía has characterized as a nihilistic "secularization of mysticism."[62]

This profane understanding corresponds to what Benjamin describes as the effect of "play and reflection" in the *Trauerspiel* and later in Romantic comedy and tragedy. In "the device of reflection," in which characters reflect upon fate, the drama of life appears as a vain succession of games. The representation of "life itself as a play" constitutes the "playful reduction of the real along with the introduction of a reflexive infinity of thought into the closed finitude of a profane space of fate."[63] In its profane representation as play, life is stripped of the aura of divine destiny.

Contrary to Wolin, then, the trajectory of Benjamin's work was not defined by a shift from a theological to a profane idea of redemption. In his later historical materialism, "Benjamin's redemptive criticism," according to Wolin, "had become thoroughly profane," ceasing to "concern itself with presenting an image of otherworldly truth."[64] However, as works like the "Coming Philosophy" appear to imply, Benjamin had already developed a profane view of religion in the early theological stage of his work. The thoroughly profane idea of redemption that appears in Benjamin's later writings, therefore, was not the result of his turn to materialism, his conversion to "the profane cause of the class struggle."[65] Rather, in both his theological and materialist phases, Benjamin embraced a completely secularized idea of salvation.

What this suggests (as Chapter 4 will consider) is that Benjamin did not feel the need "to bolster his Marxism through recourse to the theological categories of his early period."[66] Rather, he sought the aid of theology in order to develop a version of Marxism that was completely devoid of theology, including the secularized forms of the latter characteristic of modernity.

The Problem of Identity and the *Eidos* Doctrine

But if Kant had failed in his theory of knowledge to incorporate the realm of religion, in the "Program," he is also accused of the opposite error, of "abandoning the deduction of that 'empty, godless experience.'"[67] Since the scientific account of experience excludes both metaphysical speculation and immediate experience, the coming philosophy must also make room for bare life, which the Enlightenment had stripped of its proximity to God.

Such a revision of Kant would allow for a more comprehensive theory of knowledge that could grasp experience in "its total structure." Instead of merely establishing "the certainty of knowledge that is lasting," the theory would also be able to justify immediate and ephemeral experience. This "singularly temporal" experience is excluded by the concepts that appear on the Kantian table of categories. Benjamin, therefore, proposed a new theory of knowledge, based on the notion of truth as the immediate certainty of the here-and-now: The "world is knowable *now*. Truth resides in the 'now of knowability.'" The certainty of this "now," then, is distinct from the "timeless validity" of the categories employed in the natural sciences, including the principle of identity.[68]

In this way, the coming philosophy would realize the "universal philosophical interest ... directed toward both the timeless validity of knowledge and the certainty of a temporal experience which is regarded as the immediate, if not the only, object of that knowledge." Such a philosophy would justify the secular domain of the sciences, which is the "best aspect" of the "relatively empty Enlightenment concept of experience," while simultaneously rescuing the "lowest" reality of a godless "experience which ... attained its ... sad significance only through its certainty."[69]

By grasping experience in "its total structure," such a revision of Kant would comprehend the mutually exclusive character of immediate experience and the timeless categories of mechanical reason. In this way, the coming philosophy could resolve the seemingly insoluble paradox of how concepts that exist beyond time and space relate to experiences that are singularly temporal in nature.

Unable to grasp this irreducible difference, Kant artificially separated intuition and knowledge in order to avoid the risk of speculative rationalism or a deduction of reality from reason. This separation underlies the more well-known account, in the *Critique of Pure Reason*, of the necessary interaction between intuition and thought that characterizes the movement of knowledge: "Thoughts without content are empty, intuitions without concepts are blind."[70] While experience devoid of cognition remains unintelligible, thought deprived of the "material of sensation" is confined to the "empty space of pure understanding."[71]

But if knowledge and experience rely on each other, the correspondence between thought and reality, as the object of knowledge, is precluded by Kant from the outset, due to the critical limit imposed between intuition and thought. As a result of this separation (introduced arbitrarily to avoid a metaphysics in which reality is reduced to cognition), "the continuity of knowledge and experience, if not the connection between them, was disrupted," according to Benjamin.[72]

This disconnection underlies what Benjamin describes as his "disappointment" with Kant's philosophy of history, which he had originally chosen as the topic for his dissertation.[73] Because of Kant's desire to "distinguish [the forms of intuition] absolutely from the categories," the agreement between thought and experience, as the goal of knowledge itself, becomes an infinite task.[74] As Benjamin explains in a letter to Scholem, this task is eternal not because it requires an infinite duration of time to accomplish, that is, because the pursuit of knowledge is literally endless. Rather, the task is eternal because it is *a priori* impossible since its goal is an agreement between individual faculties (sensibility and understanding) whose discontinuity or disagreement is assumed arbitrarily in Kant's theory of knowledge. Because of the "[a]mbiguity of the term 'Infinite Task,'" the Kantian School conflated these two different ways of conceiving of knowledge as an interminable process.[75] "What does it mean," Benjamin writes in a letter to Scholem, "to say that science is an eternal task? ... [It is] clear ... that the subject is an 'eternal task' and not a 'solution that requires an eternally long time,' and that the first concept in no way can or may be transformed into the second."[76]

Applying this distinction to the concept of science as an infinite task, Benjamin identifies two different meanings of this task that are not clearly distinguished in Kant's conception of history. In the latter, science is understood as an infinite task not because of the truism that a knowledge of all things-in-themselves would literally be an endless endeavor. Rather, science is infinite because experience is identified with logical thinking, which can never be the "correlate of truth" since the tautological propositions of science are timeless and indifferent to the singular things they subsume.

In a 1917 letter to Scholem, Benjamin suggests one possible way of securing the "sad significance" of an immediate experience whose certainty can no longer be guaranteed by God, a certainty that Kant fails to recognize because of his "one-sided" emphasis on mechanical reason.[77] Outlining his criticism of Kant, Benjamin argues that "truth," as a unique temporal and spatial experience, can never be thought, since thinking is based on an identity principle (and a law of non-contradiction) that exists beyond time and space: "I dispute that any 'thinking' is the correlate of truth ... 'Thinking' ... may somehow be only an abstraction of the truth. The assertion of identity in thinking would be the *absolute tautology*."[78] But as such, in defining the categories of the understanding (based on the principle of identity) as the *a priori* structure of a transcendental subject, Kant confines all experience to the tautological sphere of a thinking that is constitutively separated from the ontological plane of truth. In demonstrating the timeless validity of the transcendental structure underlying the Newtonian account of the physical universe, Kant ignores the need to establish the certainty of an immediate temporal experience, which is the object of knowledge itself. In his attempt to guarantee "the certainty of knowledge [of nature] that is lasting," Kant avoided the effort to prove "the integrity of an experience that is ephemeral."[79]

This problem, as Benjamin suggests in the letter to Scholem, is one that Edmund Husserl had tried to resolve in his vitalist account of the "intuition of essence," or "eidetic intuition": "Regarding ... the problem of identity ... This in fact probably leads to the *eidos* doctrine."[80] As Adorno explained in a gloss on Benjamin's early philosophy, this doctrine was part of a phenomenological method, based on the concept of life or lived experience, "meant to replace a [Marburg School] philosophy that aims at the dissolution of ... being into categories of thought."[81]

Husserl, Descartes, and the Certainty of Ephemeral Experience

Benjamin was introduced to the doctrine while studying in Munich from 1915 to 1916, where he took two seminars on Kant which, as he described in a letter, "left me with a lasting impression."[82] The seminars were directed by Moritz Geiger, who was a disciple of Husserl. To "gain entrance into his school," the school of phenomenology, Benjamin studied Husserl's "Philosophy as a Rigorous Science," *Ideas Pertaining to a Pure Phenomenology and to a Phenomenological Philosophy* and *Logical Investigations*.[83]

In *Logical Investigations*, Husserl presents a critique of Kant's theory of knowledge that resembles the one that Benjamin proposes in the "Program for a Coming Philosophy." According to Husserl, the mechanical form of experience, the timeless validity of which Kant attempts to secure in a "critical 'saving' of mathematics, natural science," cannot be identified with experience itself as direct intuition.[84] The latter "differ[s] in principle from [the categories] which dominate objective science."

> Plainly the essential forms of all intuitive data are not ... to be brought under "exact" or "ideal" notions, such as we have in mathematics. The spatial shape of the perceived tree as such, taken precisely as a "moment" found in the relevant percept ... is no geometric shape ... Just so a seen colour as such is no ideal colour, whose Species occupies an ideal point in the colour-pyramid. The essences [of] direct [intuition] ... may not be confused with ... Ideas in the Kantian sense ...[85]

Paradoxically, then, the *a priori* concepts and perceptual forms that purportedly underlie all possible experience are not derived, in Kant's theory of knowledge, from experience at all: The "system of the forms of judgment in the Kantian deduction of what he calls the categories" is "not itself given through Intuition."[86] Instead, Kant conceived of experience on the model of the "mathematical thing," the "thing of physics," conflating its mechanical forms with intuition itself.[87] For Husserl, then, the *Critique of Pure Reason* perpetuates a confusion inherited from traditional theories of knowledge, which failed to distinguish between the "perceived object," which "has a unique place in spatio-temporality," and the "categorial object as such," which is "outside of space and time." The "Kantian doctrine," therefore, "rested entirely upon ... a mixture of irreconcilable concepts. [Does ...] the object of possible experience ... refer to the object that I perceive this moment or ... an intelligible unity constituted in that network of necessary determinations 'of which we have an idea when we speak of nature?'"[88]

This account of the Kantian doctrine corresponds to Benjamin's critique of the latter's conflation of experience as defined in the sciences, which are based on concepts that are timeless and universally valid, with experience unto itself, which is ephemeral and singularly temporal. Just as the coming philosophy would complete Kant's critique by defining the certainty of "a temporal experience ... regarded as the immediate ... object of that knowledge," so, for Husserl, Kant's theory "of knowledge found its solution in ... a temporal and actually lived cogito."[89] As Benjamin described in his 1923 curriculum vitae, Husserl's "eidetic way of taking appearances" was close to his own "mode of investigation," which views artworks as "incomparable and one-time."[90] And just as the coming philosophy would establish the certainty of a "now of knowability," distinct from the timeless validity of the sciences, so Husserl wanted to demonstrate the certainty of an immediate experience of the "*hic et nunc*": a "here and now ... whose being cannot be meaningfully doubted."[91]

In the epilogue to one of the texts that Benjamin read as part of his entrance exam into the school of phenomenology, Husserl argues that this certainty can be secured through a modified version of the Cartesian method of doubt: "My *Ideas toward a pure phenomenology* ... attempts to found ... a new science ... prepared ... since Descartes, a science related to a new field of experience." In his phenomenology, Husserl will return to Descartes's *Meditations* to thematize the ephemeral form of experience that Kant had failed to secure in the *Critique of Pure Reason*.

This return to Descartes may seem surprising at first, given the unwarranted inference, made in the *Meditations*, of the existence of a "thinking substance" or *res cogitans*, as the cause of the thoughts of the *cogito*, an inference that both Husserl and Benjamin criticize.[92] As Benjamin points out in his dissertation, the "Concept of Art Criticism in German Romanticism," this inference distinguished Descartes from post-Kantian philosophers such as Johann Gottlieb Fichte. For Fichte, Descartes, in declaring *cogito, ergo sum*, mistakenly inferred an essence from the act of cognition, an act in which no "thinking substance" is thought:

> Prior to [Kant], Descartes laid down a similar basic principle: *cogito, ergo sum*, ... which he may quite well have regarded as an immediate fact of consciousness. Then it would in effect be saying: *cogitans sum, ergo sum* ... But then the addition of *cogitans* is entirely superfluous; one does not necessarily think when one exists, but one necessarily exists when one thinks. Thinking is by no means the essence but only a particular determination of being.[93]

This essence or substance, moreover, underlies the dualism of body and mind that Husserl's phenomenological method was intended precisely to "bracket" (or suspend, "parenthesize," or put "out of action").[94] Yet, despite its account of the *cogito* as an essence, Descartes's *Meditations*, unlike the *Critique of Pure Reason*, is a work that, according to Husserl, succeeds, in spite of itself, in establishing the certainty of ephemeral experience.[95] Like the "naked, primitive" form of experience that Benjamin identifies with the European Enlightenment, the experience with which *Meditations* begins is one whose indubitable character is not derived, dogmatically, by appeal to a higher authority. Rather, Descartes attempts to secure the certainty of experience on the basis of experience itself.

As in the *Critique of Pure Reason*, this certainty is one that *Meditations* identifies initially with the "best aspect" of the Enlightenment concept of experience—the timeless validity of mathematical forms. Regardless of whether our senses are being misled by the illusions of dreams or other deceptions, for Descartes, as Husserl argues, "arithmetic, geometry, and so on ... have an element of indubitable certainty." However, as in Benjamin's account of the problem with the identity principle, this kind of indubitable certainty, precisely because of its timeless validity, does not establish the truth of an immediate temporal experience: "arithmetic, geometry ... treat only of the simplest and most general subject-matter, and are indifferent to whether it exists in nature or not."[96]

Thus, as Jacques Derrida has described, it is "only after this phenomenology of mathematical evidence and with the hypothesis of the Evil Demon" that Descartes will pose "the critical ... question ... of the ground that guarantees the truth of naïve evidence."[97] In spite of the emphasis on the mechanical aspect of experience, then, Descartes, nevertheless (in a section in *Meditations* preceding the unwarranted inference of a substance that thinks), provides an approach to ascertaining the truth of naïve ephemeral experience. If the supposition of an evil demon, declares Descartes, reduces all my perceptions ("colors, figures, sounds, and all external things") to "nothing better than the illusions of dreams," I can "at least ... *suspend my judgment*, and guard ... against giving ... assent to what is false."[98]

For Husserl, what this suspension of judgment succeeds in ensuring is not a substance that underlies the subject of thought (an "I am" of the "I think"), but the certainty of an ephemeral experience that is immediately intuited:[99] "It is possible that the perceived does not exist, but the perception of it is indubitable." I can doubt my perceptions, but not the fact I perceive: "The perceived is in question, but the perception is not." Therefore, as Husserl explains in the *Ideas*, the perception is "necessary," even though the perceived in itself is "contingent."[100]

In contrast to Kant's mechanical account of experience, then, the indubitable fact of perception that Husserl derives from Descartes's *Meditations* is a "necessary" phenomenon, even if the empirical objects it appears to perceive are not. In the phenomenological reduction, therefore, the procedure applied by Descartes "with the purpose of setting up an absolutely indubitable sphere of Being"—that is, with the aim of proving the existence of God and the soul—is employed as an "methodic expedient."[101] Whereas Descartes attempts to "doubt universally … we disregard this part … *We single out only the phenomenon of 'parenthesizing' or 'excluding'* … With regard to any positing we can quite freely exercise this peculiar *epoché*, a certain *refraining from judgment.*"[102]

Rather than proving the existence of God, who could then guarantee our experience, this expedient use of the Cartesian method of doubt reveals a profane but indubitable realm of "pure phenomena" or appearances. The latter corresponds to Benjamin's account of the "godless experience" of the Enlightenment, which "attained its … sad significance only through its certainty," a certainty based on itself, rather than a higher authority, or the validity of a natural law.[103]

As Peter Fenves has argued, Husserl's account of the *epoché* as a pure act of perception informed the concept of intuition that Benjamin employs in his earlier writings: "As for what Benjamin learned upon entering into Husserl's school, this much is certain: he learned its doctrine of intuition."[104] For Benjamin, "intuition is not, as Kant proposes … a contingent appearance" that must be subsumed by the abstractions of thought. Rather, pure phenomena are characterized by their certainty.[105] As Benjamin writes in a letter to Scholem: "The object of intuition is the necessity of a content that … announces itself as perceivable. The perception of this necessity is called 'intuition.'"[106]

Language, Eidetic Intuition, and the "Fixing of the Concept of Identity"

In an early fragment titled "Imagination," the eidetic realm of immediately intuited essences is translated in theological terms in the following manner: "there is a pure appearance … at the dawn of the world … the radiance that surrounds the objects in Paradise."[107] Like *eidos*, the purity of Paradise is that of an indubitable appearance without substance, an intuition whose veracity is irrelevant in the absence of judgment. Paradise, then, is identified paradoxically with a "godless experience" that has "attained its … sad significance only through its certainty" as a necessary appearance or indisputable intuition.[108]

This paradisal condition corresponds to what Benjamin describes in the essay "On Language as Such" as the Eden of a "pure language" that precedes logical judgment, and therefore is prior to the opposition between subject and object, as well as to the "origin of abstraction" in the Fall.[109] The original state of pure language is characterized, then, by an immediate identity of subject and object in which language "knows no means, no object, and no addressee of communication." In contrast to the "bourgeois conception of language," which "holds that the means of communication is the word, its object factual, and its addressee a human being," language, understood as language as such, communicates only itself.[110] This implies that the factual objects to which language refers are all *within language itself*. As such, language is not a means of communicating something outside of itself, but an all-encompassing medium, the contents of which are immediately present within it.

As Benjamin emphasizes, however, this identity of subject and object is distinct from that of the identity principle, A = A. While the "assertion of identity in thinking would be the absolute tautology," the identity of language with what it communicates is absolutely untautological.[111]

> For in language the situation is this: *the linguistic being of all things is their language.* The understanding of linguistic theory depends on giving this proposition a clarity that annihilates even the appearance of tautology. This proposition is untautological, for it means, "That which in a mental entity is communicable *is* its language." On this "is" (equivalent to "is immediately") everything depends.[112]

The proposition, therefore, that language communicates language is not a formula of identity, an identity that, by renouncing the "realm of truth" as singular temporal experience, would establish a timeless relationship of validity between subject and predicate. The copula "is," in Benjamin's proposition, is not a sign of equality indicating a relationship of identity that exists beyond space and time.

In his dissertation, "The Concept of Criticism in German Romanticism," Benjamin makes a similar claim about the idea of reflection in the work of Novalis and Schlegel. In the epistemology that underlies German Romanticism, "objective knowledge" of nature is based on "knowledge ... of the absolute." As in the essay on language, the absolute is defined in the dissertation as an all-encompassing medium: "The object, like everything real, lies within the medium of reflection."[113] Just as language in paradise, then, communicates language in an untautological manner, so, in reflection, defined as a "thinking of thinking," thought reflects on itself, instead of something external.

This immediate coincidence of subject and object in the act of reflection is not a correlation between cognition and being, as in the traditional concept of knowledge as *adaequatio*. Rather, like the "identity between mental and linguistic being" within language, it is an untautological unity that precedes the "origin of abstraction," including the abstractions that the Kantian subject uses to schematize the contingent intuitions it receives from the "material of sensation."[114] The identity of subject and object in the act of reflection, then, is not a correlation or equivalence between the one and the other. Rather, as Benjamin explains, in an Husserlian account of the "medium of thinking" in German Romanticism, it "would ... be ... more correct to leave this correlation generally out of play, and to speak of a coincidence of the objective and the subjective side in knowledge."[115] As the immediate coincidence of subject and object within the medium of reflection, thinking, like language as such, "knows no means, no object, and no addressee."

In the dissertation and the treatise on language, Benjamin appears to apply the "*eidos* doctrine" toward what he describes in the "Coming Philosophy" as the "fixing of the concept of identity, unknown to Kant."[116] In order to correct Kant's theory of knowledge, in which science is understood as an infinite task, "we have to ask about the medium in which truth and true being are conjoined. What is this neutral medium?" Since the medium in which knowledge coincides with absolute being, as Benjamin explains in another early philosophical fragment, is neutral "in regard to the concepts of both subject and object," knowledge cannot be understood as a function of either one or the other. "The task of future epistemology," then, "is to discover the ... sphere of knowledge in which this concept in no way continues to designate the relation between two metaphysical entities," or a correlation between subject and object.[117]

In the "Coming Philosophy," Benjamin describes this untautological concept of identity as "another relation between thesis and antithesis ... besides synthesis," "that of a certain nonsynthesis of two concepts in another."[118] In this relation of non-synthesis, subject and object are not equated conceptually. Rather, they are suspended in a state of indifferentiation. It is in this Husserlian fashion perhaps that Benjamin overcomes what Caygill describes as the main "difficulty at this early stage" of his work. This difficulty consists in "discovering a method by which ... to present the immanent absolute without translating it into an ideal totality in the manner of Hegelian speculative philosophy."[119] Instead of a conceptual synthesis of identity and difference, the coming philosophy, then, will be characterized by the idea of an unmediated coincidence of subject and object in the purity of an appearance that is revealed by putting judgment itself out of play.

However, as a theory "directed toward both ... the certainty of a temporal experience which is ... immediate" as well as "the timeless validity of knowledge," the coming philosophy will also require a dialectical complement to this Husserlian critique of abstraction or mechanical reason. If the latter reduces immediate experience to the categories of judgment, the "*eidos* doctrine" will be taken to task for the opposite error in its account of the origin of abstraction, the reduction of mechanical reason to *eidos*.

Eidos and Concept

In the *Ideas*, Husserl distinguishes *eidos* from the abstractions of science and "Ideas in the Kantian sense." In contrast to the latter, an *eidos* is not an "'exact' or 'ideal' notion" that subsumes contingent perceptions.[120] Nor is *eidos* derived as a common element or an average by means of abstraction from individual empirical examples. In the *Ideas*, in fact, Husserl uses an empiricist proof of the impossibility of abstraction in order to establish the necessity of an essence or *eidos* that is immediately "seen" or directly intuited. The proof, proposed by George Berkeley, asserts that it is impossible to abstract a general conception of color from particular sense impressions, since it is impossible to imagine a color that does not appear on a particular surface.

For Husserl, this empiricist refutation of eternal ideas demonstrates an undeniable truth: it belongs to the essence of color to always appear with extension. In this eidetic procedure, therefore, an invariant essence or *eidos*, which is necessary insofar as it applies to every perception, is directly intuited in the very *impossibility* of deriving a general concept through abstraction.[121] Instead of disproving the existence of universal ideas, the empiricist critique of abstraction demonstrates, according to Husserl, the "capacity to ideate universals in singulars, to have a 'seeing' grasp of a concept in an empirical presentation."[122] In revealing an invariant essence that is immanent to a particular appearance (as the impossibility that the appearance could be otherwise than it is), eidetic intuition accounts for the origin of the abstract conceptions that the empiricists claimed to disprove.

Benjamin may have encountered this account of the origin of abstraction in a seminar on metaphysics and epistemology that Rickert directed in 1912, a seminar which Martin Heidegger also attended.[123] The year before, Rickert had published a review of one of the texts by Husserl that Benjamin studied to enter the school of phenomenology, "Philosophy as a Rigorous Science." According to Rickert, Husserl's phenomenology was the "doctrine of a newly discovered kind of intuitive and immediate phenomenon," belonging to a "contemporary trend connected to the tendencies towards lived-experience [*Erlebnis*]."[124] This doctrine was based on the claim that abstractions could be directly derived from intuition, which was a *contradictio in adjecto*. Insisting upon the Kantian principle that "thoughts without content are empty, intuitions without concepts are blind," Rickert argued that knowledge cannot be derived from experience since "[g]enuine knowledge ... is always the result of conceptual mediation." Because knowledge necessarily "implies a departure from a mutely receptive intuitive dimension," contrary to Husserl, it cannot be said to originate within lived experience.[125]

In following the contemporary trend of *Erlebnis*—a trend which, for Rickert, also included "Bergson's ... and Simmel's *Lebensphilosophie* and various forms of biological vitalism"—Husserl had developed a philosophy that was "devoid of principles." His phenomenology of lived experience elevated "the lack of principles to a philosophical principle." For Rickert, then, phenomenology was a form of "vitalism" that "concerns itself only with 'bare life' ... and cannot therefore pose the philosophical question of how life gains value and thus acquires meaning and direction."[126]

Benjamin appears to rehearse this critique of Husserl's account of the origin of abstraction in his dissertation on the mourning-play. In the "Epistemo-Critical Prologue," Benjamin asks "whether it is necessary to hand over the task of accounting for the structure of the world of ideas to a much-cited intellectual vision" (*intellektuelle Anschauung*).[127] Does eidetic intuition, as "a 'seeing' grasp of a concept in an empirical presentation," explain the genesis of universal ideas and abstraction?[128] The answer is negative: "Ideas are not given in the world of phenomena. ... The being of ideas simply cannot be conceived as the object of an intuition—not even an intellectual intuition." Eidetic intuition does not provide an account of the formation of concepts.[129]

The critique of eidetic intuition in the *Trauerspiel* book would appear to contradict Benjamin's assertion, in the letter to Scholem, that "the problem of identity" (its exclusion of immediate, ephemeral experience) "probably leads to the *eidos* doctrine." Yet, in his description of the dissertation in the 1923 curriculum vitae, Benjamin explains that his "mode of investigation" is close to the "eidetic way of taking appearances" in its emphasis on the "incomparable and one-time." This suggests that the critique of Husserl's account of the origin of abstraction does not imply a rejection of eidetic intuition as a means of ascertaining the certainty of singularly temporal experience. This experience remains irreducible to the abstractions of thinking, even though it cannot be understood as their origin. Although the "*eidos* doctrine," in other words, provides a solution to the exclusion of immediate, ephemeral experience, it cannot account for the genesis of abstraction.

If Benjamin, then, learned Husserl's doctrine of intuition and regarded it as a probable solution to the reduction of experience to mechanical reason in Kant, he was also wary, nevertheless, of Husserl's attempt to derive abstract ideas from *Erlebnis* or lived experience. This perspective, which differs from Rickert's wholesale rejection of phenomenology as a philosophy devoid of philosophical principles, is one that Benjamin presents in a research paper written in 1916, titled "*Eidos* and Concept." In the essay, Benjamin argues that the technique of eidetic intuition is based upon a conflation of *eidos* and concept. Rehearsing the phenomenological reduction, Benjamin declares that "the *eidos* of this red blotter in front of me … exists at this point of real time, of real space." But insofar as this *eidos* is an immediately given experience—in Husserl's terms, "a 'this-there,' something unique"—it cannot be identified with a general concept, which "is timeless" and therefore indifferent to the "singular factual" character of immediate experience in the here-and-now. Although Husserl's procedure, therefore, proves that the "eidetic facts of phenomenology," as necessary appearances, are indeed "immediately given," it fails to account for the origin of the abstract conceptions, whose timeless validity cannot be equated with the certainty derived from a "seeing of essences."

The "*eidos* doctrine," in other words, does not explain the genesis of universal ideas from an immediate intuition of essence, from the necessity of the phenomenological realm of pure appearances. Insofar as the doctrine conflates concept and *eidos*—therefore confusing the timeless validity of categorial objects with the certainty of immediate perception—Husserl's "view that … concepts are eidetically given is … untenable."[130]

But insofar as Husserl's theory simply assumes that abstractions are "eidetically given," instead of explaining their genesis, the "*eidos* doctrine," as Benjamin suggests, is marked by a conflation of different kinds of experience similar to the one that Husserl identifies in the *Critique of Pure Reason*. In claiming to derive universal abstractions from an *eidos* that is "singular factual," Husserl collapses the very fundamental distinction that constitutes the central insight of his phenomenological method: that categorial knowledge, which "concerns timeless matters, differ[s] completely in kind" from direct intuition, which "concerns the temporal, and … therefore … the factual." Thus, despite the discovery of an indubitable essence within the sphere of ephemeral experience (revealed through the phenomenological reduction), Husserl's account of eidetic intuition, like Kant's *Critique of Pure Reason*, confuses experience in the context of (categorial) knowledge with experience unto itself. As a result, Husserl, like Kant, fails to ground the universal categories of knowledge in the realm of experience, or, to borrow Benjamin's criticism of Kant, "to create the closest possible connection between knowledge and experience through a speculative deduction of the world."

The theory of knowledge outlined in Benjamin's early philosophical essays and fragments dialectically synthesizes the neo-Kantian criticism of the philosophical trend of "lived experience" with "vitalist" criticisms of the Kantian system. If the latter conflates *eidos* and essence, immediate experience and conceptual knowledge, the former reduces "experience itself and unto itself" to mechanical reason. The coming philosophy, therefore, will oppose both the "extreme extension," in neo-Kantianism, "of the mechanical aspect of the relatively empty Enlightenment concept of experience," and the reduction of knowledge to experience in Husserl's phenomenology. Because of these opposite problems, neither vitalism nor neo-Kantianism can realize the "philosophical interest ... directed toward both the timeless validity of knowledge and the certainty of a temporal experience ... regarded as the immediate ... object of that knowledge." This implies the need for a coming philosophy that will be "a truly time- and eternity-conscious philosophy."

As Adorno noted, therefore, "what distinguishes [Benjamin's] philosophy is its kind of concretion," its emphasis upon "singularity—something which, according to conventional philosophical mores, would have been held for contingent, ephemeral, utterly worthless." In that way, "Benjamin's metaphysics" (which he never "deigned to write") "seems to converge with the general intellectual current ... demanding 'the things themselves' instead of their conceptual form, and which found ... expression in phenomenology."

This convergence, however, is a qualified one. Contrary to those who would "align him with the representatives of 'intuition', eidetic or otherwise," Benjamin, as Adorno points out, was equally critical of "accepted ideologies of the 'concrete.'" Contrary to Adorno, however, Benjamin's objection to Husserl's theory of concrete experience was not that "essence ... did not permit itself to be ... reveal[ed] ... to dubious intuition." Rather, Benjamin argues the opposite: essence, which is excluded by mechanical reason, is immediately apprehended in the eidetic procedure. But since *eidos* and concept are different, the abstractions of reason cannot be derived from immediate experience. If Benjamin, then, "was impelled to break the bonds of a logic which covers over the particular with the universal," he also broke with philosophies of concrete experience which, by conflating concept and *eidos*, cover over the universal with the particular.[131]

This aspect of Benjamin's early philosophy has often been overlooked. In his discussion of the "Coming Philosophy," Wolin, for example, characterizes Benjamin's criticism of Kant in the following manner: "Kant's grave error was his uncritical acceptance of the standard of 'valid' cognitive experience of his epoch, the concept of reality advanced by the natural sciences, 'a reality of an inferior rank.'" This account does not fully acknowledge the dialectical character of Benjamin's criticism of mechanical reason, a feature which distinguishes it from Nietzsche's rejection of the "shallow rationalism" of the sciences as well as the Frankfurt School's critique of instrumental rationality. For Benjamin, Kant's error was not "his selection of [an] ... inferior object domain," that of the sciences.[132] On the contrary, Benjamin argues in fact that Kant, by taking his concept of experience from Newtonian physics, succeeded in justifying the certainty of knowledge that is lasting. The criticism of Kant in the "Coming Philosophy" is directed instead at Kant's exclusive concern for the "best aspect" of the "relatively empty Enlightenment concept of experience," of the inferior reality revealed by the Enlightenment's rejection of dogma. Because the inferior form of experience underlying natural science is identified with experience unto itself, Kant ignores the need to secure the "integrity of an experience that is ephemeral," an ephemeral experience that could no longer be guaranteed by any higher authority. "The problem faced by Kantian epistemology … has two sides, and Kant managed to give a valid explanation for only one of them." A revision of Kant, then, would produce a theory of knowledge capable of demonstrating the eternal validity of mechanical reason and the certainty of immediate experience, in an age when experience and knowledge have both been reduced to a "bare, naked" form by the disappearance of God.

2

The Doctrine of Right and the Critique of Violence: Benjamin's Anarchist Revision of Kant's Moral Philosophy

Introduction: Kant, Violence, and the Unfinished Treatise on Politics

In the late 1910s and early '20s, Benjamin, "concerned with determining the relation of politics to the idea of philosophy,"[1] composed a series of essays and fragments that were intended as part of a "politics" in which "'anarchism' would be a principal point of reference."[2] This anarchist politics was expressed in Kantian terms, as a revision of a portion of Kant's moral philosophy, following a program that, as the chapter will argue, broadly resembles the one proposed in the "Coming Philosophy" with regard to Kant's theory of knowledge. Like the coming philosophy, Benjamin's politics will "take the deepest intimations ... from our times ... and turn them into knowledge by relating them to the Kantian system," while also revising this system in light of historical events in the present.[3] This period, in particular, was marked by a wave of revolutionary and counter-revolutionary violence: the Bolshevik Revolution, the Kapp Putsch, the short-lived Munich Soviet Republic in 1919, and the suppression of the Ruhr and Spartacist Uprisings by the Social Democratic Party. "It may confidently be asserted," has Benjamin noted in retrospect, "that the [German] revolution of 1918, which was defeated by the petty-bourgeois, parvenu spirit of German Social Democracy, did more to radicalize this generation than did the war itself."[4]

In Benjamin's "politics," the revision to Kant's moral philosophy in terms of the latter events will register Benjamin's "disappointment" with the concept of history presented in *Ideas for a Universal History* and *Perpetual Peace*, which he had originally chosen as the topic for his dissertation. As he described in a 1917 letter to Gershom Scholem, the two texts provoked a "purely critical attitude" due to the fact that "Kant is less concerned with history than with certain historical constellations of ethical interest," because history was subordinated to morality.[5]

This "critical attitude" is expressed in the essays and fragments that Benjamin intended to incorporate into his "politics," including "Notes Toward a Work on the

Category of Justice," the "Theological-Political Fragment," and the "Critique of Violence."

Property and the Doctrine of Right

In the "Notes Toward a Work on the Category of Justice," Benjamin presents a critique of the "Doctrine of Right" in the *Metaphysics of Morals*, in which Kant attempts to deduce the idea of legal possession or property. In the doctrine, right is defined as the external expression of practical reason. Right provides the legal authorization for the use of external force to ensure the laws of morality. According to Kant, the use of force is justified only if it accords with the rational character of practical reason, which is defined by its conformity to laws that can be willed universally. Right, then, or externally enforceable law, is legitimate only if it possesses the rational form of the categorical imperative: "act outwardly in such a way that the free use of your elective will can cohere with the freedom of everyone according to universal laws."[6] As Kant argues in *Toward Perpetual Peace*, only a doctrine of right that is consistent with the theory of morals can be called a "true politics": "True politics can take no steps forward without first paying tribute to morality."[7]

True politics, then, requires a universal law of right which, like the categorical imperative, applies at all times and in all situations. In the "Doctrine of Right," the axiom is formulated as follows: "act externally that the free use of your choice can coexist with the freedom of everyone in accordance with a universal law."[8] In terms of property, the axiom implies that persons have the right to possess anything so long as their actions do not interfere with the freedom of others to exercise the same right of possession. As Kant adds, moreover, violating this axiom would be equivalent to treating other people as things, rather than ends-unto-themselves. Such an act would be "self-contradictory," since the possibility of possession presupposes the concept of the person, who cannot be possessed or used as a thing. As a being who is capable of exercising the freedom to appropriate property, the "person cannot be a thing which can be owned, for it is impossible to be a person and a thing, the proprietor and the property."

As such, the basic axiom of right, to act externally in such a way that is "consistent with everyone's freedom in accordance with universal laws," can also be formulated as follows: people must "use themselves as well as things without thereby degrading themselves into the things they use."[9] In the "Doctrine of Right," this axiom is applied to both people and things to determine how property can be used without interfering with the freedom of others, as well as how the use of other people's "sexual properties" can accord with morality (see Chapter 7).

As Kant realized, however, this basic principle, which conforms to the universal character of the categorical imperative, is insufficient for determining the rightness of actions with regard to possession.[10] This is because the "immediate applicability" of the axiom, as Peter Fenves describes, is "exceedingly small." It applies only to the "human body ... plus whatever the body happens to hold [and] ... minus its 'sexual properties,' which, for Kant, are not one's own to use as one chooses, insofar as the use of these properties tends to degrade the personhood of their user."[11] By itself, then, the axiom of right only grants persons the freedom to use their own bodies (but not their sexual organs) together with whatever they happen to carry.

As Fenves points out, however, this freedom effectively amounts to no freedom at all: "everyone is free to do anything that does not interfere with everyone else; but since almost everything anyone does potentially interferes with someone else, everyone is actually permitted to do almost nothing." As such, in order to determine the right to use things without interfering with the freedom of others, Kant must deduce a concept of legal possession, allowing individuals an exclusive right over things that are external to their own bodies. In order for this concept, moreover, to honor morality, possession must have a rational basis, which means that the rightful acquisition of property cannot have its origins in an act that cannot be categorically willed.

The Doctrine of Right and the Suspension of Law

In the *Doctrine of Right*, however, Kant does not provide such a concept. Rather than presenting a rational moral justification for legal possession, he argues instead that it is impossible for property *not* to exist since such a state of affairs *cannot* become a universal imperative. Assuming that the use of a thing presupposes possession, Kant insists that, without ownership, no one could use anything at all. But as such, to will or demand the absence of property would be irrational.[12] Property, therefore, is necessary because the existence of a world that does not have an owner—a world of *res nullius* or "possessor-less" things—cannot be willed without contradiction, and thus it cannot be established as law.

Unable to demonstrate the rational necessity of legal possession, Kant, then, asserts that its absence would be immoral since a world of possessor-less things cannot cohere with the freedom of everyone: "[P]utting ... objects beyond any possibility of being used ... would annihilate them ... practical[ly] and make them into *res nullius*, even though in the use of things choice was formally consistent with everyone's outer freedom in accordance with universal laws."[13]

As Fenves points out, the absence of a right to possession that can be willed categorically leads Kant to employ the trope of personification in order to avoid the anarchic conclusion that ownership is contrary to the nature of things. "It is possible for me to have *any* external object of my elective will as mine; that is, a maxim which states that an object of the elective will would in itself (objectively) have to be without a lord (*res nullius*) is contrary to right, if it were to become law."[14] Thus, instead of providing a proof for the right to legal possession, one which honors morality and its rational structure, Kant grounds his doctrine of right on the rational necessity of *the rightlessness of the object*.

In his deduction of the concept of property, then, Kant uses the same illegitimate trope that he criticizes in the labor theory of property associated with John Locke. According to Kant, the theory is based on the fiction that, by expending our labor upon something, we can compel it to acknowledge our ownership: The "tacit prevalent deception of personifying things and of thinking of a right to things ... as if someone could, by the work he expends upon them, put things under an obligation to serve him and no one else."[15]

This deception, however, is also employed in the "Doctrine of Right." Kant's account of how people can rightfully "use themselves as well as things without ... degrading themselves into the things they use" is based on the premise that things can degrade themselves by relinquishing their rights to their owners. The right of possession, therefore, is based upon an unlawful violence imposed upon objects, which Kant personifies as bondsmen who are forced to surrender themselves to their masters. Thus, the "possession of a parcel of land" requires the "capacity to place it in one's charge [*Gewalt*] ... as if the piece of land itself were to say, 'if you cannot protect me, you cannot command me.'"[16]

For Kant, this act of *Gewalt* not only subjugates things. It also imposes a limit upon the freedom of others, who are forced to refrain from using an object that has been seized as property by somebody else. But as such, this violence, which limits the freedom of both people and things, is not the exercise of a right that honors morality, in the sense that it possesses the universality of the categorical imperative. Rather, for Kant, the impossibility of a possessor-less thing implies the necessity of *a law that suspends the universal principle of enforceable right*, "provisionally violating" the maxim that one's acts should cohere with the freedom of everyone.[17]

This necessity appears to possess the rational form of a law since it supposed to arise from the fact that it is impossible to universalize the demand that no one can use anything. Kant's assertion, however, that such a demand would practically "annihilate" the goods that people require suggests that the necessity of possession is not moral in character, but natural. And as Kant argues in his discussion of emergency law (see Chapter 3), "necessity has no law."

In the "Doctrine of Right," then, the concept of legal possession is not based upon a political right that honors morality, but on an exception to its universality, on a *lex permissiva* or a law that permits the violation of right. This "permissive law" gives us "an authorization that could not be got from mere concepts of right ... namely to put all others under an obligation ... to refrain from using certain objects of our choice because we ... first ... take them into our possession."[18]

The doctrine of right, then, emerges out of an original wrong, an unlawful act of lawmaking violence. The "crux of Kant's *Rechtslehre*" is a *lex permissiva* that "functions as a suspension of the universal law of right." But since "rightful possession is possible," paradoxically, "only by suspending the universal law of right," the latter depends upon "licensing a violation of a universal law, which is wrong."[19] In the immoral act that constitutes property, people are treated as things, insofar as their freedom is limited, and personified things are enslaved. Since this wrong is the very condition of right, true politics, contrary to Kant, *cannot* take a step without *dishonoring* morality.

History, Justice, and the Anti-Juridical Right of the Thing

In "Notes Toward a Work on the Category of Justice," Benjamin criticizes this doctrine of right, challenging its very foundation in the permissive law. For Kant, it is "possible for me to have *any* external object ... as mine" since "an object ... without a lord (*res nullius*) is contrary to right."[20] For Benjamin, on the other hand, the fact that, in the absence of right, it is possible to claim any object implies that right is necessarily contrary to justice. Although there is indeed, as Kant's doctrine asserts, an "entirely abstract claim of the subject in principle to every good," and although every good, therefore, can be turned into a possession, possession, nevertheless, "is always unjust." "To every good," then, "there accrues a possession-character," but no "order of possession, however articulated, can therefore lead to justice."[21] Against Kant's deduction of right—which claims that everything must be subject to possession since otherwise no one could use anything—Benjamin asserts that "useable things can be possessed, but no one can possess them" without committing injustice.[22] The "Notes," then, address a fundamental issue in Benjamin's anarchist politics that is left undeveloped in the "Critique of Violence," the issue of violence "concerning objects," rather than "conflict between man and man."[23]

As Benjamin argues, moreover, the injustice that legal possession commits against usable things is not something specific to the institution of private property, which Kant sought to defend in his bourgeois doctrine of rights. Even a "socialist or communist theory" of property "misses its goal precisely because the claim of the individual ranges over every good."[24] Because everyone has a claim upon everything, justice cannot be achieved by either a communist or bourgeois legal philosophy that recognizes only the "possession-right of the person." A doctrine that only considers the property rights of the person can never be just. It can never determine a just distribution of property, since every order of property must deny the claim that everyone has upon everything, just as every order excludes the idea of a possessor-less thing, or an object that is not ruled by a lord, as the very condition of ownership.

Benjamin's anarchist moral philosophy, then, was opposed to both collective and individual ownership since right is conceived by these doctrines only in terms of the person. Asserting the "primacy of the thingly over the personal,"[25] Benjamin argues that justice requires a doctrine that acknowledges the right of the thing: The "entirely abstract claim of the subject in principle to every good ... does not point toward the possession-right of the person but possibly toward a good-right of the good."[26]

This right, which is identified with justice itself, can be characterized as the practical correlate to the concept of truth proposed in Benjamin's early theory of knowledge. For Benjamin, truth is neither "in the consciousness of a knowing subject [nor] ... in the object ([nor] alternatively, identical with it)." Truth does not "designate the relation between two metaphysical entities"—a relation of correspondence or identity between subject and object—since the identity principle excludes the singular objects of knowledge. Rather, truth arises as a result of a putting-out-of-play of judgment as such, which presupposes the distinction between a cognizing subject and an object that is known, a suspension of judgment that reveals that "truth and true being are conjoined" in an all-encompassing medium that is entirely "neutral." "The task of future epistemology," therefore, "is to find for knowledge the sphere of total neutrality in regard to the concepts of both subject and object."

Just as truth, in the coming philosophy, is not defined as a correlation between subject and object, so justice, in Benjamin's "coming moral philosophy," or his anarchist politics, is not understood as the conformity of the world to our moral intentions. While morality "can be demanded" as an imperative that is willed by the subject, "justice in the final analysis can only be a state of the world."[27] If truth, then, requires that the "subject nature of the cognizing consciousness ... be eliminated," justice, which "constitutes a state of the world," must be detached from "the good will of the subject."[28]

Justice, therefore, is not an objective condition that conforms to morality. Rather, it is the return to a neutral state of the world that precedes moral judgment, as the practical counterpart to the epistemological paradise of a pure language which "knows no means, no object, and no addressee of communication." With regard to the problem of legal possession, the sphere of total neutrality excluded by Kant in his deduction of property is that of a moral indifference in which everyone can possess anything, even while everything has the right to refuse being appropriated as property. In this peculiar notion of justice, the moral subject is redeemed in its natural state, that of an "unimproved humanity" (to refer to Benjamin's definition of politics), while objects (to borrow an expression from Lukács [see Chapter 6]) are restored to a "defetishized thinghood," free of all moral relations.

In the "Notes," this condition of moral neutrality is asserted, in a sort of affirmative use of Kant's personification of property, as the right of a thing that is opposed to all forms of ownership. The claim that everyone has upon everything can only be addressed by a doctrine in which goods are granted the right to resist the requirement, imposed upon them by every order of property, that things must conform to the possession-right of the person. In the name of the "abstract claim of the subject in principle to every good," things, according to Benjamin, assert the right to oppose their enslavement in "true" doctrines of politics, which impose a moral obligation upon them to comply with the property rights of their owners.[29] If things, then, cannot resist being possessed because of their possession-character, it remains the case, nevertheless, that every attempt "to assign a possessor to ... good[s]" violates their right to be without a possessor, as well as the right of everyone else to possess them.[30]

But as such, this doctrine of justice would appear to be directly opposed to a "true" doctrine of right, prescribing the legitimate use of objects by persons in accordance with "virtue," that is, in accordance with whether the use can be universalized without contradiction. As Benjamin explains in the "Notes": "Justice does not appear to refer to the good will of the subject but, instead, constitutes a state of the world. ... Virtue can be demanded; justice in the final analysis can only be a state of the world."[31]

In contrast to virtue, therefore, justice is not an "ethical category of the demanded." It is not a moral demand that can be rationally willed in the form of a universal imperative. As such, its accomplishment cannot be understood with reference to the good will of the subject. Justice is not the "fulfillment of what is demanded," the fulfillment of a universalizable maxim, cohering with everyone's freedom. Since possession, in Kant's deduction of property, is not based on the universal law of morality, but on a suspension of right violating the claim of everyone has upon everything as well as the right of the good to resist being property, such a demand cannot be fulfilled and thus can never be just.

In "the final analysis," then, justice does not refer to subject's morality. Rather, it "can only be ... a state of the world," one which, like the real state of exception, can never conform to the law. Like the Messianic, therefore, justice "is not the *telos* of the historical dynamic," as it is in the Kantian conception of history as the progressive fulfillment of right. As Benjamin discovered to his disappointment, this conception is "less concerned with history than with certain historical constellations of ethical interest." Kant's conception of history is more concerned with the moral demands of the subject and the possession-right of the person than with the objective state of the world and its indisputable claim to be without a possessor.

"Justice," however, does not "refer to the good will of the subject." Rather, it "lies in the conditions of a good that cannot be possessed—a good through which all goods become propertyless." Unlike Kant's ideal of perpetual peace, justice, then, is not an ethical demand that the world must conform to morality, but a "striving to make the world into the highest good."

This concept of justice implies an historical movement similar to the one that Benjamin attributes to the Baroque (see Chapter 3). Whereas the Enlightenment regarded the "moral felicity" of humanity as the "supreme purpose of nature" and the ultimate end of historical progress, history, from the perspective of the Baroque, reveals the meaning of nature: "nature is considered as functioning for the purpose of expressing its meaning." In the *Trauerspiel*, this historical end is portrayed by a theatrical setting characterized by the "primacy [of] the thingly over the personal."

Similarly, in the "Notes," justice is characterized as a final state of affairs in which the good-right of the good is asserted over the possession-right of the person. As such, justice cannot be identified with a completely rightful order of property, an order which could only deny the right of the thing not to be a possession, and the concomitant claim that everyone has to possess it. Rather, as the "highest good," justice is a state of the world in which property is released from possession and the ownership of all things is rescinded,[32] so that things can be used without being property. In such a state of the world, the possession-right of the person, then, would be replaced by the principle of "a proprietor that is able to transcend [the] ... possessive character" of property.

This anomic state of the world, which justice requires, is one that Kant attempts to exclude by means of a suspension of right that establishes legal possession: it is "possible for me to have *any* external object ... as mine" since "an object ... without a lord (*res nullius*) is contrary to right." In this way, "Kant shrank from ... the legal vacuum of 'anarchy' or 'lawlessness,'" which he uncovered in the attempt to deduce a concept of legal possession.[33] On the other hand, Benjamin's "Notes" affirm the anarchy of an original condition of propertylessness. Kant's *lex permissiva* is opposed to a real state of permission without property, "a condition where things can be legally possessed, but it would be unjust for anyone to possess anything in particular."[34] Against the lawmaking violence of Kant's original seizure of property, Benjamin proposes the "pure *Gewalt*" of an appropriation without property, in a real state of exception in which "useable things can be possessed, but no one can possess them."[35]

Insofar as this state cannot be subsumed by the law, including one that allows for the legal suspension of right, the good-right of the good, which could potentially answer the claim that everyone has upon everything, must be seen as a right to refuse every possession-right of the person. The right that the object possesses, in other words, is a right to resist the fulfillment of right. Excluded in every juridical order, the complete permissiveness that prevailed in the original state of the world asserts itself against every system of property, as a justice that was originally denied for the sake of morality and possession.

The Missing Criterion of Violence

In the "Critique of Violence," which was Benjamin's "last great work on politics before his Marxist turn in 1924,"[36] Benjamin reiterates Kant's basic principle of right: "the most elementary relationship within any legal system is that of ends to means."[37] Right is the authority to use force to achieve moral ends, ends that are moral because they can be willed universally. This concept of right appears to already contain a standard with which to evaluate the rightness of means. In Benjamin's words, "a criterion for criticizing [violence or force] might seem immediately available … in the question whether violence, in a given case, is a means to a just or an unjust end."[38] The elementary relation of right is based upon the assumption that any means, including violence, can be "criticized," or judged as either lawful or unlawful, according to the morality of its ends, that is, by the standard of whether its ends can be willed universally.

In his deduction of legal possession, however, Kant reveals that the elementary relationship of means to ends presupposes an original suspension of its applicability, a permissive law that allows for a violence that cannot be categorically willed. In this particular case, then, moral laws cannot justify violent means. Rather, the law only *permits* them by suspending itself in an immoral manner. As such, the "question would remain open whether violence, as a principle, could be a moral means even to just ends."[39] The problem, as Benjamin further explains, is that violence considered as means, unlike its ends, cannot be criticized according to whether it can be universally willed. The "appeal … to the categorical imperative, with its doubtless incontestable minimum program—act in such a way that at all times you use humanity both in your person and in the person of all others as an end, and never merely as a means—is in itself inadequate," as a criterion for criticizing violence as means.[40]

Violence, therefore, requires a standard that is different from the rational test of the categorical imperative "[M]utually independent criteria both of just ends and of justified means [must be] established."[41] To resolve the question of whether violence can be a morally justified means, independently of whether its end can be willed universally, "a more exact criterion is needed, which would discriminate within the sphere of means themselves, without regard for the ends they serve."[42] The doctrine of right, then, remains incomplete without a critique of violence that could identify a "criterion … to assess the legality of violence" itself.[43]

According to Fenves, it is precisely such a critique that Kant fails to provide in the "Doctrine of Right." In his deduction of property, Kant does not apply the universal principle of right (act in a way that coheres with the freedom of everyone, treating them as ends-unto-themselves rather than things), an axiom which is consistent with the criterion of all moral ends, the categorical imperative. Instead, he grounds the right to possession in a legal exception to the axiom's universality. Right, then, presupposes an originary law-making violence that lacks the rational character of morality and therefore is wrong.⁴⁴ Contrary to Kant's assertion, therefore, that "[t]rue politics cannot take a step without having already honored morality,"⁴⁵ the *Doctrine of Right* appears to reveal that politics must dishonor morality so that legal possession can be categorically willed.

The basic principle of right, then, to act in a way that accords with the freedom of everyone, presupposes an outward act of violent expropriation, which transgresses morality in order to ensure its universal applicability. For Benjamin, as Fenves observes, this predicament of practical reason implies the need for a "fourth critique … for only a critique of *Gewalt* can distinguish between legitimate *potestas* and illegitimate *violentia*."⁴⁶

The Necessity of Ends and the Contingency of Means

As Benjamin points out in the "Critique of Violence," this critique is omitted in both natural and positive doctrines of law, which, despite their "antinomy," make the "common … assumption" that "just ends can be attained by justified means, justified means used for just ends."⁴⁷ In natural law, violence is understood as a "natural datum" as well as a juridical category that paradoxically precedes the very foundation of law. It is understood as natural means that can be legally exercised in the state of nature. Before "people give up all their violence for the sake of the state … the individual, before the conclusion of this rational contract, has *de jure* the right to use at will the violence that is *de facto* at his disposal." Once the contract is concluded and the state is established, violence is judged according to the lawfulness of its ends. For natural law, violence "is a product of nature … the use of which is in no way problematical, unless force is misused for unjust ends."⁴⁸

On the other hand, "positive law … sees violence as a product of history," as opposed to a natural datum. From the perspective of positive law, violence is justified not by its ends, but by its origin. Positive law "demands of all violence a proof of its historical origin, which under certain conditions is declared legal, sanctioned."⁴⁹ If natural law evaluates means according to the criterion that applies only to their ends, positive law judges the rightness of ends by the historical legitimacy of the violence employed to achieve them: "Natural law attempts, by the justness of the ends, to 'justify' the means, positive law to 'guarantee' the justness of the ends through the justification of the means."⁵⁰

For Benjamin, these two attempts to justify violence constitute an antinomy of two doctrines of right with opposing deficiencies. On the one hand, by grounding legality in the contingency of historical violence, positive law shows itself to be "blind to the absoluteness of ends," which, according to Kant, is determined by whether the ends can be rationally willed. On the other hand, natural law, which evaluates violence according to the criterion that determines the "unconditionality of ends," is "equally [blind] to the conditionality of means," to the fact that violence does not possess the rational necessity of the categorical imperative.⁵¹

Against this antinomy, Benjamin insists upon a "historico-philosophical view of law" that grasps both the absoluteness of ends and the contingency of means, recognizing both the rationality of the law and the irrational character of the violence from which it originates. Such an approach requires, of course, an independent criterion with which to evaluate violence itself, a standard of criticism specific to the "sphere of means themselves, without regard for [their] ends," which is missing in Kant as well as in both positive and natural doctrines of law.

In order to define this criterion, Benjamin examines a "distinction supplied by positive law ... based on the nature of violence" itself, as opposed to that of morality—the distinction between "sanctioned force and unsanctioned force."[52] What distinguishes these two kinds of violence is not whether their ends can be willed universally, but "the presence or absence of a general historical acknowledgment of its ends," as in the case of conquest or victory in war.[53] Obtained by violence rather than reason, this universal acknowledgment legitimates unlawful ends. Like the *lex permissiva* in Kant's "rational" deduction of property, the acknowledgment confers a moral necessity upon ends that are natural: "legal subjects sanction violence whose ends remain for the sanctioners natural ends." The sanction, then, is applied to amoral objectives that are pursued with such violence that the latter succeeds in replacing an existing political order and its system of law.

From the vantage point of the state, such violence must be opposed not because its ends are unlawful, but because the magnitude of its force undermines the state's monopoly over the means required to maintain legal order: "the law's interest in a monopoly of violence ... is not explained by the intention of preserving legal ends but, rather, by that of preserving the law itself." The difference, then, between sanctioned and unsanctioned violence is not determined by whether the ends correspond to a universalizable maxim. Rather, it rests on what Benjamin calls the "general maxim ... that all the natural ends ... must collide with legal ends if pursued with a greater or lesser degree of violence," a maxim pertaining to means rather than ends.

For Benjamin, this maxim points to a more fundamental function of violence with regard to the law. Evaluated as a means of greater or lesser degree, violence *either violates law or constitutes it as such*. It is either violence directed at unlawful ends or "mythic, lawmaking violence"[54] that does not "punish the infringement of law but ... establish[es] new law."[55] In its lawmaking capacity, then, violence is the foundation of right. This truth—which Kant overlooks in the doctrine of right, ignoring the need for a critique of violence itself—is one that Benjamin attributes to Georges Sorel (whom he would later describe as "the great, truly significant theoretician of syndicalism").[56] Sorel's reflections on violence "touch ... on a metaphysical truth in surmising that in the beginning all right was the prerogative of the kings ... in short, of the mighty; and that, *mutatis mutandis*, it will remain so as long as it exists."[57]

For Benjamin, this metaphysical truth—the *a priori* principle of a contingent lawmaking violence, underlying the absoluteness of right—provides a "more exact" standard for a critique of violence itself, as opposed to a critique of the ends it is used to accomplish. Just as ends are moral or immoral depending on whether they can be universally willed, violence is unlawful or lawmaking depending upon whether it fails or succeeds in overturning the whole legal order. If the categorical imperative, then, is the criterion for determining the justness of ends, the criterion for criticizing violence as means is whether the state is "obliged to acknowledge it as lawmaking."[58]

In the "Critique of Violence," therefore, Benjamin provides an account of the law from a point of departure that differs from that of the *Doctrine of Right*. The latter presents a moral justification for the violence, underlying the right of legal possession, in accordance with the ideal of a "true politics" in which law always honors morality. On the other hand, Benjamin's "politics" begins with a critique of violence as such, as distinct from its moral justification, a critique that discloses lawmaking violence as the basis of right: "violence ... alone can guarantee law."[59] By establishing "mutually independent criteria both of just ends and of justified means," this critique, moreover, which Kant had omitted, resolves the antinomy between natural and positive law, between the contingency of means and the absoluteness of ends.[60] Adopting a "historico-philosophical view of the law," then, Benjamin posits a lawmaking violence whose contingency, paradoxically, guarantees the necessity of all moral ends.[61]

The criticism of the "Doctrine of Right" in the "Critique of Violence" is consistent with the revision of Kant's theory of knowledge, proposed in the "Program of the Coming Philosophy." Just as Kant, in the *Critique of Pure Reason*, succeeds in demonstrating the "timeless validity of knowledge,"[62] so, in his critique of practical reason, he establishes a "incontestable minimum program" for a morality that would apply universally to all situations and times.[63] But just as the timeless validity of knowledge excludes "a temporal experience which is regarded as the immediate" and transient, so the categorical imperative fails to account for the contingency of the means employed to achieve the universal ends of morality.[64] If a revision of the first critique, therefore, requires a coming philosophy "directed toward both the timeless validity of knowledge" and the "integrity" of ephemeral experience, a revision of the doctrine of right must recognize both rational ends and the irrational violence that underlies right. In this "coming moral philosophy," the doctrine of right, which establishes the absoluteness of ends, would be completed by a critique of violence, used to evaluate the contingency of means.[65]

The Perpetual Violence of Peace

In the essay on violence, this dialectic of contingency and necessity is exemplified in the peace ceremony that follows defeat in a conflict. As "the primal phenomenon of all lawmaking violence,"[66] the peace ceremony, according to Benjamin, is "entirely necessary" even in instances of military violence when the "victor has established himself in invulnerable possession."[67] The ceremony serves to confer a moral necessity upon a contingent act of lawmaking violence. In this context, "the word 'peace' ... denotes [an] ... a priori, necessary sanctioning, regardless of all other legal conditions, of every victory. This sanction consists precisely in recognizing the new conditions as a new 'law,' quite regardless of whether they need de facto any guarantee of their continuation."[68]

Even in instances, then, when violence or military might by itself is sufficient to overcome an opponent, a peace ceremony is necessary in order to confer upon the constitutive power the *a priori* appearance of right. In this way, violence, "crowned by fate," becomes "the origin of law."[69] Through this gesture, a chance occurrence is transformed into a fateful event, "provoked by an offense against [some] ... unwritten and unknown law," such that the law appears to precede the contingent violence upon which it is founded.[70] As fate, then, violence is legitimated "under the title of power."[71]

As Benjamin emphasizes, however, the peace ceremony does not simply convert might into right, such that violence, having founded a new legal order, completely gives way to the peaceful operation of law. Just as lawmaking violence requires moral legitimacy, so the normal functioning of the juridical system depends upon violence. Thus, the legal contract, for example, owes its binding character to the fact that it "confers on both parties the right to take recourse to violence in some form," should the agreement be broken.[72] Likewise, without the "latent presence of violence," the rule of law in parliamentary government, which seeks to "cultivate in compromise a supposedly nonviolent manner of dealing with political affairs," would be incapable of both obtaining consensus and enforcing decrees.[73]

Without the latent presence of a legitimate violence required to achieve its juridical ends, government would be compelled to depend on the "ignominy" of police force, which possesses the contingency of lawmaking violence but lacks the legitimacy of the sovereign decision: "Unlike law, which acknowledges in the 'decision' determined by place and time a metaphysical category that gives it a claim to critical evaluation, a consideration of the police institution encounters nothing essential at all."[74] As such, the use of police can provoke violence against the state, violence that could potentially become a new lawmaking power.

Thus, from the perspective of a critique of its means, the juridical order appears not only as a system of rights, but also as a structure in which violence, in its "lawmaking" and "law-preserving" capacities, must be used to create and sustain all legality. In terms of the Kantian conception of history, what the critique of violence implies is that law, because it presupposes and perpetuates violence as its end and its origin, can never establish an eternal or perpetual peace. Rather, peace, which transfigures violence as fate, only prolongs a "dialectical rising and falling in the lawmaking and law-preserving formations of violence." The ignominious violence of the police, required to preserve the normal operation of law, gradually deprives it of the *a priori* appearance of fate, provoking a violence of greater degree that could constitute a new legal order. The "oscillation rests on the circumstance that all law-preserving violence, in its duration, indirectly weakens the lawmaking violence represented by it, through the suppression of hostile counterviolence."[75]

This dialectic of violence and law is perpetuated by the assumption that the contingency of means can be evaluated like the absoluteness of ends, by the dogma that "just ends can be attained by justified means, justified means used for just ends."[76] This dogma is blind to the fact that the violence that originates law necessarily exceeds legal ends, just as these ends, in a situation of peace, are enforced by the arbitrary violence of the police, which eventually undermines law by eroding its aura of moral necessity. By ignoring the need for a critique of violence itself, the natural and positive doctrines of law perpetuate two opposing illusions: that law can be rid of the violence upon which it is founded, and that violence can be justified by its ends. Based upon the conflation of the mutually exclusive criteria for means and ends, these illusions impose an infinite task. The attempt to realize the ideal of either a completely justified violence or that a system of right that completely conforms with morality serves to prolong the "dialectical rising and falling in the lawmaking and law-preserving formations of violence."

On the other hand, by establishing "independent criteria both of just ends and of justified means," Benjamin shows that "all the violence imposed by fate, using justified means ... [is] in irreconcilable conflict with just ends."[77] Since violence, as a means, is either lawless or lawmaking depending upon whether it can overturn the whole legal order (an order that would presume to judge it according to ends), the use of justified means is inherently inconsistent with achieving just ends. As such, the historical oscillation between constituting and constituted power precludes the possibility of arriving at justice. If the "task of a critique of violence," as Benjamin explains in the essay's opening paragraph, is to "expound ... its relation to law and justice," the critique appears to conclude that the law, which arises from lawmaking violence, cannot lead to justice.[78]

Pure Means and the Categorical Imperative

As Benjamin argues, however, this problem (that just ends and justified means are irreconcilable), underlying the "at first discouraging discovery of the ultimate insolubility of all legal problems," is one that can be illuminated by considering "a different kind of violence." In contrast to both lawmaking violence and violence that merely infringes the law, this third function of violence is "not related to [ends] as means at all but in some different way."[79] This "pure immediate violence," or "pure means" without legal ends, is one "that might be able to call a halt to mythical violence," and thus put an end to the cycle of lawmaking and law-preserving violence that forecloses the possibility of justice and perpetual peace.[80]

As an example of such a pure means, one that is nonviolent in nature, Benjamin points to the "peaceful intercourse between private persons," in which conflicts are resolved outside of the law, and without the latent threat of legal violence.[81] In the political realm, this kind of intercourse, according to Benjamin, is analogous to the role of diplomats, who "resolve conflicts case by case ... peacefully and without contracts."[82] This approach is contrasted with what Benjamin describes as the Kantian assumption that justice can be rationally willed, that "reason ... decides on the justification of means and the justness of ends."[83] The assumption is based on the obstinate tendency to criticize or evaluate both means and ends according to the criterion of the categorical imperative, on the "stubborn prevailing habit of conceiving ... just ends ... as capable of generalization, which ... contradicts the nature of justice."[84]

Rather than utilizing the pure means of a case-by-case resolution to conflict, such a conception of right assumes that, for an end to be just, it must be applicable to all similar instances. For Benjamin, this contradicts the nature of justice because "ends that for one situation are just, universally acceptable, and valid, are so for no other situation, no matter how similar it may be in other respects."[85] Since it is unjust to judge diverse situations by the same legal standard, the very universality that defines the law's moral character is precisely the reason that right is contrary to justice.

Hence, just as the timeless validity of mechanical reason in Kant's theory of knowledge excludes ephemeral and "singularly temporal" experience, so the general character of the categorical imperative makes it constitutively incapable of rendering justice in the individual case. In that sense, the "insolubility of all legal problems" is similar to the one that underlies the paradox of the Cretan, which is "insoluble" only in "in the realm of logic." Because this realm exists beyond space and time, logical propositions can never apply to singular temporal experience.[86]

This account of the relationship between justice and law corresponds to the one outlined in "Notes Toward a Work on the Category of Justice." Because of its categorical character, morality excludes justice itself. Justice cannot be demanded or willed in the rational form of a universal imperative since it does not "refer to the good will of the subject but, instead, constitutes a state of the world."[87] As such, it cannot be fulfilled through the use of violence as means toward a morally justified end. Rather, it requires a pure means without legal ends, a means which, in "striving to make the world into the highest good," renders justice to the situation itself, as opposed to enforcing the rights of juridical persons.[88] Just as justice, as Benjamin writes in the "Notes," can only be realized by recognizing the "good-right of the good" to deny the "possession-right of the person," so, in "Critique of Violence," justice is related to the indisputable claim of each situation to resist the good will of the subject.

The General and the Political Strike: Anarchism and Social Democracy

But if the non-legal, situation-specific approach to dealing with conflicts constitutes a nonviolent form of pure means, for Benjamin, the primary example "of a pure immediate violence that might be able to call a halt to mythical violence" is, of course, the general strike. For Benjamin, the general strike exemplifies a "function of violence" that is distinct from that of both founding and preserving the law, a function of "which it is the object [of the essay] ... to identify as the only secure foundation of its critique."[89] A critique of violence, therefore, which grasps the "dialectical rising and falling in the lawmaking and law-preserving formations of violence," must be able to delineate a function of violence that cannot be reduced to either formations, a function performed by the general strike.

According to Benjamin, the "workers' guaranteed right to strike" is a right to exercise violence, one that the state is compelled to concede, even though it is directly opposed to its claim of having the exclusive authority to enforce legal ends.[90] As such, the strike poses a threat to the law not because its ends are unlawful, but because it possesses a potentially "lawmaking character," because, like the violence employed by the state, the strike can assume the appearance of a force that is sanctioned. During crises, therefore, what is ordinarily recognized by the state as a right is condemned as an abuse of the law, one that must be confronted by means of a suspension of law and the declaration of a state of emergency:

> [L]abor will always appeal to its right to strike, and the state will call this appeal an abuse ... and will take emergency measures. ... In this difference of interpretation

is expressed the objective contradiction in the legal situation, whereby the state acknowledges a violence whose ends ... it sometimes regards with indifference but in a crisis [*Ernstfall*] ... confronts inimically.[91]

As Benjamin argues in the essay, however, this violence, which the state must confront with its own during moments of crisis, is not always directed at a juridical end. Drawing on Sorel's distinction between the general proletarian strike and the political strike, Benjamin argues that the two embody opposing functions of violence. In the political strike, which is limited to a particular sector, violence is used as a means toward an end, that of obtaining better working conditions or wages through the interruption of labor. Such an "omission of services" is violent because of its "extortionate" character; it serves as an extra-economic means of coercion for winning concessions from the capitalist class.[92]

As Sorel explains in *Reflections on Violence*, the strategy was favored by "moderate socialists." The latter regarded the political strike as a means of "preparing the ground for a strong centralized ... power that will be impervious to criticism from the opposition, and capable of imposing silence and issuing its mendacious decrees."[93] Although this strategy can reverse the "decay" of state institutions which, no longer "conscious of the revolutionary forces to which they owe their existence," "cannot achieve decrees worthy of this violence," it also leaves these institutions in place, changing only their managers:[94] "The political general strike demonstrates how the state will lose none of its strength, how power is transferred from the privileged to the privileged, how the mass of producers will change their masters."[95] To use to description of Social Democracy from "On the Concept of History," the moderate socialists' view of the political strike was defined by a "stubborn faith in progress ... confidence in their 'base in the masses,' and ... servile integration in an uncontrollable apparatus."[96]

As Sorel argued, moreover, the state apparatus that the moderate socialists wanted to conquer was not a democratic invention of the French Revolution. Rather, the Revolution inherited it from the absolute monarchy: The "most characteristic institutions of modern France dated from the *ancien régime* (centralization, excessive regulation)."[97] Instead of dissolving these institutions, "parliamentary socialists," who believed that they were "destined one day to take possession of the State," considered it "unwise to destroy by violence a force which is destined to become theirs."[98] Because they knew "nothing outside the ideology of the State," they regarded the pure immediate violence of the general strike with suspicion, looking "with terror on movements which might lead to the ruin of the institutions by which they live."[99] Thus, when "they attacked the upholders of the authority of the law, they did not at all seek to suppress that authority, because they wished one day to utilize it for their own ends." As a result, the "revolutionary disturbances of the nineteenth century ended by strengthening the State."[100]

This tendency was one that Marx himself had opposed, as Sorel pointed out, underscoring the need to be "careful not to confuse Marx's theories with the programs of the parties which claim the author of *Capital*."[101] Against the centralized political structure that the French Revolution had inherited from the *ancien régime*, Marx proposed the working-class council, as it emerged in the Paris Commune, as a means of abolishing the state and the alienation of labor in capitalism. For Marx, the council was the "political form at last discovered under which to work out the economical emancipation of labor."[102] Through this form of organization, the "smashed state machine" and its police apparatus would be superseded by a "fuller democracy," based upon directly elected governing bodies. Using the pure means of a non-parliamentary form of direct political intercourse, these bodies would suppress the instruments of violence employed by state power to enforce its legal decrees. In this way, democracy, according to Marx, would be "transformed from bourgeois into proletarian democracy; from the state ... into something which is no longer a state proper."[103]

Similarly, Sorel regarded the soviet commune in Russia as a new political form capable of supplanting the "arrogant bourgeois democracies."[104] As such, he rejected the parliamentary socialist program of utilizing the general strike for the purpose of seizing state power and subordinating its institutions to socialist ends. Such a program conceives of the "transmission of power ... in terms of the replacement of one intellectual elite by another." For Sorel, on the other hand, revolution required a diffusion of "authority down into the workers' own organizations."[105] As such, it could not be achieved by putting the state in the hands of representatives of the working class, but only by establishing a decentralized "republic of *soviets* against the coalition of great capitalist powers."[106]

The Critique of Violence and the Permanent Withdrawal from Capitalism and State Power

In Germany, this revolutionary project would be undermined by the parliamentarism of the Social Democratic Party, which, according to Sorel, "included in its program proposals of which Marx had pointed out the error".[107] This parliamentarism would serve to "further the interests of the bourgeoisie." In the late nineteenth and early twentieth centuries, the Party excluded anarchist members who proposed to dissolve the state institutions that it wished to control. To that end, it limited "admission solely to groups prepared to accept the legitimacy of parliamentary channels and democratic structures in the pursuit of socialist objectives."[108]

The parliamentarism of German Social Democracy was strongly opposed by figures including Gustav Landauer, "the most influential German anarchist intellectual of the twentieth century." According to James Horrox, Landauer's "ideas were important to ... thinkers including ... Ernst Bloch, Gershom Scholem [and] Walter Benjamin." In "Capitalism as Religion," a fragment that was supposed to be developed as part of his anarchist politics, Benjamin cites Landauer's most influential work, *A Call to Socialism*.[109]

As an alternative to the parliamentarianism of Social Democracy, as well as its use of the political strike as a form of extortionate violence, Landauer proposed a "restructuring of society from below." To that end, he advocated the "self-emancipation of the workers rather than a call to acts of terrorism or the violent destruction of capitalism and the state." As James Horrox describes, Landauer conceived of the general strike not merely as "a bargaining mechanism." Rather, for Landauer, "'direct action' came to mean the setting up of peaceful cooperatives and passive resistance to the state." Its "real use to the socialist cause" was not a:

> ... temporary cessation of work in capitalist enterprise, but the permanent withdrawal from capitalism altogether and the continuation of work outside of it as workers put together their own self-sufficient co-operative ventures under self-management and for their own benefit. Socialism ... would come about neither through parliamentary mechanisms, nor by resorting to acts of violence, but by means of "building the new society within the shell of the old" as workers dropped out of the present system and constructed their own cooperative enterprises as enclaves of libertarianism as an alternative to the existing society. As these societies grew they would act as an example ... siphoning workers out of the state-capitalist system and eventually reaching a critical mass after which *they* would be the prevalent form of organisation, and the state-capitalist order would become the alternative society.[110]

Landauer, then, was opposed to the use of the political strike as a form of lawmaking violence that could serve to legitimate the seizure of state power by a socialist party, a strategy which, according to Benjamin, was "summed up by the abortive German revolution" of 1918–19.[111] As such, he opposed the use of the strike as a form of extortionate violence, as a temporary interruption of labor, employed in order to obtain better terms for the worker in the contract with capital, a contract whose alleged violation, in moments of crisis, can provoke state violence. Against the political strike, Landauer proposed the general strike as a pure means without ends, which could not be evaluated as either lawful or unlawful in the eyes of the state. As a form of direct action, the general strike would establish a "stateless society based on voluntary cooperation and mutual aid," an act that would overcome capitalism and the centralized state not by coopting their organizations, but by making the latter irrelevant.[112]

The Suspension of Law and the Total Transformation of Labor

This idea of the general strike corresponds to Benjamin's account of the latter as an "entirely nonviolent, pure means," an "omission of ... service," aimed not at material gain, but which rather announces a permanent withdrawal from the contract: It "amounts simply to a 'severing of relations,'" legal relations that presuppose and perpetuate a lawmaking violence.[113] Unlike the political strike, the aim of disrupting production in a general strike is not to win concessions from capital through the use of an extra-economic means of coercion. In spite of the harm it can inflict upon the capitalist economy—which, deprived of the labor upon which it depends, "resembles ... less a machine that stands idle ... than a beast who goes berserk as soon as its tamer turns his back"—the general strike is not a violent bargaining mechanism.[114] As Sorel explained, "the general strike clearly announces its indifference toward material gain through conquest."[115]

The omission of service in the general strike is not intended as a temporary cessation of labor with a "readiness to resume work following external concessions and this or that modification to working conditions." The violence of the general strike is a pure and immediate one that does not occur so that workers can negotiate a better contract with capital, a contract guaranteed by state violence. On the contrary, the effect of the general strike is to dissolve the contract relation itself in order to change the nature of work. The general strike takes place "in the determination to resume only a wholly transformed work, no longer enforced by the state, an upheaval that this kind of strike not so much causes as consummates."[116]

As this description suggests, the pure, non-mediate violence of the general strike cannot be evaluated according to either of the "mutually independent criteria ... of just ends and of justified means." On the one hand, it is not an action that can be judged as either lawful or unlawful according to the test of the categorical imperative since its aim is not simply to compel the employer to accept a fairer contract agreement. Rather, the effect that it consummates is a "severing" of the legal relation itself, along with the violence underlying the law. But as such, like the concept of justice as a state of the world, the "determination to resume only a wholly transformed work" cannot be accomplished through a "fulfillment of what is demanded," the fulfillment of a universalizable maxim, cohering with everyone's right.[117]

It is perhaps for this reason that the total transformation of labor is something that is consummated rather than caused. The transformation is not the product of a moral causality whose ends correspond to the categorical imperative. Because this causality, in Kant's deduction of property, only relates to the possession-right of the person, it cannot abolish the right, a right that is based on the wrong of an original expropriation that subjugates things and limits the freedom of persons. And because the political strike conforms to this moral causality, asserting the possession-right of the proletariat, it is a violence that constitutes law. In contrast, the general strike, which consummates a total transformation of labor, is "anarchistic" in nature.[118]

The general strike, then, is not a lawmaking violence, one whose legitimacy depends upon whether it succeeds in supplanting the existing political order. As a form of "divine end-making" violence that is opposed to the "power ... of all mythic lawmaking," the general strike does not grant workers their rights but liberates them from law.[119] Insofar as its violence cannot be subsumed under the disparate criteria applied to means and ends, that is, insofar as it is neither a legally justified violence nor a violence that establishes law, it is capable of breaking the "cycle maintained by mythic forms of law." The violence of the general strike, then, can suspend the "dialectical rising and falling in the lawmaking and law-preserving formations of violence," a "suspension of law" upon which "the abolition of state power [and] a new historical epoch is founded."[120]

In contrast to the peace ceremony, therefore, what is consummated by the general strike is not a mythical crowning of violence as legitimate power, but a justice that puts an end to the law that violence creates in its lawmaking capacity: "Justice is the principle of all divine end-making, power the principle of all mythical lawmaking."[121] In the "Critique of Violence," then, the delineation of an independent criterion for violence as such not only allows Benjamin to complete the Kantian doctrine of right, in providing it with a way to criticize or to judge the violence upon which it is founded. By identifying a violence that is entirely outside of the law, it also establishes the possibility of a different kind of society that would no longer be based on a right that perpetuates injustice and violence: "But if the existence of violence outside the law, as pure immediate violence, is assured, this furnishes proof that revolutionary violence, the highest manifestation of unalloyed violence by man, is possible, and shows by what means."[122]

Means without Ends and Ends without Means: Hiller and Benjamin on the German Revolution

As Benjamin would later acknowledge, the notion of "unalloyed violence," as it appears in the "Critique of Violence," is an indeterminate concept, lacking concrete political content. In the essay, as Fenves has noted:

> Nowhere does Benjamin mention, for instance, the revolutionary regimes in Munich or the assassinations of their leaders, including Kurt Eisner and Gustav Landauer... the subsequent assassinations of Karl Liebknecht and Rosa Luxemburg; the general strike in March 1920 that led to the defeat of the Kapp-Lüttwitz putsch, allowing constitutional governance to resume; or the continuation of the general strike in the Ruhr region, where it was brutally suppressed by governmental and right-wing paramilitary forces in tandem.[123]

The lack of any clear reference to the dramatic events of the period would confirm Benjamin's own admission that the idea of a pure non-mediate violence was only a philosophical notion, "an empty spot, a limit concept, a regulative idea." It was only after his ambiguous turn to Marxism that the abstraction, apparently, would be filled by the idea of class conflict: "just law," as Benjamin reportedly explained to Werner Kraft in 1934, "is what benefits the oppressed in class conflict.—Class conflict is the center of all philosophical questions, even the highest."[124]

Yet, in spite of the absence of references to the events of the German Revolution, the idea of pure violence appears to have been developed at least partly in dialogue with debates on the role of violence in the rise and fall of the revolutionary regimes of the period. In the "Critique of Violence," Benjamin singles out, in particular, Kurt Hiller's "Anti-Cain," which considers the struggle between Social Democracy and those who supported soviet-style councils, the 1919 Spartacus uprising, and its defeat by the paramilitary Freikorps. Benjamin repudiates Hiller's "false, even ignoble" claim that "the revolutionary killing of oppressors" is an "intellectual terrorism" which, like the tyranny it opposes, violates the "dogma of the sanctity of life."[125]

As Hiller argued, the idea that violence as means can be justified by its ends is an error that was espoused by both the Spartacist leaders and the "noblest Bolshevik" as well as their counterrevolutionary opponents.[126] Hiller, therefore, condemned "those trigger-happy 'socialists'" who use terror but are "indignant when others use it."[127]

If I do not brutalize, if I do not kill, then I will never establish the empire of justice, of eternal peace, of joy. This ... was the reasoning of the Spartacist leaders who were deliberately and treacherously slain by military officers loyal to Ebert. We profess, however, that higher still than the happiness and justice of an existence—stands existence itself [*Dasein an sich*]. We demand that no one be permitted to take the life of one brother in order to bring freedom to another.

For Hiller, what the cycle of violence in the German Revolution reveals is that the method of Cain can never be used as a means for achieving just ends, since it violates the sanctity of bare life: "Indeed: eternal injustice for all is preferable to the killing of a single individual!" Hiller's conclusion, then, is that: "*We anti-terrorists must make a start. Abhor Cain's instrument unconditionally. We cannot simply hurl terror against terror.*"[128]

For Benjamin, of course, the alternative to this ignoble perspective is not to simply affirm the use of violence for revolutionary ends, which would be a return to the dogma that the essay sets out to attack: "just ends can be attained by justified means, and justified means can be used for just ends." On the contrary, Benjamin argues, in a manner consistent with Hiller, that this dogma "provided the ideological foundation for the terrorism during the French Revolution," and can lead to an endless "rising and falling" of lawmaking and law-preserving violence. For Benjamin, however, the "irreconcilable conflict" between violence and the ends for which it serves as a means (a conflict that produces the "discouraging experience of the ultimate undecidability of all legal problems") does not imply the need for an ignoble rejection of Cain. On the contrary, the argument in the "Critique of Violence" is directly opposed to Hiller's prescription that we must adhere to revolutionary ideals while completely renouncing the method of Cain as a means of achieving them: "Abhor Cain's instrument unconditionally. Stand to the left of Spartacus, perhaps, in terms of policy—but stand there without the instruments of death."[129]

In the "Critique of Violence," this position is criticized as a "childish anarchism" that "acknowledges absolutely no constraints on the person," severing "'action' ... from the domain of reality."[130] This critique is repeated in "The Author as Producer," where Hiller is disparaged as a "theoretician of Activism," lacking a clear program of action. Hiller's idea of "logocracy," or the rule of an intellectual elite, which was supposed to be an improvement upon the worker's council, did not provide the "slightest basis for organizing them."[131] This assessment, which Benjamin proposed to elaborate in a separate essay on Hiller that was never completed, titled "There are no intellectual workers,"[132] is consistent with Landauer's opinion of Hiller's logocracy: "I am in total opposition to the pompousness of 'intellectual councils!' There shall be no more divisions between manual and intellectual workers—and hence nothing that resembles the idea of Hiller."[133]

As a set of revolutionary ideals without a practical program for action, Hiller's position corresponds to the characterization of anarchism that appears in a letter to Scholem, anarchism as a politics with "unserviceable" methods.[134] If natural and positive law subscribe to the dogma that violence can be used for just ends,

Hiller's unconditional rejection of Cain is based upon the ignoble assumption that revolutionary aims can be achieved without violence. Whereas both natural and positive law are unable to recognize that violent means are irreconcilable with just ends, Hiller, in his thoroughgoing anti-terrorism, fails to perceive that revolutionary ends cannot be achieved without violent means.

On the other hand, in the "Critique of Violence," Benjamin rejects both revolutionary terrorism, which assumes that means can be justified by their ends, and the refusal of all violent means for the sake of preserving just ends. Against these perspectives, Benjamin adopts a position that is completely excluded from Hiller's analysis of the cycle of violence marking the events of the German Revolution. This position is not that of a "pure will," to borrow a category from Hermann Cohen's moral philosophy, a will that preserves its morality by refusing the violence that would be necessary to realize its laws. Instead, Benjamin proposes a pure violence, a revolutionary means without ends, which he identifies with the strategy of the general strike, as a total withdrawal from state power and capitalism.

The General Strike: Mythology and Demystification

As Werner Kraft pointed out, in the conversation on the "Critique of Violence," which he recorded in a diary entry, Sorel promoted this strategy as a mythology that could be used to mobilize the masses. In *The Crisis of Parliamentary Democracy*, Carl Schmitt described this mythology as the "warlike image of a bloody, definitive, destructive ... battle," which he opposed to the "bourgeois ideal of peaceful agreement" and the "cowardly intellectualism" of "parliamentary proceedings."[135] As Chryssoula Kambas argued, however, the tendency to identify Sorel exclusively with the idea of the general strike as a myth was in part the result of the German reception of his work. In this reception, Sorel appears as an "'irrationalist' and the 'spiritual father of fascism,' a formula nourished by Mussolini himself."[136]

In Benjamin's account of the general strike, on the other hand, the latter is presented not as a myth, but as a form of unalloyed "divine end-making" violence that is opposed to the "power ... of all mythic lawmaking." This power is one that Sorel also appears to attribute to the general strike. In *Reflections on Violence*, Sorel not only insists on the need to mythologize the general strike in order to inspire the masses, a strategy, later adapted by fascism, which, as Alberto Toscano has argued, is "often taken to be the sole contribution of this ... compendious book."[137] In a passage from *Reflections*, referenced in "Capitalism as Religion" – a passage which relates, in Benjamin's words, to the "heathen character of law" within capitalism – Sorel also suggests that the general strike produces a kind of demythologization.[138] In particular, its violence can serve to unmask the seemingly "natural laws" of the bourgeois economy, which perpetuate the worker's dependence on capital. Citing Marx's critique of political economy, Sorel argues that the eternal appearance of the capitalist order was the product of a process of mystification that paradoxically appears as its opposite, as the development of a scientific theory that purports to explain the immutable laws of society. In "a progress which should enchant the minds of all enlightened men," a "science of economics" emerged in which capitalism, as a contingent system of contracts established through historical violence, appears as a natural necessity.[139]

Just as the peace ceremony confers the aura of fate and moral necessity upon an act of historical violence, so economics, using "the simplest, surest and most elegant formulas," naturalizes an "unstable structure," which "could be destroyed by force, as it had been created by ... force."[140] In contrast, however, to classical drama, fate, in the modern mythology of political economy, is not portrayed as a result of the will of the gods. Rather, the tragic "submission of the masses to the conditions of the capitalist economic system" appears as the product of a natural mechanism.[141] As a result of the fetishistic religion which underlies capitalism, "the action of independent wills disappears and the whole of society resembles an organized body, working automatically; observers can then establish an economic science which appears to them as exact as the sciences of physical nature." By making the subordination of labor to capital seem like a product of natural laws, political economy not only conceals the original violence of expropriation that created the working class. It also enables the state, serving the interest of capital, to "dispense with any direct appeal to the forces of repression, except in very exceptional circumstances."[142]

What appears, then, as progress toward an enlightened society, based on rational laws, is in fact a "history of bourgeois force," a history whose various stages are distinguished only by "differences of degree" in the violence used to create and recreate the conditions for capitalism. Whether "force manifests itself under the aspect of historical acts of coercion, or ... conquest, or labour legislation, or whether it is wholly bound up with the economic system, it is always bourgeois force labouring, with more or less skill, to bring about the capitalist order."[143]

In the general strike, the apparently automatic operation of the economy is interrupted, revealing the violence required to preserve its mythological appearance as a natural mechanism. "Thus we see that economic forces are closely bound up with political power." In this way, the myth of the general strike exposes the mythology underlying the cultic religion of capitalism.[144]

3

The Aesthetic Extreme and the Dialectic of Allegory: Schmitt, Lukács, and the Origin of the *Trauerspiel* Book

The *Eidos* and The Extreme: The Methodology of *The Origin of the German* Trauerspiel

The methodology that Benjamin develops in his habilitation, a study of the *Trauerspiel* play, combines different approaches taken from various disciplines. As Benjamin explains, the habilitation "embraces on the one hand the methodological ideas of Alois Riegl with his idea of the *Kunstwollen*, and on the other the contemporary essays of Carl Schmitt."[1]

In Riegl's work, *Kunstwollen* refers to a contingent historical tendency of a particular era that drives the development of aesthetic forms.[2] In the *Trauerspiel* book, Benjamin argues that the appearance of a Baroque "doctrine of princely power" during the Wars of Religion coincided with the emergence of a "Baroque theory of drama,"[3] which was neglected as a result of a "classicist misinterpretation of the trauerspiel."[4]

Riegl's contribution to Benjamin's study, however, was overshadowed by Schmitt's. In his infamous letter to the Nazi philosopher, Benjamin acknowledged that the *Trauerspiel* book was "indebted to you for its presentation of the doctrine of sovereignty in the seventeenth century." In Schmitt's approach to the "philosophy of the state," Benjamin found confirmation of his own "modes of research in the philosophy of art."[5] Adapted to the study of art, Schmitt's method, as Benjamin writes in the short curriculum vitae of 1928, is the "prerequisite for any penetrating physiognomic interpretation of works of art, to the extent that they are unique and inimitable."[6]

In Schmitt's writings, the political equivalent to unique and inimitable artworks is the extreme or the exceptional case. In the "Epistemo-Critical Preface" (which was written after Benjamin submitted his habilitation),[7] this political concept is employed as an epistemological principle, one that Benjamin opposes to deductive and "inductive method[s] of aesthetic research." While the later derives concepts from particulars, the former deduces particulars from concepts.[8]

Benjamin's criticism of these opposing approaches, however, was not taken from Schmitt, but from one of his professors at the University of Munich, Moritz Geiger, a phenomenologist who, as Benjamin recalled in a letter, "left me with a lasting impression."[9] In the *Significance of Art*, Geiger proposes a "phenomenological method in aesthetics" as an alternative to both inductive and deductive theories of art.[10]

For Geiger, the fundamental flaw of deductive theories is that they try to "reach results from above, from some single first principle, such as the principle that art is imitation or that the aesthetically valuable is unity in variety."[11] Such an approach is inappropriate for aesthetics because it presupposes the very essence of art that it uses to understand individual works. As such, the essence is not really derived by means of a "deduction for the aesthetic attitude. If a person does not himself experience the [artistic] value, no deductive reasoning can ... instruct him."[12] Such a deduction in fact only serves to reduce diverse individual artworks to a general concept or category. But since this sort of "purely intellectual comprehension is extra-aesthetic, 'deduction' has no proper place in the aesthetic realm."[13]

As Geiger argues, however, the same problem arises with the "opposite procedure," which "approaches the problem from below instead of from above, to advance inductively".

> In order to establish the general essence of tragedy ... we consider the tragic in Sophocles, in Racine, in Shakespeare, in Schiller, and so on, and that which we find everywhere and in every writer is the essence of tragedy. But this inductive procedure ... always miscarries. For in order to point out the tragic in even a single poet, one must implicitly be already familiar with the essence of the tragic.[14]

The essence of tragedy, then, can "be grasped neither by way of deduction nor induction," since both methods presuppose what they purport to explain. The essence can be neither deduced from first principles nor discovered "through an inductive accumulation of particular examples."[15] Rather, it can only be ascertained by means of a "phenomenological attitude [that] ... attacks its problems neither 'from above' nor 'from below,' but 'from the front,'" by directly examining artworks "in so far as they are given as *phenomena*," in the experience of the senses.[16]

The particular method that Geiger prescribes for this purpose is the "intuitive grasp of essences," or "eidetic intuition," which was developed by Edmund Husserl in an early version of his phenomenology.[17] For Husserl, the technique of eidetic intuition provided an alternative to theories of concept formation in which concepts are said to arise from the process of abstraction, as well as an empirical skepticism that denied the existence of abstract ideas altogether.[18] Against theories that seek to determine the essence of things from either above or below, Husserl argued that an essence or *eidos* can be directly intuited by establishing, phenomenologically, that a specific appearance could not be otherwise than it is. Eidetic intuition, then, is the intuition of the impossibility that a phenomenon could appear differently than how the subject perceives it (see Chapter 1).

For Husserl, however, the essence that is obtained in this manner is not a universal conception, which exists above the phenomena, but an invariant *eidos* that is grasped through the necessity of its appearance.[19] Underscoring this particular aspect of the intuition of essence, Benjamin, in a letter to Gershom Scholem, defines eidetic intuition as a perception whose "object ... is the necessity of a content that ... announces itself as perceivable. The perception of this necessity is called 'intuition.'"[20]

Extending Husserl's method to the study of art, Geiger argued that the essence of tragedy can be immediately grasped "by observing intuitively in the single example the universal essence."[21] As Peter Fenves has noted, what "Geiger says about the tragic ... will find reverberation in the *Habilitationsschrift*."[22] If Benjamin's mode of aesthetic analysis, then, which viewed art as unique and inimitable, found confirmation in Schmitt's political theory, the analysis was also indebted "to an eidetic way of observing phenomena," which views every artwork as "incomparable and one-time." As Benjamin described in his curriculum vitae, the method employed in the *Trauerspiel* book is "closer" to "eidetic intuition" than to other approaches.[23]

Yet, despite this methodological closeness, Benjamin, in the end, would only adopt Geiger's Husserlian critique of inductive and deductive theories of art, while rejecting his phenomenological approach to aesthetics. Thus, in the habilitation, Benjamin asks, "whether the responsibility for an accounting of the structure of the idea-world is to be unavoidably left to a much-vaunted intellectual intuition?"[24] Does eidetic intuition, in other words, as "a 'seeing' grasp of a concept in an empirical presentation," succeed, in fact, in explaining the existence of abstract ideas and conceptions?[25] Benjamin responds in the negative: "Ideas are not among the given elements of the world of phenomena. ... The being of ideas simply cannot be conceived of as the object of vision, even intellectual vision."[26]

In the habilitation, therefore, Benjamin appropriates Geiger's critique of induction and deduction, while unequivocally rejecting his phenomenological approach to aesthetics as a method for the study of tragedy. As Fenves points out, therefore, the "methodological program underlying the *Origin of the German* Trauerspiel is distinguished from that of Husserl's phenomenology."[27] Setting aside the technique of eidetic intuition or intellectual vision, Benjamin develops, instead, an epistemology that employs the principle of the extreme, taken from Schmitt's philosophy of the state, in order to reconsider the problem of how knowledge relates to the world.

The Epistemology of the Extreme

An early version of this epistemology is outlined in the fragment titled, "Language and Logic" (1921), in which Benjamin describes the relation between language and the world in terms of the bond between ruler and subject. In the text, Benjamin distinguishes logic from what he will later describe in the *Trauerspiel* book as "genuine knowledge ... of the realm of truth," the realm of essences, "intended by languages," which is renounced by mathematics and formal reasoning.[28] In the latter, the "relation between concepts [which] ... governs the sphere of knowledge ... is one of subsumption. The lower concepts are contained in the higher ones," such that "what is known loses its autonomy for the sake of what it is known as."[29] In logic, then, the unique and inimitable are known through general concepts that deny their uniqueness. As a result, the objects of knowledge lose their independence and individuality to the abstractions that are used to subsume them.

On the other hand, in the "sphere of essences, the higher does not devour the lower. Instead, it rules over it," such that the difference between knowledge and that which is known "remains as irreducible as the gulf between monarch and people." This relation of essence, therefore, is not one in which knowledge subsumes what is known, but rather one in which an "essential unity reigns over a multiplicity of essences in which it manifests itself, but from which it always remains distinct."[30]

But if knowledge encompasses that which is known while recognizing its difference, the one cannot be deduced from the other as its *Ursprung* or origin. Knowledge is not the origin of that which is known, nor the opposite. Such a "derivation," in fact, "is only an appearance," one that posits a "pseudo-original relationship between concept and subconcept." Against this erroneous conception of origin, Benjamin proposed a concept of *Ursprung* based upon the relation between sovereign and subject: the "relation between monarch and people makes very clear that in the sphere of essence questions of legitimacy are … ultimately of origins."[31] *Ursprung* or origin, then, including the origin of the *Trauerspiel*, must be understood, not as the pseudo-origin of an inductive derivation, but as a relation analogous to sovereignty, which unifies the people without completely subsuming them. As Samuel Weber has argued, therefore, "Benjamin encounters the question of sovereignty not simply as a theme of German baroque theater, but as a methodological … problem."[32]

In the "Epistemo-Critical Preface," however, the concept of origin will not be defined with reference to sovereignty, but rather in terms of the exception to the norm, which, according to Schmitt, is that which the sovereign alone can determine. Reiterating his criticism of inductive and deductive theories of knowledge, Benjamin contends that "it is a mistake to understand the most general references of language as concepts, instead of recognizing them as ideas." In the sphere of essences, or "the realm of truth, intended by languages," the general unity that knowledge imposes on that which is known is not that of an "average," the average of all the particulars that a concept subsumes. "To insist on explaining the general as an average is wrongheaded." Instead, Benjamin argues that the "general is the idea."[33] Like the relationship between the sovereign and the people, the idea, in contrast to the concept, does not subsume what it governs. Instead, it relates itself to the elements that it unifies while recognizing their independence or difference. These elements, then, are not simply specific empirical examples of the idea, understood as a general concept. Rather, the "empirical," as Benjamin writes, "is more deeply penetrated the more distinctly it is seen as an extreme," an extreme that is irreducible to the idea of which it is an element, just as the people are irreducible to the monarch who unifies them as their supreme representative.[34]

In the "Epistemo-Critical Preface," Benjamin describes the relationship between the idea and the extreme as a *constellation*: "Ideas are eternal constellations" that "issue … from the extreme." "[I]deas come to life only where extremes gather around them." The elements that make up a constellation "are manifest most distinctly at the extremes. The idea can be described as the formation of the nexus in which the uniquely occurring extreme stands with its like."[35]

The idea, then, is a constellation composed of the "unique and extreme," formed into a unity that rescues their singular character. As Weber explains, the method of aesthetic research that Benjamin develops, using Schmitt's theory of sovereignty, is one that attempts to "think the 'idea' as a configuration of singular extremes."[36] In this way, according to Benjamin, the constellation "achieves a twofold result: the salvation of phenomena," whose irreducibility is rescued, "and the presentation of ideas," whose role in unifying extremes is preserved.[37]

Aesthetics as a Study of Extremes

In the *Trauerspiel* book, then, this theory of knowledge as a constellation of extremes, which was indebted in part to Schmitt's theory of sovereignty, is applied to the study of the *Trauerspiel*. As a method of literary-historical analysis, the theory will allow Benjamin to avoid the pitfalls of both deductive approaches, which subsume unique works of art under general classifications, as well as inductive theories, which, by "clinging to the particular ... forfeit ... the essential."[38]

In the introduction, however, Benjamin appears at first to align himself with the latter perspective, specifically with Benedetto Croce's nominalistic conception of art and the medievalist Konrad Burdach's nominalistic theory of history. Benjamin acknowledges the merits of "Croce's vehement critique of the deduced concept of genre in the philosophy of art," which "sees in classification ... the basis of a superficially schematizing criticism." In this kind of criticism, aimed at the "marshaling of artworks with a view toward what they share in common," unique works of art are measured "against the genre ... [to] which, in the critic's opinion, they belong." According to Croce, this deductive approach is an "idle undertaking" since "individual works of art ... are numberless: all are original, and none translatable into any other." Deducing a common literary genre or form is impossible since "there is no mediating element interposed between the universal and the particular, no sequence of genres or types, no *generalia*."[39]

For Benjamin, the historiographical counterpart to Croce's nominalistic critique of the idea of genre is Burdach's conception of history, which rejected the notion of an historical epoch, as a general classification that seeks to subsume irreducibly diverse historical phenomena. According to Burdach, "one should never assume that ideas such as 'the Renaissance' or 'the Baroque' are capable of mastering the material conceptually."[40] Like unique works of art, historical events resist the attempt to organize them into general categories.

According to Benjamin, these two forms of nominalism are consistent with his own theory of knowledge, based on the principle that the "idea [is] not classificatory,"[41] and that "ideas constitute an irreducible multiplicity."[42] Croce's "critique of the hypostasizing of general concepts,"[43] "as regards the concepts of aesthetic genres," therefore, "is certainly well taken."[44] The problem, however, as Benjamin argues, is that this critique "stops halfway." In particular, it fails to achieve the "twofold result" that constitutes the aim of Benjamin's theory of knowledge as a constellation composed of irreducible extremes: to save phenomena as well as their unity in the form of ideas.

Thus, despite his agreement with inductive critiques of deductive approaches to aesthetics and history, Benjamin, in a dialectical gesture, also insists that his method is exactly the opposite of the nominalistic rejection of general concepts in favor of difference: "The trauerspiel, as treated in the philosophy of art, is an idea. Such a treatment is distinguished ... by the fact that ... it presupposes unity, [while] literary history is obliged to demonstrate diversity."

As Benjamin explains, however, the contradiction between unity and diversity in both historiography and literary-historical analysis is resolved when unity is understood as an *idea*, as opposed to a concept, and diversity is conceived as an *extreme*: "But what such names cannot accomplish as concepts they can achieve as ideas—in which it is not the similar that is brought into congruence but the extremes that attain to synthesis." The idea, then, does not subsume the diversity that it unifies, reducing it to the similar or the same. Rather, it synthesizes extremes, which remain as "irreducible as the gulf between monarch and people."

From the perspective of Benjamin's notion of knowledge as a constellation of extremes, or the synthesis of an "irreducible multiplicity," both inductive and deductive approaches to history and art commit a similar error.[45] In the two apparently opposite theories, the idea is reduced to a general concept or average, which can then be either rejected as a unity that reduces diversity to the same or affirmed as the essence underlying diverse historical and artistic developments: "Whereas induction reduces ideas to concepts by dispensing with their ... coordination, deduction ends up doing the same by projecting them into a pseudo-logical continuum. The realm of philosophic thought unfolds not in an unbroken line of conceptual deductions but in a description of the world of ideas."[46]

Benjamin's study, therefore, will be based neither on a deductive approach that attempts to define an element common to all *Trauerspiel* plays, nor on an inductive method, seeking to save the diversity of individual works by rejecting all general concepts. Instead, the thesis will be a "study of extremes,"[47] unifying unique and inimitable works into an *idea* that relates them precisely as different, rather than similar: "Research should ... always be guided by the assumption that ... what is disparate and diffuse appears bound together as elements of a synthesis."[48]

The German Literary Baroque: The Virtual History of an Aesthetic Extreme

For Benjamin, this assumption implies that literary-historical analysis cannot be exclusively concerned with great works of art, with the most outstanding examples of a particular genre that can be said to embody the genre itself as a whole. In a study of extremes, "the creations of lesser writers in whose works the outlandish is frequently present will be valued no less than those of greater writers. It is one thing to embody a form, but quite another to shape it."[49]

As an aesthetic category, therefore, the extreme cannot be identified with the excellent or the exemplary. Its difference or diversity with respect to the norm is not necessarily that of an outstanding production. And in fact, as Benjamin seems to suggest, the extreme and the excellent can be inversely related: In "the historical drama," "aesthetic aporias ... necessarily emerged most clearly ... in their most radical and therefore least artistic development."⁵⁰ Like allegory, therefore, the extreme is an aesthetic category that "positions itself beyond beauty."⁵¹ But as such, the exemplary is not the only kind of extreme that can determine the history of an artform. An extreme can also be unique or inimitable in its oddity or "extreme coarseness,"⁵² and a work of poor quality can influence a genre as much as artworks produced by the "writerly elect."⁵³

Although Benjamin, then, opposed the reduction of individual artworks as average illustrations of a particular genre, contrary to Wolin, he did not "focus ... his attention ... on the *extreme characteristics* ... in order that *Trauerspiel* might be revealed not as an example, but as *exemplary*."⁵⁴ On the contrary, a focus on exemplary artworks tends to exclude aesthetic extremes like the *Trauerspiel*, consigning them to a "virtual history."

Unable to grasp its inimitable qualities as an aesthetic extreme, critics associated the *Trauerspiel* with more refined forms of drama. Viewing the failure to conform to a classical precedent (which the *Trauerspiel* poets did not understand) as an aesthetic deficiency, critics mistook the extreme distinguishing features of a new German literary Baroque as signs of a degraded form of "Renaissance tragedy." Consequently, the period was never "assign[ed] a particular title ... in German literary history."⁵⁵ Thus, the existence of a German literary Baroque in the seventeenth century, of which the *Trauerspiel* is an example, was concealed by an "all too comfortable periodization" that imposed a classical standard on the plays belonging to this unrecognized style.⁵⁶ The "thesis that the German drama of the seventeenth century was a Renaissance form is supported by the Aristotelian orientation of the theorists," who applied the principles of tragedy in the *Poetics* (like the theory of tragic effect and purgation) to evaluate the *Trauerspiel* plays.⁵⁷

This "classicist misinterpretation," however, was one that the Baroque had "put into practice in misinterpreting itself."⁵⁸ According to Benjamin, the *Trauerspiel*'s Baroque characteristics were also concealed by the playwrights themselves, who achieved their singular style unintentionally in the very attempt to conform to classical models they did not understand and were unable to imitate: "[T]hese works confronted ... formal tasks to which they were, for lack of any training, wholly unequal. Every attempt to draw closer to classical form ... served, through its very violence, to predispose the enterprise to a highly baroque elaboration."⁵⁹

For these reasons, the *Trauerspiel*, as an aesthetic extreme, as opposed to a genre (or rather as the "extreme ... of a genre [which] is the idea"), did "not enter as such into the history of literature."⁶⁰ Its existence in the "course of history" (understood, deductively, as either a "pseudo-logical continuum" of general concepts or forms, or, inductively, as an irreducible diversity of individual artworks) is a "virtual" one.⁶¹ Although the *Trauerspiel*, as a literary extreme, as opposed to a general form, "would fit into the series of aesthetic classifications without any problem," it "relates to the realm of classifications in a different manner." Because it "does not contain in itself that generality on which, in the system of classifications, each conceptual gradation depends—namely, that of the average," the *Trauerspiel* is concealed by both deductive and inductive approaches to literary-historical analysis.[62] Like the development of Baroque allegory, therefore, its history was "played out in silence because it was without conceptual formation."[63]

With regard to this problem, Benjamin singles out, in particular, a "certain [Herbert] Cysarz" as a subject of criticism. As he described in a letter to Scholem, Cysarz, who had written a successful habilitation thesis (published in 1924 as *German Baroque Poetry: Renaissance, Baroque, Rococo*), was both Benjamin's "immediate forerunner and occasionally [his] obvious opponent in this area of literary history."[64] As a forerunner to the *Trauerspiel* book, Cysarz' book had already challenged the tendency to view the Baroque as a decadent stage of the Renaissance. Rejecting this caricature, Cysarz argued that the Baroque was in fact "our modern literature's first struggle with antiquity." For Cysarz, however, this struggle was ultimately "unsuccessful" due to the "imitation of antiquity," in a "chain of receptions"[65] by poets who "obediently go to the schools of Romance literatures and the Ancients." Ironically, then, Cysarz's conclusion concerning the seventeenth century is similar to the caricature he set out to disprove: The Baroque was merely a "pseudo-Renaissance," an argument of which Benjamin was an "obvious opponent."[66]

Benjamin's criticism of Cysarz, however, is not that "his ... viewpoints" about the Baroque "are in error," but that, in immersing himself in its poetry, his perspective had become too close to that of the era itself, whose style he appropriated as awkwardly as the Baroque had imitated antiquity: "It is quite characteristic of baroque style that anyone who stops thinking rigorously while studying it immediately slips into a hysterical imitation of it." In his "attempt to part the hair of the degenerate boor," to see past the caricature of the baroque as the Renaissance in decline, Cysarz, then, had failed to maintain the critical distance required to separate its achievement from its own idea of itself, or of the poets' awareness of their work.[67]

The originality, or extremity, of an artform, however, does not depend upon the poet's intention, on whether the latter's deliberate aim was to invent or to imitate, which is why "the creations of lesser writers" are capable of "virtually" shaping a genre. As Benjamin suggests, moreover, the virtual history of the *Trauerspiel*, as revealed in his study of aesthetic extremes, is one that largely occurred without the agency or awareness of the authors, authors who wrote in a genre that "was never capable ... of self-reflection in its interior." "The German *trauerspiel* ... remained astonishingly obscure to itself."[68] But precisely because of this, the difference between the *Trauerspiel* and its classical model is concealed in histories that focus only on the superior qualities of exemplary plays from the period, produced by the writerly elite. As Benjamin argues, however, the defining characteristics of the *Trauerspiel* plays were not a purposeful product of artistic excellence. Rather, as Weber points out, "the German baroque ... is ... tied ... to a certain *lack* of sovereignty, to a certain incapacity of producing consummate artistic forms."[69]

The *Trauerspiel*'s "baroque elaboration," therefore, was not a result of artistic genius. Rather, it arose out of the *inability* of playwrights of the period to conform to the classical model of tragedy, which masked the uniqueness (or extremity) of the plays they produced. The "Aristotelian theory of tragic effect ... would have been especially [in]accessible to the seventeenth-century understanding. Nevertheless, the more impossible it was to fathom this doctrine … the more room there would have been for the free play of interpretation."[70] The originality of the form, then, was not the result of the artistry of its authors, but of their ignorance of the classical precedent they wanted to imitate.

But as such, the *Trauerspiel*, as an extreme, can only exist as a virtual presence in histories that grasp its development as a series of deliberate aesthetic decisions, just as, in Schmitt's theory of sovereignty, "the exceptional becomes exemplary once dictatorial prerogatives are developed."[71] Subsumed under the sovereign prerogative, the real state of exception, to borrow an expression from one of Benjamin's last pieces of writing, is excluded from the official record of history, as a causal series of exemplary sovereign decisions.

Genius and Sovereignty

It is for this reason perhaps that knowledge is defined in the *Trauerspiel book* as a constellation of extremes, rather than as a relation resembling the bond between ruler and subject. And in fact, in the text, Benjamin attempts to completely detach the extreme from its relation to sovereignty. Adapting Schmitt's philosophy of the state to the study of art, Benjamin develops a concept of the extreme that departs from Schmitt's explanation of its role within politics, as the occasion for an exemplary sovereign decision.

As Peter Bürger has argued, this explanation was conceived, "following the model of the free act of the artistic genius," taken from Kant's account of aesthetic judgment.[72] For Kant, art cannot be created by simply applying a formula or a general principle. "The concept of … art … does not permit of the judgement upon the beauty of its product being derived from any rule." Rather, art is the result of a "natural endowment," or an "innate mental aptitude (*ingenium*)," whose creations defy existing norms and conventions. But since "art must necessarily be regarded as art … of genius," it cannot be subjected to rules. Rather, like sovereignty, it creates its own law, and "gives the rule to art."[73] As a product of genius, art "surpasses the ordering categories of the understanding,"[74] just as the exception surpasses the general rule, embodying a unity that does not correspond to "any determinate concept of reason,"[75] and exhibiting "a conformity to law without a law."[76] As Victoria Kahn has argued, therefore, the Schmittian "sovereign who freely decides is the political equivalent of the Kantian genius who gives rules to himself."[77]

In "Art in the Age of Its Mechanical Reproducibility," Benjamin will insist on the need to "neutralize" the "traditional concepts" of "creativity and genius," whose "uncontrolled" use, in the era of film and photography, could "allow factual material to be manipulated in the interests of fascism."[78] The task proposed in the essay, of making concepts like genius "useless for the purposes of fascism," would seem to be the artistic equivalent to the political task of realizing a "real state of exception," a state that the sovereign, presumably, could no longer decide: "Then we will clearly see that it is our task to bring about a real state of exception, and this will improve our position in the struggle against fascism."[79]

In both Schmitt's philosophy of the state and Kant's critique of judgment, the exception is reduced to the exemplary acts and decisions of a sovereign subject. As Benjamin notes in "Program of the Coming Philosophy," this problem is also apparent in the *Critique of Pure Reason*, which failed to perceive that "there remains the subject nature of ... consciousness to be eliminated."[80] For Benjamin, on the other hand, the real state of exception, or what Benjamin refers to in the *Trauerspiel* book as the "plane of the creaturely state," exceeds the intentions of the artistic genius as well as the monarch. If the sovereign, according to Schmitt, decides on the state of exception, the decision, according to Benjamin, is also determined by the creaturely state in which it occurs, a real state of exception devoid of transcendence: "The plane of the creaturely state, the terrain on which the trauerspiel unfolds, quite unmistakably determines the sovereign as well. As highly enthroned as he is over his subjects and his state, his status is circumscribed by the world of creation; he is the lord of creatures, but he remains a creature."[81]

If the executive decision, therefore, surpasses the general rule, the exception on which the sovereign decides also surpasses his sovereignty, even though its presence can only be virtually felt. Likewise, the *Trauerspiel*, as an aesthetic extreme, shaped by the outlandish works of lesser writers, exceeds the narrow conception of art as the exemplary creation of an artistic genius, defying all rules and conventions. In contrast to the exception on which the sovereign decides, the *Trauerspiel* is an extreme upon which "no sovereign genius [has] imprinted his personality."[82]

Myth and Historical Life: The Tragic Hero and the Baroque Tyrant

According to Aristotle's *Poetics*, pity is produced by the fate of a pious hero who, in the "dramatic peripeteia"[83] or "reversal in classical tragedy," suffers unjustly as a consequence precisely of a virtuous act to uphold the law.[84] In Benjamin's words, "fate it is nothing but the act that, by a malicious chance, thrusts the guiltless into the abyss of universal guilt."[85] A purgation of feelings, then, is aroused by "a pathological breakdown in the face of a dreadful fate," by the tragic representation of an exception to law.[86] As Benjamin argues, however, this "part of the *Poetics*, which ... bespeaks its determination by the cultic character of Greek theater, would have been ... [in]accessible to the seventeenth-century understanding."[87] Because the "German trauerspiel of the Baroque [was] ... distinguished by a great poverty of non-Christian conceptions ... it could not become a drama of [tragic] fate."[88]

The purpose of the *Trauerspiel*, then, was not to arouse pity, but rather to humble the audience, watching the downfall of the most powerful, who utterly failed to be pious. Whereas in Greek tragedy, an exception to the law results from the ethical action of a virtuous hero, the "trauerspiel exists to temper the virtue of its spectators"[89] by portraying a sovereign whose "despicable feebleness of ... actions" undermines his "sublime status."[90] The purpose of such a representation is not to provoke pity. In the *Trauerspiel*, what "fascinate[s] in the downfall of the tyrant" is not the undeserved fate of a hero, who dooms himself by acting in accord with the law, but "the conflict ...

between the impotence and depravity of his person and ... belief in the sacrosanct power of his role."[91]

According to Benjamin, this "law of the trauerspiel" is directly opposed to the reversal of ethical action that characterizes the drama in classical tragedy.[92] Thus, in Shakespeare's great *Trauerspiel*, *The Tragedy of Hamlet*, the death of the prince, who "goes to pieces inwardly because he could find no other solution to the problem of existence than the negation of life," has "absolutely no relation" to his tragic fate. Hamlet's death is the result of an "entirely external contingency" with respect to the action, which "completely undermines the tragic character of the drama."[93] "The death of Hamlet," therefore, "has no more in common with tragic deaths than the prince has with Ajax." "If tragedy ends with decision, entirely uncertain though it may be," in *Hamlet*, fate—in conformity with the anomic "law of the trauerspiel"—is reduced to contingency: "He wants to die by chance."[94]

But as a result of this theatrical difference—the replacement of the pious hero of classical tragedy by the depraved and impotent sovereign—the *Trauerspiel* was deprived of the "cultic character" of its Aristotelian precedent. As such, its aim, according to Benjamin, was not the representation of myth, but the dramatization of historical life, "putting history pure and simple on view": "Historical life, as that epoch represented it to itself, is its content, its true object. In this respect it differs from tragedy. For the object of the latter is not history but myth."[95]

In Greek drama, therefore, an exception to the law is mythologized as an inevitable fate, a fate of which, as Hegel described, it is "the honor of ... great characters to be culpable."[96] In the *Trauerspiel* plays, on the other hand, sovereignty is desacralized, reduced to a mere "historical life" from which fate is excluded. "For fate is no purely natural occurrence, any more than it is purely historical," just as a precarious historical occurrence is not a moral event that can be subsumed by the universality of ethical laws.[97] In the *Trauerspiel*, tragedy is not the result of a "moral transgression," as it is in classical drama. Rather, it is the "creaturely state of the human being that is the cause of the downfall," making it completely "different from the extraordinary downfall of the tragic hero."[98] In the *Trauerspiel*, then, the downfall does not arise from a mere moral failure to act in accord with the law, but rather from the inherent inability of humanity to transcend its bare life, to make its human existence completely conform to a moral or religious ideal. In that sense, the *Trauerspiel* plays have "nothing in common with religious conceptions; the perfect martyr escapes immanence as little as does the ideal image of the monarch."[99]

According to Benjamin, this demythologized representation of historical life, exposed by the conflict between the sacred role of the sovereign and the depravity of his person, is directly opposed to Schmitt's political theology of sovereignty. Whereas for Schmitt, the sovereign is he who decides on exceptional cases that cannot be subsumed under a law, the tyrant portrayed in the *Trauerspiel* plays is a prince who, because of the conflict between himself and his sovereignty, cannot decide upon the exception:

> The antithesis between the power of the ruler and his ability to rule entailed for the trauerspiel a characteristic feature ... which stands out in all clarity only when viewed against the background of the theory of sovereignty. This is the

indecisiveness of the tyrant. The prince, with whom rests the decision concerning the state of exception, shows that, as soon as the situation arises, a decision is nearly impossible for him.[100]

Through a "study of extremes," then, Benjamin uncovers the "indecisiveness of the tyrant," as a fundamental feature of the *Trauerspiel* (which had been disguised by its reduction to a classical norm), and proposes this representation as a critique of Schmitt's theory of sovereignty. If Benjamin's analysis of the *Trauerspiel* as an aesthetic extreme is indebted, therefore, to Schmitt's "presentation of the doctrine of sovereignty in the seventeenth century," the Baroque idea of the tyrant, discovered in this analysis, is also used to dispute Schmitt's account of this doctrine.[101]

Schmitt and the Political Theology of the Seventeenth Century

In *Political Theology*, Schmitt presents a critique of the "modern concept of sovereignty," which regarded the ruler as the "supreme executive power."[102] For Schmitt, the "contemporary theory of the state" lacks the "vivid awareness of the meaning of the exception that was reflected in the doctrine of natural law of the seventeenth century."[103] In contrast to its modern counterpart, the latter had "understood the question of sovereignty to mean the question of the decision on the exception."[104] For Schmitt, then, the modern conception of sovereignty as the supreme executive power is insufficient insofar as this power must be further defined in terms of its exclusive ability to decide on the state of exception. The latter is "more interesting than the rule" because the sovereign's supreme executive function is not to determine the law, but to suspend its applicability in the case of emergency.

For Schmitt, moreover, the question of sovereignty and the decision upon the exception was an inherently theological one: "The exception in jurisprudence is analogous to the miracle in theology." Just as the miracle is a "transgression of the laws of nature through an exception brought about by [divine] intervention," so the sovereign transgresses the laws of society by suspending their power.[105] This is why in "the theory of the state of the seventeenth century, the monarch is identified with God," a God who transcends the world just as the sovereign's right of decision transcends the law it suspends in a moment of crisis:[106]

> To the conception of God in the seventeenth [century] ... belongs the idea of his transcendence vis-a-vis the world, just as to that period's philosophy of state belongs the notion of the transcendence of the sovereign vis-à-vis the state. The nineteenth century was increasingly governed by representations of immanence.[107]

The transcendent meaning of the exception, therefore, was "lost in the eighteenth century," in the age of Enlightenment, "when a relatively lasting order was established." Because of the political stability that prevailed during this period, Kant, who was the representative of a "rationalist tendency, which ignores the emergency," did not understand that, through the right of the sovereign, "the legal system itself can anticipate the exception and can 'suspend itself.'" Because the "greater stability of political relations in the eighteenth century" served to obscure the definitive role of the sovereign in deciding upon the exception, "[e]mergency law was no law at all for Kant."[108] The political stability that followed the seventeenth century, then, resulted in a rationalist tendency that served to conceal the theological origins of the modern state, and the meaning of the state of exception: "The rationalism of the Enlightenment rejected the exception in every form."[109] The aim of *Political Theology*, therefore, will be to prove that: "All significant concepts of the modern theory of the state are secularized theological concepts not only because of their historical development—in which ... the omnipotent God became the omnipotent lawgiver—but also because of their systematic structure."[110] For Schmitt, therefore, "the point of the analysis of the centrality of the exception for sovereignty is precisely to restore, in a democratic age, the element of transcendence that had been there in the sixteenth and even the seventeenth centuries."[111]

The Baroque: A World without Transcendence

For Benjamin, on the other hand, this transcendence was, in large part, only appearance. Although Schmitt is correct in asserting that the seventeenth-century conception of sovereignty differed from the contemporary one in terms of its awareness of the meaning of the exception, this meaning, contrary to Schmitt, was not theological.

In the seventeenth century, according to Benjamin, the development of the *Trauerspiel* (the "theater of a secular society"[112] whose Baroque characteristics were concealed by a classicist reading) coincided with a "final confrontation with juridical doctrines of the Middle Ages." The outcome of the Wars of Religion between Catholics and Protestants was a "new concept of sovereignty," one that paradoxically broke with the political theology of the Middle Ages: "[P]recisely in a century of religious wars ... [the] theocratic claim [of the clergy] was rejected by Protestantism ... And with the appearance of the Gallican articles of 1682, the last bulwark of the theocratic doctrine of state collapsed."[113]

Although this "extreme doctrine of princely power was ... more spiritual and more profound than its modern reconception,"[114] which did not grasp the meaning of the state of exception, this meaning, according to Benjamin, does not conform to Schmitt's explanation.[115] For Schmitt, the miracle of the sovereign decision was performed in order to realize what Benjamin called "the ideal of a complete stabilization, a restoration as much ecclesiastical as political."[116] The sovereign suspends the law in a state of exception for the sake of saving the law. On the other hand, in the Baroque conception of sovereignty, the supreme function of the prince was not to perform the mysterious act of suspending the law so as to restore it, but rather to *exorcise* this originary political superstition, exposing it as a juridical fiction: "If the modern concept of sovereignty amounts to a supreme executive power on the part of the ruler, the Baroque concept develops on the basis of a discussion of the state of exception, and makes it the most important function of the prince to exclude this."[117]

By excluding the state of exception, the Baroque sovereign exposes the foundational myth that the law can prevail even where it no longer exists, revealing the extreme character of a bare historical life that is no longer bound to a juridical-ecclesiastical order: "The concern of the tyrant is the restoration of order in the state of exception: a dictatorship whose utopia will always be to set the iron constitution of laws of nature in place of precarious historical occurrence."[118] In "antithesis to the historical ideal of the Restoration," the seventeenth-century theory of sovereignty, on the other hand, "is faced with the idea of catastrophe. And it is on the basis of this antithetic that the theory of the state of exception is conceived."[119]

If this Baroque concept of sovereignty, for Benjamin, then, was more "spiritual" than its contemporary counterpart, this spirituality was that of the "religious man of the Baroque," who, confronting catastrophe, "holds fast to the world," instead of the promise of religious salvation. But as such, the spirituality of the seventeenth century was one that was oriented toward a "Baroque eschatology,"[120] an empty "eskhaton," or "an end of time [that] ... knows neither redemption nor a hereafter and remains immanent to this world."[121] Just as the *Trauerspiel*, then, was defined by a "repudiation of eschatology in religious plays," so the Baroque theory of sovereignty was characterized by its rejection of the ideal of a final theological political moment of restoration, when the law at last possesses "validity without exception."[122] "Such redemption as [the *Trauerspiel*] knows will lie more" in "worldly events and the transitoriness of the creature" than "in the fulfillment of a divine plan of salvation."[123]

The Baroque, then, was defined by a religious perspective on history that was oriented toward an *irreligious* finality, the profane end to a "salvation history" in which "the tension between world and transcendence" is resolved in the catastrophe of a *world without transcendence*.[124] Like the new "secular drama" in the *Trauerspiel* plays, the Baroque conception of history was one that "stop[s] at the boundaries of transcendence."[125] In the secularization of the divine plan of salvation, "political-religious problems," which were "the reigning problems of the Baroque,"[126] were denied a "religious solution ... so as to summon from them, or impose upon them, a worldly solution in its place."[127]

Contrary to Peter Gordon, therefore, the *Trauerspiel*, on Benjamin's reading at least, does not show a "fidelity to [the] Lutheran doctrine [that] ... fallenness opens itself to grace."[128] Such a "contrast between history and redemption"—which, according to Gordon, recurs "with some frequency throughout [Benjamin's] career"—would constitute a religious rather than a worldly solution, restoring the eschatology repudiated in the *Trauerspiel* plays.[129] In the latter, history does not appear as a movement leading to an eschatological end in which humanity finally transcends all creation, along with its own creaturely nature. Fallenness does not open itself onto grace. Instead, history becomes a "headlong flight into a nature without grace," "a graceless Creation."[130]

What this suggests is that the "nihilism" underlying Benjamin's interpretation of the *Trauerspiel* play is distinct from that of Nietzsche, who held that nihilism must be completed by a revaluation or re-enchantment of the world, redeeming it from the meaninglessness of existence. In contrast, the irreligious form of redemption dramatized in the *Trauerspiel* plays is one that seeks "consolation in the renunciation of a state of grace," in the "collapse of all eschatology," allowing for a "reversion to the bare creaturely condition,"[131] devoid of religious significance. This feature of the *Trauerspiel* plays corresponds to what Weber describes as "the function assigned to the sovereign by the baroque ... that of *transcending transcendence* by making it immanent, an internal part ... of the world."[132]

In contrast, therefore, to Schmitt's transcendent account of the seventeenth-century sovereign, the Baroque prince of the *Trauerspiel* plays "remains pagan. In the trauerspiel, [the] monarch ... do[es] not escape immanence."[133] In order to exclude the state of exception, catastrophe has to be emptied of every kind of transcendence, while "everything earthborn" is "exalted" "before it is delivered over to its end."[134] As a result, the tension between the world and the law (possessing a universality which transcends the world) is removed by means of what Benjamin calls "the decelerating hypertension of transcendence that lies at the bottom of all the provocative this-worldly accents of the Baroque." In this movement of apocatastasis, the exaltation of life becomes completely "this-worldly," while the transcendence of law, which no longer applies to a world that is wholly profane, is reduced to a mere empty form or a "vacuum." "The beyond is emptied of everything in which even the slightest breath of world can be felt."[135]

This Baroque eschatology is directly opposed to the religious idea of salvation that is often attributed to Benjamin. According to Wolin, for example, "Benjamin's historico-philosophical methodology appears analogous to ... *negative theology*" insofar as the "*mortification of historical life serves*," in Benjamin's view, "*as the negative indication of the path to redeemed life.*" "For Benjamin, the more manifestly historical life appears destitute of salvation ... the more it refers to that sphere *beyond* historical life where redemption lies in store. This sphere can only be reached through the utter *devaluation of ... all worldly values.*"[136]

This idea of redemption, however, which denies the creaturely existence of "everything earth-born" exalted by the seventeenth century, presupposes precisely the tension between historical life and transcendence that Baroque eschatology aims to decelerate. In his account of the negative theology to which Benjamin supposedly subscribed, Wolin oddly reverses the formula that Benjamin uses to characterize the process of profanation associated with the allegorical mode of perception. Whereas for Wolin, the "*mortification of historical life serves as the negative indication of the path to redeemed life*," for Benjamin, spiritual meaning is dissipated by the transience of human existence to the same degree to which it seeks to transcend historical life. "So much meaning, so much forfeiture to death, for at the deepest level death incises the jagged line of demarcation between physis and meaning."[137]

In Wolin's reading, therefore, the "this-worldly" salvation which Benjamin identifies with the Baroque idea of "an end of time ... [that] remains immanent to this world" is replaced by a religious eschatology oriented toward a "sphere *beyond* historical life." In contrast to the image of the afterlife that Wolin attributes to negative theology, the form of redemption that Benjamin perceives in the *Trauerspiel* is not an inverted reflection of a wretched worldly reality that the allegorist wishes to mortify. Rather, like the "wisdom of the melancholic," this worldly redemption "is won from immersion in the life of creaturely things, and nothing of the voice of revelation reaches it."[138]

Rational Theology and Emergency Law

But if the Baroque conception of sovereignty, contrary to Schmitt, was not religious in nature, neither can its contemporary counterpart be characterized as a rationalism that denies its theological origins. As Benjamin argues, moreover, the vivid awareness of the state of exception in the seventeenth century cannot be explained by the prevalence of conflicts during the period. Conversely, "it will not suffice to refer only to the greater stability of political relations in the eighteenth century if one wishes to explain how" the purportedly theological meaning of the exception was lost in the modern theory of sovereignty. Contrary to Schmitt, Kant did not simply believe that "emergency law was no law at all" because he lived in an Age of Enlightenment, marked by relative peace and security. Rather, his inability to understand that the exception is more interesting than the rule "goes together with his *theological* rationalism."[139]

In this rational political theology, reason, extending beyond its own limits, postulates God as a necessary condition for realizing the law. But precisely because of this, the law, in Kant's theological rationalism, can never cease to apply, any more than God can cease to exist. For Kant, therefore, the idea of a *Notrecht*, an emergency law or "law of necessity (*Ius Necessitatis*)," is a contradiction because "[n]ecessity," like the natural endowment of genius, "has no law (*necessitas non habet legem*)," and therefore it cannot be claimed as a right. An emergency law cannot be a law since it suspends the whole legal order to allow unlawful acts to occur: "Yet there could be no necessity that would make what is wrong conform with Law." As such, emergency law contradicts the very concept of law: "[W]ere there such a right [of necessity] the doctrine of right would have to be in contradiction with itself."[140] Kant, therefore, denied that such an exceptional right could be legally exercised either by a sovereign in a moment of crisis or by a people opposing a tyrant:

> Nor can some kind of emergency law [*Notrecht*], having a presumed right to do what is unlawful in the most extreme crisis ... provide the key for closing the gate to restrict the power of the people. The head of state may believe that he can justify his harsh procedure by the insubordination of the subjects, as readily as the subjects can justify their rebellion from complaints regarding their exceptional suffering. Who then shall decide?[141]

For Kant, then, the contradictory notion that the sovereign can rightfully decide an exception, or can lawfully commit unlawful acts with impunity, is a result of an "ambiguity (*aequivocatio*) [that] arises from confusing the objective with the subjective basis of exercising" the right of necessity. Since no penal law could prevent someone from acting out of necessity to save their own life—or, in the case of the sovereign, to save the juridical order[142]—a crime committed out of necessity cannot be "judged inculpable (*culpabile*), but only unpunishable (*impunible*)."[143]

The idea of emergency law, then, arises from what Kant describes as a "strange confusion" that conflates a "subjective impunity" for an "objective impunity" that would be in "conformity with law."[144] For Kant, the sovereign decision is not a *legal* suspension of law (which would be contradictory), but an "objectively" unlawful act whose culpable subject is immune from all legal sanction because of the lawless necessity of the action.

This contradiction, however, is one that Kant himself commits in his doctrine of right. In the latter, Kant argues that a suspension of law, or *lex permissiva*, which constitutes the origin of legal possession, must be rationally willed as a law since, without the right of ownership, no one would be allowed to use anything (see Chapter 2). In the case of first acquisition, therefore, a suspension of law to permit a wrong to occur is justified because it is necessary. In the case of the *Notrecht* or emergency law, on the other hand, Kant makes the opposite argument. The *Notrecht* is not legal since "no necessity ... would make what is wrong conform with Law."

In his account of emergency law, Kant, therefore, defines an action, or, rather, a form of *Gewalt*, similar to one he excludes in his deduction of property: the anarchistic possibility of a use or possession of things that cannot be possessed because of their inviolable right to be goods. Just as "useable things can be possessed, but no one can possess them," so rulers and subjects can employ violent means without legal sanction to preserve or overturn law, but no one can claim that this violence is right.[145]

In deciding on the exception, therefore, the sovereign, in Kant's account of the *Notrecht*, acts with an extra-juridical impunity that cannot be recognized by the law. As a legally or objectively culpable figure with total subjective impunity, the sovereign is included in the juridical order from which he is excluded from punishment, an extra-juridical immunity that mirrors the "sacredness" that Giorgio Agamben famously attributed to the figure of *homo sacer*. The figure's capacity to be killed without legal sanction (the "unpunishability of his killing") corresponds to the culpable impunity of the sovereign decision upon the exception.[146] Like the violence imposed by the state in an emergency crisis, the sacred capacity to be killed without sanction exists both inside and outside of the law. If emergency law, then, according to Kant, cannot be understood as a right, its impunity, or external character with regard to the law, remains, nevertheless, a legal conception, one that, for Kant, is ultimately grounded in a rational conviction in God.

This legally recognized form of illegal violence that the sovereign commits is one that Benjamin will compare, in "Critique of Violence," to the extra-juridical character of the general strike as a means without legal ends.[147] Or, to put it in terms of the Baroque conception of sovereignty, Benjamin will oppose the legally unpunishable violence of the state to a "pure revolutionary violence" without eschatology, a violence that repudiates the restoration of law. But in that case, the Baroque theory of sovereignty was distinguished from its contemporary counterpart not only by its awareness of the state of exception, but also by its rejection of theology, including the rationalist theology that underlies Kant's account of emergency law.

Political Theology and *Trauerspiel*

If Kant, then, did not believe in the miracle of the sovereign exception, this was not because his rationalist account of the state was unable to recognize that its "omnipotent lawgiver" or sovereign was actually a secularization of "the omnipotent God" of the seventeenth century. Kant's disbelief cannot be attributed to his secularized notion of sovereignty, since the theological concept from which he purportedly derived it *was already secularized*, or already immanent. The Baroque theory of sovereignty both recognized and rejected the ecclesiastical and political idea of the state of exception, which Schmitt had defined, incorrectly, as its very foundation.

If the Baroque doctrine of sovereignty, then, was "more spiritual and more profound than its modern reconception," it was not because the latter lacked an awareness of the theological meaning of the state of exception in the seventeenth century. Rather, the era's spirituality was that of the "religious man of the Baroque," who, confronting catastrophe, "holds fast to the world," rejecting all religious eschatology, including the "historical ideal of ... Restoration," for which the sovereign decides upon the state of exception.[148]

In his "study of extremes," then, Benjamin (for whom Schmitt's philosophy of the state was a "prerequisite" for a "penetrating ... interpretation" of unique works of art), uncovers a virtual history of sovereignty that directly refutes the principal thesis of *Political Theology*: "All significant concepts of the modern theory of the state are secularized theological concepts." Tracing a virtual history of "sovereign indecision" in the Baroque, as a series of exemplary decisions in states of emergency, Benjamin shows, to the contrary, that the modern idea of the state *theologizes* a profane conception of politics.

Contrary to Jacob Taubes, therefore, Benjamin's references to Schmitt's philosophy of the state in the *Trauerspiel* book do not demonstrate that its "entire elaboration of the function of the sovereign in baroque drama is transposed from ... *Political Theology*."[149] If Benjamin found confirmation for his method of aesthetic research in Schmitt's political theory, the method was only confirmed by disproving the philosophy of the state from which it derived its epistemological principle of the extreme. Against Schmitt's theological political conception of sovereignty, as the miraculous power to decide upon the exception, Benjamin presents a profane "theory of 'sovereign indecision,'" in a study of aesthetic extremes in the seventeenth century.[150]

Scientific and Theological Analogies to Sovereignty in the Seventeenth Century

Benjamin's study, however, does not merely present a historical critique of Schmitt's theory of sovereignty, disputing the chronology or periodization of the process of secularization proposed in the theory. What appears in the *Trauerspiel* book to be a mere transposition of the "entire elaboration of the function of the sovereign in ... *Political Theology*" is in fact an immanent critique of the method that Schmitt employs to substantiate his principal thesis. This method is that of a "sociology of the concept of sovereignty":

> All significant concepts of the modern theory of the state are secularized theological concepts not only because of their historical development ... whereby, for example, the omnipotent God became the omnipotent lawgiver—but also because of their systematic structure, the recognition of which is necessary for a sociological consideration of these concepts.[151]

Schmitt, then, will not only attempt to prove his thesis historically, by showing that the modern idea of the state originates in theology. The argument will also be demonstrated synchronically, by examining how a shift in the systemic structure of society transformed the meaning of sovereignty.

As Schmitt argues, however, "it would be erroneous" to assume that this structure can be adequately understood by either "a spiritualist philosophy of history [or] ... a materialist one."[152] The sociology of sovereignty that Schmitt proposes, therefore, departs from both materialist and idealist conceptions of history. Whereas materialist philosophies like Marxism consider ideas such as sovereignty to be merely "'reflexes', 'reflections', and 'disguises' of economic relations," spiritualist philosophies view social and political change as the product of the history of ideas.[153] These two opposing positions, however, share a common assumption. Both "construct a contrast between two spheres," the spiritual and material, in order to "seek causal relations" by "reducing one to the other."

Schmitt's sociology of sovereignty, then, rejects both the materialist view that "idealities ... are a reflex of sociological reality," and the spiritualist conception of "social reality ... as a result of a particular kind of thinking."[154] Instead of attempting to understand the "systematic structure" of society, materialist and spiritualist philosophies simply identify one part of the structure as the cause of the other, a procedure that "must necessarily culminate in a caricature."[155] Rejecting these causal accounts, Schmitt will attempt to prove his interpretation of sovereignty in the seventeenth century by showing that his interpretation of the latter "correspond[s] to the general state of consciousness" during that period.[156]

The thesis of *Political Theology*, then, will be confirmed by a sociology of sovereignty that demonstrates that the concept pervaded both spiritual and material dimensions of life in the seventeenth century. By revealing a "continuous thread [that] runs through the metaphysical, political, and sociological conceptions that postulate the sovereign as ... primeval creator," the sociology will verify that the postulate was part of the systematic structure of the period.[157] The aim of a sociology of the concept, then, is to prove that the postulate was a fundamental presupposition of a specific social milieu, permeating all aspects of the era, such that the concept appears as an ontological given within the consciousness of the period:

> But it is a sociology of the concept of sovereignty when ... the juristic construction of the historical-political reality can find a concept whose structure is in accord with the structure of metaphysical concepts. Monarchy thus becomes as self-evident in the consciousness of that period as democracy does in a later epoch.[158]

The correspondence between the legal conception of sovereignty and the structure of metaphysical concepts in the seventeenth century, then, is not a causal relation, such that the one can be understood as a reflex of the other: "It is thus not a sociology of the concept of sovereignty when ... the monarchy of the seventeenth century is characterized as the real that is 'mirrored' in the Cartesian concept of God."[159]

In the political discourse of the seventeenth century, moreover, analogies to theology, such as the one between the miracle and the legal exception, were not simply a "kind of playing with ideas [that] yields colorful symbols and pictures." Rather, they were "fundamentally systematic and methodical analogies,"[160] pointing to an ontological assumption common to both politics and theology, an assumption that distinguishes the seventeenth century and its "inner heterogeneity"[161] with respect to the modern secular era:

> In the theory of the state of the seventeenth century, the monarch is identified with God and has in the state a position exactly analogous to that attributed to God in the Cartesian system of the world. According to Atger, "The prince develops all the inherent characteristics of the state by a sort of continual creation. The prince is the Cartesian god transposed to the political world."[162]

After the seventeenth century, the origins of the modern state in this political theology would be concealed as a result of the increasing rationalization of politics. Embracing the model of natural science, politics, then, became "depoliticized" as a result of its secularization. Losing its faith in the miracle of the exception, the modern era adopted a rationalist tendency that understood politics only as the "calculable functioning of human relationships ... as a mere function of predetermined, calculable, general rules."[163]

Theology and Natural Science: Sovereignty and the Spatialization of Time

In the habilitation, Benjamin will adapt elements of this sociology of sovereignty in his study of the *Trauerspiel*. But just as Benjamin turns the concept of the extreme against Schmitt's own political theory, so he applies his sociology of sovereignty to the purpose of disproving the thesis it is supposed to confirm. Drawing upon Schmitt's account of the function of "systematic and methodical analogies," Benjamin asserts that the *Trauerspiel* "should be cleared of any suspicion of idle analogizing."[164] The analogies that appear in the plays should not be understood, as they are in "simpleminded art-theoretical debates [on the] ... concept of symbol,"[165] as mere "embellishment ... which ... misses the content in the analysis of form and the form in the aesthetic of content."[166] Rather, like the "genuine concept" of the symbol "belonging properly to the field of theology," the analogies used in the plays must be understood dialectically as figures defined by "an indissoluble union of form and content."[167] The figures in the *Trauerspiel*, then, are not a "kind of playing with ideas [that] yields colorful symbols and pictures." Rather, the plays employ systematic analogies that correspond to a general state of consciousness in the seventeenth century.

As Benjamin argues, however, the fundamental analogy that distinguishes the *Trauerspiel* plays was not to theology. Rather, the Baroque was defined by a systematic "metaphoric that analogizes historical events with natural occurrence." In "political activity," the "poet of the seventeenth century" heard "only the horror of a destructive will, arising periodically in the manner of natural forces."[168] In the "practice of natural-historical troping," "moral transgression justifies itself purely and simply through appeal to natural conduct. 'One avoids trees that are about to fall.'"[169]

What this metaphorics suggests is that the "continuous thread [that] runs through the metaphysical, political, and sociological conceptions" of the seventeenth century was not the "postulate [of] the sovereign as a ... primeval creator." Rather, it was the representation of political life as a mechanical force. The "events of high politics" were portrayed as a "natural mode of behavior ... Great was the wealth of images the authors had at their disposal for the compelling resolution of historical-ethical conflicts into demonstrations of natural history."[170]

In his examination of the "systematic and methodical analogies" of the seventeenth century, then, what Benjamin uncovers is not a political theology, but a natural science of politics. As Hugo Grotius (a Dutch jurist cited in the *Trauerspiel* book) described, "the general appearance of political works" in the seventeenth century "is still abstract and logical." Writers pursued "the dream of a political geometry, of a rational policy. Political science takes the mathematical form that Descartes assigns to science," becoming a "political algebra." Thus, Hobbes, who "thought of pacifying the spirits and bringing back to concord the citizens divided by the civil wars," employed a "method of abstract analysis." And the preface to Spinoza's *Theologico-Political Treatise* "looks like a declamation against the religious fanaticism which was rife in Holland at that time."[171]

Contrary to Schmitt, this period, then, was not an historical moment that preceded the process of rationalization in which politics, understood on the secular model of the natural sciences, would become both "depoliticized" and detached from its theological origins. Rather, according to Benjamin, the "practice of natural-historical troping" points to a concept of the political that was characterized by an "intimate fusion of historical and moral concepts ... almost as unknown to the pre-rationalist West as it is wholly alien to antiquity."[172]

Using Schmitt's sociology of the concept of sovereignty, then, Benjamin arrives at the opposite conclusion. What the systematic analogies of the seventeenth century reveal is not a theology that pervaded all spheres of life, from metaphysics to politics, a theology that was later concealed by a rationalization that reduced its analogies to a reflex of economic relations. Rather, they reveal a far-reaching process of secularization, encompassing politics as well as aesthetics. Thus, by applying Schmitt's analysis of systematic analogies, Benjamin shows that the purportedly theological origin of the modern theory of the state is largely a historical fiction.

Mechanical Causation and God in Kant and Descartes

In the *Trauerspiel* book, Benjamin, moreover, argues that this secularization is evident precisely in the analogies that Schmitt uses to prove that the "sovereign as ... primeval creator" runs through the "metaphysical, political, and sociological conceptions" of the seventeenth century. In particular, Benjamin quotes the analogy by Frédéric Atger that Schmitt uses in order to show that the monarch during that period had "a position exactly analogous to that attributed to God in the Cartesian system of the world": "The prince develops all the virtualities of the state by a sort of continuous action. The prince is the Cartesian God transposed into the political world."[173]

As Benjamin suggests, the parallel between politics and theology is based on a more fundamental analogy between theology and natural science. This analogy is discussed in Henri Bergson's *Time and Free Will*, a text that was assigned in a seminar that Heinrich Rickert directed in 1913, "Seminar on Metaphysics in Conjunction with the Writings of H. Bergson."[174] For Descartes, as Bergson points out, the mechanical law of causality, which governs the natural world, presupposes God's continuous action at every moment in order to guarantee its authority. As Bergson describes, Descartes believed that the intervention of God was needed in order to ensure the law of causality because he was keenly aware that:

> ... causality, in so far as it is supposed to bind the future to the present, could never take the form of a necessary principle; for the successive moments of real time are not bound up with one another, and no effort of logic will succeed in proving that what has been will be or will continue to be, that the same antecedents will always give rise to identical consequents.[175]

In "On the Concept of History," Benjamin alludes to another version of this argument, made by Émile Meyerson, a Polish chemist and philosopher of science who Bergson admired: The "substitution of homogeneous configurations [of time] for changes in the physical world ... has been identified by Meyerson as the basis of the natural sciences (*De l'explication dans les sciences*)."[176] In this text, Meyerson cites another of Benjamin's teachers, Alois Riehl, who directed a course that Benjamin attended in the summer semester of 1913 on Kant's *Prolegomena to Any Future Metaphysics*. According to Riehl, the principle of causality, as the basis of natural science, arises from the "application of the principle of identity to time or ... the succession of events." The "prior condition for a causal conclusion is an equation between the antecedent and the consequent ... We explain a change if ... we succeed in reducing it to an immutable being or to an identical sequence."[177]

Causality, then, presupposes the application of the identity principle to actual change, to a singular succession of specific events, such that the latter can be equated to all similar cases. But by establishing a necessary relationship between antecedent and consequent in this manner, the principle of identity, as Benjamin explains in "Theses on the Problem of Identity," excludes immediate, ephemeral experience, which constitutes the object of knowledge itself (see Chapter 1): "The formula of identity ... 'A = A' ... does not assert the equality of two spatially or temporally distinct stages of A. But neither can it express the identity of any A existing in space or time," since the "identity-relation ... exist[s] beyond time and space."[178]

The necessity, then, of the principle of causality, which can never "succeed in proving that ... the same antecedents will always give rise to identical consequents," excludes the certainty of immediate experience, a certainty that Descartes, in the *Meditations*, had grounded in God. In this way, the identity principle, as Benjamin describes in the fragment, serves as a conceptual version of Descartes's evil demon, "transposed from the sphere of perception to that of logic."[179] Just as the supposition of a demon, manipulating our senses, threatens to reduce all our perceptions to the "illusions of dreams," so the principle of identity deprives us of certainty as to our knowledge of change in the physical world.

As Bergson points out, this problem would lead Descartes to postulate an "instantaneous physics, intended for a universe the whole duration of which might as well be confined to the present moment." Such a physics could only belong to a being who possesses a simultaneous knowledge of all events, events that, to our finite human intelligence, would only appear in succession. It "could ... not be said that that the duration of the human mind was all at once [*tota simul*] in the manner of God's duration; for our thoughts manifest a succession which cannot be found in the divine thoughts."[180] As the only being capable of observing every physical change that has and will ever occur, God alone can ensure that the universe moves in a uniform manner. Descartes' universal mechanics, therefore, presupposes a "superhuman intelligence which would know at any given moment the location, speed, and direction of all the particles of matter [and] could foresee ... if it were endowed with infinite mathematical aptitude, everything that would happen." Natural science, then, studies a system whose mechanical movement in time is sustained at each moment by the continuous act of a God who conceives of this movement instantaneously and in its entirety: "*And, in fact, the systems on which science operates are in an instantaneous present which is constantly renewing itself.*"[181]

In Descartes' mathematical physics, therefore, God's continuous action must be assumed, since the principle of identity employed in the sciences can never ensure that the movement of the natural world conforms to its mechanical laws. It was precisely because Descartes, according to Bergson, understood that physical change cannot be reduced to an identical sequence that he "attributed the regularity of the physical world and the continuation of the same effects to the constantly renewed grace of Providence."[182]

If Kant, then (as discussed in Chapter 1), had been forced to establish the eternal validity of the natural sciences upon the finite foundation of mere human experience due to the "godlessness" of his age, Descartes had sought to show that the deficiencies of mechanical reason necessitated the existence of God. Conceived in an era when experience had been "stripped of its proximity to God,"[183] Kant's philosophical system could only begin with experience, which placed the objects of theology beyond the reach of human cognition. In Descartes' mathematical physics, on the other hand, it was still possible to determine the limits of mechanical reason, of our knowledge of nature, by beginning with God: It "is very clear that the best path to follow when we philosophize will be to start from the knowledge of God himself, and try to deduce an explanation of the things created by him."[184] Beginning with God, then, what the deduction uncovers is that natural science is based on a law of causality of which it can never be certain. This led Descartes to conclude that causation did not really occur in the physical world.

If Descartes, then, affirmed a universal mechanics in which everything in the world is subject to causal relations, he did not believe, nevertheless, that these relations were *truly* causal in character. For Descartes, matter is "devoid of all active causal powers. ... [T]he physical world is, when left to its own devices, inert." In Descartes' physics, therefore, causal relations in the physical world "are not properly, and in their own nature, efficient causes."[185]

As the neo-Kantian philosopher, Wilhelm Windelband points out (in a history of philosophy which Benjamin consulted in writing the habilitation), the "efficient principle derives, not from [finite] ... substances themselves, but from the deity." As such, causal relations in the natural world are "only occasions in connection with which the consequences determined by divine contrivance appear ... not as *causa efficientes*, but *causce occasionales*. The true 'cause' for the causal connection ... is God."[186]

As such, the claim that science can discover true causes in the natural world was "vilified" by seventeenth-century Cartesians "as impious or ridiculed as absurd."[187] The seemingly necessary relations between antecedent and consequent discovered by natural science are, in fact, only accidental or "occasional" in character. Since the law of causality is based upon an identity principle that can never ensure that the "same antecedents will always give rise to identical consequents," God's divine intervention in the physical world is the only true mechanical cause: Thus, Descartes did "not hesitate to call the cause that sustains [everything] an efficient cause."[188]

Just as the "practice of natural-historical troping" belonged to a natural science of politics that was "as unknown to the pre-rationalist West as it is wholly alien to antiquity,"[189] so the Cartesian conception of God as the only true mechanical force in the universe was specific to the Baroque.[190] As Bergson points out, "*the idea of creation is absolutely absent [...] from Greek philosophy: when God intervenes in the world, it is as the arranger of the world ... God created the world.*"[191]

Space and Homogeneous Time

The continuous action of this divine mechanical power serves to connect what Benjamin calls "otherworldly phenomena with a predominantly temporal character" with "immanent, predominantly spatial phenomena of the world of things."[192] The eternal motion of God sustains the "occasional" causes that govern the natural world, a world whose successive unfolding within a *temporis naturam* exists all at once in the simultaneous duration through which God conceives of creation.

For Descartes, this implied that the concept of time employed in mathematical physics differs from time as it exists in itself. The *temporis naturam* employed in the sciences is not "duration *per se*," but merely "its measure or number," which is derived by identifying duration with the external perception of movement, by comparing "duration with the greatest and most regular motions." The result is the concept of time as the "number of movement," as a measurable and infinitely divisible duration that is "simply a mode of thought," and not time as it exists in itself.[193]

According to Benjamin, this comparison, which gives rise to the concept of time in the natural sciences, was one that "fascinated" the seventeenth century.[194] During the period, the analogy between time and external movement was symbolized by the clock, "in frequent use at that time" because it was "ideally suited to represent a mechanism," as well as the "general 'mechanization of the world view' of that time."¹⁹⁵ "It is no accident," therefore, as Benjamin argues, "that the image of the clock dominates" during the era.¹⁹⁶

The movement of the hands of a clock provides a spatial representation of time or duration. To use Kant's terminology, time, which is intuited internally, is represented by space, which is the form of all external experience. As Kant explains in the *Critique of Pure Reason*, this analogy between space and time gives rise to the measurable time employed in the sciences: Because

> inner intuition yields no shape we ... must attempt to remedy this lack through analogies, and represent the temporal sequence through a line progressing to infinity ... and infer from the properties of this line to all the properties of time, with the sole difference that the parts of the former are simultaneous but those of the latter always exist successively.¹⁹⁷

This analogy is the subject of criticism in Bergson's *Time and Free Will*, as well as in Husserl's "Philosophy as a Rigorous Science." In the latter text, Husserl (who cites Bergson's theory of time as *durée* in the essay) criticizes what he calls a "false naturalism that absurdly misconstrues ... problems ... regarding representations of time."¹⁹⁸ In this naturalism, time, as an internal or "psychical" experience is conceived by analogy to the spatial form of the physical objects of science: "Through the medium of thing-experience," the perception of time, represented as space, becomes a "sort of mediate seeing of the psychical."¹⁹⁹ In that sense, to extend the "model of the natural sciences" to the representations of time "inevitably means to reify consciousness," reducing a psychic phenomenon to a physical thing.²⁰⁰ For Husserl, then, natural science is based on what Benjamin calls a "psychophysical parallelism" between time and space.

In *Time and Free Will*, the term that Bergson employs to describe this parallelism is "endosmosis," a process which Benjamin defines in the essay on Hölderlin as the "interpenetration of individual forms of perception," of the internal and external forms of pure intuition.²⁰¹ For Bergson, the spatialized time that emerged from this process is the product of an "illegitimate translation of the unextended" (time) "into the extended" (space), "of quality into quantity."²⁰² This spatialized time, then, is based on a "confusion of duration with extensity, of succession with simultaneity, of quality with quantity," a conflation in which pure time or *durée* is reduced to "a fourth dimension of space, which we call homogeneous time."²⁰³ Translated as space, the intensive quality of time is reduced to a quantifiable form of extension: "In place of a heterogeneous duration ... we thus get a homogeneous time whose moments are strung on a spatial line."²⁰⁴

In the *Trauerspiel* book, Benjamin summarizes this thesis as follows: "The image of the moving hand is, as Bergson has shown, indispensable for the representation of the nonqualitative, repeatable time of mathematical natural science."²⁰⁵ The analogy of time to the intuition of space, then, creates the quantitative conception of time, underlying the concept of causality in the natural sciences.

By reducing duration to an infinite series of homogeneous units, the spatialization of time, based on the image of the moving hand, makes it possible to conceive of an observable change or succession as a necessary sequence, conforming to a causal relation that is the same in all cases. But since causality, according to Bergson, is based upon the illegitimate translation of time into space, it could never become a necessary principle. For Descartes, as Benjamin seems to suggest, this meant that God's continuous action not only ensures that causation occurs in the physical universe. It also guarantees the comparison between time in itself, or "duration *per se*," and external change, an analogy from which the concept of time as the "number of movement" emerges as a mere "mode of thought" that measures the accidental or occasional causality of the natural world.[206]

The Psychophysical Parallelism and the Baroque Sovereign

The role of "God," then, "in the Cartesian system of the world" was to guarantee the analogy between space and time, underlying the mechanical movement of nature, as measured by natural science.[207] As Benjamin argues in the *Trauerspiel* book, the latter was a fundamental analogy for the seventeenth century: "It is not only the [mind-body] dualism of Descartes that is Baroque," but also his "doctrine of psychophysical influence."[208] In the seventeenth century, this divine function was symbolized in "the celebrated clock metaphor of Geulincx, which schematizes the psychophysical parallelism in terms of the operation of two … synchronized clocks, the second hand beats time, so to speak, for what happens in both worlds."[209]

Geulincx' clock, then, is a metaphor for the analogy between space and time, underlying the concept of causality. The parallel is ensured by "a constantly renewed regulation of the clocks," a miracle performed by a God who, as the only efficient cause, is symbolized as a watchmaker who synchronizes the incommensurable realms of internal and external experience, time and extension.[210] As Geulincx describes, the two spheres are connected by God in an absolute relationship of identity that cannot be reduced to the mere *causae occasionales* that apparently govern the natural world:

> There is no causality: neither clock rings because the other makes it do so, but because they share a mutual dependence, each having been carefully constructed and dedicated to fulfil the same purpose. … [B]oth depend on that supreme artificer, who has so ineffably wedded and fused them together.[211]

Geulincx' clock, then, is a figure for the supreme power of God, who coordinates what Benjamin refers to as "otherworldly phenomena with a predominantly temporal character" with "immanent, predominantly spatial phenomena of the world of things." That "the epoch appears fascinated by this notion" implies that the "systematic analogy" that defined the Baroque was not between politics and theology, but that of the psychophysical parallelism which constituted the measurable time of the natural sciences.

In the seventeenth century, the "nonqualitative, repeatable time of mathematical natural science" would become the temporal setting in which was "enacted not only the organic life of the human being," but also its politics, "the doings of the courtier and the acts of the sovereign."[212] Just as the postulate of a Cartesian God establishes the possibility of spatialized time underlying the causal laws of natural science, so the sovereign, who "represents history" and can "be considered its incarnation," was conceived in the seventeenth century:[213]

> ... according to the occasionalist image of the divine potentate ... [who] immediately intervenes in the affairs of state at every moment in order to arrange the data of the historical process in a, so to speak, spatially measurable, regular and harmonious succession. "The prince develops all the virtualities of the state by a sort of continuous action. The prince is the Cartesian God transposed into the political world."[214]

In this passage, Frédéric Atger's analogy, which Schmitt uses to prove that the postulate of the sovereign as primeval creator was part of the systematic structure of the seventeenth century, is situated by Benjamin in the context of a more fundamental analogy. Contrary to Schmitt, the juridical miracle performed by the sovereign in the seventeenth century was not that of a suspension of the legal order, analogous to the theological mystery of a "transgression of the laws of nature ... brought about by [divine] intervention."[215] Although Descartes contends that God possesses even the power to alter the principles of natural science, just as a king can alter the law,[216] as Bergson points out, the miraculous power that defines the Cartesian God is not the ability to interrupt the mechanical laws he created. Rather, owing to God's continuous action, these mechanical laws are sustained, "by a true miracle at each moment of duration," despite the fact that the laws are based on an identity principle that can never prove their necessity, and on a notion of time that is built on an analogy.[217]

Unlike the Kantian genius and the Schmittian sovereign, therefore, whose reflective judgment miraculously transgresses every mechanical principle, the Cartesian God guarantees the integrity of a mechanical knowledge that cannot account for the natural world on its own. If the Baroque sovereign occupied "a position exactly analogous to that attributed to God in the Cartesian system of the world," what the analogy shows, contrary to Schmitt, is not the existence of a political theology, but something like a natural science of God. Just as God, for Descartes, ensured the psychophysical parallelism that underlies all causal laws, so the sovereign, as a transposition of the Cartesian God, guarantees the regular operation of a juridical order whose laws can never conform to reality. And just as God ensures the analogy from which time arises as an infinite homogeneous quantity, so the sovereign decision on the state of exception ensures the progression of history through the medium of empty, homogeneous time.

Mechanism, Theology, and Secularization

This account of the occasionalist clock, as the metaphor for a Cartesian God who ensures the parallelism between space and time, suggests a more complicated conception of the relationship between theology and natural science than the one that critics have often attributed to Benjamin. According to Peter Gordon, for example, the figures of mechanical automata which appear in Benjamin's texts imply a critique of the rationalization of politics in modern society similar to the one developed by Schmitt. "Schmitt believed that any genuinely political order must find its ultimate grounding in a sovereign whose ... irrationalistic intrusion into politics represents the functional analogue to a miraculous event."[218] Against the modern theory of the state, Schmitt argued the "machine" cannot be allowed to "run ... by itself."[219]

This political theology, according to Gordon, is congruent with Benjamin's Marxist messianism, which is expressed in the form of analogies such as that of the chess-playing Turk in "On the Concept of History": "In Benjamin's interpretation, the ... Turk illustrates the dull and lifeless repetition of modern politics that functions as a mere machine and has banished all that is messianic or miraculous from the world."[220] "For Benjamin," then, "the Turk is only *apparently* a secular mechanism. Its movements may appear automatic, just as the movements of history will appear automatic for those who subscribe to speciously mechanistic philosophies of historical progress."[221]

As Gordon argues, however, this "allegorical interpretation of the Turk as animated by the hidden powers of 'theology' marks a radical departure from the earlier, naturalistic explanations" of such machines. In the eighteenth century, the enthusiasm for inventions like the mechanical Turk arose because of the fact that the latter was seen as "an object of purely secular wonder":

> No one believed that it was an *actual* miracle in the religious sense, just as no one would take the existence of an actual clock as a validation of Deist principles. ... [People] admired it as an especially fine specimen of technical design, no different in kind from ... elaborate clocks whose perfection testified to merely human ingenuity.[222]

The metaphor of the chess-playing automaton, therefore, expresses Benjamin's view that modernity is not defined by the "disappearance of religion but only its *concealment*."[223] Mechanism is merely a cover for a theology that persists beneath the appearance of a completely desacralized world. Thus, despite the criticism of Schmitt implicit in Benjamin's demand for a "real state of exception," the meaning of the chess-playing Turk corresponds to the thesis of *Political Theology*: "All significant concepts of the modern theory of the state are secularized theological concepts." The machine, then, is a figure that "invokes but ultimately contests the classical theory of secularization," in a manner resembling Schmitt's critique of modernity, but which departs from the Marxist ideal of total demystification:

> Weber presents us with a vision of a disenchanted modernity that has lost all contact with the explosive powers of religion. Against Weber, Benjamin appeals to the "messianic" as the enduring but hidden force within history. This not only marks a decisive break with Weber; it also signals Benjamin's ambivalent stance toward the broader ideal of thoroughgoing secularization that underwrites classical Marxism.[224]

This analysis of Benjamin's use of mechanical metaphors ignores the fundamental analogy that defines the Baroque, the analogy of time to space that constitutes the condition of mechanism itself, expressed in the image of the occasionalist clock. "It is no accident that the image of the clock dominate[d]" the seventeenth century since it is "ideally suited to represent a mechanism," symbolizing the "general 'mechanization of the world view' of that time."²²⁵

Unlike Gordon's interpretation of the mechanical chess-player, Benjamin's account of the occasionalist clock does not depart from "earlier, naturalistic explanations." Nor does the clock, however, represent the perfection of a "merely human ingenuity." Instead of opposing mechanical and theological forms of explanation, Benjamin argues that the clock embodied a naturalistic understanding of "otherworldly phenomena with a predominantly temporal character." In the Cartesian metaphysical physics for which the clock served as a symbol, God is conceived as the only true mechanical force in the universe. If no one, therefore, "would take … an actual clock as a validation of Deist principles," in the seventeenth century, the clock served, nevertheless, as the "systematic analogy" for a "supreme artificer" whose action is analogous to a machine that represents time by its movement in space.²²⁶ By attributing to God the ability to guarantee this analogy, the metaphor acknowledges the "miracle" underlying the mechanical concept of time, which can never establish the certainty of a singular experience of the vanishing present. At the same time, it represents God as a purely secular function, as the power of mechanism itself.

But in that case, the occasionalist clock is not a machine that is secretly operated by a supernatural power. Nor is it a metaphor that expresses what Gordon calls the ambivalence between mechanism and theology that purportedly characterizes all of Benjamin's work, including that of his materialist phase, defined by an "ambivalent secularization, poised … between Marxism and messianism."²²⁷ Rather, it points to the messianic (and nihilistic) possibility of a fully secularized epistemology that can demonstrate, without reference to God, both the timeless validity of mechanical reason and the immediate certainty of ephemeral experience: "Thus, the task of the coming philosophy can be conceived as the discovery … of that concept of knowledge which …. makes not only mechanical but also religious experience logically possible."²²⁸

In contrast to the Kantian theory of knowledge, the coming philosophy, then, does not limit the scope of mechanical reason in order to make room for religion. Instead, it reduces religion to a logical possibility, just as the critical philosophy defines the conditions of possibility underlying the laws of natural science. In that way, the coming philosophy would allow for a profane understanding of natural science as well as theology, whose objects exceed mechanical explanation.

This possibility was already implicit in Descartes' metaphysical physics, whose universal mechanical laws depend upon the action of God and his ability to ensure that its laws will apply to the singular objects of experience. Although Kant, who lived in an age of "extraordinary superficiality and godlessness," will succeed in establishing the validity of these laws without reference to God, his one-sided theory of knowledge failed to provide a "deduction of … 'empty, godless experience.'"²²⁹ Kant's epistemology, in other words, remains incomplete without an undogmatic demonstration of "the certainty of a temporal experience which is regarded as the immediate … object of knowledge." In his phenomenology, Husserl, on the other hand, will turn to Descartes' *Meditations* as a "methodic expedient," using it not to prove the existence of God, but to establish the "sad" certainty of a bare or "naked" form of existence, "stripped of its proximity to God."[230] Although this "*eidos* doctrine," however, demonstrates the necessity of immediate experience without relying on God, it also conflates this experience with conceptual knowledge, identifying a pure intuition that is necessarily excluded by mechanical reason as the origin of abstraction itself. What appears, then, as a "striking ambivalence" between "mechanism and messianism" is in fact a dialectical and twofold critique of rationalist and irrationalist theories of knowledge, which recognizes the limits of each.

This account of the history of modern philosophy, implicit in Benjamin's work, suggests a critique of the classical theory of secularization that differs from the one that Gordon attributes to Benjamin. If Benjamin rejected the thesis of "a disenchanted modernity that has lost all contact with ... religion," it was not because of his "ambivalent stance toward the broader ideal of thoroughgoing secularization," such as the one that "underwrites classical Marxism." On the contrary, in the habilitation, Benjamin affirms the "total secularization of the historical in the state of creation," which defines the Baroque,[231] a "secularization of time" that is "hidden in the worldview of the natural sciences."

For Benjamin, however, this total secularization did not occur during the eighteenth century, which had supposedly created a disenchanted modernity, completely detached from religion, but rather during the period directly *preceding* it. Thus, in "Capitalism as Religion" (1921), Benjamin attacks Weber's account of modernity, arguing that capitalism is "not only a religiously conditioned construction ... but an essentially religious phenomenon." Capitalism, therefore, is not a secular form of society that arose from religion, from the protestant ethic in the seventeenth century. Rather, capitalism is itself a religion, one that replaced the religion that conditioned its historical rise: "Capitalism has developed as a parasite of Christianity in the West ... until it reached the point where Christianity's history is essentially that of its parasite—... capitalism."[232]

In contrast to Schmitt, then, Benjamin's critique of Weber's account of modernity is not that it conceals religion by continuing it in a secularized form. On the contrary, he argues that modernity is itself a form of religion that only seems to be secular. What appears as a process of secularization, therefore, is in fact a re-enchantment of the world, which was secularized in the seventeenth century. "Capitalism was a natural phenomenon with which a new dream-filled sleep came over Europe."[233] For Benjamin, then, modernity is not defined by an "ambivalent secularization" that disguises its theological basis, but by the shift to a new form of religion that seems to be no religion at all. If "Benjamin, then, was a theorist of ambivalent secularization," it was not because he "conceived of his [own] work as the secularized trace of theological ideas," but because he conceived of modernity as a new form of religion, one that he sought to unmask and demystify.[234] Benjamin, therefore, does not reject the "ideal of thoroughgoing secularization," but rather the thesis that modernity can be identified with this principle.

To borrow Benjamin's account of the work of the Austrian writer and poet, Adalbert Stifter, Benjamin's thinking is not defined by an ambivalent secularization, but by an insolent one. In Stifter's writings, the "concept of creation," which is a "theological inheritance of speculations that last possessed contemporary validity ...

in the seventeenth century," is "insolently secularized" such that it coincides with "the cosmopolitan credo of ... worldliness." Creation is "made ... into a church in which nothing remained to recall the rite except an occasional whiff of incense in the mists," which is all that is left of theology.[235]

Theology, however, is revived under capitalism, a religion that Benjamin, as Gordon correctly observes, will analyze in the late stage of his work by "rely[ing] on the Marxist critique of commodity fetishism."[236] In this critique, however, which is presented in *Capital*, the bourgeoisie is not understood, as it is in the *Manifesto*, as "the historical agent of disenchantment," dissolving all "religious and political illusions" by creating a market based on "naked self-interest," and "callous 'cash payment.'" Rather, as in Benjamin's account of capitalism as a new kind of religion, the development of the capitalist mode of production is characterized in Marx's critique of commodity fetishism as the shift from one set of religious illusions to another. Just as in the "misty realm of religion ... the products of the human brain appear as autonomous figures, endowed with a life of their own," so, "in the world of commodities ... the products of men's hands" appear to control their producers. "I call this the fetishism which attaches itself to the products of labour as soon as they are produced as commodities."[237]

As Chapter 5 will argue, the mechanical character of the bourgeois economy, which arises out of this fetishism, will lead neo-Kantian thinkers, like Friedrich Lange, to identify capitalism with the mechanical view of the natural world developed in the empirical sciences. As a result, the secularized *Weltanschauung* of the sciences would serve to conceal and to naturalize the cultic religion of capitalism. In the *Arcades Project*, Benjamin will define modernity itself as a "phantasmagoria" in which a worldview based on "mechanistic natural science" provides the foundation for a mythology in which capitalism has existed for all of eternity: "The world dominated by its phantasmagorias—this ... is 'modernity.'"[238] In contrast to Schmitt, Benjamin's critique of modernity is not that the "machine now runs by itself," but that the mechanism that appears to prevail within bourgeois society serves to disguise its historical character: As such, a "'critique' of the nineteenth century ... ought to begin ... [with a] critique not of its mechanism and cult of machinery but of its narcotic historicism."[239]

Contrary to Gordon, therefore, Benjamin's thinking was not "poised in indecision between a theological and a nontheological understanding of modernity," wavering between mechanism and messianism.[240] Rather, in texts like the *Arcades*, which criticizes the simultaneously mythical and mechanical representation of bourgeois society that appears in Blanqui's final work, Benjamin seems to affirm the ideal of total secularization against the seemingly secular religion of capitalism.

What this suggests is that Benjamin's historical materialism is not based on what Michael Löwy describes as a romantic "opposition between life and the automaton in the context of a Marxist-inspired analysis of the transformation of the proletarian into an automaton."[241] The latter would be a more accurate account of Lukács's Marxism, which opposed the lived experience of the laborer to a capitalist process of "rational mechanisation [that] extends right into the worker's 'soul.'"[242] On the other hand, in the reflections on Blanqui and Nietzsche that are used to frame the *Arcades*, Benjamin appears to coordinate his early critique of *both* vitalist and mechanical conceptions of knowledge with Marx's critique of political economy.

In contrast to Lukács' theory of reification, this critique distinguishes capital as an "automatic subject" from the "self-acting" automata or automated machinery that it animates in order to augment itself through the accumulation of surplus value.[243] Subject to the seemingly eternal and natural law underlying the bourgeois economy, the law that value is determined by labor time, the tendency of technology to reduce the need for direct human labor only expands the exploitation of labor (see Chapter 6).

While Aristotle, then, assumed that the invention of self-moving automata could liberate slaves, political economy eternalizes the "economic paradox" within capitalism whereby machinery becomes an "unfailing means for turning the ... lifetime of the worker ... into labour-time at capital's disposal for its own valorization."[244] Instead of abstractly opposing the automaton to life, Benjamin, combining Marx's critique with his own early philosophy, rejected the "cult of machinery" as well as vitalist forms of philosophy that serve as a cover for a "narcotic historicism" that conceals the historical nature of capitalism.

The Secularization of History and the Spatialization of Time

In the seventeenth century, according to Benjamin, the "repeatable time of mathematical natural science" would extend into politics. As befitting an era that "analogizes historical events with natural occurrence," the "doings of the courtier and the acts of the sovereign" were treated as a mechanical process. A "political science" emerged that "understand[s] the human being as a force of nature," developing a "calculable mechanics in the creature," based on the idea of the "uniformity of human nature." Hence, "a turn of phrase such as 'In the clockwork of power, councilors may be the moving gears, but the prince must ... be nothing less than the hand and balance.'"[245]

In the *Trauerspiel* plays, the result of this fundamental analogy between nature and politics is a representation of history as a mechanical movement: "The ... repeated spectacle of the rise and fall of princes ... stood before the eyes of the writers less as morality than as the natural side of historical process."[246] Like the psychophysical parallelism between time and space, underlying the concept of causality in natural science, this analogy is characterized by "a projection of temporal process into space."[247]

The result, according to Benjamin, was a change in theatrical form. Whereas the deep moral meaning of the political drama in classical tragedy depends upon the irreversible character of the sequence of actions unfolded in time, the *Trauerspiel* represents historical tragedy as a predictable progression that appears to conform to a natural law. Hence, the irrelevance of the Aristotelian principle of the "unity of action as a complement to temporal unity" with regard to the *Trauerspiel*.[248] In the plays, the profound moral dilemma of the sovereign decision is replaced by "an exacting ... political calculus in intrigue. Baroque drama knows historical activity not otherwise than as the base machination of schemers."[249]

These machinations (in which "the new theater has its god") are those of an intriguer who, seeing politics as a natural process, plays out in advance, as though on the space of a miniature model, the plot or scenario that will appear to its victim, the sovereign, as an irreversible tragedy:[250]

> In contrast to the spasmodic temporal progression that tragedy presents, the trauerspiel unfolds—choreographically, one might say—in the continuum of space. The organizer of the plot strands ... is the intriguer. ... His depraved calculations interest the spectator ... insofar as the latter recognizes ... a mastery of the political machine ...²⁵¹

In the *Trauerspiel* book, moreover, Benjamin equates this spatialization of time with the "total secularization of the historical in the state of creation," leading to a world without the transcendence of law.²⁵² The process of secularization is identified with the "metaphysical tendency" whereby the quantitative time of natural science is extended into the domain of history and politics:

> If history is secularized in the setting, this bespeaks the same metaphysical tendency that in the exact sciences at that time led to the infinitesimal method. In both cases temporal process is caught up and analyzed in a spatial image. The image of the setting—or, more precisely, the court—becomes the key to historical understanding.²⁵³

What this passage suggests is that the "plane of the creaturely state, the terrain on which the trauerspiel unfolds,"²⁵⁴ and which "quite unmistakably determines the sovereign as well,"²⁵⁵ is spatialized time. Instead of rejecting what Husserl called the "false naturalism" of the sciences, which reifies time through the figure of space, or what Bergson called the "illegitimate translation" of *durée* as extension, Benjamin identifies homogeneous time as the inescapable setting of all creaturely life. To borrow Benjamin's account of the "spatiotemporal unity" that distinguishes Hölderlin's poetry from its ancient Greek models, "the living are always clearly the *extension* of space."²⁵⁶

Like the plane of the creature, the homogeneous time resulting from the analogy to space must be emptied of every kind of transcendence in order to arrive at the this-worldly form of salvation portrayed in the *Trauerspiel*. In "the attempt to find consolation in the renunciation of a state of grace in reversion to the bare creaturely condition ... what is decisive is the transposition of originally temporal data into a spatial unreality and simultaneity. It leads deep into the structure of this dramatic form."²⁵⁷

For Benjamin, then, the irreligious form of redemption that defines the Baroque, a redemption "consequent upon the collapse of all eschatology,"²⁵⁸ requires the reduction of "otherworldly phenomena with a predominantly temporal character" to "immanent, predominantly spatial phenomena of the world of things." In the *Trauerspiel*, then, history is secularized in its reduction to a spatial image, that of the royal court, "the setting par excellence of the trauerspiel."²⁵⁹ For writers in the seventeenth century, the court constituted a sort of representation of political history in miniature, affording the spectator a "panoramatic" perspective on its mechanical workings: The "social order and its representation, the court, is with [Pedro Calderón de la Barca] a natural phenomenon of the highest kind."²⁶⁰ Portraying the tragedies of the court, the rise and fall of successive sovereigns, as a predictable natural process, Calderón's characters "turn the order of fate around in their hands like a ball, exposing to view now one aspect, now another."²⁶¹

In this way, the theatre of the seventeenth century sought to "unfold a formal dialectic of the setting," in which the "constantly repeated spectacle of the rise and fall of princes" is portrayed as a spatialized image. In Baroque drama, therefore, the "dialectical rising and falling in the lawmaking and law-preserving formations of violence" (to borrow a phrase from the "Critique of Violence") is suspended in its spatial representation. The same point is made in the *Trauerspiel* book with regard to the "pivotal motif of the witching hour." According to Benjamin, the secularization of fate in the spatialization of history, which characterizes the *Trauerspiel*, accounts for "the association of the dramatic action with night, and ... midnight in particular." Because of the widespread belief in the seventeenth century that "time comes to a standstill" at midnight,[262] the latter could serve as a static representation for the "temporal progression ... [of] tragedy."[263] The reoccurring fate of the sovereign, the perpetual rise and fall of princes, is most authentically represented in spatialized terms: "Now, since fate ... is only inauthentically—that is, parasitically—to be conceived as temporal, its manifestations seek out space-time."[264] In the *Trauerspiel*, then, the dialectic of history appears at a standstill.

Reification and *Trauerspiel*

The analysis of figures like the witching hour and the dialectic of the setting are indicative of another significant influence on Benjamin's methodology in the *Trauerspiel* book, namely Hegel's philosophy. In the habilitation, the idiosyncratic description of the dialectic as a "turnabout of extremes" suggests that Benjamin was reading Hegel through Schmitt and vice versa.[265] Like his use of Schmitt's political theory, however, Benjamin's appropriation of Hegel's philosophy in the *Trauerspiel* book will take the form of an immanent critique that seeks to undermine the philosophy precisely by more strictly applying its own methodology. As Jan Urbich has noted, the result of this immanent critique was a departure from Hegel in which the temporal movement of the dialectic is preserved in a spatialized form:

> Benjamin makes a decisive break with Hegel that can be understood as a shift from the mode of time to the mode of space as 'transcendental' model for the dialectical order. ... [T]he ... movement has been brought to a stand-still or a freeze-frame. Nevertheless, the dialectical movement has not disappeared: its conceptual energy has turned into a logical luminescence of the extreme elements ... within the spatial structure of the constellation. Benjamin's theory of dialectics is continuously characterized by the spatial idea of a "dialectics at a standstill" ... like an image, as "imaging of dialectics" ...[266]

However, given Benjamin's avowedly shallow knowledge of Hegel during the period in which he composed the habilitation, Hegel's philosophy may have served, in fact, as a proxy for the work of another philosopher, György Lukács, whom Benjamin had begun to study during this time. In a letter to Scholem in 1924, Benjamin writes that, in *History and Class Consciousness*, "Lukács arrives at ...

epistemological [principles that] ... astonished me because these principles resonate for me and validate my own thinking."²⁶⁷

As Ferenc Fehér has argued, however, Lukács's writings did not simply confirm Benjamin's pre-existing ideas. They were in fact the source of many of the most important insights in the habilitation: "The early Benjamin ... was eager to embrace the recommendations of *The Theory of the Novel*," as well as the "Metaphysics of Tragedy," works "that led to the discovery of the special claims and the distinct features of modern, non-tragic drama, the *Trauerspiel*." In particular, Lukács' notion of reification was the "intellectual foster-father of Benjamin's conception of the *creatura*'s history as natural history," as petrified landscape "abandoned by its gods [and] ... deprived of its meaning."²⁶⁸

Although the *Trauerspiel* book indeed contains both direct and indirect references to Lukács's work, including the concept of reification, what Fehér's account overlooks, however, is that these references also suggest a critique of the concepts that they borrow. The particular kind of validation that Benjamin found in Lukács's theory of knowledge, therefore, may have been closer to the confirmation he discovered for his literary-historical method in Schmitt's philosophy of the state. Just as the latter would prove to be too theological for Benjamin's tastes, so Lukács' dialectical method would be judged to be insufficiently profane. In the same letter to Scholem, therefore, Benjamin confesses that he "would be surprised if the foundations of [his] nihilism were not to manifest themselves against communism in an antagonistic confrontation with the concepts and assertions of Hegelian dialectics."²⁶⁹

In the *Trauerspiel* book, this nihilism will assert itself in the form of a thesis about the Baroque that is directly opposed to Lukács' notion of reification, as a process that "degrades time to the dimension of space," thereby suspending the dialectical movement of time. As a result of this process, "time sheds its qualitative, variable, flowing nature; it freezes into an exactly delimited, quantifiable continuum filled with quantifiable 'things.'"²⁷⁰ In the habilitation, on the other hand, Benjamin will identify this spatialization of time with a Baroque secularization of history, in which this "temporal process is caught up and analyzed in a spatial image."²⁷¹

The political ramifications of this striking confrontation with Lukács, however (a confrontation belonging to another "esoteric dossier" in Benjamin's writing career), are never spelled out in the *Trauerspiel* book.²⁷² But the antagonism between Benjamin's account of the German Baroque and the concept of reification was one that Lukács would immediately recognize. Thus, in his response to the book, Lukács (failing perhaps to perceive that the confrontation, in fact, was deliberate) criticizes Benjamin's "entirely nihilistic" conception of allegory as an instance of reification: Benjamin's interpretation of the allegorical "emblem expresses nothing if not an uncritically affirmed fetishization," mirroring the "capitalist fetishization of human relations into things."²⁷³

Benjamin's apparent antagonism to the concept of reification, moreover, was not merely an idiosyncrasy of his early "metaphysical period." Rather, insofar as the *Arcades Project* was to be an attempt to "see the nineteenth century," and the era of industrial capitalism, "just as positively as I tried to see the seventeenth, in the work on *Trauerspiel*," the idiosyncrasy is one that would also distinguish his later historical materialist method.

In the habilitation, however, the fact that this rebuttal to the theory of reification appears in the context of a critique of Schmitt's political theology suggests that, for Benjamin, the Marxist philosopher and the Nazi political theorist shared a common methodological assumption. This assumption is that of a "political existentialism" that opposes the reduction of *Erlebnis*, or the "lived experience" of time, to the rationalist tendencies of modern society, which Schmitt associated with the predominance of "predetermined, calculable, general rules."[274]

In Lukács, this assumption is tied to the idea of a proletarian subject of history that can liberate time from its reification as space, resuming the historical process as "the uninterrupted outpouring of what is qualitatively new," as opposed to a quantifiable continuum of spatialized time.[275] For Benjamin, on the other hand, who rejected the "cult of 'experience' (*Erlebnis*),"[276] the historical process can never resolve the "dialectical rising and falling in the lawmaking and law-preserving formations of violence." Because of this, the proletarian general strike is defined as a suspension of this historical process that would serve to exclude the sovereign decision. What this suggests is that the nihilism that separates the spatial conception of dialectics at a standstill from Lukács' dialectic of time as lived experience is related to what the "Critique of Violence" calls the "discouraging discovery of the ultimate insolubility of all legal problems." While Lukács, therefore, declares the "right of the Revolution to establish its own lawful order,"[277] Benjamin proposes the concept of revolutionary violence as the deposition of law.

Allegory as the Negative of the Symbol

In the *Trauerspiel* book, however, the immanent critique of Lukács' dialectic will not proceed by way of *History and Class Consciousness*. Rather, Benjamin refers only to his early "Metaphysics of Tragedy" (1910), which he cites mostly in an approving manner. As Lukács describes in the text, "existence can have no reality except ... the reality of lived experience."[278]

In the chapter "Allegory and *Trauerspiel*," Lukács' discussion of tragedy appears as part of a virtual history of how the meaning of the "allegorical mode of perception" in the seventeenth century was lost as a result of a modern misinterpretation.[279] Because of "an antagonism between earlier and later meanings ... played out in silence because it was without conceptual formation," the "original form of allegorical expression" became "estranged" "around 1800." Subsequently, allegory was seen as "only a mirage of the symbolic."[280]

In its "genuine" theological meaning, the symbol, according to Benjamin, is not simply a "philosophical embellishment" for an idea, but "an indissoluble union of form and content," the paradoxical "unity of sensuous and supersensuous object."[281] But as such, its analysis requires a "dialectical tempering" that could grasp the necessary relationship between the form and the content, the indissolubility of the idea and its expression.[282]

On the other hand, in the "modern and untenable discourse concerning allegory and symbol," allegory is understood in opposition to the symbol, as a mode of expression lacking all of its virtues.[283] The different examples of this modern discourse cited in the *Trauerspiel* book include the writings of Lukács and the neo-Kantian philosopher Hermann Cohen and his disciples. These thinkers are identified with a "negative" concept of allegory that fails to recognize that the latter is "not exempt from a corresponding dialectic … which … immerses itself in the abyss between image-being and meaning [and] has nothing of the … sufficiency that is found in … the sign."[284]

Insisting on a positive conception of allegory, Benjamin argues that allegory, just like the symbol, is characterized by a dialectical movement. In contrast to the symbol, however, the dialectic of allegory does not guarantee its sufficiency, or its unity with its content. On the contrary, the "dialectical movement [that] storms in this abyss of allegory" results in an irreducible disunity or difference between meaning and image.[285]

In "neo-Kantian aesthetics," this dialectical movement, according to Benjamin, is "misunderstood … as ambiguity." For Hermann Cohen, "multivalence," or "the abundance of meanings is something allegory, and the Baroque, glory in." Viewing allegory as the negative of the symbol, Cohen asserts that this ambiguity is contrary to the "unity of meaning" that defines both natural harmony and the "realm of artistic … order," which, according to the "rules of metaphysics … is bound … by the law of [artistic] economy." For Cohen, therefore, allegory, and its ambiguity of meaning, is the result of an absence of symbolic unity.[286]

This neo-Kantian perspective is consistent with the "peremptory dismissals" of allegory,[287] which see it as a form of expression that "merely signifies a general concept or idea that is distinct from it."[288] Instead of an "indissoluble union of form and content," allegory is only "a conventional relation between a signifying image and its signification," in which an image is "intentionally and avowedly chosen to express a concept."[289] Whereas in allegory, therefore, the relationship between image and meaning is accidental or arbitrary, the symbol, on the other hand, is the necessary form of its content.

Allegory and Time

For Benjamin, this negative definition of allegory, as a figure that lacks the necessity of the symbol, implies a difference in relation to time. Because of its dialectical unity, the symbol possesses an immediate connection to that which it symbolizes, and, as such, it can reveal its supersensuous content in a complete and instantaneous manner. "The temporal measure for the experience of the symbol," then, "is the mystical instant," in which the idea, in assuming a sensual form, is disclosed all at once and in its entirety.[290] On the other hand, because of its conventional relationship to its content, allegory, which "lacks … [the] momentary totality" of the symbol, expresses its meaning only "progress[ively] in a series of moments." Whereas the symbol, therefore, is "closed on itself, concentrated, persisting in itself unchanged," allegory is a figure that "successively advancing … has taken on the flux of time itself."[291]

This "modern and untenable discourse concerning allegory and symbol" corresponds to Bergson's critique of the sciences, whose homogeneous conception of time is based on an "illegitimate translation of the unextended into the extended." In "a projection of temporal process into space," the intensive quality of time, immediately intuited as *durée*, is reduced to a measurable form of temporal extension. The time, then, in which allegory unfolds as a "progression in a series of moments" is spatialized time. Thus, in a letter to Florens Christian Rang, Benjamin, discussing the *Trauerspiel* book, describes "the relationship of works of art to historical life" in Bergsonian terms: "the same forces that become ... extensively temporal in ... history ... appear concentrated [*intensiv*] in ... works of art."[292]

In "Some Motifs in Baudelaire," however, Benjamin seems to suggest that the experience of *durée*, of the purely qualitative intensity of a time devoid of extensity, is no longer possible in the "age of large-scale industrialism."[293] Similarly, in the early essay on Hölderlin, the concept of *durée* is identified with a "divine order" that can no longer be reached by the living, and which can only be "intimated" through a poetic "interpenetration of individual forms of perception."[294] In the modern era, therefore, "otherworldly phenomena with a predominantly temporal character" can only be approximated through endosmosis; time as *durée* can only be known by analogy to "immanent, predominantly spatial phenomena of the world of things." Since the "living," in Hölderlin's poetry, "are always clearly the extension of space," the only time they can experience is one that is spatialized or extensively temporal.[295]

Like the living, allegory, as Benjamin argues in the *Trauerspiel* book, unfolds on the creaturely plane of homogenous time. Allegorical representation is a "matter of making time present in space—and what else is the secularization of time but its transformation into the strictly present?"[296] In the "modern and untenable discourse concerning allegory and symbol," this feature of allegory is viewed as a lack or deficiency. Whereas the symbol is a dialectical unity that expresses its content as a momentary totality, allegory possesses only an accidental relationship to its meaning, which it can only reveal over time "in a series of moments." As such, it lacks "the totality that is denied to all external temporal progression."[297]

The ability of the symbol to achieve such a totality corresponds to Lukács' account of the "metaphysical reason" for the unity of time in classical drama. This unity, as Lukács explains in a passage from "Metaphysics of Tragedy," cited by Benjamin, "is born of the desire to come as close as possible to the timelessness of this moment which yet is the whole of life," to grasp of the entirety of existence in an instant. Tragedy "interrupts the eternal flow of time [through] ... stylization at every instant of the drama; every moment is a symbol, a reduced-scale image of the whole." This stylization of time, which seeks to transcend all mere external temporal progression, is the "technically necessary condition of dramatic form-giving," which endows meaning upon the individual elements of the action. The unity of time, then, solves the fundamental metaphysical problem to which tragedy is a response: the "mystical" and "technical paradox contained in trying to give temporal duration to a moment which, by its very nature, is without such duration." "Tragic drama," therefore, "has to express the becoming-timeless of time," to reveal a pure duration that "no longer lies within the plane of temporal experience."[298] In achieving the unity of time, drama gives form to existence. The "most profound verdict which tragedy pronounces," therefore, is that form "is the highest judge of life. Form-giving is a judging force ... there is a value-judgment in everything that has been given form."[299]

The Dialectic of Allegory

For Benjamin, this metaphysics of tragedy, which views the mystical instant as the "temporal measure for the experience of the symbol,"[300] is consistent with what "may be described as a negative, a posteriori construction of allegory," typical of the modern discourse on the latter.[301] In this negative construction, allegory is understood as an inferior symbol which, lacking the dialectical unity of content and form that allows the latter to serve as an immediate "image of the whole," is confined to the plane of external temporal experience.[302]

Such a view, however, fails to perceive that "allegory is not exempt from a corresponding dialectic."[303] Reversing the modern perspective, Benjamin, therefore, proposes a positive and dialectical conception of allegory, asserting its priority over the symbol. For Benjamin, allegory is not an imperfect symbol which, because of its conventional character, lacks the power to embody a momentary totality. On the contrary, this symbolic power presupposes an extensive "progression in a series of moments," which is "sublimated" in the mystical instant.[304] As Lukács acknowledged, this sublimation can never succeed due to the paradox of "trying to give temporal duration to a moment which, by its very nature, is without ... duration," a paradox which "springs from the inadequacy of expressing a mystical experience in ... human language."[305] Because time, as *durée*, is an intensive quality, its representation in tragedy, as an act that can only occur in the "extensively temporal" duration of history, necessarily "contradicts the very nature of time."[306]

Affirming this inevitable failure as a positive dialectical feature of allegory, Benjamin, in what appears to be a direct refutation of Lukács, defines this contradiction as a sort of anti-metaphysical function of allegory. If the "metaphysical reason" for the unity of time in classical tragedy is "to express the becoming-timeless of time" (i.e., to express a pure duration that lies beyond "the plane of temporal experience"), the function of allegory is to "mak[e] time present in space." Just as the *Trauerspiel* reduces a "temporal process" (the "repeated spectacle of the rise and fall of princes") to a "spatial image" (the court), "outside of historical drama, in the [allegorical] lyric, one [also] meets with a projection of temporal process into space."

Instead of revealing a supersensuous object in a momentary totality, this projection expresses the insurmountable contradiction between the intensive quality of *durée* and the extensive temporality of spatialized time, which is sublimated in the instantaneity of the symbol. In its "corresponding dialectic" to that of the symbol as a "unity of sensuous and supersensuous object," allegory appears as the necessary expression of the irreducible difference or disunity between time and its representation. What its dialectic reveals is the impossibility of a psychophysical parallelism between the internal and external forms of experience.

But in that sense, allegory, unlike the symbol, is not a *form* of expression. Rather, to borrow Benjamin's reworking of the Bergsonian concept of endosmosis in the essay on Hölderlin, allegory expresses the necessary "deformation" (*Entstaltung*) of time in its representation as space, one which Benjamin captures in the spatial image of a "temporal plasticity."[307]

For Benjamin, of course, the lack of a unity of time, which deprives allegory of "the totality ... denied to all external temporal progression," is not an aesthetic deficiency.[308] Rather, as Paul de Man has suggested, the extensive temporality that characterizes allegory constitutes, in fact, an *Ursprung* or origin that the symbol necessarily fails to suppress. Whereas the symbol is defined by a "simultaneity, which, in truth, is spatial in kind, and in which the intervention of time is merely a matter of contingency ... in the world of allegory, time is the originary constitutive category." While the symbol seeks "refuge against the impact of time in a natural world to which, in truth, it bears no resemblance," "the prevalence of allegory always corresponds to the unveiling of an authentically temporal destiny."[309]

As de Man suggests, this image of nature, expressed in the allegorical dialectic of perceptual deformation, is more originary than the neo-Kantian notion of artistic order and natural harmony which, according to the "rules of metaphysics," is bound to the "purity and unity of meaning."[310] In the *Trauerspiel* book, the image of nature that emerges from allegory is described as a "petrified primal landscape" in which "all classical harmony of form, and everything human is lacking." This nature, then, is not one that is bound to the metaphysical law of the unity of meaning, but rather one that resists every attempt to endow it with human significance, a nature embodying "everything untimely, sorrowful, and miscarried that belongs to it from the beginning." According to Benjamin, this "is the core of the allegorical vision," which instead of perceiving a meaning, an idea or an *eidos*, intuits "the jagged line of demarcation between physis and meaning."[311]

But as such, contrary to Fehér, the "petrified primal landscape" that allegory intuits cannot be identified with the concept of "second nature" in Lukács as a "petrified estranged complex of meaning that is no longer able to awaken inwardness ... a charnel-house of rotted interiorities."[312] As Adorno describes, this second nature is that of "an alienated world of commodities," a "world of things created by man, yet lost to him, the world of convention." For Lukács, this alienation can be overcome through allegory, which deciphers the human significance in "rotted interiorities" that have been petrified in this second nature. "The reference to the charnel house," then, as Adorno describes, "includes the element of the cipher: everything must mean something ... Lukács can only think of this charnel house in terms of a theological resurrection, in an eschatological context."[313]

For Benjamin, on the other hand, what allegory intuits is not a reified meaning, but a petrified landscape that is devoid of human significance, a thesis which Lukács will characterize as an uncritical affirmation of commodity fetishism itself (see Chapter 6). Allegory does not resurrect the meaning of reified things; it represents the line that separates nature and meaning, in accordance with a Baroque eschatology that renounced the religious idea of salvation in favor of a purely profane form of redemption.

Contrary to Wolin, therefore, the "allegorist's task" is not "to provide a restoration of meaning through the 'miraculous' transfiguration of ... profane material content." Allegory is not defined by "an insatiable 'will to meaning'" that assigns religious value to the most wretched worldly phenomena, a definition that would be more appropriately applied to the symbol.[314] The allegorist does not perceive meaning, but rather intuits "the jagged line of demarcation between physis and meaning," which deprives everything of significance.

In the modern discourse on allegory and symbol, this object of allegorical vision is misconstrued as a failure of representation, indicating the absence of any necessary relationship between meaning and nature. Grasping this abyss between meaning and image in positive terms, Benjamin argues that the accidental or conventional character of the allegorical mode of expression is *the necessary form that its particular content assumes.*

In contrast to the symbol, however, the content of allegory is not a specific idea or a particular meaning. Rather, allegory expresses the failure of meaning or signification itself, a failure that undermines "all classical harmony of form." Such a content, according to Benjamin—which is "not so much signified ... as ... presented as allegory"[315]—is one that cannot be conveyed by the symbol, which, in conformity with the "rules of metaphysics," is bound to the "purity and unity of meaning." The symbol, therefore, can only reveal the "transfigured countenance of nature" through a "sublimation of downfall," a sublimation of the primal image of nature as a landscape devoid of human significance, thereby concealing the "jagged line of demarcation between physis and meaning."[316] From a dialectical perspective, such a content can only assume the form of an allegory in which the irreducible difference between *physis* and meaning is expressed by the lack of a necessary relation between content and form. If the symbol, then, is a dialectical union of content and form, the abyss between meaning and image within allegory, in its "corresponding dialectic," is the necessary mode of expression for the primal vision of nature as a setting completely devoid of human significance.

Thus, rejecting the negative notion of allegory as a symbol lacking a necessary relationship to its content, Benjamin, reversing the priority of the one over the other, characterizes the symbol as an allegory that is incapable of revealing the "demarcation between physis and meaning." Just as the symbol, which expresses its meaning in a momentary totality, is incapable of revealing the necessary deformation of time by its spatial analogy, so its form can never express the abyss between nature and human significance, which is the object of allegory.

By reconstructing the dialectic of allegory corresponding to that of the symbol, Benjamin, then, recasts the concept of nature implicit in both Lukács' metaphysics of tragedy and Cohen's conception of allegory, situating it within a more originary representation of the natural world. Contrary to Cohen's conception, allegory is not an extravagant "abundance of meanings ... everywhere in contradiction to [the] purity and unity of meaning," a principle which defines the "old rules of metaphysics" to which art and nature are bound. From the allegorical perspective, the "transfigured countenance of nature," revealed in symbolic representation, appears as something "written on nature's countenance in the sign-script of transience." Its ephemeral unity is dissolved in a primal landscape devoid of "all classical harmony of form."

But if the "undialectical mode of thought of the neo-Kantian school is incapable of grasping the synthesis that emerges ... in allegorical writing," the focus on form in Lukács' theory of tragedy, as Benjamin appears to imply, suggests an incomplete dialectic. Benjamin, therefore, proposes an allegorical dialectic of sensory deformation, corresponding to, but also encompassing, Lukács' dialectical analysis of the unity of time as the basis of "dramatic form-giving." In the dialectical movement of allegory, the revelation of nature in a momentary totality appears as an image based upon a sublimation of nature as an infinitely extended duration, condemning everything to impermanence, a concept that served to secularize time in the seventeenth century: "Nature looms before [all] … as eternal transience."

The unity of time, then, which underlies form, cannot be conceived apart from its opposite: the deformation of time in its interpenetration with space. For Benjamin, then, Lukács' account of the "profound verdict" of tragedy, that form "is the highest judge of life," lacks its antithesis, namely, the "annihilating but just verdict" that life cannot be subsumed by a judgment of form.[317] As the philosopher Arthur Hübscher observed, in an essay cited by Benjamin, the Baroque was defined by a twofold dialectic of allegory and symbol. The latter were combined in a "powerful and violent attempt … to bring about … a synthesis of the most heterogeneous elements": "longing for … harmonious unity with nature" together with the "counter-experience [of] … something different, the experience … of murderous time, of irremediable transience."[318]

Transience and Eternity: Religious Salvation and Profane Redemption

For Benjamin, this concept of transience distinguishes the metaphysics of tragedy from the profane eschatology of the *Trauerspiel*. In the latter, the metaphysical impulse "to come as close as possible to the timelessness of this moment which yet is the whole of life" is replaced by the Baroque tendency to empty a transcendent beyond and "exalt … everything earth-born before it is delivered over to its end."[319] The tragic and mythical goal of achieving eternity is repudiated in favor of the creaturely desire to live the transient moment forever. In this way, the *Trauerspiel* was directly opposed to the metaphysics of tragedy: The "flight from the world that is characteristic of the Baroque is [the] … total secularization of the historical in the state of creation. Standing opposed to the desolate course of the world chronicle is not eternity but the restoration of paradisical timelessness. History passes into the setting."[320]

Contrary to Wolin, therefore, the dialectical "turnabout of extremes" from which the "Baroque apotheosis" arises is not based upon the "theological conception of the diametrically opposite relation in which profane life stands to the life of salvation." If the "'dialectic' of allegory causes all manifest content to be transformed into its opposite," this content is not that of an "earthly life" that is to be transfigured into the "blissfulness of the life beyond," such that "*the death's head becomes an angel's countenance.*"[321] In the dialectic of allegory, the "desolate course of the world" is not opposed to a transcendent eternity that lies beyond all earthly existence. Rejecting the theological "separation of this-worldly existence from … salvation" (a dichotomy underlying the "aesthetic of redemption" that Wolin attributes to Benjamin), Benjamin identifies allegory with a purely profane form of redemption that affirms the transience of creaturely life.

In the anti-metaphysical eschatology of the *Trauerspiel*, the desolate course of the world—which, represented as setting, is confined to spatialized time—will not be redeemed in the timelessness of an eternity which, like law, transcends the creaturely plane of existence. Rather, what is to be restored is the paradise of a mere creaturely life, preceding the theological concept of an eternity in which the desolate course of the world will finally be righted. The paradisical timelessness of Baroque eschatology, then, is that of a transient present that no longer needs to conform to an ideal of eternity that creaturely life can never achieve.

This account of Baroque eschatology is directly opposed to the religious conception of history that critics have attributed to Benjamin's messianism. According to Wolin, in Benjamin's early aesthetics: "Life in the profane continuum of history was considered incapable of fulfillment *a priori* insofar as it was deemed the diametrical antithesis of the Messianic age, the sphere of redeemed life." In the *Trauerspiel* book, however, redemption is not opposed to the empty infinity of spatialized time. Rather, it is identified with the total secularization of history as the result of the reduction of "otherworldly phenomena with a predominantly temporal character" with "immanent, predominantly spatial phenomena of the world of things," which is also the plane of creaturely life.³²²

Contrary to Sigrid Weigel, therefore, "the concept of secularization in *The Origin of German Tragic Drama*" does not appear as "a kind of counter-concept to messianism." "While the *messianic*," according to Weigel, "aims at redemption through the fulfilment of history, *secularization* here means the withdrawal of sacred significance within history, the transformation of existence back into the creaturely state or of history back into nature."³²³ Benjamin, however, does not oppose the messianic to the secular, but rather identifies the moment of messianic fulfillment with a "total secularization of the historical," leading to a completely "graceless Creation."³²⁴

This worldly form of redemption corresponds to the messianic idea of an eudemonistic or merely creaturely fulfillment that Benjamin distinguishes from the religious idea of salvation. In the "Theologico-Political Fragment," the latter's "immortal" or transcendent eternity is opposed to a concept of time resembling the allegorical representation of nature as an empty infinity of "eternal transience," a concept with which Benjamin identifies his nihilistic anarchist politics:

> To the spiritual *restitutio in integrum*, which introduces immortality, corresponds a worldly restitution that leads to the eternity of downfall, and the rhythm of this eternally transient worldly existence, transient in its totality ... the rhythm of messianic nature, is happiness. For nature is messianic by reason of its eternal and total passing away. To strive after such passing, even for those stages of man that are nature, is the task of world politics, whose method must be called nihilism.³²⁵

Like the messianic historical task that Benjamin proposed in one of his first publications, "The Life of Students," the goal of Baroque eschatology is not to realize a transcendent condition, but to reach an "immanent state of perfection."³²⁶ "The secular order should be erected on the idea of happiness."³²⁷ Instead of trying to "come as close as possible to the timelessness of this moment which yet is the whole of life," the

Trauerspiel plays sought to immortalize and redeem the paradisical timelessness of the ephemeral moment. Thus, "it is precisely allegory that saved ... the insight into the transience of things, and the concern to save them and render them eternal, is one of the strongest motives in the allegorical."[328]

By redeeming the transient present, allegorical representation provides the "precondition for escaping the embarrassments of a historicism that treats its object as necessary but inessential transitional phenomenon."[329] The present is no longer conceived in negative terms as a transitional phase toward an eternity beyond the continuum of homogeneous time. To employ a spatial figure, the present becomes an extreme that is irreducible to the historical constellation to which it belongs.

4

Mechanical and Historical Time in Benjamin and Heidegger

Enlightenment and Profane Redemption: Infinite Perfectibility and Unimproved Humanity

In its account of the profane eschatology of the Baroque, the *Trauerspiel* study encapsulates much of Benjamin's early philosophy, a philosophy that regarded the question of history as its ultimate measure: The "ultimate metaphysical dignity of a philosophical view ... will always manifest itself most clearly in its confrontation with history; in other words, the specific relationship of a philosophy with the true doctrine will appear most clearly in the philosophy of history."[1]

The philosophy of history made manifest in the *Trauerspiel* book is oriented toward the creaturely paradise of a transient present, a present no longer conceived as a transition toward a transcendent ideal of salvation that is unrealizable. This Baroque eschatology accords with the messianic idea of an "immanent state of perfection,"[2] a state which Benjamin opposes in the "Life of Students" to a neo-Kantian "view of history that puts its faith in the infinite extent of time and thus concerns itself only with ... progress."[3]

This view, which is implicitly identified in the early essay with "Cohen and Rickert's neo-Kantian philosophies,"[4] is one that ambiguously posits a quasi-religious finality at the end of an infinite continuum of time conceived on the model of space. According to Scholem, the neo-Kantian notion of progress "is where the most fundamental errors of the Marburg School are to be found: the distortion ... of everything into an infinite task." "The messianic realm and mechanical time have produced, in the heads of Enlightenment thinkers (*Aufklärer*), the—bastardized, accursed—idea of Progress."[5] Benjamin criticized this idea throughout his career, rejecting the "rationalistic furor for throwing light onto vast historical expanses by means of the torch of the Ideal (whether of progress, science, or reason)."[6] In the fragment titled "World and Time," Benjamin opposes the Enlightenment notion of continual human perfectibility to a messianic "definition of politics" as the "fulfillment of an unimproved humanity."[7]

The philosophy of history implicit in this definition of politics, which appears, in Benjamin's early writings, together with a sort of history of the concept of time in different historical periods, is defined in relation to the Kantian and neo-Kantian conceptions of progress. As Benjamin points out in the *Trauerspiel* book, this concept of history was preceded by a Baroque teleology that, in contrast to that of the Enlightenment, did not conceive of humanity and its moral perfection as the "supreme purpose of nature," disclosed in the unfolding of history. For the Baroque, nature was not, as in Kant's account of the sublime, the unattainable "realm of the crossover between the theory of experience and the theory of freedom," as Benjamin describes in "Program for the Coming Philosophy."[8]

In Baroque eschatology, the final purpose of nature is not to conform to the demands of morality, so that the latter can realize its ends. Rather, nature is only "considered as functioning for the purpose of expressing its meaning."[9] This meaning, however, is only revealed when the purpose of nature is no longer conceived as the goal of realizing human morality. In that sense, the teleology of the Baroque is oriented toward the suspension of the teleology that defines the Enlightenment theory of progress. In that way, it resembles the concept of justice proposed in the "Critique of Violence" and "Notes toward a Work on the Category of Justice," a messianic conception of justice that is directly opposed to the doctrine of right insofar as it cannot be demanded as a moral imperative. From the perspective of justice, history is not the "fulfillment of what is demanded," of a universalizable maxim cohering with everyone's freedom. Rather, just as the purpose of nature in Baroque eschatology is to express its own meaning, as opposed to embodying the moral felicity of humanity, so justice can only be realized as "a state of the world," which "does not appear to refer to the good will of the subject."[10]

Based upon the profane recognition that nature is indifferent to the moral ends of humanity, Baroque eschatology aims at the salvation of a creaturely life devoid of religious transcendence. Similarly, a messianic conception of justice can only be realized in an *unethical* state of the world in which the interminable task of achieving moral perfection is at last set aside in order to reach "the fulfillment of an unimproved humanity."

If redemption, therefore, as Scholem explains in an article on kabbala, is the "return of all things to their primal state," for Benjamin, this paradisal condition is not an "original state of divine harmony."[11] Rather, the primitive state of humanity is that of a profane imperfection which, like the idea of "a pre-ethical state of humanity" that appears in the writings of Goethe and Ludwig Bachofen, does not yet desire religious salvation nor aspire to fulfill its moral ideals.[12] The "pre-lapsarian age" that preceded the fall into abstraction and ethical judgment was characterized by an originary profanity.

In Benjamin's philosophy of history, then, a "redeemed humanity" is not one that recovers an original purity, but one whose historical development makes its ethical progress unnecessary. Just as nature, in the Baroque teleology, is only "considered as functioning for the purpose of expressing its meaning," so humanity, in Benjamin's messianism, will one day be redeemed just *as it is*, without any moral improvement.

But what this suggests is that, contrary to Richard Wolin, the "inner drive behind ... Benjamin's ... oeuvre" (a drive which was realized in the *Trauerspiel* study) is not to establish "the ultimate link with that realm with which mere life in its immediacy can have no contact: *the realm of redeemed life.*"[13] Redemption is not defined in

Benjamin's work as the transcendence of mere creaturely life, as the recovery of an "original paradisiacal state, whose ultimate, eschatological meaning will fully unfold only after the profane realm of history has been surmounted."[14] On the contrary, as Samuel Weber suggests in his account of Baroque eschatology, redemption implies "*transcending transcendence*," returning human existence to an original state of bare life, an unimproved state which Benjamin identifies with happiness: "To be happy is to be able to become aware of oneself [embrace oneself] without fright."[15]

In contrast, however, to Baroque eschatology, this profane scheme of redemption, in which "Paradise is at once the origin and primal past ... of humanity as well as the Utopian image of the future," is not purely cyclical, as Scholem asserted.[16] Rather, it is cumulative in character. However, instead of realizing an impossible moral perfection, the progress of history, and its continual failure to accomplish its task, creates the conditions for a redeemed humanity to return to its original, morally unimproved state.

It is in this manner that Benjamin resolves the contradiction that, according to Jürgen Habermas, purportedly constituted the primary weakness of his historical materialism—its "conservative-revolutionary" conception of history. In "his writings of the 1930s, Benjamin," as Wolin describes, summarizing Habermas' argument:

> ... tried to reconcile the irreconcilable: a theory that takes claims concerning progressive historical development seriously ... and a messianic view of history that believes, conversely, that only those breakthroughs are meaningful that present themselves as ruptures with the continuum of history as it has been constituted thus far.[17]

Reconciling the irreconcilable, Benjamin would later develop an historical materialism in which the progress of history establishes the possibility of its own messianic suspension. "Through a series of class struggles,"[18] as Benjamin explains in the "Paralipomena to 'On the Concept of History,'" describing how "Marx secularized the idea of messianic time,"[19] "humanity attains to a classless society in the course of historical development. ... But classless society is not to be conceived as the endpoint of historical development." "Classless society is not the final goal of historical progress but its frequently miscarried, ultimately achieved interruption."[20]

This image captures the contradictory movement described in the "Theologico-Political Fragment," in which progress directed at the "telos of [an] ... historical dynamic" simultaneously pushes "in the opposite direction," toward a messianic suspension of history.[21] The storm blowing from paradise, piling rubble upon rubble, increases the Angel of History's desire to stop its ascent into the future. The inimitable task of achieving moral perfection eventually enables the return of humanity to its original pre-ethical state. The temporal progression of history unfolds contradictions that are suspended in a spatialized image. Thinking "comes to a standstill in a constellation saturated with tensions" as a result of its own dialectical movement.

As Benjamin seems to suggest in a cryptic diary entry from 1931, it is this contradictory movement that makes it possible to reconcile the "conservative" and revolutionary aspects of his theory of history: "If [my] ... approach is determined by its firm rejection of the possibility of an evolutionary or universalist dimension in history, it is determined *internally* by a productive polarity."[22] Because progress produces a momentum pushing in the opposite direction to that of its historical ends or moral demands, it itself creates the conditions for its own messianic arrest.

In "The Concept of History," Benjamin opposes this possibility to the neo-Kantian conception of socialism as an infinite task: "Once the classless society had been defined as an infinite task, the empty and homogeneous time was transformed into an anteroom, so to speak, in which one could wait for the emergence of the revolutionary situation with more or less equanimity."[23] Against this neo-Kantian account of the classless society, Benjamin proposes the messianic and Marxist conception of history as "the object of a construction whose place ... is fulfilled by the here-and-now."[24] In this "Now of Recognizability," "truth is charged to the bursting point with time," and "thinking suddenly halts in a constellation overflowing with tensions."[25] In the constellation, the "historical materialist ... cognizes ... a revolutionary chance in the struggle for the suppressed past," and seeks to "explode" the latter "out of the homogeneous course of history."[26]

This Marxist conception of history, however, which is presented in one of Benjamin's last pieces of writing, already appears in one of his first publications, "Life of Students." Against a neo-Kantian "view of history that puts its faith in the infinite extent of time and thus concerns itself only with ... progress," Benjamin insists on the "historical task" to "delineate a particular condition in which history appears to be concentrated in a single focal point."[27] This "point of explosion," "charged to the bursting point with time," is identified with a "Truth [that] resides in the 'now of recognizability.'"[28] According to Benjamin, the now is a moment that can be grasped only in "its metaphysical structure, as with the messianic domain or the idea of the French Revolution."[29]

As Michael Löwy has argued, therefore, Benjamin's early writings "contain *in nuce* many of Benjamin's future preoccupations and one can rigorously show its similarity with his last writings. ... We can see a basic continuity in his spiritual trajectory from 1914 to 1940."[30] In that way, Benjamin's latter writings are connected to his earliest works in a manner recalling the figure of the constellation, in which different events, separated in time, come into contact in a here-and-now shot through with the "splinters of messianic time."[31]

According to Howard Eiland and Michael W Jennings, it is this messianic conception of time that unifies the two separate phases of Benjamin's work: "Benjamin's youth writings constitute the workshop of his later philosophy."[32] The texts from the earlier phase, then, were "more than juvenilia." They were "suffused with the originality that would mark virtually everything Benjamin would later write," specifically with "regard to the problem of time, which exercised some of the best minds of his generation."[33] As Eiland and Jennings point out, "none of the 'romantic' motifs ... or the philosophical principles informing them, are absent from the later work."[34] The early writings, therefore, composed while Benjamin was developing his metaphysical anarchism, would also inform the later political works of his Marxist or historical materialist phase.

Jetztzeit and *Augenblick*: Tradition and Mechanical Time in Benjamin and Heidegger

The messianic conception of history, which defines both the theological and materialist phases of Benjamin's work, is often characterized as a religious conception of time that departs from the secular notion of history as a linear succession of empty, homogeneous time. Thus, according to Tamara Tagliacozzo, the *Jetztzeit* is a "theological conception of ... history [that] ... stands opposed to ... mechanical time, the mathematically measurable time of the natural sciences."[35]

This description, however, does not fully acknowledge the dialectical character of Benjamin's understanding of history, which does not oppose mechanical time to vitalist critiques of the latter, as Nietzsche does in the doctrine of eternal return. Instead, Benjamin argued that mechanical time and eternal return are "indissoluble antinomies in the face of which the dialectical conception of historical time must be developed."[36] The opposition, moreover, between messianic and mechanical time, which interpreters have attributed to Benjamin, is inconsistent with the views on mechanical time expressed in the habilitation. In the latter, Benjamin affirms the spatialization of time, identifying it with the profane form of redemption portrayed in the *Trauerspiel*. Baroque eschatology "bespeaks the same metaphysical tendency [as] ... in the exact sciences," in which the "temporal process is caught up and analyzed in a spatial image."[37] The "secularization of the historical in the state of creation" is related to the spatialization of time, which reduces the latter to a homogeneous, empty continuum, a time to which Descartes confined the continuous action of God, who ensures the mechanical laws of the universe.[38] Against the background of this image of nature as an infinite succession of spatialized time, condemning everything to impermanence, "historical life" emerges from mythology, revealing its eternal transience.

The idea of a profane form of redemption, however, which affirms the transient present of creaturely life, is not merely a feature of Benjamin's early theological phase. In his historical materialism, the idea reappears as the "now-time" or *Jetztzeit*. As Giorgio Agamben has noted, in philosophy, the term, which Benjamin supposedly used to refer to a theological notion of time, is more often employed to denote exactly the opposite, to designate the modern and secular understanding of time. In the work of other philosophers, *Jetztzeit* "harbors purely negative and anti-messianic connotations."[39] In Schopenhauer, for example, this "coined word ... as pretentious as it is cacophonic" is defined as a present that refuses to see that the future will one day sit in judgment of what is happening now and therefore will determine its meaning.[40] "This one here—our time—calls itself by a name that it bestowed upon itself, a name that is as characteristic as it is euphemistic: *Jetzt-Zeit*. Yes, precisely *Jetztzeit*, meaning, only the now is thought and the time that comes and judges is not even glanced at."[41] For Schopenhauer, then, the *Jetztzeit*, which belongs to the "present age ... intellectually impotent and remarkable for its veneration of what is bad in every form," is a now which, ignoring the future, does not perceive itself as a mere transition.[42]

In *Being and Time*, the term *Jetzt-Zeit* is used to refer to the "vulgar" and originary understanding of time as a linear "succession of nows."[43] "What we call now-time

[*Jetzt-Zeit*] is everyday time as it appears in the clock that counts the 'nows.'"[44] This mechanical time is opposed to the "moment" or the "instant" (*Augenblick*), which constitutes the "authentic" form of the present. According to Heidegger, the latter cannot be derived from the *Jetzt-Zeit*. "The phenomenon of the Moment [*Augenblicks*] can *in principle not* be clarified in terms of the *now* [*Jetzt*]. The now is a temporal phenomenon that belongs to time as within-time-ness," to time understood as an infinite and homogeneous medium *in which* events and actions unfold.[45] On the contrary, this vulgar conception of time as a linear succession of nows is the product of a process of temporalization that it serves to cover up or conceal. Because of the *Jetzt-Zeit*, then, the "ecstatic character of primordial temporality is levelled down."[46]

For Heidegger, this ecstatic movement, which transcends the now, begins in the *Augenblick*, which is distinguished from the *Jetzt-Zeit* by its futural orientation. Seizing the moment, rather than simply being carried along in the now that is continually passing away, *Dasein* anticipates its futural possibilities, possibilities which then illuminate a potential that was already there in its past, in a "heritage" that is "retrieved" or "repeated" in the future. In this movement of "historicity," the past returns from *Dasein*'s ecstatic projection of itself into the future. The "character of *having-been* arises … from the future."[47] As such, tradition is not something handed down from the past to the present. Rather, its transmission goes by way of the future. *Dasein* takes hold of the present in a "momentaneous" manner, handing "down to itself its inherited possibility."[48] In anticipating a future, which reveals what was already there in its past, *Dasein* realizes its "fate."[49]

On the other hand, in Benjamin's work, *Jetzt-Zeit* loses its "negative connotation."[50] Indeed, Benjamin accords a positive meaning to the negative characteristics that others attribute to *Jetzt-Zeit*. Thus, the transitory present, which Schopenhauer identifies with an "intellectually impotent" modernity, becomes the basis for a materialism that, to borrow a phrase from Benjamin's early metaphysical program, affirms the "superficiality and godlessness" of modern society.[51] "The historical materialist cannot do without the notion of a present which is not a transition, but in which time takes a stand … and has come to a standstill."[52]

Moreover, instead of opposing the transient present to the messianic, Benjamin does exactly the opposite, identifying the "anti-messianic connotations" of *Jetztzeit* with the messianic itself. Whereas Schopenhauer, therefore, conceives of the *Jetztzeit* as a frivolous present, refusing to glance at the future that will judge it one day, Benjamin's messianism, in accordance with Jewish tradition, turns its back on the future in order to break its mythical hold on the present. "We know that the Jews were prohibited from inquiring into the future: the Torah and the prayers instructed them in remembrance. This disenchanted the future."[53] And against the idea of a present awaiting redemption from a future messiah, Benjamin evokes the "lack of envy which every present day feels toward its future." This *Jetztzeit*, therefore, does not seek divine restitution, but longs for a profane "image of happiness … colored by the time to which the course of our own existence has assigned us."[54]

This image of happiness was abandoned by Social Democracy, which "preferred to cast the working class in the role of a redeemer of future generations, in this way cutting the sinews of its greatest strength."[55] As Benjamin argues, however, this apparently Marxist conception of the historical role of the working class in fact conforms to the bourgeois notion of progress: "Social Democratic theory [was] … shaped by a conception of progress … in keeping with an infinite perfectibility of humanity," an idea which "cannot be sundered from the concept of its progression through a homogeneous, empty time."[56]

As Benjamin explains in "Paralipomena to 'On the Concept of History,'" this mechanical conception of time is based on the "substitution of homogeneous configurations for changes in the physical world," a substitution that underlies the principle of causality.[57] Subjecting the field of history to "the modern concept of science," bourgeois historicism "contents itself with establishing a causal nexus among various moments in history."[58] As Benjamin argues, however, history is not "a construction whose site is … homogeneous, empty time, but time filled full by now-time [*Jetztzeit*]." "The concept of historical time," therefore, "forms an antithesis to the idea of a temporal continuum."[59]

Life and Spatialized Time: Benjamin and Heidegger Read Bergson

As many have noted, this antithesis appears to resemble the opposition between the *Jetztzeit* and the *Augenblick* that underlies Heidegger's account of historicity, in which the historical past or the "having-been" is constituted through its repetition in the "authentic present" of an *Augenblick*. Just as tradition, according to Heidegger, is constituted through its repetition in the present, so, for Benjamin, "no state of affairs having causal significance is for that very reason historical. It became historical posthumously, as it were, through events that may be separated from it by thousands of years."[60] Thus, the French Revolution, as Benjamin notes in "On the Concept of History," regarded itself as a repetition of Rome, creating its own revolutionary heritage through a "[t]elescoping of the past through the present."[61] To "Robespierre ancient Rome was a past charged with now-time …. The French Revolution viewed itself as Rome reincarnate."[62]

To borrow Benjamin's description of time in Marcel Proust's *In Search of Lost Time*, history, then, occurs in "intertwined time, not boundless time."[63] History is not simply a causal chain of events that happens within empty, homogeneous time. Rather, it consists of actions that unfold in a *Jetztzeit* in which the present repeats an earlier precedent that is constituted as such by the repetition itself, creating the appearance of a casual nexus that was always there in the past, the past "the way it really was."[64] Like Heidegger's *Augenblick*, the *Jetztzeit* is an ecstatic movement of temporalization in which tradition is handed down from the future, creating an intertwined present that is opposed to the mechanical notion of time as a linear succession of nows.

As Slavoj Žižek has argued, therefore, there is a "striking" parallel between Heidegger's conception of historicity and Benjamin's historical materialism:

> As for Heidegger's notion of authentic choice as a repetition, the parallel with Benjamin's notion of revolution as repetition […] is striking: here also, revolution

is conceptualized as a repetition that realizes the hidden possibility of the past, so that a proper view of the past (the one that perceives the past not as a closed set of facts but as open, as involving a possibility that failed, or was repressed, in its actuality) opens only from the standpoint of an agent engaged in a present situation.[65]

This account of the similarities between Benjamin and Heidegger, however, fails to acknowledge the twofold orientation of Benjamin's thinking with regard to the problem of time, an aspect of his early coming philosophy that was later transposed into his historical materialism. This philosophy was a critique not only of mechanical reason, but also of vitalist theories of the constitution of time, including those of Bergson and Husserl, whose student, Heidegger, as Adorno described, would carry out "the transition of phenomenology into vitalism."[66]

Against both rationalist and vitalist theories that opposed "otherworldly phenomena with a predominantly temporal character" to "immanent, predominantly spatial phenomena of the world of things,"[67] Benjamin proposed a coming philosophy that grasped the limits of each. "Thus, the task of the coming philosophy can be conceived as the discovery ... of that concept of knowledge which .... makes not only mechanical but also religious experience logically possible."[68]

Furthermore, instead of endorsing the opposition between authentic and mechanical time that underlies Heidegger's work, Benjamin rejected his account of both mechanism and history. In a letter to Scholem, written during the same period as the "Program to the Coming Philosophy," Benjamin states that "not only what [Heidegger] ... says about historical time ... which I am able to judge ... is nonsense, but ... his statements on mechanical time are, as I suspect, also askew."[69]

Heidegger distinguished his views on historical and mechanical time from those of Henri Bergson, whom he studied in a 1913 course offered by Heinrich Rickert, titled "Seminar on Metaphysics in Conjunction with the Writings of H. Bergson," which Benjamin also attended.[70] Although he would later disparage Bergson's "indeterminate and insufficient" idea that the vulgar notion of time is an "externalization of a 'qualitative time' into space,"[71] "Heidegger nevertheless also incorporates Bergson's views about the difference between time and duration."[72]

The distinction between spatialized time and *durée* is developed in one of the text assigned in the seminar that Rickert directed, *Essai Sur Les Données Immédiates De La Conscience*, whose critique of the "repeatable time of ... natural science" is evoked in the *Trauerspiel* book.[73] In "The Problem of Historical Time" (which Benjamin criticized in the letter to Scholem), Heidegger rehearses this criticism in the following manner: "The flow freezes, becomes a flat surface, and only as a flat surface can it be measured. Time becomes a homogeneous arrangement of places."[74] In the text, moreover, the problem of "intratemporality" or within-time-ness is explained in Bergsonian terms, as the spatialization of time or *durée*: "Motions run their course in time. What exactly does this mean? 'In' time has a spatial meaning; however, time is obviously nothing spatial. ... In the relation between motion and time, what is clearly at issue is measurement of motion by means of time."[75] "Like Bergson," therefore, as Heath Massey has argued, "Heidegger maintains that the time we measure and divide into discrete units, the time of the natural sciences, is fundamentally different from the qualitative, heterogeneous time of human life."[76]

On the other hand, Benjamin, who reported "harvesting seminar laurels ... with papers on Bergson" during his time as a student, appears to have developed a different perspective on Bergson's philosophy.[77] In his early "Metaphysics of Youth," Benjamin gives a response to a question that Heidegger will pose as the fundamental problem of *Being and Time*, the question of the origin of time: "Are we time?"

Benjamin's conclusion is that a positive answer must be rejected out of humility with regard to the transcendental ability of the subject to constitute nature itself. "As landscape all events surround us, for we [are] ... the time of things," things which respond to "the shudder of temporality with which we assault the landscape." "Are we time? Arrogance tempts us to answer yes," but "then the landscape would vanish," since the world would be reduced to the subject.[78] To avoid such a reduction—a risk which is taken by Heidegger, whose "temporal idealism" derives mechanical time from *Dasein*'s authentic temporalization[79]—time, according to Benjamin, must be conceived as arising from our bodily movement in space. "The only answer is that we set out on a path. As we advance ... we define things with the movement of our bodies ... flood them with the time of our existence."[80]

What the answer suggests is that "we" do not constitute the ordinary conception of time as a linear succession of *Jetztzeit* that conceals the process of authentic temporalization. Rather, we *are* the spatialization of time, the process of endosmosis, based on the "confusion of duration with extensity," which produces the vulgar, "repeatable time of ... natural science." The "path," moreover, that constitutes time resembles what Benjamin, using Bergson's terminology, refers to in the Hölderlin essay as "the intensive activity of the gait as an inner, plastically temporal form."[81] In Benjamin's reading of Hölderlin's poem, "Timidity," the gait is analyzed as a figure for the process of endosmosis, or what Benjamin describes as the movement of "spatiotemporal interpenetration."[82]

Just as Baroque drama and science, then, were defined by the reduction of "otherworldly phenomena with a ... temporal character" to the "spatial phenomena of the world of things,"[83] so, in "Timidity," the "divine order" of time as *durée* is "intimated in the image of space." In the gait, or the path on which we set out, the intensive quality of time is reduced to a quantifiable form of extension, such that in "place of a heterogeneous duration ... we thus get a homogeneous time whose moments are strung on a spatial line."[84]

If, for Bergson and Heidegger, this homogeneous time, employed in the sciences, arises from the authentic temporality of *Dasein* or from the pure duration of "life," for Benjamin, on the other hand, life is confined to the creaturely plane of spatialized time. "In this world of Hölderlin's," a profane world in which the pure intensity of time can only be intimated through the "interpenetration of individual forms of perception," the "living are always clearly the extension of space, the plane spread out."[85] "Temporal existence in infinite extension, the truth of the situation, binds the living."[86] The identification of life with the spatialization of time and experience is also expressed in an idea, described in Benjamin's account of his youth, which he had "for years, played with ... the idea of setting out the sphere of life—*bios*—graphically on a map."[87] As Alexander Gelley has noted, the idea "suggests ... a form of autobiographical exploration guided by a spatial schematism," inspired by Marcel Proust's "exercises in spatializing a life sequence."[88]

It is this spatialization of life, as Benjamin explains in "Berlin Chronicle," that distinguishes the form of recollection employed in the latter from that of autobiography. Whereas autobiography "has to do with time, with sequence and what makes up the continuous flow of life," the chronicle records "space ... moments and discontinuities."[89] "The determining experiences of childhood survive, then, not in the manner of a continuous narrative but as images whose form bears the imprint of the moment of recovery."[90] In "Berlin Chronicle," the recollection of infancy is captured in a spatialized form, just as history, for the historical materialist, "decays into images, not into stories."[91] This spatialization of time also distinguishes the form of classical tragedy from that of the *Trauerspiel*. In the latter, the temporal sequence of tragic events appears, to the character-type of the intriguer, in a "panoramatic" perspective. The schemer turns the temporal "order of fate around in their hands like a ball, exposing to view now one aspect, now another."[92]

Historicity and Historical Materialism

In his later historical materialist phase, the suspicion that Benjamin harbored toward Heidegger's view of historical and mechanical time would become a conviction. In notes compiled in the early stage of his research on the *Arcades*, Benjamin describes the concept of history developed in *Being and Time*, "the new book by Heidegger," as a "reactionary" "view on the historical world."[93] In a 1930 letter to Scholem, Benjamin, therefore, announced plans "to annihilate Heidegger."[94]

In another letter earlier that year, Benjamin mentions his intent to compose an epistemological introduction to the *Arcades*, incorporating "some aspects of Hegel and some parts of Marx's *Capital* ... to provide a solid scaffolding for my work." The introduction would contain a "discussion of the theory of historical knowledge. This is where I will find Heidegger, and I expect sparks will fly from the shock of the confrontation between our two very different ways of looking at history."[95]

Although the introduction was never completed, the convolute that Benjamin compiled for that purpose (Convolute N, "On the Theory of Knowledge, Theory of Progress") contains an entry comparing Heidegger's concept of historicity to Benjamin's own theory of the dialectical image. In the entry, Benjamin asserts that "authentic" time is not linear but intertwined. "Every present day is determined by the images that are synchronic with it." Contrary, however, to Heidegger's account of historicity, it "is not that what is past casts its light on what is present, or what is present its light on what is past," such that tradition is handed down from a future that *Dasein* projects backwards in time in the *Augenblick*. Rather, "image is that wherein what has been comes together in a flash with the now to form a constellation. In other words: image is dialectics at a standstill. For while the relation of the present to the past is purely temporal, the relation of *what-has-been* to the now [*Jetzt*] is dialectical."[96]

In the dialectical image, then, the "ecstasies" that constitute time in Heidegger's account of historicity are grasped as a static constellation saturated with tensions, as opposed to a temporal movement from the future into the past, ensuring the transmission of "heritage" and the fulfilment of fate. As Benjamin explains later on in Convolute N, it is precisely this kind of redemption or continual recuperation of the past by the present that must be suspended: "What are phenomena rescued from? Not only, and not in the main, from the discredit and neglect into which they have fallen, but from the catastrophe represented very often by a certain strain in their dissemination, their 'enshrinement as heritage' ... There is a tradition that is catastrophe."[97]

In contrast, then, to Heidegger's account of how heritage is retrieved through repetition, Benjamin's "weak messianism" does not seek to redeem a lost heritage by retroactively incorporating it into the record of history. This idea of redemption is based upon the erroneous assumption, which has existed "from time immemorial," that "historical narration has simply [to] pick ... out an object" from the past. Having retrieved it, the "first thought was then always to reinsert the object into the continuum."[98]

For the historical materialist, on the other hand, the neglected "object of history" is not to be incorporated into the past through a rewriting of history. Rather, it must be "blasted out of the continuum of historical succession."[99] Unlike the temporal movement of historicity, the establishment of a dialectical constellation between the past and the present, the entwinement the *what-has-been* and the now, does not serve to transmit a forgotten tradition. Contrary to a commonplace view of Benjamin's messianism, the latter, as Agamben has argued, cannot be "assimilated to the dominant doctrine that conceives of the task of history writing as the recuperation of alternative heredities that must then be consigned to ... tradition."

> The idea that is presupposed in this practice is that the tradition of the oppressed classes is, in its goals and in its structures, altogether analogous to the tradition of the ruling classes (whose heir it would be); the oppressed class, according to this theory, would differ from the ruling classes only with respect to its content.[100]

For Benjamin, however, the historical materialist does not merely seek to recover a different tradition, that of the oppressed as opposed to the rulers. If it is "more difficult to honor the memory of the anonymous than it is to honor the memory of the famous, the celebrated," it is not only because the history of the oppressed has been buried by their oppressors, making its content more difficult to retrieve and transmit as tradition. Rather, it is because an "historical construction ... dedicated to the memory of the anonymous" must differ in form from the history of the rulers.[101] For this reason, the "historical materialist ... dissociates himself from this *process* of transmission," and, therefore, from the "barbarism" that "taints the *manner* in which [heritage] was transmitted from one hand to another."[102]

The memory of the anonymous, then, can only be honored by interrupting the process through which tradition itself is transmitted, as opposed to reconstructing their history and removing their anonymity. The oppressed are redeemed through the destruction of the process of inheritance that perpetuates their exclusion. Unlike the famous and the celebrated, therefore, the anonymous can only be honored *in anonymity*.

Mechanism, Messianism, and the Image of Transience

This profane form of redemption is achieved through the "destructive or critical momentum of materialist historiography ... registered in that blasting of historical continuity with which the historical object first constitutes itself."[103] But as such, materialist historiography is opposed to the practice of historical narration. Thus, as Benjamin explains in the *Arcades*, in a statement on the "elementary doctrine of historical materialism," "[h]istory decays into images, not into stories."[104]

The messianic task of redeeming the past by blasting it out of the continuum of history, rather than reinserting it into the historical record, corresponds exactly to Benjamin's account of the revolutionary potential of mass reproduction. In contrast to historical narration, mass reproduction does not transmit tradition through stories. Rather, it disseminates images in a manner that "detaches the reproduced object from the sphere of tradition," depriving it of the "cult value" accorded to objects of cultural heritage (see Chapter 7).[105] In that sense, mass reproduction is directly opposed to the repetition of the past which, in Heidegger's account of historicity, constitutes tradition and fate. Through mass reproduction, the masses appropriate images that have been freed from their "embeddedness in the context of tradition," and from the rules and conventions restricting their use.[106]

The messianic potential that Benjamin ascribes to mass reproduction suggests a more complex relationship between mechanical time and the *Jetztzeit*, as the "a model of messianic time," than the one that readers like Žižek have identified. Instead of opposing the two, Benjamin, in "On the Concept of History," in fact uses one form of time as a figure for the other. In thesis XV, the apparently ecstatic "moment of action" when the "revolutionary classes ... are about to make the continuum of history explode" is likened to mechanical reproduction, "history in time-lapse mode."[107] Like montage, time-lapse photography abbreviates the succession of time by juxtaposing non-contiguous moments, in accordance with the messianic principle, recorded in Convolute N, that "for a part of the past to be touched by the present instant, there must be no continuity between them."[108]

In contrast to Heidegger's account of historicity, however, the result of this contact between the past and the present, between "events that may be separated ... by thousands of years," is not an authentic temporalization in which *Dasein* constitutes its own tradition and destiny.[109] Such an argument, as Adorno asserted in a lecture whose arguments are informed by the *Trauerspiel* book, reduces history to "the realm of subjectivity."[110] Rather, the messianic abbreviation of the passage of empty, homogeneous time, which resembles the effect of decreasing the frame rate in film, apprehends, in the flash of an image, the eternal transience of humanity and the whole of its history.

"In relation to the history of all organic life on earth," writes a modern biologist, "the paltry fifty-millennia history of *homo sapiens* equates to something like two seconds at the close of a twenty-four-hour day. On this scale, the history of civilized mankind would take up one-fifth of the last second of the last hour." Now-time, which, as a model of messianic time, comprises the entire history of mankind in a tremendous abbreviation, coincides exactly with the figure which the history of mankind describes in the universe.[111]

Whereas for Heidegger, then, *Dasein* constitutes time by anticipating a future that redeems the past, transmitting it as tradition, for Benjamin, the *Jetztzeit* is a messianic representation of nature as an empty eternity that seizes the truth of every tradition in recognizing its transience. "To grasp the eternity of historical events," as Benjamin writes in "On the Concept of History," "is really to appreciate the eternity of their transience."[112] If the *Augenblick* is redeemed by the future that retroactively recognizes the past that produced it, the *Jetztzeit* recovers an abbreviated infinity, completely devoid of transcendence.

In the messianic now, empty, homogeneous time is fulfilled by its contact with an empty eternity, or what Benjamin describes in the "Theologico-Political Fragment" as an "eternity of downfall, and the rhythm of this eternally transient worldly existence, transient in its totality."[113] If the *Jetztzeit*, then, is a "full ... time" whose "theological name ... is messianic time," what fills its emptiness is not a final judgment from a future that retroactively justifies its occurrence. Rather, it is fulfilled by an image of this emptiness captured at an infinitely slower frame rate.[114] In this dialectical image, in which the passage of homogeneous time is brought to a standstill in a mechanical reproduction that abbreviates its infinity, the present appears not as a moment that will be redeemed by the future, handing the past to itself as tradition. Rather, the now that passes away in mechanical time appears as a transition within an eternity of transience, and, as such, it no longer appears as a transition at all.

What this implies, then, is that, in Benjamin's philosophy of history, "mechanical time, the mathematically measurable time of the natural sciences," is not opposed to the *Jetztzeit* as a secular to a theological notion of time. Nor is Benjamin's objection to empty, homogeneous time merely that it is a modern conception devoid of religious significance. On the contrary, his critique of "the schema of progression within an empty and homogeneous time" suggests that the latter is *too religious* in character. Against the insufficiently secularized modern conception of history as an infinite task that occurs in mechanical time, Benjamin, therefore, in "On the Concept of History," opposes the theological notion of transience, as a completely profane form of life.

As Benjamin argued in his early philosophical writings, the "ambiguous" idea of the infinite task is a result of the one-sided character of the Kantian theory of knowledge, which was inherited by the Marburg school of neo-Kantianism (see Chapter 1). By situating the objects of religion beyond human experience, while reducing experience to mechanical reason, this theory preserved the illusion that it is possible to transcend the creaturely plane of spatialized time. Benjamin's criticism of Kant, then, is not that his critique of pure reason could only save natural science by denying the existence of God. On the contrary, Kant makes room for religion by denying that science applies to the objects of theology. Although Kant, then, according to Benjamin, demonstrated the timeless validity of the laws of natural science without reference to God, by conflating the mechanical view of experience with experience unto itself, he also excluded the possibility of a completely profane account of theology. Hence, "the task of the coming philosophy can be conceived as the discovery ... of that concept of knowledge which .... makes not only mechanical but also religious experience logically possible,"[115] including the experience of God as the "circumference" of the "realm of Ideas."[116]

Marxism and Messianism

The idea of a secularized theory of knowledge was later transposed into a Marxist perspective, producing an historical materialism based on a profane understanding of nature, which exists in spatialized time, and of the ultimate ends of human existence, which is "transient in its totality." This eternal transience, which was the aim of Baroque eschatology, would become reenchanted after the seventeenth century with the rise of capitalism as a new form of religion. In the "phantasmagoria" that characterizes modernity, the eternal transience of a cosmos without God is pressed into the service of a new form of mythology. As Benjamin argues in his remarks on Blanqui—which were intended as a frame for the *Arcades Project* as a whole—the mechanical view of the universe as an empty infinity will serve as the eternal appearance of an historically specific and transitory form of society. In the doctrine of eternal recurrence, capitalism projects its image "across the heavens" (see Chapter 6).[117]

This critique of modernity differs from those of Benjamin's contemporaries on both the right and the left who opposed the spiritual to the mechanical, identifying the latter with modern society, which is condemned for its reification, vulgar conception of time, and instrumental rationality. In Lukács's Marxism, for example, which was informed by the Baden School of Neo-Kantianism, "modernity" was viewed as "afflicted with the domination of abstract rationalization over spiritual profundity."[118] This opposition, which underlies the neo-Kantian socialism of Hermann Cohen and his disciples as well as the Hegelian Marxism of Adorno and Lukács, corresponds to the Kantian distinction between the moral autonomy of persons and the mechanism that governs the material world. In Kant, according to Benjamin, the "concept of freedom stands in a peculiar correlation to the mechanical concept of experience and was accordingly further developed in neo-Kantianism."[119] Rejecting this dichotomy, Benjamin proposed a coming philosophy in which "not only the concept of experience but also that of freedom will undergo a decisive transformation."[120]

In the *Trauerspiel* book, this opposition between freedom and mechanism is called into question in an implied criticism of the history of secularization and the reification of time in Lukács and Schmitt. For Benjamin, these processes cannot be used to define modern society since their appearance precedes the modern theory of the state and the rise of the capitalist mode of production. Just as the Baroque conception of politics was already secularized, so time, in the seventeenth century, was already spatialized, reduced, in Lukács's terms, to "an exactly delimited, quantifiable continuum filled with quantifiable 'things.'" For Benjamin, what defines bourgeois society is not spatialized time, but the "concept of ... *progression* through a homogenous and empty time," of "*progress* into the void," as opposed to the empty continuum in which this progression occurs.[121] Whereas Baroque eschatology implied "an end of time [that] ... knows neither redemption nor a hereafter and remains immanent to this world,"[122] the notion of progress preserves the possibility of transcending the spatialized time that constitutes the "creaturely plane of existence." In that way, the Enlightenment reintroduces theology into a concept of time that was already secularized.

As Benjamin suggests in "Capitalism as Religion," this re-enchantment of history resulted from the rise of capitalism. The latter was "not only a religiously conditioned construction, as Weber thought, but an essentially religious phenomenon." According to Benjamin, then, capitalism is not a secular form of society whose development depended on a particular kind of religion. Rather, it is a new form of religion that replaced an earlier one that conditioned it: "Capitalism has developed as a parasite of Christianity in the West ... until it reached the point where Christianity's history is essentially that of its parasite—... capitalism."[123] If the seventeenth century, then, was defined by a profane form of redemption, modernity is based upon a religion that seems to be a purely secular form of society.

In the final stage of his research on the *Arcades*, Benjamin will analyze this cultic religion through Marx's critique of political economy, in which the fetishism of commodities, as a practice peculiar to capitalism, assumes an eternal appearance. As the next chapter will argue, this fetishistic appearance, as Marx pointed out, was uncritically accepted in the neo-Kantian conception of socialism, which identified the mechanical character of the bourgeois economy with the laws of natural selection. Although Marxists like Lukács argue that these apparently natural laws belonged in fact to a "second nature," constituted by the commodity, they also associated this feature of capitalism with phenomena, such as measurable time and mechanical reason, that existed in other societies. If neo-Kantian socialism, then, eternalizes a historically determinate aspect of capitalism, the theory of reification identifies capitalism with a transhistorical phenomenon, the reduction of time into space, thereby generalizing Marx's critique of commodity fetishism.

5

Neo-Kantianism and the Critique of Political Economy

Science and Socialism: Neo-Kantianism, German Idealism, and the Labor Question

According to Frederick C. Beiser, neo-Kantianism was not simply an "academic philosophy," one which, "ensconced in … ivory towers," preoccupied itself only with "abstruse questions about the logic of the sciences."[1] As Benjamin observes in "On the Concept of History," the movement was tied to Social Democracy, providing the Party with its "school philosophy" in the concept of socialism as an infinite task.[2]

The movement rose to prominence within the academy during the second half of the nineteenth century, with the publication of works like *The History of Materialism and Critique of Its Contemporary Significance* (1866), by Friedrich Albert Lange. Lange, who was considered the "father of Marburg Neo-Kantianism," was also a founder of the social-democratic movement.[3] In the 1860s and '70s, the school would come to eclipse German Idealism in academic philosophy, just as Fichte, Hegel, and Schelling had previously claimed to surpass the Kantian system.

As Beiser points out, the decline of German Idealism coincided with the growing predominance of the empirical sciences. During this period, the latter's achievements served to discredit the idea of a speculative deduction of natural science, such as the one that Hegel proposed in the *Logic*. As the empirical sciences began to encompass "every sphere of reality … the old *a priori* methods of speculative idealism" appeared increasingly "bankrupt," having "nothing more to offer than the hocus-pocus of metaphysics."[4] As a result of the development of the sciences, the "detail of [Hegel's] philosophy of nature" (to borrow Friedrich Engels's account of Lange's critique of the latter) seemed "full of nonsense."[5]

This perception may have informed Benjamin's early understanding of Hegel. From his university seminars, which were directed by prominent neo-Kantian thinkers, Benjamin acquired the impression of Hegel as an "intellectual brute, a mystic of brute force, the worst sort there is."[6] And yet Benjamin would go on to defend the intellectual brute against the "presumptuous" claim, made by Scholem, that Hegel's *a priori* deduction of the empirical sciences was more mysticism than rational thought: Hegel's "speculative philosophy of nature ... greatly offended my mathematical soul even as it impressed my mystical soul."[7]

Confronted with the growing prestige of the empirical sciences in the late nineteenth century, the neo-Kantian school rejected Hegel's speculative form of philosophy, attempting instead to redefine the relationship of philosophy to science. In this connection, the school returned to the *Critique of Pure Reason*, reinterpreting the latter as a "theory of knowledge," and specifically that of natural science: "The neo-Kantians had in mind a very specific conception of epistemology: the examination of the methods, standards and presuppositions of the empirical sciences."[8]

For neo-Kantian thinkers, therefore, the legitimacy of philosophy could only be reestablished by limiting its role to elaborating a scientific epistemology. This restriction, however, did not imply that the neo-Kantian school concerned itself only with questions pertaining to science and its methodology. On the contrary, its theory of knowledge had a considerable effect on the politics of the period, giving rise to a conception of socialism that competed with Marxism in its influence over the labor movement.

For neo-Kantian thinkers, this concept of socialism, as Ernst Cassirer described, "was a necessary consequence of the ... categorical imperative," just as Kant's moral philosophy, from the point of view of the school, was a necessity for the socialist movement: the latter "was essentially a moral movement whose philosophic basis is best expressed in the Kantian moral philosophy."[9] Neo-Kantian philosophers believed that a "Kantian foundation would grant the socialist movement academic respectability, a moral critique, an inviolable foundation for the infusion of an ethical will, a sense of … moral purpose into the working class."[10]

This Kantian socialism attracted figures like Eduard Bernstein, a social democrat and a prominent leader in the Second International, who argued that socialism could be achieved without revolution by working within the structures of bourgeois democracy. As Bernstein acknowledged, it was "Lange's work that led him to both Kant and revisionism."[11] Together with Cohen, Lange "played a decisive role" in shaping Bernstein's political views.[12] "The idea of socialism as a movement toward an unattainable goal, popularized by Bernstein, stems from Cohen's point of departure."[13] This concept of socialism as an infinite task was further developed by students of Cohen, including Karl Vorländer and August Stadler, who established the "tradition of Marburg socialist theory," providing social democracy with its "school philosophy."[14]

This philosophy was opposed by communist critics of social democracy, including Rosa Luxemburg, who, in a letter to Kurt Eisner, wrote, "may you drown in the moral absolutes of your beloved *Critique of Pure Reason*."[15] According to Franz Mehring, a leader in the Spartacus League whose "rigor," according to Benjamin, "made him immune to revisionism,"[16] the socialism of the Marburg School was an attempt to revitalize an old bourgeois ideology for the purpose of undermining the proletariat. For Marxism, neo-Kantianism "represented historically the moral expression of the German bourgeoisie at the end of the 18th century, and in its intended reapplication it could only emasculate the worker movement."[17]

For Benjamin, on the other hand, the neo-Kantian school marked "the withering of the [eighteenth century] bourgeoisie's oppositional resolve, and the withering of the historical ambition which had lived in that resolve." While the school continued Kant's theoretical program of grounding "all knowledge in ... the exact sciences," this rationalist program no longer served the revolutionary role it had in the "early period of the German bourgeoisie," and its struggle against feudal society.[18]

As Mehring argued, moreover, the concept of a socialism founded on *a priori* ethical principles appealed to those without a knowledge of history. A purely formal criterion for socialism was attractive to those who "suffer from a lack of a sense of history, which one comprehends when one has it, but never learns to comprehend when one doesn't have it." As Mehring argued, therefore, the attempt to "graft Marx onto Kant or Kant onto Marx" could serve no other purpose than to "obscure the hard-fought insights into its historical tasks achieved by the German working class." The "objective essence" of neo-Kantian socialism could be "nothing more than the attempt to shatter historical materialism."[19] In "his confrontation with neo-Kantianism," then, Mehring sought to expose "the bourgeois-reactionary character of the entire 'Back to Kant' movement."[20]

By the end of the nineteenth century, this movement would become as influential in political discourse as in academic philosophy, assuming a stature similar to that of Hegel's idealism in the 1830s and '40s. According to Philip Moran, one of the most significant intellectual changes from this period to the end of the century, "from the time of Marx and Engels to the time of Lenin was the shift from the dominance of Hegelianism to the dominance of neo-Kantianism." The doctrine, which appealed to reformists and moderate socialists, constituted "the main political and ideological opponents of Marxism during this period of monopoly capitalism."[21] Thus, Lenin's writings frequently targeted arguments by neo-Kantian thinkers, including Lange, Hermann Cohen, Rudolf Stammler, Georg Simmel, and Sergei Bulgakov. According to Moran, "One of the key issues involved in Lenin's ongoing fight with revisionism concerns ... whether one strives to improve capitalism, to reform it, and to think of socialism as a kind of Kantian regulative idea which cannot be achieved in reality."[22] According to Lenin, this "theory of bourgeois philosophers," which "serves as the basis of the tactics of the bourgeoisie," could not be reconciled with Marxism, which "serves as the basis for the tactics of the proletariat in modern capitalist countries."[23]

Socialist Darwinism and the Critique of Political Economy

The tradition of Marburg School socialist theory can be traced to the work of one of its founding figures, Friedrich Lange. In his *History of Materialism*, Lange, as Beiser describes, presents a critique of Hegel's idealism as well as materialist forms of philosophy. While the latter purportedly reduces human activity to the mechanical causality that governs the material world, Hegel's philosophy constitutes a regression to a pre-Kantian dogmatic metaphysics that cannot be justified on the basis of experience. "If materialism stands for the triumph of a complete mechanism and naturalism, which undermines moral ... ideals, speculative idealism represents a revival of metaphysical rationalism, which," like theology, saves "these ideals but only by going beyond the limits of reason."[24]

As Cohen suggests in his introduction to the *History of Materialism*, Lange's critique of materialism would appear to imply a rejection of Marx's purportedly exclusive concern for "problems of the stomach," and his tendency to ignore the moral basis of action.[25] To borrow Benjamin's description of the "historian schooled in Marx," historical materialism understands history only as a "fight for the crude and material things," while failing to recognize that socialism can only be actualized through the exercise of practical reason.[26] In his critique of materialism, Lange anticipates the neo-Kantian conception of socialism, which follows "straightforwardly from a proper understanding of Kant's categorical imperative."

For Cohen, however, this understanding was one that Lange did not correctly apply in his political theory, a theory which, like Marx's, purportedly, adopts a "naturalistic foundation" that is inconsistent with Lange's own critique of materialism.[27] In the *Labor Question* (1866), Lange, attempting to "derive the conditions which produce the [problem of] labor ... from the principles developed by Darwin," defines market competition as an expression of the evolutionary struggle for survival. The market, then, is a social institution that conforms to natural laws, in particular, the law of overpopulation associated with Thomas Malthus. Just "as nature produces an abundance of seed to create a single plant, so there is an enormous supply of workers where only a lucky few get a living wage. Natural selection and the struggle for existence mean that the strong will rule over the weak not only in nature but also in society."[28]

Cohen, however, was incorrect to assume that this naturalism was the foundation of Lange's political theory. As Beiser points out, Lange "believed that the mechanisms of natural selection were leading to greater oppression and misery, not greater progress and perfection." As such, "the task of ethics was to work *against* these forces and demand greater social equality."[29] Lange's theory, therefore, departs from Benjamin's account of the socialism adopted by revisionists such as Bernstein, for whom "the Darwinian influence served to maintain the party's faith and determination in the struggle."[30] According to Benjamin, this tendency "affirmed that the materialism of natural science 'automatically' turned into historical materialism." Using the "concept of the 'self-acting'" which arose "when the self-regulation of the market was beginning," and which "celebrated its triumph in Kant, in the form of 'spontaneity,'" thinkers associated with Social Democracy developed a deterministic conception of history.[31] In the latter, the "automatic subject" of capital, which emerges from what Marx characterized as a fetishistic inversion in which the producers are ruled by the process of production, is eternalized as a natural process.[32]

For Lange, on the other hand, socialism could only be realized by going against the mechanical determinism of the market, a determinism which he identified with the natural process of selection. The theory of evolution, then, was not the naturalistic basis of Lange's political thought. Rather, Darwinism was the scientific foundation from which Lange developed a naturalized understanding of the society he wished to reform. In this view, the market is identified with the evolutionary struggle for survival based on the fact that both appear to conform to mechanical laws. This naturalized conception of capitalism, then, is opposed to a politics that is thoroughly Kantian in its dualism of morality and nature and in its categorical demand for equality: "There were two conflicting forces at work in Lange's social and political universe: *natural* ones, which worked toward inequality ... and *moral* ones, which strive for equality and freedom for all."[33] Lange's naturalism, therefore, was not a *social* Darwinism that affirms the law of natural selection. Rather, the theory was a *socialist* Darwinism in which an ahistorical criticism of capitalism, as a continuation of the struggle for survival, is opposed to the Kantian ideal of morality, as conformity to a universal criterion that applies at all places and times.

Despite his objection to the purportedly naturalistic foundation of Lange's social theory, Cohen's own political philosophy, moreover, was founded on a similarly dualistic account of society as characterized by a conflict between moral and natural forces. On the one hand, Cohen identifies the realm of economics with what he calls a "labor society" (*Verkehrsgebiet*), which operates mechanistically. The latter is opposed to a "legal society" (*Herrschaftsgebiet*) in which relations between moral persons are regulated according to the principle of freedom or moral autonomy. According to Moran, "Cohen opposes in an abstract way freedom to causality, the moral to the economic. And he asserts the priority of freedom over necessity, of the moral over the economic."[34]

Neither was Cohen, however, correct in his characterization of the naturalistic foundation of Marx's materialism, which Cohen believed was similar to Lange's political theory. This identification (which Lange himself had assumed) was one that Marx and Engels expressly repudiated. As Marx mentions in *Capital*, the dismissal of Hegel by "mediocre" thinkers who derived their idea of materialism from empirical science was entirely different from his own attack against the "mystificatory side of ... dialectic nearly thirty years ago."[35]

In the 1870s, the view of Hegel's philosophy as an unscientific idealism, popularized by figures like Dühring and Lange, encouraged misreadings of *Capital* and its "Hegelian sophistry," compelling Marx to declare himself a "pupil of that mighty thinker."[36] Unwilling to believe that Marx had adopted a speculative method which had been completely discredited, neo-Kantian thinkers like Karl Vorländer argued that Marx had only "flirted" with Hegelian concepts in several parts of his writings.[37] In *History and Class Consciousness*, Lukács criticizes this view as that of philosophers who believed "that for Marx the dialectic was no more than a superficial stylistic ornament and that in the interest of 'scientific precision' all traces of it should be eradicated systematically from the method of historical materialism."[38]

The same argument is presented in Lange's review of *Capital*, which praises Marx's "astounding" empirical analysis of capitalism but complains that the Hegelian "speculative form ... tiresomely intrudes on the content ... to the disadvantage of its effectiveness."[39] As Marx argues, however, what Lange fails to perceive is that the empirical analysis in *Capital* is based on the same speculative method that apparently undermines its scientific precision:

> Mr Lange expresses surprise that ... I ... take *au serieux* the dead dog Hegel, after Büchner, Lange, Dr Dühring ... etc., had long agreed that they ... buried him. Lange is naïve enough to say that I "move with rare freedom" in empirical matter.

He has not the slightest idea that this "free movement in matter" is nothing but ... the dialectical method.[40]

For Marx, then, Lange's inability to recognize the dialectical character of the critique of political economy in *Capital* indicated an inadequate understanding of the speculative philosophy he assumed he had already buried. Having misunderstood Hegel's idealism, Lange, as Marx goes on to explain, inevitably misconstrued the materialistic critique of the latter implicit in *Capital*: "[W]hat ... Lange has to say about the Hegelian method and my application of the same is simply childish. ... [H]e understands *rien* about Hegel's method and, therefore ... still less about my critical manner of applying it."[41]

As Karl Korsch suggests in a quotation that appears in the *Arcades*, the critique of Hegel implicit in *Capital* is not simply that his dialectical method is inverted or upside-down such that ideas appear to determine reality. Rather, Marx's criticism of Hegel's idealism is also directed at its claim to universality, the fact in the dialectic denies its own historicity as a movement that arises from a specific form of society. Such an idealism, as Korsch emphasizes, cannot be overcome by simply putting it back on its feet and replacing it with an equally abstract and ahistorical form of materialism. It is for this reason precisely that *Capital* does not present an "all-comprehensive 'materialistic philosophy' embracing both nature and society, or a general philosophical interpretation of the universe."[42] Unlike Hegel, Marx does not "lay down any general propositions as to the essential nature of all society but merely describes the particular conditions and developmental tendencies inherent in the historical form of contemporary bourgeois society." What defines Marx's critical application of Hegel, therefore, is not just its materialism, but what Benjamin called the "[r]estriction of the materialist conception of history," the fact that Marx's use of the dialectical method recognizes its historical character.[43]

As both Marx and Engels insisted, it is this restriction that fundamentally distinguished their own historical method from Lange's naturalistic account of the bourgeois economy in *The Labor Question*. Instead of considering the specific conditions in which the struggle for existence occurs within capitalism, Lange, as Marx describes in a letter to Engels, does exactly the opposite. He begins with an apparently universal mechanical principle and then applies it to bourgeois society. "All history may be subsumed in one single great natural law ... the Malthusian law of ... over-population. Thus, instead of analysing this 'struggle for life' as it manifests itself historically in various specific forms of society," Lange "transpose[s] every given struggle into the phrase 'struggle for life.'"[44]

For Lange, then, the law of natural selection and overpopulation that underlies competition in capitalism applies to all forms of society. As Engels argued, however, survival in modern society does not solely depend upon natural conditions. For workers in capitalism, it also depends on the sale of their labor power as a commodity, which is an historically specific relationship of production: "the population exerts pressure on the means—not of subsistence, but of employment."[45] In capitalism, in other words, subsistence is mediated by the wage-labor relation. Labor must be exchanged for wages in order for workers to acquire what they need to survive. The survival of the population, therefore, does not rest solely on natural laws, laws that determine what Thomas Malthus referred to as "the power in the earth to produce subsistence for man."[46] Rather, survival also depends upon the economic law that regulates the exchange of commodities, a law that does not exist either in nature or in non-capitalist modes of production where products are not primarily produced for exchange.

As Engels suggests in his letter to Lange, this law underlies the paradox in industrial capitalism whereby "modern machinery [creates] … unending commercial crises."[47] These crises are caused by the development of the forces of production, which increases the quantity of goods that can be created while reducing the labor required in order to do so. Since the value of goods is determined by labor time, in accordance with the law of exchange, by reducing the labor required to produce the means of subsistence, technology potentially reduces employment, which is a condition for obtaining the means of subsistence. As Marx argues, therefore, "The decrease of … necessary labour appears as increase of the relatively superfluous labouring capacities—i.e. as the positing of surplus population, hence becomes a tramp and a pauper."[48]

These superfluous individuals, then, are not the result of the Malthusian law of overpopulation. As Marx emphasizes, "it is … the means of *employment* and not of *subsistence* which put [the worker] into the category of surplus population."[49] In capitalism, therefore, the development of technology creates what Marx and Engels describe as crises "that, in all earlier epochs, would have seemed an absurdity … Society suddenly finds itself … cut off [from] the supply of every means of subsistence … [b]ecause there is … too much means of subsistence."[50] In capitalism, therefore, an increase in the means of subsistence which, in the natural world and in "all earlier epochs," would have alleviated the struggle for life, paradoxically increases its pressure.

In Lange's political theory, the resulting appearance of overpopulation and the increased competition for wage labor is understood, transhistorically, as an expression of the Darwinian process of evolution. To borrow Marx's criticism of Malthus, Lange explains "'over-population' by the eternal laws of nature, rather than the merely historical laws of the nature of capitalist production." As a result, "a particular kind of social production of a historical and transitory character" appears as a "necessity ordained by nature."[51]

As Engels argues, therefore, in his letter to Lange, Marx's critique of bourgeois political economy applies equally to Lange's socialist view of the labor question:

> The so-called "economic laws" are not eternal laws of nature but historical laws that appear and disappear, and … political economy … is for us merely a summary of the laws and conditions in which modern bourgeois society can exist … For us, therefore, none of these laws, insofar as it is an expression of purely bourgeois relations, is older than modern bourgeois society.[52]

Like political economy, then, Lange's socialism assumes that the relations and laws that exist within capitalism are eternal and unchangeable. In contrast to Marx's materialism, therefore, Lange's naturalistic account of the bourgeois economy disguises the transitory character of the society that it criticizes, the fact that its historical laws can "appear and disappear."[53]

Lange's neo-Kantian theory of socialism, in other words, is based on what Engels described in a letter to Mehring, which Benjamin cites, as "the bourgeois illusion of the eternity and finality of capitalist production."⁵⁴

As Marx argues in "Critique of the Gotha Program" (a program that Bernstein helped to develop), this ahistorical aspect of Lange's socialist Darwinism not only serves to undermine the possibility of abolishing capitalism. It leads to the concept of socialism as a morally rational accommodation to supposedly natural laws that belong to an historical and transitory mode of production. If the capitalist economy is a natural expression of the struggle for survival, then the poverty of the working class cannot be eliminated by abolishing the wage-labor relation. It can only be more fairly distributed in accordance with universal moral criteria.

> [I]f ... the Malthusian law of population (preached by Lange himself) ... is correct, then ... I cannot abolish the law even if I abolish wage labor ... because the law ... governs not only the system of wage labor but *every* social system. Basing themselves directly on this, the economists have been proving ... that socialism cannot abolish poverty, which has its basis in nature, but can only make it *general*, distributed simultaneously over the whole surface of society!⁵⁵

For Marx, therefore, Lang's account of the labor question leads to the concept of socialism as a morally rational version of capitalism, one in which the relations of production specific to bourgeois society are organized in a more equitable manner, in accordance with Kantian ethics.

This neo-Kantian conception of socialism is taken to task in Ernst Bloch's review of *History and Class Consciousness*, which Benjamin praised as "by far the best thing he has done in a long time," as a remarkable review of a book that is "very important, especially for me."⁵⁶ For Lukács, the work of the neo-Kantian school was defined by the "antinomies of bourgeois thought," a thought for which the "binary opposition of subject and object is fundamentally unsurpassable."⁵⁷ Unable to overcome the dichotomy, the neo-Kantian school was compelled to repeat it in various forms, including in the opposition between "historical materialism," caricatured as a reductive economism, and the categorical imperative, which transcends the empirical given. For the Marburg School, "all these dualistic pairs of concepts are equivalent: fact and ought—necessity and freedom—determinism and intuitive irrationalism—economically isolated vulgar Marxism and ethical supplement—fatalism and voluntarism—mechanism and religious utopia; they all stem from an immediate, undialectical attitude."⁵⁸ In the neo-Kantian criticism of capitalism, a purportedly eternal moral ideal is opposed to a particular form of society that is taken to be an eternal reality. As Lukács argues, therefore:

> Whenever the refusal of the subject simply to accept his empirically given existence takes the form of an "ought," this means that the immediately given empirical reality receives affirmation and consecration at the hands of philosophy: it is philosophically immortalised. "Nothing in the world of phenomena can be explained by the concept of freedom," Kant states, "the guiding thread in that sphere must always be the mechanics of nature."⁵⁹

Ethical Socialism and the Infinite Task

The Marxian critique of the neo-Kantian school was completely ignored by virtually all of its members, including Lange himself, who responded to Engel's reply by reasserting his ahistorical concept of capitalism. As Beiser describes, Lange, in later editions of the *Labor Question*, affirmed that "Competition and the need to subsist were basic natural facts behind social conflict. The power of a captain of industry over his workers was simply an expression of his dominant position in the struggle for existence."[60] Socialism, therefore, can only be achieved through an ethical struggle against this natural state of affairs.

In his theory of "ethical socialism," Cohen—despite his objection to the naturalistic foundation of Lange's political philosophy—would propose a similarly dualistic account of society. Society, according to Cohen, was divided, on the one hand, into a "labor society" (*Verkehrsgebiet*), which operates according to mechanical laws, and a "legal society" (*Herrschaftsgebiet*), in which relations between moral individuals are regulated according to the principle of freedom or moral autonomy "Cohen opposes in an abstract way freedom to causality, the moral to the economic."[61]

This opposition corresponds to the Kantian distinction between persons and property. While property can be exchanged for an equivalent, persons can never be treated as property. "Whatever has a price can be replaced by something else as its equivalent; on the other hand, whatever is above all price, and therefore admits of no equivalent, has a dignity."[62] As Kevin E. Dodson has argued, this distinction "provides the moral basis in Kant for the condemnation of capitalist relations of production."[63] Since the latter is based upon wage labor, and "wage-labor is nothing other than the sale of the use of one's body for a wage," persons are deprived of their dignity under capitalism.[64]

For Cohen, such a state of affairs would be one in which the mechanical causality of the "labor society" deprives individuals of their moral autonomy. "Consequently, a capitalist labor market is incompatible with one's dignity as a member of the realm of ends."[65] The "Marburg neo-Kantians," therefore, "insisted that the economic basis of liberalism was morally inconsistent with the Kantian idea of freedom," emphasizing the "incompatibility of the categorical imperative with capitalism."[66]

Against the reduction of people to things in bourgeois society, Cohen "asserts the priority of freedom over necessity, of the moral over the economic," identifying the Kantian "realm of ends," in which persons are all treated with dignity, with socialism itself: "For Cohen, that moral order in which the person becomes an independent value, an end and not merely a means, in which the categorical imperative becomes the norm of behavior, is socialism."

As Cohen argued, however, the dignity of the person, which is based on her moral autonomy, cannot be conceived as a thing that a person possesses, a view which he attributed to Kant.[67] Freedom is not a property that can be acquired or lost. Rather, it is an *activity* of the person that defines the latter as such: "Such an absolute beginning of action can be thought only in connection with the absolute ego of the acting person." For Cohen, therefore, the person is not a passive adherent of ethical maxims. Rather, the moral individual is only constituted as such through the exercise of its freedom, through the act of undertaking its ethical duty: "the ego should not be considered as given, but as a task."[68]

Since the ego as well as its freedom exists only in the task of achieving its moral autonomy, what "is important," from Cohen's perspective, "is not that attainment of the goals, but the moral movement towards it."[69] And because this movement is what constitutes freedom itself, it can never come to an end. "The whole content of moral willing," therefore, according to Cohen, "wishes nothing other than to remain an eternal task, which can never be an inert possession."[70]

For Cohen, moreover, the task of realizing a socialism conceived in Kantian terms as a kingdom of ends was one that he assigned to the "legal society," and specifically to the state, which was supposed to ensure that the economy conforms to morality. Because Cohen considered the state to be the "central agent for the institution and enforcement of ... economic justice," he "disapproved of anarchists and communists who wanted to abolish the state."[71]

For the latter, the state is only "an agent to protect the interests of the ruling class." As Cohen argued, however, this view fails to distinguish between the state as it is and as it ought to be, "between the empirical state and the state of right or justice." Because of this difference, it would be a *non sequitur* to assume that the state will always be an instrument of oppression, based on its present, empirical form. In politics, it is imprudent "to take experience and history as the guide for how things ought to be."[72]

This critique of anarchism and Marxism is based on the neo-Kantian notion of the infinite task. For Cohen, the latter defines the progress of science as well as society, as the latter develops toward ethical socialism. "In the Marburg view ... history was a never ending process of ... appropriation by man of the *a priori* principles of reason ... in scientific progress ... In the state and in society this process was marked by ethical progress ... [toward] the unreachable ideal—a ... moral existence."[73]

This idea of historical progress would appear to embody the same "ambiguity" that Benjamin attributed to the concept of science as an infinite task (see Chapter 1). Like the latter, justice appears in Cohen's philosophy as both an ideal that "requires an eternally long time" to accomplish and one that is inherently unachievable.[74] On the one hand, the ideal of an ethical state that does not serve the interest of capital is presented as a "goal of development" that the empirical state can attain, if only Marxists and anarchists were willing to wait. On the other hand, the ideal is *a priori* impossible since the difference between the ethical and empirical state is a condition of socialism itself, understood as a task as opposed to an inert possession or thing. The task, therefore, is necessarily endless, just as the movement toward moral autonomy must continue indefinitely as a condition of freedom itself. But in that case, the empirical state must remain a tool of oppression forever for the sake of preserving the ideal of ethical socialism. Because of this ambiguity, then, ethical socialism provides a permanent justification for capitalism.

This ambiguity also underlies Cohen's neo-Kantian conception of messianism, as a rational commitment to the infinite task of completely realizing the moral law and establishing the "dominion of the good on earth." For Cohen, "the Messiah's coming consists in nothing but the ultimate end of injustice ... Prophetic messianism is thus an expression of faith that humanity is making progress towards realizing ideal ethical laws," a progress that humanity can never achieve.

The ambiguity in the neo-Kantian notion of history, which Benjamin had identified in writings preceding the materialist phase of his work, is also noted in *History and Class Consciousness*. Because the ought, according to Lukács, "cannot arise" without the empirical reality to which it opposes itself, reality can never conform to morality. This "antinomy of bourgeois thought" underlies the neo-Kantian notion of the infinite task, which ambiguously attempts to achieve an ideal that is *a priori* impossible, since moral autonomy can only exist in opposition to that mechanical world that it seeks to transcend. "For the popular solution of an infinite progression [towards virtue, holiness], which Kant himself had already proposed, merely conceals the fact that the problem is insoluble." By "establishing the mechanics of nature as an unchangeable fact of existence … setting up a strict dualism of 'ought' and 'is,'" the neo-Kantian conception of history "rules out from the start" its completion. Having excluded the possibility that morality can ever be realized from the outset, neo-Kantianism then extends the task of achieving this impossible goal across the infinite duration of time. In *History and Class Consciousness*, this ambiguity is characterized in the following manner: "However, if a thing is theoretically impossible it cannot be first reduced to infinitesimal proportions and spread over an infinite process and then suddenly be made to reappear as a reality."[75] As Bloch describes in his review of Lukács's book, the result is an "abstract utopia" which, rather than reconciling morality and reality, "eternalis[es] the dualism between the kingdom of freedom and that of necessity."[76]

Neo-Kantianism and "Historical Materialism"

The concept of socialism as an infinite task is one that Cohen opposed to a sort of neo-Kantian caricature of Marxism, which Cohen and others in the Marburg School referred to as "historical materialism," an expression that Marx himself never used. According to Cohen, Marx's "understanding of history is the sharpest contradiction to ethical idealism, in which socialism both logically and historically has its roots."[77] While ethical socialism asserts the moral over the economic, historical materialism reduces people to things, freedom to mechanical causality.[78] Portraying Marxism "as vulgar materialism," Cohen argued that "man is depicted by Marxists as a passive victim of a causal chain."[79] For Cohen, then, Marx was a "narrow economic determinist."[80]

As Moran pointed out, this caricature is ubiquitous in the work of the neo-Kantian school. Despite the latter's diversity, the misrepresentation of Marx is repeated in almost identical terms by different philosophers, for whom Marx exemplifies a sort of cardinal philosophical error against which the school defined its idealism. Neo-Kantians "mostly direct their attack at Marx's philosophy." However:

> They do not make important distinctions, like some other critics of Marxism, between the position of Marx and the positions of Engels and Lenin. … Instead,

they identify Marx with ... historical materialism and argue that such a position is philosophically unsound and politically harmful.[81]

Such uninformed denunciations of "historical materialism," however, were not confined to the Marburg School. Heinrich Rickert, who criticized the school's assertion that reality is reducible to the concepts of natural science, rejected "historical materialism" in exactly the same manner as Cohen, describing it as a doctrine that collapses moral to mechanical causality. For Rickert, historical materialism is an attempt "to transform all history into economic history and then into natural science." As Georgi Plekhanov observed, this characterization of Marx's theory revealed that Rickert did not have "the foggiest notion of historical materialism." "Rickert thinks nothing of repudiating Marx's historical theory, [but] he does not consider it necessary to get to know it."[82]

In *The Problems of the Philosophy of History* (which Benjamin described as "an extremely wretched concoction"),[83] Georg Simmel presents a similarly sweeping condemnation of "so-called historical materialism" as a form of historiography. "According to this theory, the properties of economic life ... determine the whole of historical life: both ... religion and art, law and technology." As a theory of history, historical materialism is based upon the illegitimate "restriction of historical understanding ... to a certain singular province of [economic] interests." The result is a "temporal ... schematization of events" in which history is "causally reduced to relations of the productive process."[84]

Vorländer's Kantian Marxism

On the other hand, for younger members of the Marburg School, like Karl Vorländer, this reduction of history to economic conditions was not a "fundamental error," but "a defect that needs to be supplemented." The "deficiency," as Vorländer explains, "lies in the fact that Marx does not address ... the relationship between economics and ethics," but was interested only in identifying "which laws actually work within ... [the] economy." Historical materialism, then, is confined to an "objective analysis of the given," investigating only what *is* as opposed to what *ought to be*. But precisely because it only considers "social development from the causal point of view," it cannot conceive of history as a conscious ethical task.[85]

Marxism, therefore, is a "purely social-historical theory" that requires a "complementary standpoint," an "ethical standpoint," which neo-Kantianism alone was capable of providing:[86] "Vorländer believed that Cohen's critical method could provide a basis consistent with Marx' historical and political analysis." The combination, then, of Marx with Cohen's reading of Kant would create an "unshakable socialism rest[ing] on the eternally valid foundation of idealist factors!"[87] To borrow Benjamin's description of Eduard Fuchs, Vorländer was convinced by the "illusion" that a "moralistic consideration of history and ... historical materialism were in complete accord."[88]

While Cohen, therefore, had assumed that a socialism based on Kantian ethics required a rejection of historical materialism, Vorländer called for "a synthesis of Kant and Marx."[89] Despite the Kantian "reawakening" in philosophy, this reproachment had been delayed because communists were "suspicious of Neo-Kantianism," their leaders having developed their materialist doctrine on the foundation of an unscientific form of idealism.[90]

Yet, in spite of its sympathetic perspective on Marx, Vorländer's Kantian Marxism is founded on the same presupposition as Cohen's rejection of historical materialism. In both cases, a morality based on the universal criterion of the categorical imperative is opposed to a naturalized conception of the economy that identifies economic and natural laws on the basis of their mechanical character, a concept that is attributed to Marx.

This account of Marx's "objective analysis," however, conflates the *critique* of political economy with political economy itself, a discipline in which the laws that govern bourgeois society appear as a "necessity ordained by nature." For Marx, this mechanical causality is not an immutable fact, but a *social* necessity that defines a specific mode of production: The laws that "appear to the political economists' bourgeois consciousness to be ... self-evident" "bear the unmistakable stamp of belonging to a social formation in which the process of production has mastery over man."[91]

For Marx, then, the subordination of persons to the objective compulsion of economic relations, which deprives them of their moral autonomy, is not simply a given to be analyzed scientifically. Rather, it is the product of a particular kind of society that appears to be a natural condition. Marx's "objective analysis," therefore, is not solely concerned with identifying the laws underlying the bourgeois economy. Its primary aim is instead to unmask the economy as a transitory phenomenon, to reveal that "'economic laws' are not eternal laws of nature but historical laws that appear and disappear."[92]

Contrary to Vörlander, moreover, the critique of political economy does not disregard the relationship between economics and ethics. In contrast to neo-Kantianism, however, it does not abstractly oppose the one to the other in terms of the concepts of mechanical and moral causality. Rather, in Marx's analysis, the impersonal domination or heteronomy of the capitalist economy (and its apparently "nature-imposed necessity")[93] is grounded precisely in the freedom or moral autonomy that prevails in the exchange of commodities. Within the Marxian framework, the latter constitutes the historically determinate condition of the categories of Kantian ethics, including the concept of property as a thing that can be "replaced by ... its equivalent" and of the person who is inherently free and therefore cannot be exchanged. In the exchange of commodities, "the juridical moment of the Person enters ... as well as that of freedom."[94]

As Marx argues in *Capital*, the distinction between persons and property, which is assumed in Kant's axiom of right, defines the sphere of exchange within bourgeois society. As a "juridical relation ... between two wills," the exchange of commodities presupposes the freedom of the exchangers.[95] In order to voluntarily exchange what they own, individuals must be free in the sense that they are not the property of another. The juridical person, therefore, must be "the free proprietor of his own ... person," including her labor power.[96]

For Marx, however, the exchange of commodities is an act that not only coheres with the freedom of others, in accordance with the axiom of right. It also exactly conforms to the second formulation of the categorical imperative, to treat other persons "never simply as a means, but always at the same time as an end." This principle, according to Marx, is "presupposed as ... precondition of exchange." In the act of exchange, "individual A serves the need of individual B by means of the commodity *a* only in so far as ... individual B serves the need of individual A by means of the commodity *b*." "Each serves the other in order to serve himself; each makes use of the other, reciprocally, as his means." By treating the other person as means, "each arrives at his end ... each becomes means for the other ... only as end in himself."[97]

Although the "categorical imperative," then, as Ernst Bloch pointed out, in response to the neo-Kantian reading of Marx, "is by no means ... confined to the young Marx," "as alleged by [his] bisectors," it was not "transferred" without alteration "into the materialist philosophy of history." In his earlier writings, Marx appears to affirm Kant's moral philosophy as the very standpoint of critique: "The criticism of religion ends with the teaching that *man is the highest essence for man*—hence, with the *categoric imperative to overthrow all relations* in which man is a debased, enslaved, abandoned, despicable essence."[98] In *Capital*, on the other hand, the universal imperative to always treat others as ends is grounded in the historically determinate social relations that underlie capitalism, in particular, in the relation which arises from the exchange of commodities.

This relation, in which each individual is treated reciprocally as means and ends simultaneously, presupposes the commodity form. For Marx, the commodity is not only an object of utility. To borrow Kant's definition of property, it is a thing that "can be replaced by something else as its equivalent." As Marx argues, however, the value contained in commodities which allows them to be equated with other commodities is not a natural property, but a "fetishism which attaches itself to the products of labour as soon as they are produced as commodities." In a society in which use values are produced for exchange, products possess a "super-sensuous" quality, distinct from their physical properties, allowing them to be replaced for an equivalent quantity of that super-sensuous quality. Value, then, is a "super-natural" property that is created by the act of exchange:

> It is only by being exchanged that the products of labour acquire a socially uniform objectivity as values, which is distinct from their sensuously varied objectivity as articles of utility. This division of the product of labour into a useful thing and a thing possessing value appears in practice only when exchange has already acquired a sufficient extension and importance to allow useful things to be produced for the purpose of being exchanged.

Thus, the reciprocal freedom of juridical persons in the act of exchange—an act which appears in Marx's analysis as the practical basis of Kantian ethics and its "eternally valid foundations"[99]—presupposes the fetishism of commodities, as a phenomenon specific to capitalism. In the critique of political economy, as Korsch pointed out, such "high ideals of bourgeois society as that of the free, self-determining individual ... equality of all citizens in the exercise of their political rights, and ... in the eyes of the law, are now seen to be nothing but *correlative concepts to the Fetishism of the Commodity*, drawn from the existing system of exchange."[100]

As Marx argues, moreover, the fetishism that underlies the legal relations and political principles of bourgeois society also gives rise to the mechanical laws that regulate its economy. In the economy, the "magnitudes of value ... vary continually, independently of the will ... of the exchangers. Their own movement within society has for them the form of a movement made by things, and these things, far from being under their control, in fact control them."[101]

Contrary to Cohen's critique of "historical materialism," Marx, then, does not depict "man," deterministically, as a "passive victim of a causal chain."[102] Rather, in Marx's analysis, the economic laws that subsume individuals are characterized as an apparently "nature-imposed necessity," belonging to a specific mode of production, a social necessity which arises from the activity of morally autonomous persons. In capitalism, "individuals *seem* independent ... free to collide with one another and to engage in exchange within this freedom; but they appear thus only for someone who abstracts from the conditions ... [that] ... although created by society, appear as if they were natural conditions, not controllable by individuals."[103]

Contrary to Vorländer, therefore, Marx does not disregard the relationship between economics and ethics, a deficiency that can be corrected purportedly by simply adding Kant's moral philosophy to Marx's purely "objective analysis." Such a revision would result in the abstract representation of bourgeois society that Marx had already criticized, one in which a transhistorical notion of capitalism, as the product of natural conditions, is opposed to an apparently universal morality that applies to all forms of society.

But as such, the project that Kōjin Karatani proposed of transcoding "between the domains of ethics and political economy, between the Kantian critique and the Marxian critique," in order "to recover the significance of the critique common to both," is an untenable one.[104] The two forms of critique are irreconcilable. The Kantian critique of the "capitalist economy where people treat each other merely as a means" is based on a universal criterion that the critique of political economy sought to unmask as the principle of a morality that is specific to bourgeois civilization.

The Is and the Ought and the Real and the Rational: Immanent Critique and the Categorical Imperative

This disagreement between the critique of political economy and the neo-Kantian socialisms of Lange, Vorländer, and Cohen is rooted in a fundamental methodological difference. For the neo-Kantian school, "nothing could have been more regrettable and injurious from the point of view of the socialist movement than that its modern founders traced their intellectual ancestry back to Hegel." And according to Cohen, "nothing ... contributed so much to making philosophy contemptible in the prerevolutionary age than the reactionary motto of Hegel: The real is reasonable, and the reasonable is real."[105]

For Hegel, the real is rational and vice versa because society, as it exists in the present, necessarily conditions the ethical ideals that are applied in order to criticize it and to imagine a more perfect society in the future. Because "everyone is a son of his time ... [i]t is just as foolish to fancy that any philosophy can transcend its present world ... If a theory transgresses its time, and builds up a world as it ought to be, it ... gives room to every wandering fancy." Philosophy, then, "always comes too late" to "teach the world what it ought to be."[106]

For Cohen, this argument is contemptible because it collapses the Kantian distinction between the *is* and the *ought*, between society as it exists in the present and the way that it should be in a more virtuous future. In doing so, it "requires submission to every reality, however abhorrent it may appear to be from the ... socialist point of view."[107]

In the *Grundrisse* and *Capital*, Marx develops Hegel's reactionary justification for bourgeois society into a critique of "vulgar socialist" theories, like social democracy, that condemn capitalism from an ethical standpoint that claims to be universal. Because thought cannot overstep its own time, such criticisms of capitalism eternalize moral ideals that are rooted in its own social relations. The ought merely hypostatizes what is. For Marx, moral criticisms of capitalism, such as the one proposed of Pierre Proudhon, which are supposedly based on eternal ethical principles, unwittingly serve to conceal the historical and transitory character of the society that they seek to transcend:

> Proudhon creates his ideal of justice, of *"justice eternelle,"* from the juridical relations that correspond to the production of commodities: he thereby proves, to the consolation of all good petty bourgeois, that the production of commodities is a form as eternal as justice. Then he turns round and seeks to reform the actual production of commodities, and the corresponding legal system, in accordance with this ideal.[108]

In "Critique of the Gotha Program," Marx, as Benjamin notes in the "On the Concept of History," extends this argument to the founding political program of the Social Democratic Party. According to Marx, the apparently socialist idea of "equal right," proclaimed in the platform, is in fact a *"bourgeois right."* The principle that the worker should receive the equivalent "amount of labor which he has given to society" is the "same principle [that]... regulates the exchange of commodities, as far as this is exchange of equal values." As Marx argues, moreover, the existence of inequality in capitalism is not the result of an ethical failure to apply the ideal of equality in a categorical manner. On the contrary, it arises from the universal extension of this right, a right which belongs to bourgeois society. Because individuals are inherently unequal with respect to labor, applying the principle, universally, that everyone should receive the same for their work privileges those with greater ability. The right of equality thus "tacitly recognizes unequal individual endowment, and thus productive capacity, as a natural privilege. It is, therefore, a right of inequality, in its content, like every right." For Marx, then, the ideal of equality, which Social Democracy asserts as a socialist right, is directly opposed to the communist principle: "From each according to his ability, to each according to his needs!"[109]

From Marx's perspective, therefore, an ethical socialism, based on purportedly universal ideals, would only serve to eternalize legal relations specific to a society founded on the exchange of commodities, thereby foreclosing the possibility of abolishing capitalism. For thinkers such as Proudhon, who believed in a similar conception of socialism, history appears as a progressive struggle to recover an original condition of equality and freedom that has been corrupted by capitalism: "history has so far failed in every attempt to implement [freedom and equality] in their true manner, but … Proudhon … [has] discovered … and intend[s] now to supply the genuine history of these relations in place of the fake."[110] As Marx argues, however, the notion of an original state of equality is only a projection into the past of relations that arise from the exchange of commodities, a projection that conceals the latter's historically determinate character as the basis of capitalism. Thus hypostatized, these relations are then taken as socialist principles with which to establish a future society:

> [T]hose socialists … want to depict socialism as the realization of the ideals of bourgeois society articulated by the French revolution … demonstrate that exchange and exchange value … are originally (in time) or essentially (in their adequate form) a system of universal freedom and equality, but that they have been perverted by money, capital, etc.

For Marx, however, the contradictions to the ideals of freedom and equality that exist within capitalism cannot be removed by means of a more consistent application of these ideals. They result in fact from the very exercise of these rights: The "system of equality and freedom, and … the disturbances which they encounter in the further development of the system are disturbances inherent in it, are … the realization of equality and freedom, which prove to be inequality and unfreedom." As such, an ethical criticism of capitalism, such as the one proposed by Proudhon, "is just as pious as it is stupid." Since the right to equality, as Marx argues in the "Critique of the Gotha Program," creates inequality in applying an equal standard to inherently unequal individuals, the attempt to realize this right universally is a task that cannot be accomplished. Hence, Marx emphatically rejected the "superfluous business of realizing the ideal" of equality, as a principle rooted in the exchange of commodities.[111]

As the French philosopher Armand Cuvillier observed, therefore, in a passage quoted in the *Arcades*, the ideal of equal exchange was "in Proudhon's eyes, the very goal of progress. For Marx, it is quite otherwise. The determination of value by labor is not an ideal; it is a fact. It exists in our current society."[112] From Proudhon's perspective, therefore, history begins with an original state of equality and progresses toward this bourgeois ideal, which is taken as an eternal principle. Since the ideal is impossible to attain, the "superfluous business" of realizing it, according to Marx, is an unending task that serves to perpetuate the social relations that underlie bourgeois society.

In Convolute N, "On the Theory of Knowledge, Theory of Progress" (which contains passages dealing with the question of method), Benjamin presents what appears to be a succinct account of Marx's critique of Proudhon's vulgar socialism. The latter adopted a "concept of progress" that ran "counter to the critical theory of history ... the moment it ceased to be applied as a criterion to *specific* historical developments," as a criterion specific to bourgeois society.[113] The "idea of progress extended over the totality of recorded history," therefore, "is something peculiar to the satiated bourgeoisie."[114] The result was an "uncritical hypostatization rather than a critical interrogation" of the concept of progress, and its specific historical character. In this hypostatization of bourgeois society, progress serves "to measure the span between a legendary inception and a legendary end of history," between an original state of equality that never existed and the ideal of a classless society that can never be realized. A critical interrogation of this mythological view of bourgeois society must show that its development always achieves the opposite of its ideals, "outlin[ing] regression at least as sharply as it brings any progress into view."[115]

Marx's critique of the vulgar socialism of Proudhon and Social Democracy is one that Benjamin appears to appropriate in his own account of neo-Kantian socialism, as a doctrine in which the Marxian idea of "the classless society is defined as an infinite task." In the latter, according to Benjamin, the secularized conception of messianic time embodied in Marx's idea of a classless society is "elevated ... to an 'ideal,'" the ambiguous object of an infinite task: "Once the classless society had been defined as an infinite task, the empty and homogeneous time was transformed into an anteroom, so to speak, in which one could wait for the emergence of a revolutionary situation with more or less equal equanimity."

For Benjamin, then, the Marxian concept of a classless society is opposed to the neo-Kantian notion of an ethical socialism as an endless progression toward the bourgeois ideal of universal equality and freedom. In that sense, Marx's secularized messianism is incompatible with the prophetic messianism of the Marburg School, and its faith in an ideal that cannot be achieved. Against the school philosophy of Social Democracy, then, Benjamin will adopt the expression, "historical materialism," so derided by neo-Kantian thinkers, in order to define his own methodology.

This methodology, however, contrary to Wolin, will not adopt "communist principles as a compulsory ethical stance," a "vestige" of the "unyielding Kantian ethical standpoint," which Benjamin purportedly preserved from his youth. Benjamin did not embrace "the idea of communist praxis as the *historically appropriate embodiment of the categorical imperative*," an idea which resembles the neo-Kantian notion of socialism as an infinite ethical task.[116] Nor did he identify the practical application of the categorical imperative with the fulfillment of "messianic ends," as Cohen does in his own conception of messianism.[117] On the contrary, he argued that such ends do not "refer to the good will of the subject," and therefore cannot be formulated as a moral demand (see Chapter 2). But as such, Benjamin's turn to Marxism from 1924 cannot be described as the "bolshevization of an orthodox Kantian," as Sándor Radnóti asserted.[118] Rather, as the chapter will argue, his historical materialism will attempt to coordinate an unorthodox revision of Kant with an equally unorthodox reading of Marx, one that emphasizes the critique of political economy and its historically determinate analysis of bourgeois society.

Primal History and the Classless Society

The 1935 exposition on the *Arcades*, which Adorno described as "a wide-eyed presentation of mere facts" without any "theoretical answers to questions," appears in fact to present a complex theory of history in a highly condensed form.[119] According to Benjamin, the development of new means of production gives rise to "wish images" in which a "collective unconsciousness" seeks "to overcome … the inadequacies in the social organization of production."[120] The development of technology, then, arouses a collective desire to transform work and society.

The impulse to create a new future society necessitates a break with the "recent past," a break which then leads "the imagination back upon the primal past" (*Urgeschichte*), to an origin or "originary past" (*Ursprung*), which Benjamin identifies with the Marxist idea of a classless society.[121] Since the latter, in Marx's conception, as Benjamin argues in "On the Concept of History," refers to the messianic end of history, the primal past is also oriented toward the future. In the wish images inspired by technology, "the new and the old interpenetrate in fantastic fashion."[122]

This purportedly Marxist theory of history (which Adorno described as a vulgar tribute and a disservice to Marx) appears to coordinate the methodology that Benjamin developed in his habilitation on the mourning play with a particular interpretation of Marx's critical theory: The "baroque sense of history … impelled Benjamin's subsequent development of a materialist (and Marxist) conception of history."[123] As Benjamin explains in Convolute N, "On the Theory of Knowledge, Theory of Progress," the "concept of origin" was originally developed "in the *Trauerspiel* book … Now, in my work on the arcades I am equally concerned with fathoming an origin."[124]

In the dissertation, "primal history" is not used to refer to the historical past, but rather to events or phenomena that must be excluded or "sublimated" in order for history to appear as a coherent progression or process (see Chapter 3). Thus, Benjamin describes allegory as the "primal history" of the symbol because the symbol's seemingly indissoluble unity with its content or meaning denies the irreducibility of nature to symbolic representation, which is precisely the significance of allegory. Insofar as the symbol can never eliminate its irreducible difference from what it represents, the allegorical mode of perception, whose suppression is the origin of the symbol itself, is also its end, or its inevitable failure.

In the exposition, this conception of primal history as both origin and end is associated with the Marxist conception of a classless society, as the "dream" of a future that is "wedded to elements of primal history … that is, to elements of a classless society."[125] This concept, however, was not only inspired, as Adorno suggested, by "reactionary" ideas,[126] such as the theory of a prehistoric matriarchy proposed by Johann Jakob Bachofen and the notion of "collective unconscious," developed by Carl Jung and Ludwig Klages.[127] As Benjamin explains in an essay on Bachofen, the:

> picture of prehistory which swept aside everything that nineteenth-century common sense had imagined about the origins of society and religion … would … be of utmost interest to fascist theorists; but it appealed hardly less

to Marxist thinkers through its evocation of a communistic society at the dawn of history.[128]

The appeal of the concept of a primitive classless society for Marxist thinkers is a topic that is considered at length in Karl Korsch's *Karl Marx*, which was "one of Benjamin's main sources [on] ... Marxism," a source that introduced him "to an advanced understanding of Marxism."[129] According to Korsch, the existence of a "classless and Stateless 'primitive Communism'" at the origin of humanity (in "the earliest epochs of human society") was a historical fact of great methodological importance for Marx.[130] On the one hand, it presented a "critical challenge to the 'eternal truths' of the capitalist mode of production," to the tendency of political economy to portray earlier modes of production as imperfect or incomplete versions of bourgeois society.[131] For political economy, according to Marx, "forms of social production that preceded the bourgeois form, are treated by the bourgeoisie in much the same way as the Fathers of the Church treated pre-Christian religions."[132]

Contrary to Adorno's criticism, therefore, "the image of classlessness," as it appears in the exposé, is not "undialectically" "back-dated into myth, insofar as it is merely conjured up from the *arche* ... 'the Golden Age.'"[133] Such a mythological view of the classless society would not only be inconsistent with the criticism of bourgeois society developed by both Marx and Fourier, which used the concept of primitive communism to unmask capitalism's mythological understanding of its own historical origins. The notion of classlessness as a golden age also completely departs from the profane conception of paradise developed in Benjamin's pre-Marxists writings, as an origin that precedes the mythologies of both moral and mechanical reason.

In Marx's writings, however, the concept of primitive communism is used not only to criticize bourgeois political economists, but also to challenge the tendency of vulgar socialist critics of capitalism to imagine the future as a better version of bourgeois society. For thinkers like Karl Grün and Pierre Proudhon, socialism, as Marx pointed out, was simply a perfected form of present-day society, without the contradictions inherent to the capitalist mode of production.

In the seemingly opposing perspectives of political economy and vulgar socialism, therefore, history appears as progress toward the realization of the ideals of bourgeois society. In the bourgeois conception of history, the capitalist mode of production is assumed as both the origin and the end: "The idea of an historical past repeating itself in the future fits in very well with the bourgeois concept of development, with its glorification of existing bourgeois conditions."[134]

In his attempt to challenge "the 'eternal truths' of the capitalist mode of production," Fourier was "the first to break loose from the accepted single-track idea of progress." This effort would inform Benjamin's aim of developing an "historical materialism which has annihilated within itself the idea of progress." Like the concept of history proposed in Benjamin's early "metaphysical" writings, history as a unity or constellation of singular events, this historical materialism will seek to expose a virtual past concealed by the bourgeois notion of history as progress toward its own universal ideals. Just as a classicist misinterpretation concealed the existence of a German Baroque, categorizing it as a decadent form of Renaissance tragedy, so this bourgeois historicism, as

Benjamin writes in the *Arcades*, was "meant to cover up the revolutionary moments in the occurrence of history."¹³⁵

The *Arcades Project* and the Critique of Political Economy

It was only in the second stage of his research on the *Arcades*, from 1935 to 1939, that Benjamin would begin to incorporate Korsch's ideas, compiling Convolute X, devoted to Marx, which consists mainly of quotations taken from *Karl Marx*. As Susan Buck-Morss has noted, moreover, "evidence of real study of *Capital* does not appear until [this] second stage, although there is already a reference to 'the fetish character of commodities.'"¹³⁶

Benjamin met Korsch through Bertolt Brecht in 1930, three years after beginning the *Arcades Project*. The two thinkers, however, were already connected through the anarchist pedagogue, Gustav Wyneken. Korsch, who developed a theory of pedagogy based on Wyneken's teachings,¹³⁷ had been the chair of the Independent Students' Association, of which Benjamin would become the president of the Berlin University chapter in 1914.¹³⁸ Korsch's wife, Hedda Gagliardi, moreover, was a teacher at the Wickersdorf Free School Community, where Benjamin became a "strict and fanatical disciple of G. Wyneken."¹³⁹

Benjamin's engagement with Korsch's writings began in 1930, when he read *Marxism and Philosophy*.¹⁴⁰ The book, published in 1923, was written, however, at a time when Korsch "had but a simplistic understanding of the Marxian critique of political economy."¹⁴¹ In the text, Korsch argues "that the Hegelian dialectic was fundamental to Marxism,"¹⁴² a claim that was more famously made by Lukács in *History and Class Consciousness*.

This argument seems to have elicited a less than enthusiastic response from Benjamin, who described the book to Adorno as "faltering steps ... in the right direction."¹⁴³ As such, *Marxism and Philosophy* could not serve as a reliable guide to the theory in *Capital*, a theory which, as Benjamin admitted to Scholem, would have to be "stud[ied] ... [in order] to get anywhere and to provide a solid scaffolding" for the *Arcades*.¹⁴⁴ Although Korsch, therefore, was one of "Benjamin's main sources of knowledge regarding Marxism, and [is] ... cited extensively in *The Arcades Project*," *Marxism and Philosophy* is not mentioned at all in the manuscript.¹⁴⁵

Korsch's understanding of Marxism, however, had already begun to change along with his political views even before the book's publication. Following his involvement in the failed 1923 coalition between Communists and Social Democrats in Thuringia, which was crushed by the Reich, Korsch became wary of the "elitist ... prejudice" of the Communist Party, even though he would continue to adhere to its "Leninism until after his expulsion."¹⁴⁶ Korsch's rejection of Leninism, moreover, coincided with his discovery of "the fetishistic character of the categories of political economy,"¹⁴⁷ and the "principle of historical specificity," underlying Marx's critique of political economy. This critique, as Korsch explains in *Karl Marx*, published in 1938, "look[s] through those ... categories of the bourgeois economists, to disclose their 'fetish character,' and to demonstrate the specific social character of bourgeois commodity production."¹⁴⁸

In Marx's analysis, then, "fetishism" refers to the way in which theories such as political economy confer an eternal appearance upon a particular mode of production, capitalism. "It is one of the chief failings of classical political-economy that it … treat[s] the form of value as something of indifference; something external to the nature of the commodity itself." In political economy, the commodity, which "stamps the bourgeois mode of production as a particular kind of social production of a historical and transitory character," is treated as the "eternal natural form of social production." For bourgeois society, then, political economy serves as a mystified form of self-understanding that "overlook[s] the specificity of the value-form," and therefore fetishizes the commodity-form.[149] By abstracting the latter from its historical and transitory character, political economy produces the image of bourgeois society as an eternal reality. "Marx," therefore, as Korsch pointed out, "scornfully dismissed the superficial and arbitrary procedure of the bourgeois social scientists who described the various conditions of different historical stages in the terms of the same general concepts and thus 'by a sleight of hand represented bourgeois conditions as unchangeable natural laws pertaining to society *in abstracto*.'"[150]

In the *Arcades Project*, Benjamin develops this critique of the fetishism of commodities into a concept of culture in bourgeois society as a phantasmagoria, belonging to an historically determinate mode of commodity production, that assumes an eternal appearance:

> The property appertaining to the commodity as its fetish character attaches as well to the commodity-producing society—not as it is in itself, to be sure, but more as it represents itself and thinks to understand itself whenever it abstracts from the fact that it produces precisely commodities. The image that it produces of itself in this way, and that it customarily labels as its culture, corresponds to the concept of phantasmagoria.[151]

In *Karl Marx*, Marx's historically specific critique is extended to Hegel's dialectic of history. Whereas Korsch, in the earlier text, had argued that the dialectic was "fundamental to Marxism," in the later work, he criticizes "German idealistic philosophers from Kant to Hegel" for treating the categories of bourgeois society as "timeless concept[s]."[152] Marx, then, as Korsch came to recognize, had not simply applied Hegel's philosophy to his criticism of capitalism. Rather, he "transplanted the dialectical method … from an idealistic to a materialistic basis."[153] The shift in Korsch's interpretation of *Capital* from *Marxism and Philosophy* to *Karl Marx* suggests an intellectual itinerary that parallels the development that Korsch attributes to Marx, who passed "from Hegelian idealism to his later materialistic theory."[154]

As Korsch argued, however, what defines Hegel's idealism is not that his dialectical method is upside-down or inverted, such that ideas appear to determine reality. Rather, the idealism of Hegel's philosophy lies in its claim to universality, the fact that its dialectic does not appear to be a product of the particular form of society from which it emerged. Such an idealism cannot be corrected by simply replacing it with an equally ahistorical form of materialism. As Korsch explains, therefore, in a passage quoted in Convolute N, the critique of political economy does not provide an "all-comprehensive 'materialistic philosophy' embracing both nature and society, or a general philosophical interpretation of the universe."[155] Unlike Hegel, Marx does not "lay down any general propositions as to the essential nature of all society but merely describes the particular conditions and developmental tendencies inherent in the historical form of contemporary bourgeois society."[156] Instead of taking "its departure from a preconceived and dogmatic principle,"[157] like that of a universal dialectic of history, Marx attributes this movement, along with its apparently "super-historical" character, to the specific conditions that define bourgeois society. What distinguishes Marx's critique from Hegel's philosophy, then, is not its materialism, but what Benjamin calls the "[r]estriction of the materialist conception of history," the fact that Marx's materialism acknowledges its own historicity.

According to Franz Borkenau, this interpretation of *Capital*, which underscored its critique of both the historically determinant character of bourgeois society and the dialectical method that Hegel used to study it, was far more faithful to Marx than that of Korsch's contemporaries: Korsch's "Marx-study [is] most solidly close to the actual teaching of Marx. Where every other author instinctively attempts to reinterpret Marx on his own lines of thought."[158] Korsch's interpretation, therefore, was distinguished from other versions of Marxism, including that of the Communist Party, by its fidelity to "Marx's own Marxism." As Korsch argues in *Karl Marx*, the "most important point made in Marx's historical materialism was later missed ... by those 'orthodox' Marx-interpreters who themselves combatted ... all attempts ... to 'revise Marxism.'" In response to critiques by the neo-Kantian school, these interpreters "wanted to strengthen the materialistic character of the Marxian science by giving it a philosophical interpretation," transforming its historically specific analysis of capitalism into timeless materialist principles. This ahistorical reading of *Capital* "reintroduced ... backward philosophical attitudes into a theory which Marx had previously transformed from a philosophy into a veritable science."[159] In the work of "Marxist epigones," the "formulas of materialist history that were applied by Marx and Engels ... solely to the ... investigation of bourgeois society ... have been detached ... from this specific application ... and out of so-called historical materialism they have made a universal ... sociological theory."[160] In the name of orthodoxy, therefore, these strict disciples of Marx misrepresented his criticism of capitalism by elevating it to an "all-comprehensive 'materialistic philosophy,'" a form of materialism that Marx had denounced as idealism. Thus, as Benjamin observed, "*Das Kapital* has by no means passed through the hands of all Marxists," including the most orthodox ones.[161] On the other hand, by remaining "close to the actual teaching of Marx," "Korsch ... attempted to turn the critical tools of Marxism on Marxism itself."[162]

The Philosophy of Money and the Critique of Political Economy

This criticism of orthodox Marxism is one that Benjamin would incorporate into the *Arcades* during the second phase of his work on the project. In a letter to Scholem in 1935, he announced that the "focus" of the *Arcades* "will be on ... the fetish character of commodities."[163] Benjamin would begin studying *Capital* the same year, at a moment when many of his contacts in the French intellectual scene were becoming more interested in the young Hegelian Marx, popularized by Alexandre Kojève. In his celebrated lectures on Hegel, Kojève presented an "anthropologistic" (mis)interpretation of the *Phenomenology of Spirit*,[164] one which resonated with the humanism that prevailed during the period.[165] While Kojève's introduction to the dialectical method "flabbergasted" his French audience—which included André Breton, Georges Bataille, and Roger Caillois—they failed to impress Benjamin, who criticized the lectures in a letter to Horkheimer.[166] The "seminar on the 'Phenomenology,'" from which "some of the Surrealists [as well as] ... the 'Acéphale' circle," "received their information on dialectics," was "highly contestable," showing a lack of "proficiency in materialist dialectics."[167]

For Benjamin, moreover, it was precisely because the old materialist Marx now appeared to be completely outmoded that it was necessary at last to study his writings: "Brecht found me in the garden reading *Capital*. Brecht: 'I think it's very good that you're studying Marx just now, at a time when one comes across him less and less [...]' I replied that I prefer studying the most talked-about authors when they were out of fashion."[168] Several months later, Benjamin would supplement his study of *Capital* by reading Korsch's *Karl Marx*, which develops an ultra-leftist critique of orthodox Marxism by returning to Marx's later critical theory, at a time when it was more fashionable to look at his early Hegelian writings. As Eiland and Jennings describe, Korsch's "'riveting' book was in many ways Benjamin's most extensive encounter with Marx's own ideas; Korsch is cited in *The Arcades Project* more frequently than Marx himself."[169]

In the *Arcades*, furthermore, many of the quotations taken from *Karl Marx* are statements on the problem of method, on the historically determinant character of Marx's materialism, or his "[r]estriction of the materialist conception of history." Thus, in an entry in Convolute N, Korsch argues that what separates Marx's critique from Hegel's philosophy is the "rational principle of *specification*": "The real interest lies ... in the specific traits through which each particular historical society is distinguished from the common features of society in general."[170] In another passage, Korsch explains that the fetishistic "function" of political economy is to shift "responsibility for ... [the] hideousness [of] ... the present stage of development ... from the realm of human action to the sphere of so-called immutable, nature-ordained relations between things."[171] The categories of political economy, then, serve to eternalize the bourgeois mode of production, including the law that value is determined by labor, which regulates the exchange of commodities. As such, the "ultimate meaning of [the] ... law of value," discovered by political economy, is not that labor is the source of all wealth in every form of society. The aim of Marx's critique of political economy in fact was to show that the seemingly natural law is only the "*economic law of motion of modern society.*"[172]

This historical restriction, as Korsch points out in another quotation in Convolute N, is completely obscured in the orthodox interpretations of Marx, such as that of Plekhanov, which attempts to transform his historically specific critique into an all-encompassing materialist worldview. In the *Arcades* and "On the Concept of History," this critique of orthodox Marxism is applied to the concept of socialism developed by thinkers associated with the neo-Kantian school, including Georg Simmel, Paul Natorp, and August Stadler. The concept of "value" employed by this school was originally derived from political economy. Raising the concept to a "position of philosophical honour," neo-Kantian thinkers extended it beyond the restricted domain of exchange and production.[173] In "Literary History and the Study of Literature," Benjamin denounces the "proclamation of 'values'" underlying the "false universalism of the methods of cultural history ... as formulated by Rickert and Windelband." "[H]istory was distorted" by the development of "cultural sciences" based on universal values, on a "cult in which the 'eternal values' were celebrated."[174]

It was Simmel who was the first to apply this procedure to the Marxian critique of political economy, arguing that the concept of commodity fetishism is only a particular instance of a wider phenomenon: "The 'fetishism' which Marx assigned to economic commodities represents only a special case of this general fate of contents of culture," a fate in which objects "created by human subjects ... become alienated from ... their origin."[175] In this manner, a term that Marx uses in *Capital* to refer to the eternal appearance of a social relation that is specific to bourgeois society is redefined in Simmel's philosophy as the process through which culture in general reproduces itself by objectifying its contents. Thus, "Simmel deserves the reputation of being the first to claim to have generalised Marx."[176]

This project is one that Simmel pursues in the *Philosophy of Money*. In response to Adorno's criticism of the text, Benjamin defends Simmel's work as a book that contains significant insights, even though its principal arguments, which are critical of the theory developed in *Capital*, must be repudiated: "one can find much that is interesting in the book if one is resolved to disregard its basic thoughts. I was struck by the critique of Marx's theory of value."[177]

This critique is quoted at length in Convolute X.[178] As Simmel explains in the passage, there is a "fundamental connection" between Marx's conception of socialism and "the labour theory of value," which holds that "the value of a product ... is determined by the labour invested in it." The proposition, however, as Simmel points out, encounters an "insurmountable" difficulty, the existence of "valueless labour," forms of work that produce goods that do not have utility and therefore cannot be exchanged for an equivalent value. Valueless labor, then, violates the labor theory of value since it implies that "the value of labour is measured not by its amount but by the utility of its result!" If value, therefore, is determined by work, that is, if "all value is labour," the existence of valueless labor implies that this postulate cannot be reversed: It is not true that "all labour is value," since work that is useless does not possess value.[179]

But if value is not solely determined by labor, but also by its utility, this implies that some labor is more valuable than others. But as such, work is unequal. For Marx, according to Simmel, this inequality would be corrected in a classless society "in which the *utility value of objects, in relation to the labour time applied to them* forms *a constant*." A socialist society in which all workers are equal presupposes, therefore, the "equivalence of utility for all labour." As such, "to the motto of the labour theory, that [all] labour ... is of equal value," Marx, as Simmel suggests, "added the further motto, that ... no labour would be less useful than any other." In a socialist society in which the labor theory of value prevails, all work, then, must be equally useful.[180]

As Simmel argues, however, "this completely utopian state of affairs" would require that all social production be limited to "the immediately essential, unquestionably basic life necessities," restricted to "the most primitive ... and most average objects." To guarantee that all work is equal in value, the labor performed by society as a whole must be restricted only to what is necessary, and therefore undeniably useful. Only this could ensure that the "amount of labour ... performed in each sphere of production ... exactly covers the part of each need that is circumscribed by it." But in that case, socialism requires a "completely rationalized ... economic order," one in which planning ensures that production corresponds to a "unified total societal need." Such a utopia, however, would only be possible on the basis of an "absolute knowledge of needs and the labour requirements for each product."[181]

But because an absolute knowledge of needs is impossible, "no regulation of the amounts of production could bring about a situation in which the relationship between need and labour applied was everywhere the same." Socialism, therefore, according to Simmel, can never exist in reality. Instead, it must be conceived as an infinite task, an "approximation to ... [a] completely utopian state of affairs."[182] In the *Philosophy of Money*, therefore, "Simmel," as Benjamin notes, "goes on to reproach Marx, as it appears, for confusing a statement of fact with a demand," for confusing what is with what ought to be.[183] In the passage quoted in Convolute X, Simmel concludes, then, that a socialism consistent with Marx's labor theory of value would be an unachievable goal.

At the end of the entry from the *Philosophy of Money*, Benjamin states that Simmel's "critique" should be compared to "the counter-critique of this standpoint by Korsch."[184] This counter-critique, taken from *Karl Marx*, is quoted "in opposition to Simmel" a few entries later.[185] Reading it together with the passage from the *Philosophy of Money*, the quotation from Korsch appears like a direct refutation of what Simmel describes as the "motto of the labour theory, that labour is indeed labour and as such is of equal value," a motto which he incorrectly attributes to *Capital*, but which would be a better description of the neo-Kantian view on the labor question.[186]

For Marx, as Korsch explains in the counter-critique, the "idea that there is an 'equality' inherent in all kinds of labor ... which forms the basis of the economic concept of value, is [not] ... a natural condition." Equality is not a condition for socialism, a moral demand that Marx confused for a "statement of fact." Rather, it is a presupposition of "present-day capitalist 'commodity production.'"[187] The exchange of commodities presupposes the equality of all useful labor, which makes it possible to equate the different use values or goods they produce according to the law defined by the labor theory of value.

Like other neo-Kantian readers of *Capital*, then, Simmel conflates Marx's critique of political economy with political economy itself, a discipline that assumes that its labor theory of value is universally valid. For Marx, on the other hand, the law that value is determined by labor time is one that only prevails in societies in which goods are produced for exchange. Despite its discovery of the law that underlies bourgeois society, political economy, then, is unable to grasp the latter's historically determinate character. For political economy, therefore, the fetishism of commodities, in which goods appear to embody a super-sensuous quality or "phantom objectivity" that makes them exchangeable, is a natural state of affairs:

> [The] scientific discovery that the products of labour, in so far as they are values, are merely the material expression of the human labour expended to produce them ... by no means banishes the semblance of objectivity possessed by the social characteristics of labour. Something which is only valid for this particular form of production, the production of commodities ... appears ... to be just as ultimately valid as the fact that the scientific dissection of the air into its component parts left the atmosphere itself unaltered in its physical configuration.[188]

In political economy, then, the "scientific discovery" of a transitory law, which can appear and disappear, is mistaken for an immutable fact, like those uncovered by empirical science. Failing to grasp its historical character, Simmel, attributing the discovery to *Capital*, criticizes Marx's "labor theory of value by arguing more generally that people in all societies place value on items in light of their relative desirability and scarcity."[189] In this way, Simmel, as Karl Mannheim points out, "abstracted, in a completely unhistorical manner, the capitalistic money form from its capitalistic background and imputed the characteristic structural change to 'money as such.'"[190] Insofar as money, in Marx's analysis, is the universal equivalent to the super-sensuous property of value contained in commodities, Simmel's philosophy of money "general[izes] Marx's theory of commodity fetishism."[191] Whereas the latter, for Marx, is a "semblance of objectivity" that use values acquire only in capitalism, for Simmel, this semblance is a universal phenomenon, just as the law that value is determined by labor applies to every society.

In the *Philosophy of Money*, then, as Benjamin argues, summarizing Korsch counter-critique, an historically determinate theory of money and labor in bourgeois society is transformed into a theory of money as such and labor in general: "The petty-bourgeois-idealist theory of labor is given an unsurpassed formulation in Simmel, for whom it figures as the theory of labor per se. And with this, the moralistic element—here in antimaterialist form—is registered very clearly."[192]

The "moralistic element" to which Benjamin appears to refer is the concept of socialism that Simmel derives from his ahistorical and "antimaterialist" interpretation of *Capital*. In the latter, socialism appears, as it does in Lange's reply to the labor question, as a moral accommodation to a seemingly universal law that belongs, in fact, to a particular mode of production, a moral demand which Simmel describes as an impossible task. Contrary to Simmel, however, the concept of socialism that Marx proposes in *Capital* is not one in which the labor theory of value is realized by restricting society to producing only objects of utility. As Benjamin argues "in opposition to Simmel," "useful things are, according to Marx, effectively different also under the regime of the law of value," that is, under capitalism.[193]

This argument is taken from another passage in *Karl Marx*, which is also quoted in Convolute X. "With Marx," as Korsch explains in the passage, "use value is not defined as a use value in general, but as the *use value of a commodity*. This use value inherent in commodities ... is, however, not merely an extra-economic presupposition of their 'value.' It is an element of the value."[194] If Marx, then, in "*Capital*," according to Simmel, "argues that the precondition of all value, of the labour theory too, is use value," this claim is not a general one that applies to every form of society.[195] Rather, it extends only to a society in which goods are produced as commodities, which, in Marx's analysis, must possess the dual character of being both use and exchange values. Because commodities are exchanged for other commodities, all commodities must also embody a common value that is distinct from their utility, a value measured in terms of an equal "abstract human labor" that makes them equivalent and therefore exchangeable. Thus, as Marx explains in a passage cited in Convolute X: "The body of the commodity ... figures as the materialization of human labor in the abstract, and is at the same time the product of some specifically useful concrete labor. This concrete labor becomes, therefore, the medium for expressing abstract human labor."[196]

In the *Philosophy of Money*, this duality of use and exchange value, underlying the exchange of commodities (in accordance with a labor theory of value that prevails only in capitalism), is interpreted as an insuperable obstacle to creating a classless society, based on the equality of labor. As Korsch noted, however, this "'vulgar' socialism," which Marx had rejected as "economically false" in his criticism of Social Democracy, was "unjustly imputed to scientific socialism by its bourgeois critics."[197] From Marx's perspective, this vulgar socialism commits an error similar to that of political economy, portraying the future as opposed to the past in terms of relations specific to capitalism: In "attempting to portray a socialist future, [it] at bottom only idealized the existing conditions of society." As a result, the idea of a classless society becomes in unachievable goal.[198]

Benjamin's use in Convolute X of Korsch's historically specific interpretation of *Capital* as a rejoinder to Simmel's generalizing account of the commodity form suggests an understanding of Marx that departs from Wolin's characterization of the exposé. According to Wolin, "Benjamin's draft aims not at the dialectical *Aufhebung* of commodity society but at an irrationalist regression to a mythical, pristine stage of civilization which has yet to be tainted by the capitalist division of labor and the fatal separation between the 'use value' and 'exchange value' of goods."[199] What the entries in Convolute X suggest, however, is a critique of a neo-Kantian misreading of Marx that universalizes the categories of use and exchange value, projecting them into a socialist future in which the capitalist law of equal exchange is finally realized.

6

Fourier or the Arcades: The Liberation of Work and Desire or an Eternity of the New

Marx and Fourier

According to Karl Korsch, the use of the concept of a classless society to challenge the tendency to eternalize capitalism was a strategy that Marx had derived from an earlier thinker. "Marx ... only continued, in a more highly developed form, the 'criticism of civilization' which had been initiated ... by the first great Utopian socialist ... Charles Fourier in his vital attack on the self-complacent assurance of the bourgeois conception of the world."[1] Although the political impact of Fourier's writings gradually waned during the nineteenth century, his methodology, nevertheless, would leave an indelible mark upon later critics of capitalism. As Auguste Pinloche pointed out (in a work that Benjamin reviewed), Fourier's ideas had "an undeniable continuous influence on the development of socialism, less perhaps because their *practical* value ... than their *critical* value," which was "recognized by ... Marxism despite serious differences."[2]

Fourier's utopianism, then, did not precede the development of a scientific understanding of capitalism. Rather, it was "the great precursor of modern scientific socialism, the first to predict and analyze the mechanism of the capitalist regime."[3] According to Arnold Ruge, Fourier was "the father of modern scientific socialism," and "Marx and his principal collaborators recognized in Fourier ... the patriarch of contemporary socialism."[4] Marx's debt to Fourier in fact was such that: "One can understand nothing of [his] work ... if one does not know the Fourierist lineage of his principal conceptions."[5]

While the critique of political economy, moreover, provides, in large part, only a negative picture of a post-capitalist society, the few concrete descriptions of communism that do appear in Marx's writings are unmistakably colored by Fourier's account of utopia: "The constructive part of Marx is clearly Phalansterian."[6] Moreover, instead of rejecting Fourier's socialism as unscientific, Marx appropriated his method, his "attack on the self-complacent assurance of the bourgeois conception of the world," in order to develop a theory of capitalism based on the "principle of historical specification."[7] Adopting the idea of a primitive communism—excluded by the bourgeois conception of history, which sees only itself in the past and the future—Fourier was "the first to break loose from the accepted single-track idea of progress":

> It is only with a knowledge of the totally non-bourgeois forms of a primitive society that it becomes possible for the social revolutionary to imagine a further development which will go beyond the bourgeois conditions of present-day society not only by a gradual readjustment of its existing pattern but by a fundamental change of the whole system.[8]

Just as the nineteenth-century "dream" of the future was "wedded to ... primal history," so the concept of a primitive classless society is wedded to the idea of a future that could only arise through a break with bourgeois society, rather than a progressive realization of its principles. As Korsch suggests, the collective unconscious from which such a wish image emerges differs as much from the unconscious of earlier epochs as the bourgeois mode of production differs from previous social formations, formations that it sees only as less developed forms of itself.

> There need be ... as little structural likeness between those primaeval conditions of humanity ... and the future conditions of a fully developed communist society, as there is at the present time between the "unconscious" elements of the mental structure of modern bourgeois man as recently disclosed by the psychoanalysts ... and the "corresponding" state ... of either primaeval man ...[9]

As Benjamin, moreover, observes in the exposé, the future beyond bourgeois society that Fourier envisioned was one that Marx had greatly admired, opposing it to the mediocre socialism and philistine moralizing of Fourier's critics. "Marx took a stand against Carl Grün in order to defend Fourier and to accentuate his 'colossal conception of man.'"[10] "Benjamin," then, as Löwy points out, "does not counterpoise Fourier to Marx—he carefully records all the instances when Marx or Engels praise the 'colossal conception of man' of the inventor of the phalansteries and his brilliant 'intuitions of a new world'—but to the vulgar Marxism shared by the main currents of the Left."[11]

In the passage on Grün from the *German Ideology* that Benjamin cites in the *Arcades*, Marx and Engels describe Fourier's colossal conception as that of a society beyond bourgeois civilization in which "the poorest member eats from forty dishes every day ... five meals ... daily [and] ... people live to ... 144."[12] Inspired by the development of the means of production, and taking the amorality of the market as his "point of departure," Fourier imagined a world of abundance in which "morality becomes superfluous." This future society would be based on the passions, rather than virtue or economic self-interest. "Thus, Fourier," as Benjamin explains in the *Arcades*, "views immoral businesses as a complement to idealist morality. To both he opposes his hedonistic materialism."[13]

In contrast to Grün, as well as to the ethical socialism of the neo-Kantian school, Fourier, then, did not simply criticize the market from the standpoint of morality, identifying the application of the categorical imperative with the abolition of capitalism.

Instead, he regarded morality and the bourgeois economy as complementary institutions, both of which would be overcome in his hedonistic utopia. As Pierre Klossowski points out in his recollections of Benjamin's exile in Paris, the historical condition for this utopia was the development of industrial technology. "Fourier envisaged an economy of abundance resulting ... from this free play of passions. At the point when abundance is within reach," it is time "to make way for a mankind liberated from social constraints, open to all the pleasures that are its due."[14]

Morality, Capitalism, and Happiness

This Fourierist view of utopia was one that Klossowski and the other members of the Collège de Sociologie, including Georges Bataille, "perceived to be [Benjamin's] most authentic depth."[15] Fourier's eudemonistic vision of communism, a wish image born of technology, is consistent, moreover, with the messianic (and nihilistic) conception of politics that appears in the "Theologico-Political Fragment," politics as the restitution of a "transient worldly existence." Like the Greek conception of ethics, this politics, as Giorgio Agamben as argued, is not oriented toward a religious form of salvation, a "spiritual *restitutio in integrum*," but aims at a worldly happiness or *eudaimonia*. This aspect of Benjamin's politics is also apparent in "On the Concept of History," where "happiness (*Gluck*) and redemption (*Erldsung*) are [seen as] inseparable," which suggests that "Benjamin's ideas on the philosophy of history" are directly related to his "theories of happiness."[16]

Although Benjamin first mentions Fourier's name in the essay on Goethe (1928), Fourier's work, according to Florent Perrier, only enters "into the heart of his reflections" beginning with "his review of the work by Pinloche's *Fourier et le socialisme* published in 1933." In his preface to the German edition of *Four Movements*, Benjamin remarks on the irony that Fourier is so often dismissed as a utopian thinker in spite of the fact that his work, compared to other critics of capitalism, is so remarkably detailed in its attempt to imagine an alternative to bourgeois society: "No one has been more exposed to the reproach of utopianism; but in no one else do we find a doctrine so animated by the desire to give concrete content to the idea of a better world."[17]

This idea of a better world was one that Benjamin, who had "boundless admiration" for Fourier, embraced in a "personal version of a 'phalansterial' renewal," a version of utopian socialism that he opposed to the "pre-fascist aestheticism" of Bataille's Acéphale group.[18] Benjamin's Marxism, then, sought "to reconcile Marx and Fourier": "he spoke to us of it as an 'esotericism' both 'erotic and artisanal' lying beneath his explicitly Marxist conceptions." In Benjamin's Fourierist Marxism, the "common ownership of the means of production," as Klossowski recalled:

> ... would allow the abolished social classes to be replaced by a society reorganised in terms of affective classes. A liberated industrial production, instead of subjugating affectivity, would allow its forms to flourish ... in the sense that work would be made the ally of avid desires, and would cease to be the punitive recompense for having them.[19]

In accordance with the messianic principle that "origin" or *Ursprung* "is the end," this concept of a future classless society is one in which the development of industrial technology would allow for a return to an original pre-ethical state. As Benjamin describes in the *Arcades*, Fourier viewed the "advent of machines" in the industrial era as a means for creating "the land of milk and honey, the primeval wish symbol that Fourier's Utopia has filled with new life."[20] Fourier's phalanstery, then, was a wish image, "[c]orresponding to the form of new means of production," which "deflect[s] the imagination ... given impetus by the new ... back upon the primal past ... to the elements of a classless society."[21]

Contrary to Karl Grün, this idea of the future, wedded to a primal past, is not an impracticable, decadent fantasy, the selfish dream of a society in which everyone follows their own inclination, incompatible with the strict socialist morality needed to overcome the vices of bourgeois society. (Such a morality, in fact, would have been inconsistent with the concept of revolution that Benjamin attributed to Marx: "Marx ... set himself the task of showing how the revolution could arise from its complete opposite, capitalism, without the need for any ethical change.") Fourier's phalanstery— in which morality as a "systematic endeavour to repress the human passions" is replaced by play or "impassioned work" as the organizing principle of society—was not simply a frivolous "expression of civilised egoism." On the contrary, as Engels observed, Fourier's ideal of the future was a rigorous deduction made by a philosopher who "use[d] the dialectic method in the same masterly way as his contemporary, Hegel," in spite of the fact that he had never read Hegel. As Benjamin noted, therefore, "we ... find dialectical interpretations in authors of the same period who certainly had no knowledge of Hegel—for example, in Fourier's assertion that all partial improvements in social conditions during the 'civilizing' process necessarily cause a deterioration in the status quo overall."[22]

Yet, instead of elaborating a philosophical justification for bourgeois society, and embracing an "absolute idealist faith in progress," Fourier, using "these same dialectics ... argues against talk about illimitable human perfectibility,"[23] against "all of our rantings about continuous progress."[24] For this reason, Marx, as Benjamin noted, "considered Fourier the only man besides Hegel to have revealed the essential mediocrity of the ... bourgeois."[25]

In contrast to Hegel, however, and his somber depiction of the end of history in capitalism, Fourier's dialectics portended a "humorous annihilation" of bourgeois society,[26] in which its obsolete mode of production would be replaced by another, based "on the model of children's play."[27] Using the same dialectics as Hegel to analyze bourgeois society, Fourier developed a concept of utopia that "annihilated within itself the idea of progress," progress that its proponents assumed would eventually create a morally perfect society. As Benjamin noted, however, this pessimism toward humanity's ability to achieve its moral ideals was matched by an equally fervent belief that society could realize a radical happiness by freeing itself by means of technology from the hypocrisy of morality and the contradictions of capitalism. "In Fourier's extravagant fantasies about the world of the Harmonians, there is as much mockery of present-day humanity as there is faith in a humanity of the future."[28]

This future humanity is not that of a society that eventually actualizes the bourgeois ideals of the French Revolution. Rather, it is a humanity that will at last be relieved of the interminable task of ethical progress, celebrated by Enlightenment thinkers, by creating a society based on the "creatures' enjoyment."[29] As Roland Barthes explains, the "motive behind all Fourierist construction … is not justice, equality, liberty, etc., it is pleasure. Fourierism is not a radical eudemonism. Fourierist pleasure … is very easy to define: it is sensual pleasure."[30] In Fourier's words, the system of phalansteries "that is going to succeed our civilized incoherence will have no place for moderation or equality or any other philosophical outlooks: it requires pure, ardent passions."[31]

Technology and Crises of Plethora

Applying the dialectical method, Fourier argued that the civilized incoherence of bourgeois society was a result of "contradictions which it constantly reproduces without being able to solve them." Capitalism continually "arrives at the very opposite to that which it wants to attain, or pretends to want to attain, so that … 'under civilization poverty is born of superabundance itself.'"[32] Because of this contradiction, capitalism makes it impossible for society to utilize the very abundance that the system produces, and therefore to realize Fourier's colossal conception of man.

If this conception seems unrealistic, it is not because it is inherently impossible and immoral that society could consume such abundance. Rather, it is because, in bourgeois civilization, affluence creates "crises from plethora" (*crises plethoriques*),[33] crises in which poverty, paradoxically, is born of abundance: "pauperism, chronic crises, unemployment and strikes" occur "with unprecedented accuracy and breadth."[34] This absurd state of affairs was justified by political economy, which Fourier called the "last child of philosophy … and a liar like his mother," a "bastard child" that served as the "science of the wealth of nations dying of hunger."[35] Having supplanted theology as the queen of the sciences, political economy makes an idol out of the market: the "golden calf of commerce [is] … turned into a social religion and a subject of academic debate."

In *Socialism: Utopian and Scientific*, Engels describes Fourier's account of crises of plethora in the following manner: "Commerce is at a stand-still, the markets are glutted, products accumulate, as multitudinous as they are unsaleable … factories are closed, the mass of the workers are in want of the means of subsistence, because they have produced too much of the means of subsistence."[36] This dialectical and historically specific analysis of the contradictory character of capitalism—which Fourier, according to Engels, "so clearly defined"—closely corresponds to the famous description of crises in capitalism that appears in the *Communist Manifesto*.[37] In modern "bourgeois society":

> … there breaks out an epidemic that, in all earlier epochs, would have seemed an absurdity—the epidemic of over-production. … [I]t appears as if a famine, a universal war of devastation, had cut off the supply of every means of subsistence; industry and commerce seem to be destroyed; and why? Because there is

too much civilisation, too much means of subsistence, too much industry, too much commerce.[38]

For Fourier, these crises of overproduction in which poverty absurdly arises from plethora expose the fundamental contradiction of capitalism as a civilization in which the "mode of production is in rebellion against the mode of exchange."[39] As Marx and Engels described, it was precisely this contradiction that Grün, in his criticism of Fourier, was unable to grasp, due to a tendency toward "unhistorical abstraction." Grün "forgets that over-production causes crises only through its influence on the exchange value of products."[40]

As Marx argues in *Capital*, this exchange value is paradoxically diminished by the superabundance produced by technological progress, in what Fourier describes, using the trope of personification, as an act of rebellion by the means of production against the exchange of commodities. This aspect of Marx's analysis, which was inherited partly from Fourier, was ignored by "the positivists among the Social Democratic theorists." "In the development of technology," these theorists, as Benjamin explains in the essay on Eduard Fuchs, were "able to see only the progress of natural science, not the concomitant retrogression of society. Positivism overlooked the fact that this development was decisively conditioned by capitalism."[41]

Contrary to Adorno, therefore, Benjamin's account of the "wish images" aroused by the development of the forces of production is not based on an "undialectical" and "linear … historical-developmental … relation to the future as utopia."[42] Rather, it is founded on an historically specific analysis of bourgeois society that identifies the Hegelian dialectic of history with the contradictory movement of capital and that conceives of utopia as a break with the "single-track idea of progress," suspending this dialectical movement. "This standstill is utopia and the dialectical image, therefore, dream image." The latter "justifies its violent expulsion from the continuum of historical process."[43]

The Primacy of the Thingly and the Fetishism of Commodities: Lukács' Reading of the *Trauerspiel* Book

The trope of personification, which Fourier uses in order to characterize crises in capitalism, is also frequently used in Benjamin's writings. This mode of expression is one that Benjamin, for example, discusses at length in the *Trauerspiel* book. In his commentary on the text, Lukács criticizes Benjamin's analysis of this trope, the personification of things in allegory and drama. According to Benjamin, a distinguishing feature of the *Trauerspiel* is its representation of the "efficacy of the thing," which corresponds to its secularized depiction of life: "For once human life has sunk into the bonds of the merely creaturely, the life of seemingly dead or inanimate things gains power over it as well."[44] As the characters in the *Trauerspiel* lose their control, when the tyrant loses his sovereignty, "the stage property manages with unceasing virtuosity to occupy the foreground."[45]

Freed of an "anthropomorphizing response" that perceives the natural world only as a reflection of human concerns, nature, in Benjamin's interpretation of allegory, is seen, in Lukács' words, in its "unfetishized thinghood." As Benjamin describes in the *Trauerspiel* book: "Allegorical personification has always pretended that its task was not to personify the thing but rather, by fitting it out as person, to give it a form only more imposing," "granting primacy to the thingly over the personal."[46]

For Lukács, this "entirely nihilistic" conception of allegory is contrary to the function of art as a reflection of the relationship between society and the natural world. By disrupting the "anthropomorphizing response" through which art personifies nature, allegorical representation, as Benjamin characterizes it, would deprive humanity of the very ability to conceive of itself as a subject. Since "mimetic art is man's striving for self-awareness in his relations with his proper sphere of activity in nature and society, it is evident that [Benjamin's] concern with allegory must undermine that universal humanity which is always present implicitly in aesthetic reflection." In allegory, then, the representation of nature as a completely de-fetishized objectivity, in which man can no longer recognize his reflection, becomes the image of a de-subjectivized humanity.[47]

But as such, according to Lukács, this concept of a completely "unfetishized thinghood" is more accurately understood as exactly the opposite, *as fetishism itself*. Benjamin "ignores the fact that to give things a more imposing form is to fetishize them, in contrast to an anthropomorphizing mimetic art, with its inherent tendency to de-fetishization and its true knowledge of things as the mediators of human relations."[48] For Lukács, a totally de-fetishized nature, therefore, would be a completely de-humanized world, one in which objects that embody human relations appear as reified things that act independently of the persons who imbue them with meaning.

Thus, after praising the *Trauerspiel* book as "the most profound and original theorization" of the relationship between the Baroque and modernist art and ideology, Lukács goes on to describe its principal thesis as *ideology itself*, as an argument that affirms reification and capitalism.[49] Contrary to Benjamin, the "primal landscape" that allegory expresses is not an unfetishized natural world, free from all mythology and anthropomorphism. Rather, Benjamin's account of the allegorical "emblem expresses nothing if not an uncritically affirmed fetishization," a "capitalist fetishization of human relations into things."[50]

In his review of the *Trauerspiel* book, then, Lukács evokes Marx's critique of commodity fetishism against Benjamin's nihilistic conception of allegory, as the representation of an unfetishized nature. Like the commodity, this nature, which is in fact a "second nature" created by the capitalist mode of production, is a result of a "definite social relation between men" that "assumes ... the fantastic form of a relation between things."[51] If Benjamin's concept of natural history as a petrified landscape "deprived of its meaning" was taken, therefore, as Ferenc Fehér has argued, from Lukács' notion of reification, it also affirms reification in a manner that is completely opposed to Lukács' account of commodity fetishism.[52]

The critique of the nihilistic conception of allegory that Lukács presents in his review of the *Trauerspiel* book would appear to be exactly the opposite, moreover, of Adorno's critical comments on Benjamin's use of the concept of commodity fetishism. If the idea of a completely de-subjectivized thinghood amounts, in Lukács' view, to a "capitalist fetishization of human relations into things," in the Hornberg letter, Benjamin is accused of reducing commodity fetishism to a subjective illusion, just as the "dialectical image is psychologized as 'dream.'" As Adorno argues, however, the "fetish character of the commodity is not a fact of consciousness, but is dialectical in the crucial sense that it produces consciousness."[53] If Benjamin, then, interprets commodity fetishism in too subjective a manner, his concept of allegory is fetishistic because it completely eliminates all subjectivity in its account of the object.

The subjective account of commodity fetishism that Adorno attributes to Benjamin is inconsistent, however, with the non-psychologistic view of religion which Benjamin praises in "Problems in the Sociology of Language," written a year before the exposé was completed. Against the positivistic view of primitive religion embraced by "Durkheim's school," Benjamin approvingly cites the work of the anthropological economist, Olivier Leroy, which:

> counters the psychological interpretation of certain magical notions among primitives with an argument which is as simple as it is surprising. He insists that one must take account of the degree of reality, or of evidentiality, attributed to the objects of magical beliefs by the community upholding such beliefs ...[54]

In *Capital*, Marx applies a similar argument to the "political economists' bourgeois consciousness," which regards the "metaphysical subtleties and theological niceties" of the commodity form as a "self-evident and nature-imposed necessity." For Marx, then, the reality and evidentiality of magical beliefs, which ethnologists recognized in earlier modes of production, are also a fundamental feature of modern society. In capitalism, the exchange of commodities that constitutes the real economy is based on the collective illusion that products embody a supernatural property that makes them exchangeable. This critique of political economy is one that Benjamin would encounter in Korsch's interpretation of *Capital*: "By depending in their conscious actions upon such imaginary concepts [as value], the members of modern 'civilized' society are really, like the savage by his fetish, controlled by the work of their hands."[55]

As for Lukács' criticism of Benjamin's purportedly fetishistic conception of allegory, it largely reproduces the "modern and untenable discourse concerning allegory and symbol," which the *Trauerspiel* book calls into question.[56] Contrary to Lukács, Benjamin does not merely overlook or ignore the fact that his nihilistic conception of allegory undermines the concept of art as the aesthetic reflection of a universal humanity, thereby unwittingly committing the error of reification. On the contrary, this is precisely the function that Benjamin deliberately assigns to the dialectic of allegory.

If Benjamin, then, as Jan Urbich has argued, employs, in the *Trauerspiel* book, a "dialectics of subject and object," this dialectic, nevertheless, is not oriented toward the latter's identity, revealing a humanized nature that appears as the mediator of social relations.[57] In the dialectical movement of allegory, this "tendency to de-fetishization," which would realize the "anthropomorphizing response to the world," is disrupted by the revelation of an "unfetishized thinghood" that undermines the vocation of art as the aesthetic reflection of a universal humanity. In allegory, in other words, the tendency toward an identity of subject and object is suspended in the image of death, in the "*facies hippocratica* of history as a petrified, primal landscape," which represents the irreducibility of nature to meaning: "death digs most deeply the jagged line of demarcation between physical nature and significance."[58]

Universalizing Commodity Fetishism

In his assessment of Benjamin's theory of allegory as "an uncritically affirmed fetishization," Lukács, moreover, appears to extend the concept of fetishism beyond his own definition of it as "a *specific* problem of … the age of modern capitalism."[59] As Eiland and Jennings point out, "Marx's more localized theory of commodity fetishism becomes, in Lukács's reformulation, a globalizing view of society as 'second nature.'"[60]

According to Korsch, the tendency to universalize Marx's historically specific analysis was common among both its defenders and critics,[61] including neo-Kantian thinkers like Simmel who presented the "petty-bourgeois-idealist theory of labor" as a "theory of labor per se."[62] As Lukács himself acknowledged, this neo-Kantian perspective informed his own interpretation of *Capital*: "it was Marx … that attracted me—and I saw him through spectacles tinged with Simmel … my knowledge of … Marx was greatly influenced by the philosophy … of Simmel … Not the least reasons being that this approach brought me closer to Marx, through a distorted way."[63]

Moreover, according to Gillian Rose, this tendency, which also defines Adorno's version of Marxism, is rooted in an inability on Lukács' part to "break out of the neo-Kantian paradigm." The work of Adorno and Lukács "has achieved renown as a Hegelian Marxism, but … the reception of Hegel and Marx on which it is based was determined by their neo-Kantian education." This Hegelian Marxism, therefore, "constitutes a neo-Kantian Marxism," one which, like Simmel's corrective to the naïve realism of historical materialism, universalizes social relations that are specific to capitalism. Adorno and Lukács "turned the neo-Kantian paradigm into a Marxist sociology of cultural forms by combining Simmel's philosophy of form with a selective generalization of Marx's theory of commodity fetishism."[64]

Similarly, in Adorno's dialectical materialism, the historically restricted conception of value in Marx's analysis is replaced, as Martin Jay has observed, by the universal idea of the "exchange principle."[65] Thus, in his criticism of the exposé on the *Arcades*, Adorno, for example, defines the commodity as "an alienated object in which use-value perishes," as though a commodity could remain a commodity without the dual character of use and exchange value that constitutes it as such.[66] In *Negative Dialectics*, moreover, use value is defined, trans-historically, as "Marxist terminology" for everything that "defies subsumption under identity."[67] The equation of different material products in terms of a theological or supernatural substance that is not "a geometrical, physical, chemical or other natural property of commodities" is identified with abstraction itself.

Whereas Korsch (in a passage cited in the *Arcades*) argues that, in Marx's analysis, "use value is not defined as a use value in general, but as the *use value of a commodity*,"[68]

Adorno, in a manner consistent with Simmel's generalization of Marx, identifies it with heterogeneity or "non-identity" as such. Use value, then, is equated with the "irreducibly qualitative," with everything that resists and has always resisted "identity-thinking" and its purely quantitative "measurement-category of comparability."[69] Like use value, therefore, exchange value is not a historically determinant concept, but rather an "age-old injustice. For the exchange of equivalents was based since time immemorial exactly on this, that something unequal was exchanged in its name, that the surplus-value of labor was appropriated."[70]

For Marx, on the other hand, as Benjamin recognized, the twofold character of the commodity form—as a useful thing that embodies an exchange value measured by labor time—was an historically determinate feature of the capitalist mode of production: "concrete labor becomes, therefore, the medium for expressing abstract human labor. In this latter is contained, as Marx believes, all the misery of the commodity-producing society."[71]

The transhistorical notion of use and exchange value that underlies Adorno's critique of "identity thinking" is consistent with the "generalization of Marx's theory of commodity fetishism," which Lukács derived from Simmel's neo-Kantian reading of *Capital*. For Marx, however, commodity fetishism was not simply a reification of social relations *in general*, such that the charge of fetishism can be leveled at anyone who ignores the "true knowledge of things as the mediators of human relations," or who grants "primacy to the thingly over the personal."[72] Rather, it refers to a "*definite* social relation between men," the exchange relation, through which the products of labor acquire a value that appears to determine their movement independently of their producers.[73]

As Benjamin notes in the *Arcades*, this form of fetishism had not yet been generalized during the period studied in the *Trauerspiel* book: "In the Baroque age, the fetish character of the commodity was still relatively undeveloped. And the commodity had not yet so deeply engraved its stigma—the proletarianization of the producers—on the process of production. Allegorical perception could thus constitute a style in the seventeenth century, in a way that it no longer could in the nineteenth."[74]

The Slave Revolt of Technology

As the statement implies, Benjamin associated the allegorical primacy of the thingly over the personal with an historical period that preceded the primacy of commodity fetishism, which suggests that the two kinds of primacy constitute distinct forms of the "efficacy of the thing." In Engels's description, moreover, of Fourier's view of the fundamental contradiction in capitalism, the primacy of the commodity form, arising out of the exchange relationship, is opposed to that of the means of production, which is personified as an agent of rebellion. In Fourier's "fetishistic" representation of the productive forces, therefore, machinery is portrayed as fighting against the fetishism that arises from the exchange of commodities. The efficacy of technology, then, as a physical thing, is opposed to the metaphysical agency of exchange value, which is a supernatural substance as opposed to a natural property of things. Because of this second nature, the natural tendency of technology to create a superabundance becomes the condition for crisis, mass employment, and poverty.

The difference between these two kinds of efficacy is one that Adorno overlooks in his recommendation in the Hornberg letter that Benjamin should refer to Lukács' notion of reification in order to correct the vulgar Marxist view of technology expressed in the exposé on the *Arcades*:

> The overvaluation of machine technology and the machine as such has always been a peculiarity of backward-looking bourgeois theories: the relations of production are obscured by abstract reference to the means of production.—the very important Hegelian concept of the second nature, subsequently taken up by Georg [Lukács] ... is relevant [here].[75]

For Adorno, therefore, the exposé was characterized by what Ferenc Fehér calls an "uncritical infatuation with technological process and its allegedly 'progressive' trend" in abolishing aura. This "reactionary" view of technology is inconsistent with the critique of reification, and of the "inauthenticity and the mechanically lifeless culture of modernity," which Benjamin had adopted in the *Trauerspiel* book. According to Michael Löwy, the "uncritical adherence to the promises of technological progress" was the product of "a brief experimental period," when Benjamin was "tempted" by "Soviet productivism," a "Soviet variant of the ideology of progress."[76] As a result, the texts from the period "are closer to a 'classical', if not orthodox, historical materialism."[77]

As Adorno argues, moreover, the uncritical celebration of the progressive tendencies of industrial machinery and the notion of primitive communism employed in the exposé are conjoined misconceptions or errors. In the *Arcades*, the fetishism or "overvaluation of machine technology," which Adorno describes as a bourgeois ideology, is combined with an equally fetishistic conception of the historical past. "It seems to me that your uncritical acceptance of the first appearance of technology is connected with your over-valuation of the archaic as such."[78]

Contrary to such criticisms, Benjamin had not unwittingly adopted a bourgeois or Soviet view of technology, one that fails to perceive that the means of production can only be understood with reference to the social relations that determine their use. Rather, he held a different and opposing conception of the role of technology within bourgeois society. In "Theories of German Fascism," for example, Benjamin describes the primary cause of fascism and war in a manner that closely resembles Fourier's diagnosis of crises of plethora, in which the "mode of production is in rebellion against the mode of exchange." As Benjamin argues, similarly personifying the means of production, bourgeois society, "according to its economic nature ... cannot help but resolutely exclude technology's right of co-determination in the social order. Any future war will also be a slave revolt of technology."[79] Just as possessions, asserting their "good-right," resist attempts, such as Kant's, to reduce them to the status of bondsmen belonging to persons who appropriate them through labor, so in capitalist crises, technology refuses its bondage to bourgeois relations of property. War, then, as Benjamin argues in the work of art essay, is the result of "an uprising on the part of technology," rebelling against its "inadequate use in the process of production," where its ability to produce an abundance creates "unemployment and the lack of markets."[80]

As such, by enslaving technology, the bourgeois economy becomes subject to the whims of technology, which, in its "rebellion against the mode of exchange," creates crises of overproduction, leading to war: If "the natural use of productive forces is impeded by the property system, then the increase in technological means ... will press toward an unnatural use. This is found in war ... Instead of deploying power stations across the land, society deploys manpower in the form of armies."[81]

Capitalism, Life, and Technology

Benjamin's account of the slave revolt of technology differs from what Simmel, in the *Philosophy of Money*, calls the "revolt of objects." In the latter, the machines that humanity has enslaved overpower their masters, persons who, in a tragic reversal, become "slaves of the production process ... slaves of the products." The "machine, which was supposed to relieve man from his slave labour in relation to nature, has itself forced him to become a slave to it." "Man has thereby become estranged from himself."[82] In modern society, the domination of nature by means of technology results in a "dispensing of spirituality as the central point of life." Man is estranged from his human existence by the very technology that enhances his ability to exploit the natural world.

This view of machinery is consistent with the cosmic vitalism of Ludwig Klages, a vitalism which, as Wolin has argued, constituted a "defining moment" in Benjamin's "intellectual trajectory" and a "key to understanding Benjamin's development."[83] According to Klages, "technology is without the slightest capacity to enrich life" and is the principal cause of the "poverty of experience" in modern society.[84] Klages, therefore, opposed this impoverishment of existence to the "elemental" force of Eros. In the "cosmic" experience of intoxication or ecstasy, the boundary between subject and object is dissolved, while the mechanical concept of space and time is replaced by what Klages describes as a "perpetual present with a *boundlessly mobile now-point*" and a "*boundlessly mobile 'here.'*"[85]

This primal experience of the *hic et nunc* is "in complete opposition to logical consciousness, which—feeling its way along the straight line of time—considers each past thing to be destroyed." Against this impoverished conception of linear time, Klages opposed the Nietzschean "circle of time," a circle in which the "present ... sees only repetitions" of the past—"live, know, and teach the *eternal return of the origin*."[86]

As Benjamin argues, however, the "eternal return appears precisely as that 'shallow rationalism'" to which it opposes itself.[87] A universe in which every instant must be repeated *ad infinitum* is as meaningless as the concept of time in the natural sciences as an endless succession of identical moments. What this suggests is that contrary to Wolin, the "methodological cornerstone of the *Arcades Project*"—with its concepts of the "wish image" and the "primordial past"—does not "hinge ... on a theory of images or *Bilder* that is of specifically Klagean provenance."[88] Such an interpretation ignores the twofold critique of vitalism and rationalism that defines Benjamin's work as a whole.

In the early metaphysical phase of Benjamin's writings, this critique takes the form of the call for a "coming philosophy," "directed toward both the timeless validity of knowledge and the certainty of a temporal experience ... regarded as the immediate ... object of that knowledge." This theory of knowledge would demonstrate the validity of both mechanical reason and vitalist accounts of immediate ephemeral experience while simultaneously grasping the limits of each. In the *Arcades Project*, this critique takes the form of a "dialectical conception of historical time" that comprehends the concept of progress and eternal return as dialectical complements that exclude the possibility of a messianic suspension of history.

Benjamin also extends this dialectical criticism to Klages, explicitly repudiating the opposition between life and technology that underlies his "*cosmogonic Lebensphilosophie*." "There is no more insipid and shabby antithesis than that which reactionary thinkers like Klages try to set up between the symbol-space of nature and that of technology."[89] This shabby antithesis (which also informs non-Fascist theories like Lukács' account of reification) is a defining characteristic of bourgeois society. Because the latter, "according to its economic nature ... cannot help but insulate everything technological as much as possible from the so-called spiritual ... it cannot help but resolutely exclude technology's right of co-determination in the social order."

As Ricardo Ibarlucía has observed, Benjamin, then, did not share with thinkers like Ernst Jünger the "same concern about the growing mechanization of the *Lebenswelt*, which threatened to dissolve ... authentic ... experience." Benjamin's "revolutionary nihilism" was distinguished from Jünger's "anthropological nihilism" by its positive perspective on the profanatory effects of technology, which were inspired in part by Surrealism.[90] As Pierre Naville describes in *La Revolution et les intellectuels* (one of the main sources for Benjamin's 1929 article, "Surrealism: The Last Snapshot of the European Intelligentsia"), "what constitutes the riches of modern life, machines (more specifically: dominion of the metallurgic and textile industries, precision machinery, means of transport etc. and all their applications) are the matter in which the Surrealists, among others, have discovered the splendid."[91] If machinery, for Jünger and Klages, dissolved authentic experience, for the Surrealists, it was a source of profane revelation.

What this suggests is that Benjamin's affirmative view of technology was not simply the product of an "uncritical adherence to the promises of technological progress," to a vulgar "Soviet variant of the ideology of progress."[92] This ideology was opposed to the Marxian analysis of the "dialectic between the forces and relations of production," an analysis which, according to Irving Wohlfarth, provided Benjamin with a "one-way street out of Klages's *système sans issue*."[93]

Marx's analysis, however, departs from Lukács' account of the reification of labor and time. In capitalism, "time," according to Lukács, "is transformed into abstract, exactly measurable, physical space," creating an environment in which the process of production can be "scientifically and mechanically fragmented." As Konstantinos Kavoulakos has observed, this interpretation of Marx relies on "Bergson's antithesis between the mechanical-measurable time of natural science and the qualitatively determined time of experienced duration," which Benjamin viewed as dialectical complements.[94]

For Marx, however, the measurement of labor by mechanical time is not something specific to capitalism. On the contrary, the "economy of time," which presupposes its measurement, is "the first economic law on the basis of communal production. … However, this is essentially different from a measurement of exchange values (labour or products) by labour time."[95] The determination of the supernatural substance of value contained in commodities according to abstract labor time is different from the quantification of labor time required in order to organize social production in general.

This distinction is related to the one that the philosopher Hugo Fischer identifies in a work dealing with the concept of *Technik* in Marx, which is cited extensively in the *Arcades*. "'Time' in technology," according to Fischer, "has a meaning different from the one it has in modern economics, which … measures labor-time in terms of the clock."[96] Although economics uses the clock to measure the value of goods, mechanical time cannot be equated with the abstract labor time that determines the exchange value of commodities. As Benjamin notes in Convolute X, the "abstraction 'mere labor'" through which different commodities are "compared with one another quantitatively, in terms of duration … corresponds [to] nothing real."[97] Abstract labor, which embodies the socially average time it takes to produce a commodity, is not "a geometrical, physical, chemical or other natural property of commodities."[98] Rather, it quantifies an unreal "supernatural" substance, value, which, in contrast to the abstractions of science, belongs to a specific form of society, one which, by subordinating technology to the value relation, extends the domination of capital over humanity. The law that the "measurement of labour by its duration is expressed in the magnitude of the value of the product … bear[s] the unmistakable stamp of belonging to a social formation in which the process of production has mastery over man."[99]

As Marx argues, moreover, the magnitude of this property is inversely related to the productivity of concrete, useful labor, to the time required to produce particular objects of need. "In itself, an increase in the quantity of use-values constitutes an increase in material wealth. Two coats will clothe two men, one coat will only clothe one man, etc. Nevertheless, an increase in the amount of material wealth may correspond to a simultaneous fall in the magnitude of its value."[100] For Marx, therefore, the process of production in capitalism is not characterized by the quantification of labor and time, subjecting life to the alienating abstractions of mechanical reason. Rather, it is defined by the "contradictory movement," underlying crises of overproduction, which arises from the inverse relation between the time that labor, enhanced by technology, takes to produce material wealth and the abstraction of "mere labor" that is used to determine its value.

This contradiction between value and technology is elided in Simmel's account of modernity, in which the technical exploitation of nature results in a "dispensing of spirituality as the central point of life," and the enslavement of persons by the products they produce with technology. For Marx, the fetishistic inversion whereby the producers are dominated by the process of production in capitalism cannot be explained by the prevalence of technology alone. Rather, it is the result of the inverse relation between the productivity of the means of production and the law that value is determined by labor time, a historically determinate law which, for Simmel, exists in all forms of society. The law, however, that "labour is represented by the value of its product," which appears to the "a self-evident necessity imposed by Nature," belongs in fact to a particular "state of society, in which the process of production has the mastery over man, instead of being controlled by him."[101]

By generalizing the concept of value—a concept that is synonymous in Marx's analysis with commodity fetishism—Simmel deprives it of its critical function, that of unmasking the eternal appearance of an historical and transitory mode of production. As a consequence, a "dialectical inversion" arising from the "*capitalist* application of machinery"—in which "the most powerful instrument for reducing labour-time … becomes the most unfailing means" of increasing the exploitation of labor—is attributed to technology itself.

As Benjamin argued, however, the conflict that defines capitalism is not a "revolt of objects" against the producers who have become dependent upon them, thereby placing technology, rather than spirit, at the center of society. Instead, capitalism engenders a slave revolt of technology against a mode of exchange in which plethora becomes the cause of exploitation and economic catastrophe. This contradiction cannot be resolved by putting persons rather than things at the center of life, by elevating the spirit over machinery. As Benjamin notes in "The Author as Producer," "the revolutionary struggle is not between capitalism and spirit, but between capitalism and the proletariat."[102]

Contrary, however, to the doctrine of social democracy, a classless society cannot be achieved by using technology to dominate nature so as to liberate labor. "If the human being," as Benjamin explains in the *Arcades*, "were not *authentically* exploited, we would be spared the *inauthentic* talk of an exploitation of nature. This talk reinforces the semblance of 'value.'"[103] Rather, the contradiction between capitalism and technology can only be overcome by liberating the forces of production from the value relation that continually incites their rebellion: "technology will release them from their enslavement to the powers of the apparatus only when humanity's … constitution has adapted itself to the new productive forces which … technology has set free."[104]

For Benjamin, then, society will cease to be enslaved by technology only when it recognizes the right of technology to co-determine society, which would require abolishing a historically determinate mode of exchange that continually transforms abundance into catastrophe. By liberating technology, humanity could realize its genuine purpose, which is not "the mastery of nature but of the relation between nature and humanity," a relation which, in capitalism, is mediated by the commodity form. In Benjamin's words, the "description of the labor process in its relation to nature will necessarily bear the imprint of its social structure as well." In capitalism, this structure is based on "the semblance of 'value,' which accrues to raw materials only by virtue of an order of production founded on the exploitation of human labor."[105]

Since value is determined by labor, in accordance with the concept of work as the source of all wealth, the tendency of technology to reduce the need for direct human labor can never eliminate the exploitation of work, which is a condition of capital, regardless of the progress of technology. Indeed, because of the semblance of value imposed upon nature in capitalism (a nature which is assumed to be "there *gratis*" to be exploited by labor), "progress in the mastering of nature" is always accompanied by "regression in society." To suspend this contradictory movement, Benjamin, in his "personal version of a 'phalansterial' renewal," proposed a humorous annihilation of labor and the establishment of an "erotic and artisanal" future utopia in which work would be conducted "on the model of children's play." For Benjamin, only such a utopian program could avert the potential for war arising from crises of plethora, which is a result of technology revolting against its enslavement by capital.

This utopia, then, is not one in which humanity triumphs against the machine. Rather, to borrow Benjamin's description of cinema, the worker who was forced to "relinquish [his] humanity in the face of an apparatus" is redeemed in utopia not by "asserting his humanity ... against the apparatus, but by placing that apparatus in the service of his triumph."[106]

Excursus on Technology, the Impoverishment of Experience, and Play

The "personal version of a 'phalansterial' renewal," the idea of a utopia based on second technology and the transformation of work into play, which Benjamin adopted in his later historical materialist phase, is not a departure from the messianism of his early anarchist politics. Rather, it appears to be an extension of his early messianism, one that develops an seemingly marginal theme in his pre-Marxist writings—the theme of play.

In the essay, "Language in *Trauerspiel* and Tragedy," the profane form of redemption that Benjamin identifies with the *Trauerspiel* is tied to its playful representation of tragedy. In the *Trauerspiele*, it "is the necessity of redemption that constitutes the playful element." "For compared with the irrevocability of tragedy ... every product," in the *Trauerspiel*, "animated by a feeling (of sorrow) must be called a game."[107] By transforming tragedy into play, the Baroque drama separates history from its mythic appearance as destiny. The "dramatist prophetically deals a blow to the iron rule of fate." On the other hand, in "authentic tragedy," where "all playful elements are put to one side, we find not history ... but myth."[108]

This reduction of fate to a game (which reverses the process through which history is mythologized as tragedy) is achieved through the "device of reflection." "The action is playfully diminished by the reflections that Calderón's heroes always have at their fingertips."[109] In the *Trauerspiel* book, a quotation from the German playwright Daniel Casper von Lohenstein is cited as an example of the representation of the "logic of fate as a game." "As now the whole life's course of mortals tends to begin with games in childhood, so also life comes to an end in vain games."[110]

This description could also serve as a summary of Benjamin's own views on the subject of play. According to Benjamin, the habits that structure everyday life are a product of play. "For play and nothing else is the mother of every habit. Eating, sleeping, getting dressed, washing have to be instilled into the struggling little brat in a playful way, following the rhythm of nursery rhymes. Habit enters life as a game."[111] In that sense, life begins with play.

As Benjamin suggests in "Some Motifs in Baudelaire," the habits developed through play form the basis of practice, practice through which one acquires experience. Quoting Marx's account of handicraft labor, Benjamin writes that, with "practice as the basis, 'each particular area of production finds its appropriate technical form in *experience* and *slowly* perfects it."¹¹² Insofar as habits are the product of play, play, as Marina Montanelli observes, does not merely simulate practice, but constitutes its condition: "playful repetition is therefore the source of symbolic activity, the condition of possibility ... of experience and of the rules shaping it." Play, then, is not an imitation of life. Rather, play precedes *praxis* and constitutes the condition of experience itself. "For Benjamin ... the ludic repetition of children has to do with what makes a life possible: with the construction of experience, and with all those habits that form the necessary condition for any kind of orientation of an existence."¹¹³

In play, this orientation is achieved through repetition. The latter, according to Benjamin, "is the soul of play ... 'Do it again!'" The "great law that presides over the rules and rhythms of the entire world of play: the law of repetition." In play, the "obscure urge to repeat things is scarcely less powerful ... scarcely less cunning in its workings, than the sexual impulse in love. It is no accident that Freud has imagined he could detect an impulse 'beyond the pleasure principle' in it."¹¹⁴

In children, according to Freud, the urge to repeat is tied to the desire to control the environment and to contain their own fears. It "is clear that in their play children repeat everything that has made a great impression on them in real life, and that in doing so they abreact the strength of the impression and, as one might put it, make themselves master of the situation."¹¹⁵ As Michael Powers describes, "play," according to Freud, "can be seen as the first step in the development of a sort of defense mechanism, an ability to abstract oneself from, and become immune to, the intense singularity of the event."¹¹⁶ By mastering a situation through repetition, we simultaneously master ourselves, a self-mastery from which an ego emerges, according to Benjamin, opposing itself to external reality. "[W]e experiment early on with basic rhythms that proclaim themselves in their simplest forms in these sorts of games with inanimate objects. Or rather, these are the rhythms in which we first gain possession of ourselves."¹¹⁷

As that which conditions the formation of habit and experience, orienting our relationship with the world, play is also the site in which tradition itself is transmitted. "Echoing ... [the] view of play as a form of inheritance and cultural transmission, Benjamin emphasizes that the child not only receives the toy from elsewhere, but more specifically from adults, who belong to a prior generation." As Powers has noted, "play serves as the mediating figure responsible for transitioning ... carrying the child into the world of habit and convention, a world that has already been pre-coded and marked, the conventionalized perceptual world of the *Spielzeug*." Play, then, constitutes the second nature that is handed down by tradition.¹¹⁸

For Benjamin, however, repetition and play do not only serve to assimilate the child into tradition and into the world of adults. Contrary to Freud, and his famous account of the fort/da game, repetition "is not only the way to master frightening fundamental experiences—by deadening one's own response, by arbitrarily conjuring up experiences," in order to master oneself and the world.¹¹⁹ For Benjamin, this argument "adheres to the traditional, developmental view of children's play (i.e., in terms of reproductive processes of social assimilation and integration)."¹²⁰ In Benjamin's words, it assumes "the adult was the ideal in whose image the educator aspired to mold the child," and that the "child," therefore, "wants from her doll only what she sees and knows in adults," failing to see that the "infant as a creature shaped by a spirit of its own."¹²¹

Infancy, however, is not an imperfect form of adulthood. Nor is play an imitation of the activities of the parent. This is because play, according to Benjamin, does not *represent* actions but *repeats* a singular event: "Not a 'doing as if' but a 'doing the same thing over and over again,' the transformation of a shattering experience into habit— that is the essence of play." Play "means enjoying one's victories and triumphs over and over again, with total intensity. An adult relieves his heart from its terrors and doubles happiness by turning it into a story. A child creates the entire event anew and starts again right from the beginning."[122]

Thus, the impulse that animates play is not the desire to master oneself and the world. Like the epistemology the Marburg school, whose notion of consciousness was "formed in analogy to the empirical consciousness, which ... has objects confronting it," this Freudian view presupposes an opposition between subject and object that is only constituted in play. For Benjamin, on the other hand, the desire for mastery is not the origin of play, but a product of the obscure and more originary impulse to repeat. Play does not arise from a desire on the part of a subject to control its experience through representation, but from the urge of a child, who has not developed a self, to relive her experience in all of its power.

But as such, play does not simply serve as a means of learning how to perform the activities carried out by adults, allowing for the transmission of conventions through the formation of habits. Rather, just as the playful representation of tragedy robs it of the religious aura of fate, so the child's repetition of adult behavior has the "profanatory" effect of depriving it of its seriousness. According to Benjamin, this profanation is explicit in the case of the "oldest toys," which were "imposed on ... [children] as cult implements that became toys only afterward."[123] Thus secularized, cult implements, which were removed from all profane use, are returned to their original state as things existing outside of all relations of property, both human and divine.

In play, things, reduced to mere toys, are detached from the conventions that determine their value and use, just as mass reproduction decontextualizes the images it disseminates. And just as the historical materialist blasts a "specific life ... out of the homogenous course of history," so the child playing with inanimate objects detaches them from the tradition they are supposed to transmit. As Marina Montanelli describes, "in childhood ludic activity, the profanatory gesture is ... able to tear objects from their traditional and auratic context."[124] "Children thus produce their own small world of things within the greater one," a world of desacralized articles within an adult world of objects imbued with religious and practical value through repetition and play.[125] In this way, the "child disenchants the gloomy parental apartment," creating a "play space" or *Spielraum*, which Benjamin associates with the idea of a classless society. In play, "even the most princely doll becomes a capable proletarian comrade in the children's play commune."[126]

As a "site of conflict," therefore, play, which both constitutes experience and interrupts its transmission, can be understood as both the end and the origin of tradition. Repetition engenders the habits through which tradition reproduces itself even as it trivializes the conventions to which these habits conform. It assimilates children to the adult world of things while negating their sacred and economic significance, reducing the laws that regulate their use and exchange to the mere rules of a game, rules which, in contrast to tragedy, are not irrevocable. The urge to repeat that underlies play can serve to both reproduce specific social conventions and unmask their eternal appearance as second nature. To borrow Lohenstein's description of the course of an individual's life, tradition, for Benjamin, then, begins with play and "comes to an end in vain games."

In his later career, Benjamin would transpose this theory of play into a Marxist perspective, inflected by Fourier, inventing a materialism which, in contrast to the one presented in the *German Ideology*, takes play, rather than labor or *praxis*, as the "first premise of all human history."[127] As Benjamin argues in a review of Karl Gröber's *Children's Toys of Bygone Days*, both toys and play are influenced by "the economic and particularly the technological culture of the collective."[128] Play, therefore, is conditioned historically, and, as Benjamin argues in the work of art essay, it "can interest the dialectician only if it has a historical role."[129] Play, then, changes depending upon the state of technology and the economic organization of society, the rules of which are imposed upon play by adults who, assuming that children only wish to imitate their activities, try to assimilate them into the adult world of things.

As Benjamin argues, the development of technology in capitalism served to accelerate the impoverishment of experience, which already defined the context under which Kant undertook his critique, an impoverishment revealing a bare form of existence. This existence is that of the "naked man of the contemporary world who lies screaming like a newborn babe in the dirty diapers of the present."[130]

In the *Arcades*, Benjamin identifies the impoverishment that creates this naked humanity with crises in capitalism. Because "the security of the conditions of life was considerably diminished through an accelerated succession of crises," "habit," which is "the armature of long experience < *Erfahrung* >," became "decomposed." "Habit, in short, made ready to surrender some of its prerogatives."[131]

Under capitalism, traditional habits of hard work and economy appear obsolete in the face of the unpredictable fluctuation of value during crises of overproduction, just as the military expertise acquired in earlier conflicts was rendered irrelevant by the development of mechanical warfare: "For never has experience been more thoroughly belied than ... economic experience [was belied] by inflation, bodily experience by mechanical warfare."[132] Despite the mass death and destruction it engenders, modern warfare, which "appears to some ... as the highest revelation of existence," is as meaningless as mere recreation. "Gas warfare ... promises to give the war of the future a face which permanently displaces soldierly qualities by those of sports; all action will lose its military character and war will assume the countenance of record-setting."[133]

In the era of industrial capitalism, this destruction of experience is incorporated as a condition of the reproduction of capital. As Benjamin observes in "Some Motifs in Baudelaire," Marx's analysis of the industrial process of production is concerned not only with the exploitation of labor, but also with the impoverishment of experience that occurs in the "drilling" required for factory work. The latter, according to Benjamin, "must be differentiated from practice ... which was the sole determinant in handcrafting." Practice is a form of repetition through which workers acquire the experience needed to master a skill and to learn how to use the tools of their trade. In manufacturing, however, the worker, according to Marx, "does not make use of the working conditions. The working conditions make use of the worker." Since machines use the workers, their experience is irrelevant, and "practice counts for nothing in the factory." Whereas practice, in handicraft labor, improves the worker's ability, drilling develops a "greatly simplified specialty to the point of virtuosity, at the cost of overall production capacity ... turning the [worker's] lack of any development into a specialty."

Drilling, then, is a form of repetition that does not engender experience but impoverishes it, contributing to what Marx describes in a passage cited in the *Arcades* as the "abstract negation of the entire world of culture ... the regression to the *unnatural* simplicity of the *poor* ... man."[134] In the factory, the "unskilled worker ... degraded by machine training ... has been sealed off from experience," such that labor comes to resemble mechanical forms of mass entertainment. "What the amusement park achieves with its dodgem cars and other similar amusements is nothing but a taste of the training that the unskilled laborer undergoes in the factory."[135] With the rise of industrial capitalism, the destruction of experience in repetitive drilling forms the basis for extraction of value from unskilled labor. In this way, capital develops the means of exploiting the labor that machinery has made obsolete.

If drilling allows capital to appropriate value from the impoverishment of experience, in the phenomenon of fashion, the "old habit of slowly forming styles, schools, and reputations" is replaced by the endless cycle of novelty, which allows capital to overcome crises of overproduction.[136] In this way, social reproduction occurs not through the transmission of an unchanging tradition, but through its continual interruption and reconstitution. Just as capital, then, perpetuates work which technology transforms into play, so it invents new traditions and habits that it must constantly make obsolete in order to ensure its own reproduction. In this dialectic of the new and the ever-same, capitalism, refusing to die a natural death, continually increases the "scope for play" while denying the expanded potential for play for the sake of preserving the semblance of value.

This potential is one that Benjamin identifies with revolution itself, which aims to liberate labor by freeing technology from the fetters of a form of a society based on the domination of nature and work:

> This second technology is a system in which the mastering of elementary social forces is a precondition for playing ... with natural forces. ... For in revolutions, it is not only the second technology which asserts its claims vis-a-vis society. Because this technology aims at liberating human beings from drudgery, the individual suddenly sees his scope for play, his field of action [*Spielraum*], immeasurably expanded.[137]

This concept of revolution is opposed to the program of Social Democracy, which subscribed to "the illusion that the factory-labor set forth by the path of technological progress represented a political achievement."[138] For Benjamin, however, the exploitation of labor cannot be abolished by mastering nature by means of technology. Rather, in Benjamin's Marxist and messianic scheme of salvation, the development of a first technology, which aims to dominate nature, gives rise to a second which, freed from the value relation, could redeem the impoverishment of factory labor by transforming work into play. As Benjamin notes, such a program was formulated by Fourier:

> If the human being were not *authentically* exploited, we would be spared the *inauthentic* talk of an exploitation of nature. This talk reinforces the semblance of "value," which accrues to raw materials only by virtue of an order of production founded on the exploitation of human labor. Were this exploitation to come to a halt, work, in turn, could no longer be characterized as the exploitation of nature by man. It would henceforth be conducted on the model of children's play, which in Fourier forms the basis of the "impassioned work" of the Harmonians.[139]

What this suggests is that, for Benjamin, a revolution to create a classless society without exploitation cannot be realized by means of an affirmation of labor against the degradation of work by machinery. Nor would such a revolution seek to restore the link to tradition that was severed by capitalism. Rather, the complete degradation of labor in the industrial era gives rise to the messianic possibility that humanity can return, through revolution, to an original state of infancy or inexperience, a *Spielraum* expanded immeasurably by second technology.

The profane scheme of redemption implicit in Benjamin's reflections on play (a scheme in which life begins with play and ends in vain games) resembles the "historical apocatastasis" that Benjamin opposes to Hegelian dialectic in the Convolute N.[140] Unlike the "turnabout of extremes" that completes the progression of a Hegelian *Aufhebung*, the messianic movement of apocatastasis does not preserve what it cancels and supersedes, retrieving meaning from absolute loss. Instead, Benjamin locates redemption *in* the condition of total impoverishment, in the complete loss of experience, which allows humanity to return to its original "unimproved" state. But as such, a revolution to appropriate the *Spielraum* created by second technology is not one that would overcome the alienation of man by machinery. Rather, to borrow Benjamin's account of the revolutionary potential of mass reproduction, it would realize "*a highly productive use of the human being's self-alienation*," using the impoverishment of experience for the purpose of play.[141]

In the work of art essay, Benjamin defines this positive use of self-alienation through a kind of reversal of Marx's account of the impoverishment of experience in the industrial process of production. Whereas in factory labor, "working conditions make use of ... worker[s]," while making their labor increasingly useless, second technology, which has created "remote-controlled aircraft [with] ... no human crew," has the potential to "reduce ... their use to the minimum."[142] With the rise of second technology, machinery reduces the need to exploit human labor.

This argument is one that rejects the "shabby antithesis" between *physis* and *techne*, which characterizes in the work of "reactionary thinkers like Klages." For Benjamin, technology is not opposed to nature, but is "just a new configuration of nature."[143] Nor is technology, in Benjamin's view, opposed to the human. On the contrary, its development uncovers previously undisclosed aspects of humanity, aspects of its "first nature" (see Chapter 6): "Just as technology is always revealing nature from a new perspective, so also, as it impinges on human beings, it constantly makes for variations in their most primordial passions, fears, and images of longing."[144]

It is the rejection, moreover, of the reactionary antithesis between *techne* and *physis* that distinguishes Benjamin's conception of "primal history" from Klages'. Since technology, for Klages, is "the rape of nature by humanity," proving that "man ... has torn himself apart along with the planet which have him birth," the progress of technology drives humanity further and further from its original unity with a mythologized nature.[145] For Benjamin, on the other hand, the development of technology reveals new aspects of humanity and nature, such that "primal history is clearly manifest to us in the beginnings of technology."[146] Technology continually discovers new attributes of nature and human nature that were there from the very beginning. "Only a thoughtless observer," therefore, "can deny that correspondences come into play between the world of modern technology and the archaic symbol-world of mythology."[147]

What this suggests, then, is that, in Benjamin's messianism—a messianism for which the origin lies at the end—the development of machinery, and the accompanying impoverishment of experience, is not to be overcome in order to return to the natural order. Rather, the progress of technology leads to the restoration to a primal state of inexperience, expanding an original *Spielraum*, which both preceded and conditioned the domination of nature and the exploitation of labor.

In a similar vein, Benjamin argues that mass reproduction results in "a massive upheaval in the domain of objects handed down from the past—a shattering of tradition which is the reverse side of the present crisis and renewal of humanity." For Benjamin, however, this renewal will not restore the traditions whose transmission has been interrupted by capitalism. Instead, it will reinstate an original state of traditionlessness through the use of a form of second technology, contemporaneous with socialism, which "detaches the reproduced object from the sphere of tradition."[148]

In the nineteenth century, however, the revolutionary potential for a transformation of work into play, inspired by second technology, would remain unrealized. "The century was incapable of responding to the new technological possibilities with a new social order."[149] After its period of ascendency, the bourgeoisie ceased to be concerned with "the future of the productive forces which it had set going," since, in order to realize a new social order, it would abolish itself as a class.[150]

This "bungled reception of technology" would be repeated in the twentieth century.[151] Because of "the lust for profit of the ruling class," and the belief that "mastery of nature ... is the purpose of all technology," machinery "betrayed man and turned the bridal bed into a bloodbath." The enslavement of the forces of production under capitalism prevented technology from revealing new aspects of humanity and nature: "Men as a species completed their development thousands of years ago; but mankind as a species is just beginning his. In technology, a *physis* is being organized through which mankind's contact with the cosmos takes a new and different form."[152] Meanwhile, fascism would use mass reproduction to overcome the "uprising on the part of technology" against its inadequate use under capitalism, which generates crisis and war.[153] Only "war makes it possible to mobilize all of today's technological resources while maintaining property relations,"[154] and its destruction "furnishes proof that society was not mature enough to make technology its organ."[155] In the

Arcades, the bungled reception of technology, leading to fascism, is opposed to Fourier's plan of utopia, based on a transformation of work into play. "The unfolding of work in play presupposes highly developed forces of production, such as only today stand at the disposal of humanity, and stand mobilized in a direction contrary to their possibilities—that is, they are poised for an extreme case of war" (*Ernstfall des Krieges*).[156]

Art and Technology

As Giorgio Agamben has noted, the term *Ernstfall* appears in the writings of Carl Schmitt as a synonym for *Ausnahmezustand*, or state of exception.[157] In a surprising juxtaposition, Benjamin, who intended the *Arcades Project* as "a pictorial atlas of the secret history of National Socialism," opposes Fourier's critique of bourgeois civilization to Schmitt's theory of the political, which Benjamin critically appropriated in his earlier writings.[158] What the juxtaposition suggests is that the account of technology's right to co-determine society, which Benjamin's develops in his historical materialism, should be understood in relation to the critique of the sovereign right of exception, which appears in the earlier phase of his work.

In the *Trauerspiel* book, Benjamin opposes the extreme situation upon which the sovereign decides to the purely immanent "plane of the creaturely state," a state which "quite unmistakably determines the sovereign" and his right of decision.[159] For Benjamin, this state is defined as everything within the extreme situation that is beyond the sovereign's control. In the *Trauerspiel* plays, the primacy of the creaturely state is represented by the efficacy of the stage props and the setting and by the passivity of the actors. As a representation of the plane of the creaturely state, this personified setting, acting in the background of the performance, brings about the downfall of the irresolute tyrant of the *Trauerspiel*.

The idea of the efficacy of the setting would seem to correspond to what Benjamin refers to in "Notes toward a Work on the Category of Justice" as the "good-right of the good," or the right of things not to be possessions. As discussed in Chapter 2, this concept, which Benjamin had hoped to develop as part of an anarchist politics, is proposed as a critique of the deduction of legal possession in Kant's *Doctrine of Right*. In spite of his criticism of the use of personification in the labor theory of property, Kant's argument assumes it is necessary that things be deprived of their rights in order for people to employ them as property. Property is rational since it would be a contradiction to will a world of possessor-less things that refuse to let people own them. The right of possession, therefore, or what Benjamin calls the "possession-right of the person," is based upon an unlawful violence imposed upon objects, which Kant personifies as bondsmen who are forced to surrender their rights to their masters.

As Benjamin explains in the "Notes," what is excluded in this deduction of right is an original state of permissiveness in which everyone has a claim upon everything, and in which every good has the right to be without a possessor. Because of this right (which Kant violates in order to justify ownership), no "order of possession ... can therefore lead to justice."[160] No system of property, whether collective or private, can be just if it recognizes only the right of people to subjugate objects. Rather, the original claim that everyone has upon everything can only be realized by recognizing the right of the thing to refuse its appropriation as property, its right to be without a possessor, to be a *res nullius*. The claim, then, that everyone has upon everything can only be assured by a doctrine in which goods are granted the right to resist the requirement to conform to the possession-right of the person.

In his later writings, this good right is one that Benjamin appears to extend to technology (which, for Benjamin, is not opposed to nature, but is a different form of it). Thus, in the essay on reproduction, film and photography are credited for undermining the cultic value of sacred objects, which, in the Roman legal tradition, were excluded by divine law from all profane use, in direct violation of Kant's *lex permissiva*. By anarchically increasing their ability to be seen, technological reproduction annuls the sacred laws that strictly regulated the use of these objects.

And in the *Arcades*, the doctrine of justice, in which the "claim of the subject … to every good" points "toward a good-right of the good," reappears as a historical materialism oriented toward a classless society that recognizes "technology's right of co-determination in the social order." It is in fact this perspective that underlies the purportedly vulgar Marxist criticism of art for art's sake that Löwy attributes to Benjamin's "uncritical adherence" to the "Soviet variant of the ideology of progress."[161] Just as Kant excluded the right of the thing in his deduction of property, so the reactionary artistic and political tendencies of the nineteenth century, according to Benjamin, excluded this right of technology, "which makes revolutionary demands."[162]

Thus, the *Jugendstil* movement in the decorative arts represented the "last attempted sortie of an art besieged in its ivory tower … confronted by the technologically armed world."[163] In a similar manner, Benjamin argues that the Empire style, which was "the style of revolutionary terrorism," mistook the new technology of iron construction for "a contribution to the revival of architecture in the classical Greek sense."[164] What the movement failed to perceive was that, "with the first appearance of iron construction, [architecture] begins to outgrow art," a shortcoming that Benjamin likens to Napoleon's failure to see that, with the rise of the capitalist class, the state had outgrown its old imperial grandeur:[165] "Just as Napoleon failed to understand the functional nature of the state as an instrument of domination by the bourgeoisie, so the architects of his time failed to appreciate the functional characteristics of iron construction."[166]

This tendency would continue into the twentieth century. The failure to "neutralize … traditional concepts" of art, "such as creativity and genius, eternal value and mystery" in the age of technological reproduction would allow fascism to manipulate the masses through media while preserving capitalist relations of property.[167] In the work of art essay, this development is described as "the consummation of *l'art pour l'art*" and its reactionary rejection of the right of technology.[168] As Benjamin argues in the *Arcades*, the proponents of art for art's sake sought to "seal art off from the developments of technology."

Adorno regarded this "disquieting" argument as a result of Brecht's disastrous influence on Benjamin's view of aesthetics and politics, leading him to reject the more nuanced understanding of art presented in his pre-Marxist writings:

In ... your earlier writings, the great continuity of which ... your present essay dissolves, you differentiated the concept of the work of art as an image from the symbol of theology as well as from the taboo of magic. I find it questionable, then—and here I see a sublimated remnant of certain Brechtian motifs—that you now casually transfer the concept of magical aura to the "autonomous work of art" and flatly assign to the latter a counter-revolutionary function.[169]

For Adorno, therefore, Benjamin's vulgar Marxist critique of art for art's sake (which is directly opposed to the aesthetic theory that Adorno developed by returning to Kant's theory of judgment) constituted a betrayal of Marxism as well as Benjamin's earlier reflections on art. In "aping the official line of the Communist Party," Benjamin turned his back on the Kantian account of aesthetics, which he had supposedly shared with Adorno, espousing a "backward-looking bourgeois" technological determinism that denied the autonomy of artworks.[170] For Adorno, this Brechtian denunciation of the bourgeois idea of art was yet another example of Benjamin's lack of dialectical rigor, compelling him once again to prescribe "*more* dialectics": "If you defend the kitsch film against the 'quality' film, no one can be more in agreement with you than I am; but *l'art pour l'art* is just as much in need of a defense."[171]

This criticism of Benjamin is more fully developed in *Aesthetic Theory*, which, according to Robert Hullot-Kentor, is in large part a response to the work of art essay.[172] "It was plausible that socially progressive critics should have accused the program of *l'art pour l'art*, which has often been in league with political reaction, of promoting a fetish with the concept of a pure, exclusively self-sufficient artwork." This is because the fetishistic nature of artworks—their autonomy vis-à-vis society, the fact that "they posit something spiritual as being independent from the conditions of its material production"—is indeed a "theological heritage," as Benjamin claimed in the work of art essay.[173] It is the product of a "secularization of revelation" or religious experience.[174] Contrary to Benjamin, however, the "contamination of art with revelation ... does not disqualify art" by exposing it as an empty illusion. Rather, the mystification constitutes the very "truth content of artworks."[175] It is precisely because of the fetishistic appearance of autonomy or spiritual transcendence that art can cast a critical light upon a society based on the fetishism of commodities, a "society in which everything is heteronomously defined" since everything is subject to the "principle of exchange."

> By crystallizing in itself as something unique to itself, rather than complying with existing social norms and qualifying as 'socially useful,' it criticizes society by merely existing ... There is nothing pure, nothing structured strictly according to its own immanent law, that does not implicitly criticize the debasement of a situation evolving in the direction of a total exchange society ...[176]

For Adorno, then, this implies that the theological heritage of the artwork must be preserved in order to criticize the heteronomy of a disenchanted society based on the fetishism of commodities or the principle of exchange. Art "can outmaneuver the demystified world and cancel the spell that this world casts by the overwhelming force of its appearance, the fetish character of the commodity." Art, in other words, can criticize the theological niceties of the commodity fetish only if it preserves the fetishistic appearance that constitutes its theological heritage. The ability of the artwork to demystify the cultic religion of capitalism depends, therefore, precisely on what Benjamin denounced as its "negative theology": "The eradication of every trace of revelation from art would ... degrade it to the undifferentiated repetition of the status quo."[177]

As Benjamin argues, however, in the "Little History of Photography," the fetishistic autonomy that enables art to criticize the heteronomy of existing society is itself a product of capitalism: "The more far-reaching the crisis of the present social order, and the more rigidly its individual components are locked together ... the more the creative ... becomes a fetish, whose lineaments live only in the fitful illumination of changing fashion."[178] From Benjamin's perspective, therefore, the fetishism of the artwork is a dialectical complement to the fetish character of the commodity that it criticizes. The opposition of art to existing society presupposes the principle of exchange that it repudiates by its existence as an autonomous object. But as such, the fetishism of commodities cannot be abolished without simultaneously canceling the fetishistic appearance of artworks, whose uniqueness and aura are opposed to the principle of exchange. The heteronomous religion of capitalism, based on the supernatural substance of value, cannot be demystified, in other words, without also annulling the autonomy that constitutes the theological heritage of the artwork and its basis in "cult value." But in that case, the attempt to preserve the fetishistic appearance of artworks reenforces the fetish character of the commodity, which constitutes its dialectical complement.

What is excluded in Adorno's dialectical justification of art for art's sake is the concept of a dialectic that is realized only in its self-abolition. Marx suggests such a dialectic in his early critique of Hegel's philosophy of right, arguing that one "cannot abolish [*aufheben*] philosophy without making it a reality." In his account of the limitations of Surrealist and Dadaist art, Guy Debord, applying a similar principle to the bourgeois notion of art, asserted that "the abolition and the realization of art are inseparable aspects of a single transcendence of art."[179]

Contrary to Adorno, moreover, the increase in the "exhibition value" of images resulting from the rise of mass reproduction, which Benjamin assumed would lead to the suppression and secularization of art, cannot be identified with the exchange of commodities. "The 'exhibition value' that, according to Benjamin, supplants 'cult value' is an *imago* of the exchange process. Art that devotes itself to its exhibition value is ruled by the exchange process."[180] This criticism collapses the difference between mass reproduction and the mode of exchange within capitalism. It assumes that the dissemination of images, which deprives them of their sacred or spiritual power, is necessarily tied to commodity circulation.

But if mass reproduction, as Benjamin noted, has made "more segments of the field of optical perception into saleable commodities ... conquer[ing] for commodity circulation objects which ... had been ... excluded from it,"[181] it also "emerged at the same time as socialism."[182] This suggests that the impact of "the first truly revolutionary means of reproduction" should be distinguished from their capitalist application, including advertising and fascism, which uses technology to save the sacred aura of images while preserving property relations in capitalism.

Benjamin's account of mass reproduction, moreover, would appear to conform to the Marxian analysis of the contradictory character of the capitalist mode of production, which Benjamin evokes in the opening of the work of art essay. Just as the plethora produced by machinery can diminish the supernatural substance of value contained in commodities, so the proliferation of images made possible by mass reproduction undermines the cult value that constitutes the theological heritage of the artwork.

This critique of art for art's sake is not based on a "backward-looking bourgeois" technological determinism, marking a departure from Benjamin's earlier and more nuanced understanding of art. Rather, it is fully consistent with both his earlier views on aesthetics and politics, which emphasized the "primacy of the thingly," as well as with an unorthodox reading of Marx, which considered crises in bourgeois society as revolts by technology to realize its right to undermine capitalism. Contrary to Adorno, this society is not defined by an "overvaluation of machine technology," but by a tendency to "insulate everything technological … from the so-called spiritual," compelling it to "exclude technology's right of co-determination in the social order."

As Jan Sieber has argued, this insistence upon the right of technology distinguishes Benjamin's criticism of capitalism from those of contemporaries on the political right and the left, from thinkers like Lukács and Schmitt who identified modern society with the dominance of technology and calculative reason. Unlike "Max Weber, Martin Heidegger, or T. W. Adorno and Max Horkheimer, Benjamin does not formulate his concept of technique in relation to the modern concept of rationalist subjectivity for which the natural sciences are the role model. Rather, he criticizes such a perception insofar as it takes technique to be merely an expression of instrumental reason."[183]

Thus, in "On the Concept of History," Benjamin's critique of the "technocratic" tendencies of German social democracy (which would "later emerge in fascism") is not simply that the latter takes an affirmative view of technology. Rather, the problem is that it affirms an instrumental conception of it. For social democracy, technology is an instrument of labor which, used in order to dominate nature, will create the wealth required to abolish the exploitation of labor. "Labor … [thus] conceived, is tantamount to the exploitation of nature, which is contrasted to the exploitation of the proletariat with naïve self-satisfaction."[184] Adopting the vulgar-Marxist conception of labor as "the source of all wealth," while denying the "good-right of the good," social democracy regarded technology as a tool for exploiting a natural world, which "is there *gratis*," an exploitation that would supposedly lead to the liberation of labor.[185]

As Marx argued, however, in a section from the "Critique of the Gotha Program" cited in "On the Concept of History," this supposedly socialist conception of work corresponds in fact to the specific function of labor in capitalism. Contrary to the Gotha Program, labor "is *not the source* of all wealth" in every society, although the "bourgeois have very good grounds for falsely ascribing *supernatural creative power* to labor." Like Locke's theory of property, this fetishistic notion of labor is based on the personification of nature, which is presumed to surrender its freedom to labor. In capitalism, according to Marx, this personification makes it possible for labor to appear as the source of all wealth. It is only "insofar as man … behaves toward nature, [which is] the primary source of all instruments … of labor, as an owner, treats her as belonging to him [that] … his labor becomes the source of use values, therefore also of wealth."

Labor, then, can only appear as the source of all wealth insofar as the natural world, which provides the technologies used in order to dominate it, is personified as a subject who must be enslaved in order to emancipate labor. But since labor "is *not the source* of all wealth," workers who possess only their labor power, but not the technology required for the exploitation of nature, are compelled to let others exploit them: "the man who possesses no other property than his labor power must ... be the slave of other men who have made themselves the owners of the material conditions of labor."[186] Contrary to social democracy, then, the instrumental conception of work as the domination of nature is not antithetical to the exploitation of labor. Rather, the one conditions the other.

Revolution and Second Technology

As Benjamin argues, moreover, the instrumental view of technology, which corresponds to the fetishistic conception of labor as the source of all wealth, refuses to recognize the fundamental change in the nature of technology itself that began in the industrial era. In the second version of the work of art essay, Benjamin describes this transformation as a shift from a "first" to a "second technology." The aim of first technology is to increase the power of labor in order to dominate nature. "It should be noted, however, that to describe the goal of the second technology as 'mastery over nature' is highly questionable, since this implies viewing the second technology from the standpoint of the first."[187] Instead of extending the power of labor, the goal of second technology is to make labor unnecessary. It "aims at liberating human beings from drudgery,"[188] an aim that is opposed to the bourgeois tendency to "falsely ascrib[e] ... *supernatural creative power* to labor," as the alleged source of all wealth and culture.

Since this concept of labor is the basis of wealth in bourgeois society, this society must resolutely deny the right of second technology to completely transform it, a right that Benjamin identifies with revolution itself: In "revolutions ... the second technology ... asserts its claims vis-a-vis society." "Revolutions are ... efforts at innervation on the part of the new, historically unique collective which has its organs in the new technology."[189] Revolution, then, is an effort by a collective unconscious to realize the wish images that arise from technology.

But as such, by viewing "second technology from the standpoint of the first," and seeking to seal off its corrupted concept of labor from technological change, social democracy perpetuates a property relation, wage labor, that has been rendered irrelevant by the development of the forces of production. Deprived of its right to co-determine society, technology rebels against the capitalist law that labor power must be sold in exchange for a wage, creating crises of overproduction and mass unemployment, which can only be solved through mass mobilization for war.[190]

For Benjamin, this rebellion of technology can only be averted by realizing the revolutionary demand to be liberated from the "dominion of the first technology," a demand of which "Fourier's work is the first historical evidence."[191] In contrast to the vulgar conception of socialism proposed in the Gotha Program, "the Fourierist utopia ... never advocated the exploitation of nature by man." Instead, Fourier recognized that "man's exploitation of nature reflects the actual exploitation of man by the owners of the means of production," and that, "if the integration of the technological into social life failed, the fault lies in this exploitation."[192]

Because of this failure, the superabundance created by second technology leads to crises of plethora, rather than to a transformation of work into play. For Fourier, as Pinloche pointed out: "It is industrial warfare and trade warfare that are most often the origin of military warfare."[193] As Benjamin suggests in "Theories of German Fascism," this tendency is exasperated by the counter-revolutionary desire to recreate heroic features of war that have been permanently displaced by technology. For Benjamin, the attempt to restore an authentic idea of the political, as a sovereign decision upon an "extreme case of war," ignores the true nature of crises in capitalism as "slave revolt[s] of technology."[194]

With the rise of second technology, society, then, arrives at an historical crossroads. For Benjamin, however, the choice is not barbarism or social democracy. Rather, the alternatives are the possibility of a Fourierist utopia based upon a transformation of work into play or the catastrophe of states of emergency in the era of mechanical warfare, the "unfolding of work in play [which] presupposes highly developed forces of production" or the use of industrial means of production in "an extreme case of war."[195]

The alternative, then, is either a revolution to collectively realize the wish images that arise from second technology or mass mobilization to preserve property relations in capitalism: either the humorous annihilation of morality and the capitalist mode of production (which, for Fourier, implied the abolition of wage labor, "la suppression du salariat") or the recurrence of crises of plethora, which compel sovereignty to suspend the rule of law so as to save it.[196] Through imperialist war, fascism can overcome the mass unemployment created by the "inadequate use" of the means of production in bourgeois society, creating a semblance of socialism that preserves the capitalist institution of wage-labor. The "Third Reich mimics socialism. Unemployment comes to an end because forced labor is made legal."[197]

Against the fascist reaction to second technology, Benjamin proposed the creation of a state of abundance which, no longer bound by capitalist relations of property, would resemble an original state of permissiveness in which everyone has a claim upon everything. This imperative corresponds to what Benjamin characterizes, in his notes on the journalist Carl Gustav Jochmann, as a political project of the greatest importance:

> The mode of generating wealth by means of machinery spreads the enjoyment otherwise confined to a few to all … becoming a bountiful means of producing riches. But to prevent this from becoming a misfortune for the majority through the increasingly unequal distribution of the wealth produced, nature requires a further restructuring of social forms. To discover this new structure is the task of our time.[198]

Benjamin's historical materialism, then, was not characterized by an uncritical vulgar Marxist conception of technological progress. Rather, as Irving Wohlfarth has argued, Benjamin incorporated a Marxian analysis of the contradictory relationship between the development of technology and social relations in capitalism.

> Benjamin's scattered comments on modern technological warfare can be pieced together ... roughly as follows. According to the Marxian dialectic, new forces of production blast open (*sprengen*) old relations of production. Where this dynamic is diverted from its "natural," revolutionary goal, the dammed-up forces of production find an unnatural, counter-revolutionary outlet in imperialist and inter-capitalist war.[199]

Class Struggle and Sexual Fetishism in Fashion

Inspired by the abundance resulting from the "advent of machines," Fourier adopted the "task of our time" in his utopian socialism. In the nineteenth century, the development of second technology created what Benjamin called the "architectural canon" for Fourier's utopian vision of a world in which work is transformed into play: the Paris arcades.[200] As "a recent invention of industrial luxury," the arcades, which were "the forerunners of department stores," were a "center of commerce in luxury items," carrying "large stocks of merchandise on the premises." With their "glass-roofed, marble-paneled corridors extending through whole blocks of buildings," the arcades were a new construction in which art and technology were mobilized in "the service of the merchant."[201] Whereas this construction, however, "originally serve[d] commercial ends, they become, for [Fourier], places of habitation," phalansteries that would replace the shops, factories, and phantasmagoric bourgeois interiors that defined the topography of capitalist civilization.[202]

For Benjamin, the industrial luxury sold in the arcades provided compensation for a sense of historical "impotence" that afflicted the bourgeoisie in "the middle of the century [when] ... the ... class ceases to be occupied with the future of the productive forces it had unleashed."[203] As Korsch described, this complacency came about when "the revolutionary fight of the bourgeoisie against feudal society had come to its end and a new divergence of classes had begun to manifest itself within the hitherto united industrial society."[204]

According to Benjamin, the disinterest of the bourgeoisie in the socially transformative potential of industrial technology was due to the desire to preserve capitalist relations of property: "In order to concern itself further with the future of the productive forces which it had set going, the bourgeoisie would first of all have had to renounce the idea of private income."[205] This situation, according to Benjamin, is also reflected in the vulgar socialist utopias that appeared after Fourier, in the work of writers like Edward Bellamy, who imagined the future merely as a better version of bourgeois society. For Benjamin, these later conceptions of socialism, which preceded the industrial revolution and appeared at a time when the proletariat had developed its consciousness as a class, were not more realistic than the earlier utopias of Thomas More or Tommaso Campanella.[206] On the contrary, the earlier utopias were more radical than the ones that came after, including the vulgar version of socialism espoused by Social Democracy, to which Benjamin opposed Fourier's non-positivistic fantasies of the future. Because they preceded the establishment of industrial capitalism and the rise of its social classes, the earlier utopian thinkers were able to imagine a world *without wage-labor and capital* in a way that their successors could not.[207]

In the nineteenth century, the bourgeoisie's inability to recognize technology's right to suppress the "salariat," to acknowledge "the inextinguishable claim of the Fourierist utopia ... which Marx had recognized," produced a sense of impotency for which the arcades provided distraction: "That the habit of 'coziness' so typical of bourgeois comfort around midcentury goes together with this lassitude of the bourgeois imagination, that it is one with the luxury of 'never having to think about how the forces of production must develop in their hands'—these things admit of very little doubt."[208]

Refusing the right of technology to co-determine society and unwilling to renounce the relations of property it had struggled to establish, the bourgeoisie sought comfort in new kinds of industrial luxury. As the fragments and notes devoted to the subject in Convolute B suggest, the development of these new kinds of commodities, of which fashion was a privileged example, was determined by what Marx and Fourier characterized as the contradictory relations that structure bourgeois society.

As Balzac observed, the revolutionary struggle of the capitalist class against the nobility created the modern phenomenon of fashion. After the French Revolution and the abolition of sumptuary laws—laws that had prescribed for "each class of society ... its costume" ("one recognized by his dress the lord, the bourgeois, the artisan")—"all became equal in their rights as well as their toilette, and the difference in the fabric and cut of their clothing could no longer distinguish their [social] conditions." But despite the establishment of universal equality, the class struggle, as Balzac suggests, would persist, after the revolution, in the form of changes in fashion. In the new "milieu de ... [l']uniformité," fashion "was called upon to reestablish all of the nuances" of social station and status. It became an "external sign that distinguished the rank of each individual."[209]

As Rudolf von Jhering, a German legal scholar cited in Convolute B, argued, fashion, therefore, is "the mad pursuit of ... class vanity." Its "motive is the effort to distinguish the higher classes of society from the lower." Changes in fashion arise from the "endeavor of one group to establish a lead, however minimal, over its pursuers, and the endeavor of the other group to make up the distance by immediately adopting the newest fashions of the leaders."[210]

This analysis, however, as Eduard Fuchs argued in another treatise on fashion quoted in the *Arcades*, is not sufficient. The class motive alone cannot entirely account for the phenomenon of fashion. Fuchs, therefore, identifies two further causes, the first sexual and the second of a social and technological nature.

The first "cause [that] has escaped Jhering entirely ... [is] the function of erotic stimulation in fashion."[211] According to Benjamin, this stimulation is the product of a synthesis between sexual fetishism and commodity fetishism. "The modern advertisement shows, from another angle, to what extent the attractions of the woman and those of the commodity can be merged."[212] On the one hand, sexual arousal in fashion is achieved by creating a fixation on a nonliving thing. In "every fashion, perversities are suggested by the most ruthless means. ... Every fashion couples the living body to the inorganic world. ... The fetishism that succumbs to the sex appeal of the inorganic is its vital nerve."[213] As an example, Benjamin cites Blanqui's description of the fetish behind the fashion of steel-hooped cage crinolines: "Sensational event! The belles dames, one fine day, decide to puff up the derriere. ... But what is a simple refinement on illustrious coccyxes? A trumpery, no more ... Away with the rump! Long live crinolines!"[214]

In fashion, however, this sexual fetishism is inflected by another kind of fixation, a fixation not for physical objects, but for what Marx called the "metaphysical" substance of exchange value, or the "supersensual" property that makes all commodities equal and exchangeable. "Under the dominion of the commodity fetish, the sex appeal of the woman is ... tinged with the appeal of the commodity. It is no accident that the relations of the pimp to his girlfriend, whom he sells as an 'article' on the market, have so inflamed the sexual fantasies of the bourgeoisie."[215]

In his response to Adorno's criticism of the exposé on the *Arcades Project*, Benjamin describes this kind of desire as an "empathy with exchange value": "Basically ... empathy with the commodity is ... empathy with exchange value itself. And in fact, one can hardly imagine the 'consumption' of exchange-value as anything else but an empathy with it."[216] In a society based on commodity fetishism, sexual desire is not only aroused by advertising, which seeks to couple parts of the body to inanimate objects, such as the crinoline. Rather, erotic stimulation is also excited by imbuing the body with the "supernatural" property of exchange value: "salability itself can become a sexual stimulus."[217] As Benjamin explains in the essay on Karl Kraus, "it is only the interlacing of sexual with commercial intercourse that constitutes the character of prostitution."[218]

What inflamed bourgeois fantasies about the prostitute, then, was the fact that the sexual pleasure the latter embodied provoked the desire to purchase it, a desire fulfilled by the pimp, who possesses his lover as a commodity that is exchanged to others for money. Insofar as exchange value, in *Capital*, is a synonym for the commodity fetish, the "empathy for exchange value," which defines the figure of the prostitute, amounts to something like a sexual fetish for the commodity fetish itself.

In the *Arcades Project*, Benjamin suggests that the development of the function of erotic stimulation in fashion is a privileged example of the displacement, characteristic of capitalist modernity, of eternal ideals in favor of "newness" or novelty. In modernity, as Paul Valéry argued in a passage cited in Convolute B, the "idea of creating works of lasting value lost force and gave way ... to the desire to astonish":

> There arose an automatic audacity, which became as obligatory as tradition had been. Finally, that switching—at high frequency—of the tastes of a given public, which is called Fashion replaced with its essential changeableness the old habit of slowly forming styles, schools, and reputations. To say that Fashion took over the destinies of the fine arts is as much as to say that commercial interests were creeping in.[219]

By subordinating art to commercial interests, thus shifting its aim from the creation of eternal works to the eternal production of newness, capitalism simultaneously developed a new means of promoting commodities, ensuring its own reproduction. Thus, "art's last line of resistance," its reduction to fashion, "coincid[ed] with the commodity's most advanced line of attack."[220]

This shift from a society based upon the transmission of an unchanging tradition to one whose essential characteristic is the newness of fashion is bound up with a change in the mode of production. Thus, as Fuchs argued, the frequency of changes in fashion cannot be explained only in terms of either the commodified sexual fetishism it arouses or "the mad pursuit of ... class vanity." The function of erotic stimulation in fashion and the "concern for segregating the classes" are not sufficient to explain "the frequent variation in fashions." Another "cause—the private-capitalist mode of production, which in the interests of its profit margin must continually multiply the possibilities of turnover—is of equal importance."[221]

Thus, the increasingly fetishistic character of fashion and its function in distinguishing the different classes in capitalism were phenomena rooted in the process of production in bourgeois society, a process that Fourier had described as inherently contradictory in character. By increasing the quantity of fashion that can be produced within a given period of time, the development of the forces of production simultaneously reduces its exchange value, thereby increasing its availability to the masses. In a passage from *Philosophy and Culture*, cited by Benjamin, Simmel describes this contradictory movement in the following manner:

> The quick changing of fashion means that fashions can no longer be so expensive... as they were in earlier times. ... A peculiar circle ... arises here: the more an article becomes subject to rapid changes of fashion, the greater the demand for cheap products of its kind; and the cheaper they become, the more they invite consumers and constrain producers to a quick change of fashion.[222]

The result is what Jhering describes as an inverse relationship between, on the one hand, the development of the forces of production and mass reproduction and, on the other, the rate of turnover for fashion, or the velocity of the mad pursuit of class vanity: "The duration of a fashion is inversely proportional to the swiftness of its diffusion; the ephemerality of fashions has increased in our day as the means for their diffusion have expanded via our perfected communications techniques."[223]

This inverse relation would appear to be rooted in the same contradiction that, in Fourier's criticism of bourgeois civilization, creates crises of plethora. In *Capital*, the relation is characterized as a product of the "contradictory movement [that] arises out of the twofold character of labor."[224] Since the exchange value of commodities is measured by the quantity of abstract or socially necessary labor time required to produce them, an increase in productivity, owing to improvements in particular kinds of concrete, useful labor, reduces exchange value: "Two coats will clothe two men, one coat will only clothe one man, etc. Nevertheless, an increase in the amount of material wealth may correspond to a simultaneous fall in the magnitude of its value."[225]

During the industrial revolution, this contradictory movement, as Marx described in a section in *Capital* cited by Benjamin, would lead to a reduction in the price of fashion, while dramatically expanding the exploitation of labor in dressmaking and related industries. In accordance with the Fourierist law that bourgeois civilization "constantly arrives at the ... opposite," the introduction of labor-saving devices, which created the "boom in the textile trade," the "first condition" of the Paris arcades, led to an extension of the working day.[226] To secure savings to the costs of production that could be achieved through machinery, factory-owners were compelled to operate them continually, using their capital up before its value could be depreciated by the development of new and better technology. This forced factory-owners to continually prolong the hours of work. Instead of reducing the burden of labor, therefore, the "capitalist application of machinery ... supplies new and powerful incentives for an unbounded prolongation of the working day."[227]

As a result of its capitalist application, then, the "machines," to borrow Benjamin's gloss on this section from *Capital*, served only to "aggravate exploitation rather than alleviate the human lot."[228] "Hence," according to Marx, "the economic paradox, that the most powerful instrument for shortening labour-time, becomes the most unfailing means for placing every moment of the labourer's time ... for the purpose of expanding ... capital."[229] In the industries related to fashion, the paradox produced an increase in incidences of death from overwork, which would eventually lead the British government to limit the working-day, in what Marx described as the "first rational bridle on the murderous, meaningless caprices of fashion."[230] As another observer concluded, therefore (in a remark cited by both Marx and Benjamin): "The uncertainty of fashions does increase necessitous poor."[231]

The same movement, therefore, in which "poverty is born of superabundance" also accounts for the accelerated cycles of fashion, whose perpetual production of *nouveautés* expands the exploitation of labor by fueling class vanity and sexual fetishism. In that sense, fashion is an expression of a bourgeois society in which the "mode of production is in rebellion against the mode of exchange." The "tyranny of fashion" is rooted in the abstract domination of capital,[232] based on the "dominion of the commodity fetish," a dominion that denies the right of technology.[233]

Novelty

The dominion of the commodity fetish, then, was extended by the newness of fashion, which emerged in the era of industrial capitalism as a means of escaping from crises of plethora. As Benjamin seems to suggest, this phenomenon was one that Marx did not fully account for in *Capital*. In the *Arcades Project*, therefore, Benjamin distinguishes the category of newness from both use and exchange value. Although newness turns the commodity fetish into an erotic fixation, such that exchange value or "salability itself can become a sexual stimulus," its "luster" (*Schein*) cannot be identified with the "semblance of 'value'" (*Schein des "Wertes"*), which it serves to sexualize.[234] The luster of newness can arouse the desire to purchase commodities, and thus persuade buyers to pay higher prices, but this cannot be identified with an increase in exchange value itself, which is determined only by socially necessary labor time.

At the same time, newness, as Benjamin argues, is also "a quality independent of the use value of the commodity."[235] Two coats can clothe two men, regardless of the quantity of exchange value they represent, but the utility of the coat by itself cannot stimulate either a sexual desire for the inorganic or a social desire to belong to the upper classes. This desire, then, is distinct from the "wants" arising from either "from the stomach, or the imagination," which are satisfied by the physical properties of goods considered as use-values.[236]

In the *Arcades*, Benjamin describes this desire as a sort of impotent and degraded form of the "wish images" within the collective unconscious, inspired by the advent of machines, wish images that receive their authentic expression in Fourier's utopia. This utopia, however, was directly opposed to the moralistic conceptions of socialism espoused by figures like Carl Grün and Rudolf von Jhering. For Jhering, the tyranny of fashion—which continually stokes both sexual fetishism and class vanity—pointed to the need for a return to an eternal standard of beauty, and a moral regard for visible markers of class:

> If the classes that are weak and foolish enough to imitate [fashion] ... were to gain a sense of their own proper worth ... it would be all up with fashion, and beauty could once again assume the position it has had with all those peoples who ... did not feel the need to accentuate class differences through clothing or, where this occurred, were sensible enough to respect them.[237]

For Fourier, on the other hand, the development of the forces of production, which, in capitalism, "promotes waste" through "changes of fashion" that stimulate fetishism, provided the condition for a new "amorous regime," based upon the abolition of wage labor and bourgeois morality.[238] Rather than simply eliminating the new forms of vice created by the capitalist mode of production, this amorous regime, founded on "nonsalaried but impassioned work,"[239] would "promote the gratification of many desires that civilized society condemned as perversions."[240]

In capitalism, such perversions, continually stimulated by newness, inevitably provoke the philistine moralizing of both bourgeois and vulgar socialist critics of capitalism, which serves only to further sensationalize fashion. Fashion functions in this context to relieve what Fourier called the "ennui of existing society [that] was largely the result of the systematic denial of passion embodied in the two main foundations of civilisation: marriage and work."[241] Because of the contradictory character of the capitalist mode of production, these institutions always engender their opposites, the exploitation of labor and "conjugal slavery." Fourier's phalanstery, then, was to be an attempt to "seek [a] better arrangement for the union of the sexes and the exchange of industrial products," a total transformation of affective relations and social production.[242] For Fourier, "communism could not possibly be achieved without a complete alteration in sexual relations."[243] In a truly communist society, these relations would be arranged with the aim of fulfilling the different sexual wants of women and men, which diverged at various stages of life, necessitating a "complicated and subtle combination of polygamy and polyandry."[244] Thus, Fourier wanted "every woman to have ... a husband with whom she could conceive two children ... a breeder ... with whom she could have only one child ... a lover ... who has lived with her and retained this title; fourth and last, mere possessors ... who are nothing in the eyes of the law."

In the mid-nineteenth century, however, the collective unconscious desire, aroused by technology, to realize the image of a future society of erotic freedom and unalienated labor was undermined by the "false consciousness whose indefatigable agent is fashion."[245] With the rise of fashion, the utopian sexual fantasies of a world in which desire and labor are simultaneously liberated were redirected toward the consumption of new industrial luxuries that sexualized the commodity and commodified sexuality: "The sexuality that in former times—on a social level—was stimulated through imagining the future of the productive forces is mobilized now through imagining the power of capital."[246]

For Benjamin, then, the arcades were a commodification of the utopian impulse for a better arrangement of labor and love, one that Fourier hoped to convert into an amorous regime of impassioned work, into "the Fourierist phalanstery ... based on consumption and pleasure."[247] To borrow Benjamin's characterization of the New Objectivity movement in painting, they allowed for a "conversion of revolutionary impulses, insofar as they occurred among bourgeoisie, into objects of distraction, of amusement." The pursuit of fashion constitutes a "transformation of the political struggle from a call-to-decision into an object of contemplative enjoyment ... into a consumer article."[248]

In the new products of industrial luxury sold in the *magasins de nouveautés*, the illusion of sexualized newness provided comfort to the impotent imagination of the bourgeoisie, who enjoyed the luxury of not having to "think about how the forces of production must develop."[249] In fashion, therefore, the wish for a classless society of sexual freedom is both disavowed and expressed in the form of private industrial pleasures that fulfill sexual fetishism as well as the desire to belong to the upper class of society, thereby diverting the political demand to abolish it. Insofar as the desire for a classless society is "wedded to elements of primal history," or to the concept of a primitive communism that is constitutively excluded in the bourgeois conception of progress, "*la modernité*," in the phenomenon of fashion, "is always citing primal history."[250] In the newness of fashion, therefore, "primal history," to borrow Benjamin's account of Nietzsche's idea of eternal return, "enters the scene in ultramodern get-up."[251]

The very primal desire for a better arrangement of labor and love is pressed into the service of capital, as a means of perpetuating class exploitation and of renewing the interminable cycle of production and overproduction. For Benjamin, therefore, capitalism is a system whose reproduction requires the constant invention of newness or novelty, tinged with a commodified sexual fetishism. Because this newness, moreover, in the era of industrial capitalism is as "obligatory as tradition had been" in the past, the rise of fashion revealed an historically determinate feature of the capitalist mode of production, distinguishing it from all other forms of society.[252] Whereas the reproduction of other societies presupposed the transmission of an eternal tradition, capitalism depends upon the production of newness as an unchanging condition.

As Marx and Engels argue in the *Communist Manifesto*, this unchanging condition necessitates the "constant revolutionising of production, uninterrupted disturbance of all social conditions, everlasting uncertainty and agitation distinguish the bourgeois epoch from all earlier ones."[253] While earlier societies depended upon the reproduction of traditional habits, manners and styles of dress, capitalism, according to Benjamin, is characterized by the "accelerated succession of crises," which undermines the "security of the conditions of life." As a result, individuals became "incapable of developing regular habits." Habits that preserved "experience over time" (*Erfahrung*) are undermined by the "isolated experience of the moment" (*Erlebnis*), which prevails during crises in capitalism: "Habits are the armature of long experience [*Erfahrung*], whereas they are decomposed by individual experiences [*Erlebnisse*]."[254]

The Eternal Return of the Capitalist Mode of Production

Just as the *Trauerspiel* book recovered a Baroque understanding of allegory as the primal history of the symbol, so the *Arcades Project* was intended to "wrest from primal history a portion of the nineteenth century."[255] In Convolute D, "Boredom, Eternal Return," this history is identified with the notion of eternal recurrence. This notion, according to Benjamin, appears in its "fundamental form" not only in the writings of Nietzsche, but also in *Eternity by the Stars*, written by the revolutionary, Louis Auguste Blanqui, ten years before the publication of *Thus Spoke Zarathustra*.[256]

In Convolute D, Benjamin cites Nietzsche's famous account of the concept in *The Gay Science*: "This life, as thou livest it at present, and hast lived it, thou must live it … innumerable times; and there will be nothing new in it, but every pain and … joy … all the … small and great in thy life must come to thee again, and all in the same series and sequence."[257] Like the *nouveautés* that alleviated the boredom of the bourgeoisie at the moment it "cease[d] to be occupied with the future of the productive forces," the "notion of eternal return appeared … when the bourgeoisie no longer dared count on the … development of the system of production."[258] The idea, in other words, appeared at a time when the bourgeoisie had rescinded its revolutionary role, abandoning the struggle for historical progress.

In *Eternity by the Stars*, Blanqui, in his own version of the doctrine of eternal return, condemns the notion of progress, which was once invoked by bourgeois civilization to justify its establishment, while declaring his total submission to that civilization. "It is an unconditional surrender, but it is simultaneously the most terrible indictment of a society that projects this image of the cosmos—understood as an image of itself—across the heavens."[259] In his final work, then, the civilization that Blanqui had tried to destroy is eternalized in the image of an infinite cosmos in which progress toward the ideals of bourgeois society has and will be repeated forever, throughout time and across infinite worlds. The "life of our planet … is being lived … on myriad kindred planets":

> What we call "progress" is confined to each particular world, and vanishes with it. Always and everywhere … the same drama, the same setting, on the same narrow stage … a noisy humanity infatuated with its own grandeur, believing itself to be the universe and living in its prison as though in some immense realm … [T]he universe repeats itself endlessly.[260]

Imprisoned at the end of his life for repeatedly conspiring to destroy bourgeois society, Blanqui, stricken with a form of acedia, is seized by a vision in which this society is coextensive with the unlimited extent of the cosmos. In this mechanical universe, the struggle to realize the principles of bourgeois civilization must be endlessly reenacted. In "his last place of captivity," the Château du Taureau during the Paris Commune, Blanqui "writes this book in order to open new doors in his dungeon."[261] In the book, the dungeon becomes the prison house of a determinate mode of production that has expanded to encompass the whole of space and time, and appears as the inescapable fate of all human generations in the past, present, and future. Blanqui succumbs to what Engels described as "the bourgeois illusion of the eternity and finality of capitalist production."[262]

According to Benjamin, the indictment of bourgeois society implied in Blanqui's concession to its inescapable power is so terrible that it rattles the power to which it capitulates: "Blanqui yields to bourgeois society. But he's brought to his knees with such force that the throne begins to totter."[263] His "infernal vision" of the infinite repetition of history undermines the bourgeois conception of progress: "In the idea of eternal recurrence, the historicism of the nineteenth century capsizes."[264] "Until now, the past, for us," as Blanqui laments, "meant barbarism, whereas the future has signified progress, science, happiness, illusion!"[265]

In *Eternity by the Stars*, this historicism is seen within the broader expanse of its own primal history, a history which Benjamin defines, in spatial terms, as a setting or background. "Primal history forms part of the recent past, just as mountains, seen from a great distance, appear to form part of the landscape lying before them."[266] As a fundamental form of primal history, the idea of eternal return places the bourgeois conception of progress within the "prodigious distances" of the stars and the infinite duration of time, in which this progress, endlessly repeated, appears as a meaningless drama.[267] "The people of the nineteenth century see the stars against a sky which is spread out in this text."[268] Against this background, the historical present merely reproduces "the same drama ... on the same narrow stage"[269] performed by "a noisy humanity infatuated with its own grandeur,"[270] and unaware that is reenacting a play that had already been staged innumerable times in the past.[271]

Like the "formal dialectic of the setting"[272] that unfolds in the *Trauerspiel* plays, in which the "constantly repeated spectacle of the rise and fall of princes" is portrayed as a spatialized image, Blanqui's infernal vision reduces the temporal movement of progress to space.[273] This spatial representation reveals an immense meaningless cosmos that resembles the allegorical representation of nature as a "petrified primal landscape," in which "all classical harmony of form, and everything human is lacking."[274] From the perspective of Blanqui's cosmic eternity, human history runs its "course without even scratching the terrestrial surfaces. The disappearance of the disruptors would leave no trace of their self-styled sovereign presence, and would suffice to return nature to its virtually unmolested virginity."[275] The "most brilliant civilizations disappear without leaving a trace."[276] Like allegorical perception, therefore, Blanqui's infernal vision perceives "the jagged line of demarcation between physis and meaning," or the irreducibility of nature to meaning.[277]

In Nietzsche, such a perception is identified with the head of Medusa, in which "all features of the world become motionless, a frozen death throe."[278] The image corresponds to the idea of eternal recurrence as the thought of existence in "its most terrible form: existence as it is, without meaning or aim, yet recurring inevitably without any finale of nothingness."[279] For Nietzsche, according to Benjamin, the terrible thought "that nothing new will occur" had to be met with "heroic composure." Whereas in Blanqui's view of eternal recurrence, "resignation predominates," in Nietzsche, the idea is joyfully willed or affirmed: "We deny end goals: if existence had one it would have to have been reached."[280]

For Nietzsche, the absence of end goals implies that the universe is not mechanistic, "for if it were that, it would not condition an infinite recurrence of identical cases but a final state. Because the world has not reached this, mechanistic theory must be considered an imperfect and merely provisional hypothesis."[281] The affirmation of eternal recurrence, therefore, is not the affirmation of a mere mechanical law, since a mechanical series can never arrive at the thought of existence without meaning or purpose. For Blanqui, on the other hand, who took "his data from the mechanistic natural science of bourgeois society,"[282] the idea of an infinite repetition of history was an inescapable scientific deduction to which we must be resigned without hope: "Is it a windfall? Let us profit from it. Is it a mystification? Let us resign ourselves to it."[283]

In spite of this difference, the significance of the idea of eternal return with regard to bourgeois historicism was the same for Blanqui and Nietzsche, according to Benjamin. Viewed from the vantage point of eternity, the present (that of the nineteenth century), with all of its *nouveautés*, appears as a phantasmagoria in which the latest fashions have already been rolled out and worn by innumerable other versions of ourselves throughout time: "The number of our doubles," as Blanqui describes, "is infinite in time and space. These doubles exist in flesh and bone—indeed trousers and jacket, in crinoline and chignon. They are by no means phantoms; they are the present eternalized."[284] For Blanqui, what appears to be progress is actually an "immemorial antiquity parading as up-to-date novelty."[285] Time is the "monotonous flow of an hourglass that eternally empties and turns itself over. The new is always old, and the old always new."[286] Thus, in the concept of eternal return, "every tradition, even the most recent, becomes the legacy of something that has already run its course in the immemorial night of the ages. Tradition henceforth assumes the character of a phantasmagoria in which primal history enters the scene in ultramodern get-up."[287]

If this primal history, however, succeeded in capsizing the bourgeois conception of progress, the idea of eternal recurrence, in its both mechanical and non-mechanical forms, remains *mythic* in character. While denying all end goals—as either "ungodly" or unscientific—it preserves the "essence of the mythical event [which] is return. ... Thinking once again the thought of eternal recurrence in the nineteenth century makes Nietzsche the figure in whom a mythic fatality is realized anew."[288] As Karl Löwith suggests, therefore, in a statement cited in the *Arcades*, Nietzsche's repudiation of religious eschatology maintains the very form the latter: The doctrine of eternal return is "an atheistic surrogate for religion ... which down to its tiniest details often imitates the New Testament."[289] To use Benjamin's account of the difference between tragedy and *Trauerspiel*, what Nietzsche affirms, then, "is not history but myth."[290] And it is for this reason that his philosophy is taken as an object of criticism in the *Arcades*, whose aim is precisely "the dissolution of 'mythology' into the space of history."[291] The notion of eternal return, then, is not a concept of history as a purely "precarious historical occurrence."[292] On the contrary, it denies the contingency of the bourgeois conception of progress in affirming it as an endless "*répétition du mythe*,"[293] an assessment that corresponds to Benjamin's early criticism of Nietzsche as formulating the "paradigm of capitalist religious thought."[294] Although Nietzsche's philosophy, as Benjamin argues in "Capitalism as Religion," shows that "God's transcendence is at an end," God, nevertheless, "is not dead; he has been incorporated into human fate."[295]

In contrast, however, to the melancholy that characterizes the *Trauerspiel*, the acedia expressed in Blanqui's account of eternal recurrence, and its "unconditional surrender" to capitalism, is not aroused by "the omnipotence of fate which removes all value from human activities."[296] Rather, it is a melancholy that belongs to an historically determinate form of society whose mechanical characteristics paradoxically produce the appearance of a destiny that must be repeated for all of eternity. As a consequence, apparently, of the mechanical view of the universe, humanity, trapped in a mythical cycle, is forever condemned to rehearse the inevitable failure of bourgeois humanity to realize its principles. Insofar as the bourgeois conception of progress is eternalized in Blanqui's account of eternal recurrence, his infernal "vision has the entire universe entering … modernity."[297] In that sense, the notion of eternal return is a "primal history *of* the nineteenth century," the historically determinate representation of the immemorial past produced by the capitalist mode of production.[298] The concept of progress, therefore, that is capsized by the doctrine of eternal return is also its dialectical complement:

> The belief in progress—in an infinite perfectibility understood as an infinite ethical task—and the representation of eternal return are complementary. They are the indissoluble antinomies in the face of which the dialectical conception of historical time must be developed. In this conception … faith in progress seems no less to belong to the mythic mode of thought than does the idea of eternal return.[299]

In the failure to grasp its unity with its dialectical complement, the doctrine of eternal return commits the opposite error to that of the modern discourse of the symbol, criticized in the *Trauerspiel* book, a discourse of which Lukács' metaphysics of tragedy is an example. In this discourse, the allegorical image of nature as an infinitely extended duration, condemning everything to impermanence, is sublimated so that the symbol can emerge as an "indissoluble union of form and content," capable of expressing its content as a momentary totality. On the other hand, in the doctrine of eternal return, the infernal image of an infinite cosmos in which "civilizations disappear without leaving a trace" fails to acknowledge its necessary relationship to its antinomy, the task of human perfectibility, whose moral significance is nullified by the thought of eternal return. Unable to grasp its identity with its opposite, the idea of eternal recurrence capsizes the concept of progress while also affirming it as an interminable task, like the labor of Sisyphus. Against this one-sided and mythical construction of history, which is presented as a scientific deduction, Benjamin, then, proposes a dialectical theory of historical time that, by grasping the concepts of progress and eternal return as indissoluble opposites, dissolves the appearance of fate.

This twofold critique of rationalist and vitalist theories of history, as an indissoluble antinomy concealing the historical character of bourgeois society, is also presented in the "Paralipomena to 'On the Concept of History.'" In the text, Benjamin opposes Marx's "secularized ... idea of messianic time"[300] to both the neo-Kantian conception of progress and the Nietzschean notion of eternal return. The problem with neo-Kantianism, however, is not that its rational concept of history reduces the latter to the empty infinity of mechanical time. Rather, Benjamin argues that, in the concept of the classless society as an infinite task, "empty and homogeneous time was transformed into an anteroom ... in which one could wait for the emergence of the revolutionary situation with more or less equanimity."[301] Whereas history, then, in Baroque eschatology, is secularized by the spatialization of time, in the concept of the infinite task, the eternal transience of historical time becomes re-enchanted—the present is transformed into a transition awaiting the arrival of a transcendent ideal. The "idea of messianic time" that "Marx secularized" ("And that was a good thing") is theologized once again in the neo-Kantian version of a classless society.[302] Against the bourgeois conception of history, which throws "light onto vast historical expanses by means of the torch of the Ideal (whether of progress, science, or reason),"[303] Benjamin proposes a secularized messianism that grasps "historical events" in the "eternity of their transience."[304]

From the standpoint of this Marxist Messianism, "faith in progress seems no less to belong to the mythic mode of thought than does the idea of eternal return."[305] For Benjamin, therefore, the rational concept of modernity as an endless ethical task is identical to the vitalist account of the latter as eternal damnation in a circular cosmos without meaning or aim: "The basic conception in myth is the world as punishment ... Eternal recurrence is the punishment of being held back in school, projected onto the cosmic sphere: humanity has to copy out its text in endless repetitions."[306]

As Benjamin suggests in the exposé, these dialectical complements concealed the fact that the society to which Blanqui was forced to concede could not be upended through progress. Rather, its overcoming required a "humorous annihilation" of the contradictions of capitalism, which Fourier had prescribed as a way of recognizing the right of technology, a utopian prescription that conflicted with Blanqui's mechanical view of the universe: "Blanqui expressly emphasizes the scientific character of his theses [on eternal return], which would have nothing to do with Fourierist frivolities."[307] As a result, Blanqui, who embodied his century, could only condemn bourgeois society, while surrendering to the phantasmagoria of its eternal appearance, a modern mythology which Benjamin opposed to Fourier's future utopia, inspired by the "advent of machines." "This resignation without hope is the last word of the great revolutionary. The century was incapable of responding to the new technological possibilities with a new social order."[308]

Like the novelty of fashion, therefore, the notion of eternal return, in which the contradictions of bourgeois society appear as a cosmological fate, both excludes and expresses the wish for a new social order. "Everything new it could hope for turns out to be a reality that has always been present; and this newness will be as little capable of furnishing it with a liberating solution as a new fashion is capable of rejuvenating society."[309]

As Adorno recalled, this analysis of modernity as a phantasmagoria was the result of a "second, materialist" layer that Benjamin added at the later stage of his research on the *Arcades* "probably because he happened to come across a forgotten work, written in prison by Auguste Blanqui." The fortuitous discovery provided Benjamin with the chance to revisit, and to rework within a Marxian framework, a central theme of his earlier writings—the concept of fate. In these works, Benjamin sought to unmask "the deception of 'the universally human' … From time immemorial, the masters have used such categories to set themselves up as God." In spite of its cosmological proof against progress, *Eternity by the Stars* portrays the struggle of bourgeois humanity to achieve the universal ideals of liberty and equality as an implacable fate. It is this eternal appearance, which is identified with modernity, that Benjamin attempts to dissolve in the materialist criticism of the myth of modernity that he began to develop in the *Arcades*: "That links [Benjamin's] materialistic period with his theological one. He viewed the modern world as archaic not in order to conserve the traces of a purportedly eternal truth but rather to escape the trance-like captivity of bourgeois immanence."[310]

7

Benjamin and Bataille: The General Economy of the Arcades or Expenditure in the Age of Mechanical Reproduction

Morality, Happiness, and the Final Purpose of Creation

In an entry in the *Arcades*, Benjamin identifies the concept of revolution developed as part of his historical materialism as a point of convergence with Fourier's utopian socialism: "Fourier's conception of the propagation of the phalansteries through 'explosions' may be compared to two articles of my 'politics': the idea of revolution as an innervation of the technical organs of the collective ... and the idea of the 'cracking open of natural teleology.'"[1] The conception of revolution as an "innervation" of the collective, liberating itself by realizing the right of technology to transform work into play and to render morality irrelevant, is comparable to the idea that bourgeois civilization will at last be dissolved in an "*explosion du phalanstère*."[2]

As philosopher Giuseppe Ferrari describes in an essay cited in the *Arcades*, this explosion, for Fourier, would be ignited by the radical eudemonism created by the abolition of the bourgeois mode of exchange. Freed from the relations of production in capitalism, the superabundance produced by technology would cause the phalansteries to spontaneously multiply: "Once the phalanstery is a given, happiness spreads by explosion, civilization is overthrown. How would it resist the spectacle of happiness?"[3]

In the entry on Fourier, moreover, the "politics" to which this idea is compared is put in quotations by Benjamin. This is perhaps because the work to which it refers was never completed. In October 1920, Benjamin began writing a letter (also unfinished) describing a plan to compile a series of essays encapsulating his "politics," a politics of which anarchy would be the primary focus.[4] The work, as he explains in another letter to Scholem, would consist of three different chapters, the first of which would be titled "The True Politician," and the second, "The True Politics."[5] Both titles refer to Kant's "Toward Eternal Peace," in which he argues that "[t]rue politics cannot take a step without having already honored morality."[6]

"The True Politics," moreover, would be broken up into two different sections. The first, titled "The Dismantling of Violence," would likely have been a revision of the critique of Kant's doctrine of right that Benjamin outlines in the essay on violence. The second, "Teleology Without Final Purpose," refers to Kant's account of teleological judgment, which ends with a reflection on the "final purpose of the existence of the world, that is, of creation itself."[7]

As Wilhelm Windelband describes in his history of philosophy, the critique of teleological judgment was an attempt to overcome the "*dualism of Nature and morality*" that underlies Kant's theory of ethics.[8] The theory is marked by a tendency to "see ... in all motivation of moral action by natural impulses a falsification of pure morality."[9] Opposing desire and duty, Kant conceived of morality as a perpetual "warfare against ... inclinations."[10] Conversely, freedom or the "autonomy of the practical reason" is identified with the suppression of natural impulses, which frees the subject from the bonds of sensual pleasure. Happiness is in continual conflict with morality: "The goal of the sensuous will is happiness; the goal of the ethical will is virtue; these two cannot sustain to each other the relation of means to end."[11]

Because of the opposition between morality and sensual pleasure, "the development of civilization succeeds only at the cost of individual happiness."[12] The "*progress of history*," then, as the continual "approximation to ethical perfection," proves antithetical to "a *growth of human happiness*." As an infinite ethical task, history, therefore, is also a perpetual war against human nature, one that progress continually serves to intensify. As the development of industry multiplies "individual wants," the duty to deny them for the sake of moral autonomy increases accordingly, removing the "prospect of satisfying" desire. Just as bourgeois society, then, is defined by a contradictory movement in which abundance creates mass immiseration and poverty, so in Kant's conception of progress, the "ethical development of the whole ... grows in an *inverse ratio* to the empirical satisfaction of the individual." In that sense, the infinite progress of practical reason toward the impossible goal of moral perfection is also a perpetual "retrogression in history."[13]

As Benjamin mentions in the "Coming Philosophy," the opposition that underlies this conception of history is one that Kant tried to overcome in the *Critique of Judgement*, which seeks to define "the realm of ... crossover" between morality and nature. This realm is identified with the "knowledge of an experience which is ... nonmechanical," "those scientific types of experience (the biological ones)," which Kant had neglected in the *Critique of Pure Reason*.[14] In a letter to Scholem in 1921, Benjamin announced that the "Politics" he was writing would engage with this particular part of Kant's philosophical system. He was therefore studying "the epistemology ... of biology for the last or penultimate part of my political works."[15]

In the third critique, Kant acknowledges that the principle of mechanical causality cannot explain the fact that organisms (or "organized beings") and biological systems are characterized by an interdependence that makes it appear as though they had been designed for a particular purpose. To account for this, we must conceive of a "natural teleology," one that considers nature with regard to its ends, that is, in terms of the final as opposed to the efficient causality that defines the domain of the empirical sciences.

This natural teleology, moreover, would investigate not only individual organized beings, but also their interrelation in the natural world as a system of ends. As Kant argued, however, such a system can only be understood on the presupposition of a final purpose of the whole of creation, a purpose which he identified with humanity. Because human beings are the only creatures capable of investigating creation as a system of ends, man must be the ultimate purpose of nature. Our teleological knowledge of "all these ... creatures," so "artfully devised ... and ... diversely, coherently, and purposively interrelated," "would exist for nothing" if the natural world "did not include human beings." In order to understand organisms as ends, we must therefore "presuppose that man is the final purpose of creation," since "without man all of creation would be ... gratuitous and without a final purpose."[16]

As Windelband argues, however, this natural teleology only reintroduces the opposition between nature and freedom and the duality of happiness and morality which it is supposed to resolve. If humanity, according to Kant, is the final purpose of nature, this is true only with respect to its moral being, not to its happiness. Creation was not "given a final purpose with reference to the feeling of pleasure, and to the sum of that pleasure." Rather, "it is only as a moral being that man can be a final purpose of creation." Since pleasure is a natural inclination, it cannot be willed as an ethical imperative. As such, the purpose of nature cannot be the happiness of humanity. "For the fact that man ... makes happiness his own final intention gives us no concept ... for what [end] he exists at all."[17]

And because happiness, as Kant suggests, cannot be the aim of a moral imperative, even a perfectly happy state of affairs, in which everyone acts in a manner that pleases everyone else, could not be considered the final end of creation if those acts are not intended to fulfill moral ends.

> If this person does not possess a good will, what point is there in his having all this talent, assuming even that he ... exerts a useful influence on his community, so that he is very valuable in relation both to his own state of happiness and to the benefit of others? If we consider what this person is like inwardly, then he is ... worthy of contempt; and if creation is indeed to have a final purpose, then the only way for this person's existence to be consistent with that final purpose is on ... condition [that he] ... forfeit his ... happiness.[18]

For Kant, then, the final purpose of creation is the moral being of a creature that denies its own creaturely character. Because the purpose of the natural world is to transcend human nature, it is an aim that exists outside of creation itself: "what is at issue is not an end of nature (within it) ... but the end of its existence" in the supposition of an eternal realm of moral perfection that surpasses mere creaturely life. A teleological investigation of nature, therefore, "supplies a basis for a theology."[19] Although Kant, then, according to Windelband, argued that "the 'highest good' must consist ... in the union of virtue and happiness," his natural teleology demonstrates that the "last synthesis of practical conception ... can be morally thought only in the form that virtue alone is worthy of happiness." Conceived only in terms of the moral being of humanity, the final end of creation excludes human happiness.[20]

The "Cracking Open of Natural Teleology" in Fourier

This account of the final purpose of creation is one that Benjamin had apparently wanted to criticize in the second article of his anarchist politics, in the section titled "Teleology without Final Purpose." Although this critique was never developed, the entry in the *Arcades* comparing Fourier's view to Benjamin's "politics" provides some indication of what it might have contained. If the first point of connection is the concept of revolution as an "innervation of the technical organs of the collective," comparable to Fourier's claim that the phalansteries will propagate by explosion, the second is what Benjamin calls the "cracking open of natural teleology."[21]

This peculiar expression suggests a progression toward an unachievable goal that is at last set aside, a teleology in which the moral being of humanity, as the purpose of all of creation, is renounced in the end, rather than actualized. To borrow Benjamin's description of the "hedonistic impulse" that underlies the work of Karl Kraus, progress, in its continual failure to achieve moral perfection, "arrives at a conception of happiness that is as resigned as it is sensual."[22] The concept corresponds to Fourier's account of a humorous end to bourgeois morality in the establishment of a hedonistic utopia in which labor as well as technology is finally liberated. In the *Arcades* entry, then, Fourier's utopian socialism is presented as a critique of Kant's conception of history. If the final purpose of nature, for Kant, is the moral being of mankind, "Fourier's constant objective," as Auguste Pinloche pointed out, was "the happiness of humanity" and its creaturely pleasures.[23]

Whereas Kant, moreover, defines the goal of creation by means of a teleology that investigates nature as a system of organized beings, in Fourier's work, the possibility of a hedonistic utopia is derived from a mechanics of sensual pleasure. In the phalansteries, individuals will no longer be subject to a morality in which freedom requires a perpetual war against inclinations. Such a system, according to Fourier, "teaches man to be at war with himself, to resist his passions, to repress them." Moral philosophy, however, is "not qualified to estimate the natural impulses or passional attractions, which morality proscribes and relegates to the rank of vices."[24] As such, morality is "incapable of organizing … our passions wisely." In Fourier's phalansteries, therefore, pleasure replaces morality, becoming the basis of social cohesion: "the sole tendency of the passions is towards concord and the social unity which we believed was so far removed from them." For Fourier, man is a social animal not because of his reason, but because of his impulses: "A man indifferent to everything and having no passions, sufficient to himself, would cease to be a social being."[25]

In Fourier's utopia, therefore, passion provides the foundation for constructing a "mechanism made of men," one in which the happiness of the whole is achieved by aligning the work of each individual with their personal passion in such a way that "morality becomes superfluous."[26] In Fourier's words, "mechanism produces coincidence in every respect between individual … and collective interest," eliminating the need for the "doctrine termed MORALITY, which is a mortal enemy of passional attraction."[27] As Benjamin explains in the *Arcades Project*, therefore, "Fourier does not dream of relying on virtue" in order to create his utopia. Instead, "he relies on an efficient functioning of society, driven by passions. In the gearing of the passions, in the complex meshing of the *passions mécanistes* with the *passion cabaliste*, Fourier imagines the collective psychology as a clockwork mechanism."[28]

In this amoral mechanism for organizing desire, the natural inclinations of individuals, which continually threaten to undermine their morality, are aligned with the interest of the whole through an intermeshing of communal labor and individual passion. In "the state of harmony, what is vice for us becomes virtue, and *vice versa*."[29] If even the most useful person, then, in Kant's conception of the final purpose of nature, is unworthy without a good will, in Fourier's eudemonistic machine, the most depraved individual will serve to create the most human happiness: "Nero, in such a context, would become a more useful member of society than Fénelon."[30]

Whereas Kant's teleological judgment, moreover, is based upon the assumption that "without man all of creation would be … without a final purpose," Fourier's utopian speculations foresaw the "termination of the human race … after it has enjoyed the benefits of the boreal light: for 70,000 years."[31] In contrast to Kant's natural teleology, then, Fourier's "colossal conception of man," based on a mechanics of the latter's natural inclinations, does not "presuppose that man is the final purpose of creation." Rather, it assumes that his happiness as a transient creature is possible in a natural world of which he is not the ultimate end.

To return to the entry in the *Arcades*, the comparison to Fourier would seem to suggest a conjunction or constellation of Benjamin's early anarchist politics, based upon a revision of Kant, and the utopian socialism that informed his later historical materialism. The "two articles" from Benjamin's "politics" that are related to Fourier's theory correspond to the two sections from the incomplete anarchist treatise. Fourier's "*l'explosion du phalanstère*" is similar to the arguments that Benjamin had intended to make in "The Dismantling of Violence," which would have been a revision of the "Critique of Violence." The latter attempts to establish the possibility of a pure revolutionary violence without ends, one that could lead to both a transformation of labor and the abolition of state power. In his later historical materialism, this possibility is identified with the concept of revolution as an "innervation of the technical organs of the collective," which Benjamin compares to the idea that Fourier's hedonistic utopia would propagate by explosion.

If the first article of the politics, then, pertains to the possibility of abolishing bourgeois society, the second was perhaps supposed to provide an account of the new kind of society that such a revolution would serve to establish. This hedonistic society would overcome the duality of morality and nature underlying the dialectical movement in Kant's teleology whereby the progress of freedom is always accompanied by the retrogression of happiness.

In Benjamin's incomplete anarchist treatise, the two chapters to which these articles of his politics correspond were to be preceded by a discussion of Paul Scheerbart's 1913 "intergalactic utopian novel." The "first part of my *Politik* … is the philosophical critique of the *Lesabéndio*,"[32] a work which is "imbued with an idea which could not have been more foreign to the notions then widespread,"[33] and whose author "sometimes seems like the twin brother of Fourier."[34] This idea is that of "a humanity which had deployed the full range of its technology and put it to humane use," which recalls Benjamin's Marxist-Fourierist critique of the "inadequate use" of the forces of production in capitalism.³⁵ Just as the "the Fourierist utopia ... never advocated the exploitation of nature by man,"³⁶ so "Scheerbart believed that ... people should discard the base and primitive belief that their task was to 'exploit' the forces of nature."³⁷ And just as Fourier argued that "labor ... far from exploiting nature, is instead capable of delivering creations whose possibility slumbers in her womb,"³⁸ so Scheerbart believed that people "should be true to the conviction that technology, by liberating human beings, would fraternally liberate the whole of creation."³⁹

A Different Utopian Will

In a fragment titled "A Different Utopian Will," which was written at the same time as the work of art essay, Benjamin suggests that the dialectic that underlies Kant's teleology can be suspended by adopting an affirmative view of the regression accompanying the progress of freedom. The fragment begins by distinguishing between a "first" and "second nature." While first nature refers to the natural impulses (to the "bodily organism of the individual human being"), second nature relates to technology and the social relations of production.⁴⁰ According to Benjamin, the "problems of the second nature, the social and technological ones, must be very close to resolution before those of the first—love and death—can be distinguished even in outline." The solution, then, to the problems associated with the human body and its desires ("love and death") clearly comes into view only when humanity is close to resolving its social and technological problems.⁴¹

In the fragment, this possibility is identified with the development of a second technology that no longer aims at the domination of nature (and therefore no longer perpetuates the exploitation of labor), enabling the transformation of work into play. When humanity's second nature has evolved from first to second technology, the solution to its bodily problems, its desires, becomes recognizable. For Benjamin, this implies that the "goal of revolutions" is twofold in character. Revolutions must strive to emancipate the human body (or first nature) "by the liquidation of the first technology," while appropriating second technology as humanity's second nature. As "innervations of the collective," therefore, revolutions are characterized by a "twofold utopian will." This will, which is opposed to the traditional concept of technology as an instrument for mastering nature, affirms the "revolutionary demands" of second technology to liberate the bodily organism.⁴²

According to Benjamin, this "different utopian will" was one that even "the most far-sighted minds of the bourgeois revolution refused to acknowledge."⁴³ These thinkers—including Kant first and foremost—regarded the manifestations of this utopian will as a regression of history, of history understood as the continual "work of civilisation" toward the ideal of realizing the moral being of humanity. But what appears as decadence from the standpoint of the concept of history as a progression toward moral perfection is, in fact, the assertion of a utopian will that aims to abolish morality and put an end to its perpetual war against human nature. "When the powers that be disseminate a hypocritical morality, the socialist Charles Fourier observed, a countermorality immediately springs up among the oppressed, who close ranks around it to resist their oppressors."⁴⁴

Thus, in the wake of the French Revolution, the Marquis de "Sade and Fourier envision the direct realization of hedonistic life." Instead of rejecting this hedonism as a regression from the final purpose of nature, Benjamin, therefore, defines it in positive terms, as a utopia "based on the first nature (and especially the human body)," rather than on eternal moral ideals that transcend all creation and creaturely life.[45]

By asserting the revolutionary demand to liberate desire as well as second technology, the "twofold utopian will" would presumably serve to dissolve the antinomies that underlie bourgeois production as well as Kantian ethics. On the one hand, it arrests the dialectical movement in the Kantian conception of progress that arises from the "*inverse ratio*" between "ethical development" and the "empirical satisfaction of the individual." On the other, it suspends what Marx (following Fourier) referred to as the "inverse relation" between value and technological progress, underlying the outbreak of crises of plethora in bourgeois society.[46] In the fragment, then, a different utopian will is affirmed against both the perpetual war against inclinations in Kant's critique of morality and the constant rebellion against capitalism by its own means of production, which Marx analyzed in his critique of political economy.

In the teleology without final purpose implied in Fourier's different idea of utopia, the history of capitalism and civilization ends, unexpectedly, in a state of radical hedonism that makes practical reason irrelevant rather than realizing its principles. In this way, Kant's natural teleology, with its taxonomy of species and genera organized into a hierarchical system of ends, comes to a comical conclusion, one which, for Benjamin, was embodied in the figure of Mickey Mouse: "Mickey Mouse proves that a creature can still survive even when it has thrown off all resemblance to a human being. He disrupts the entire hierarchy of creatures that is supposed to culminate in mankind."[47]

As the figure for a creaturely life that is no longer compelled to conform to the moral being of humanity as the final purpose of nature, Mickey Mouse, then, represents the possibility of a humorous end to the infinite work of civilization and its perpetual war against inclination: "In these films, mankind makes preparations to survive civilization."[48] For Benjamin, the Mickey Mouse movies confirm the "cracking open of natural teleology," realized in Fourier's writings, a "humorous annihilation" of morality, in which the pathologies born of repression achieve a socially useful expression by finding release in a comical form:

> For the purpose of elucidating the Fourierist extravagances, we may adduce the figure of Mickey Mouse, in which we find carried out, entirely in the spirit of Fourier's conceptions, the moral mobilization of nature. Humor, here, puts politics to the test. Mickey Mouse shows how right Marx was to see in Fourier, above all else, a great humorist. The cracking open of natural teleology proceeds in accordance with the plan of humor.[49]

As Benjamin suggests, Marx's praise for Fourier as a satirist was in no way meant to diminish his acuity as a philosopher or a critic of capitalism. Rather, it correctly identifies his philosophical approach to the problem, opposing a hedonistic humor to the seriousness of a bourgeois morality that continually excites immorality in its pursuit of the infinite task of moral perfection. (This approach may have informed

Marx's account of commodity fetishism and its depiction of capitalism as a society in which people are ruled by the things they produce. "Marx," as Benjamin notes in "Brecht's *Threepenny Novel*," "who was the first to try to bring back the relations between people from their debasement and obfuscation in capitalist economics into the light of criticism, became, in doing so ... a master ... of satire."[50])

Against a natural teleology that subordinates nature to the moral ends of humanity, Benjamin proposed Fourier's notion of a "moral mobilization of nature," in which natural inclinations, no longer denied for the sake of autonomy, are deployed in an immoral but socially beneficial direction. This mobilization is opposed to the fascist use of perversion to manipulate the masses. Just as fascism grants political "expression to the masses" while "leaving intact the property relations which they strive to abolish,"[51] so it allows them to express their perversions while leaving intact the bourgeois morality that creates perversion through their repression: "ever since the bourgeoisie came to power ... taboos against more or less broad areas of sexual pleasure ... engender masochistic and sadistic complexes. Those in power then further these complexes by delivering up to the masses those objects which prove most favorable to their own politics."[52]

In the work of art essay, Benjamin opposes the humorous use of technology for the public display of perversion in mass entertainment to the fascist deployment of media, which permits the expression of fantasies denied by morality for the purpose of controlling the masses:

> technologization has created the possibility of psychic immunization against such mass psychoses. It does so by means of certain films in which the forced development of sadistic fantasies or masochistic delusions can prevent their natural and dangerous maturation in the masses. Collective laughter is one such preemptive and healing outbreak of mass psychosis.[53]

In this passage, Fourier's program, then, is proposed as an antidote against fascism: mass reproduction, applied to a "cracking open of natural teleology ... in accordance with the plan of humor," could serve as a means of preempting the mass psychosis created by the fascist use of technology. By exhibiting the sadistic fantasies and masochistic delusions of the collective in a comical form, mass reproduction permits a "direct realization of hedonistic life," while preventing its fascist manipulation by transforming the passions released into play.

Benjamin and Acéphale

The Fourierist notion of a humorous end to morality, accompanying the "advent of machines," would become a fundamental point of dispute between Benjamin and the members of the secret society known as Acéphale, formed by Georges Bataille. According to Michel Surya, it was Bataille "who first welcomed Benjamin to Paris," as he had welcomed other emigres, including Theodor Adorno and Max Horkheimer.[54] Before fleeing Paris in 1940, Benjamin entrusted Bataille with several of his manuscripts and with the painting, "Angelus Novus" by Paul Klee, which Scholem had given to him as a present.[55]

In the course of conducting his research on the *Arcades* in the reading rooms on rue Richelieu, Benjamin befriended Bataille, who was a librarian in the Département des Médailles at the Bibliothèque Nationale.[56] It was through Bataille that he became acquainted with Pierre Klossowski, a brilliant philosopher, artist, and translator, who was hired by the Institute of Social Research to translate the work of art essay into French. According to Eiland and Jennings: "It was only via the development of an intensive interchange with Klossowski concerning the work of art essay ... that Benjamin began to make his way at the margins of Bataille's intellectual world." "And Bataille, in turn, would figure in Walter Benjamin's approach to the most advanced French intellectual circles of the late 1930s."[57]

In 1936, Benjamin attended a meeting organized by Contre-Attaque, a collaboration between Bataille and André Breton. The aim of the organization was "nothing less than the liberation of children from parental educational tutelage ... the free expression of sexual urges ... the free play of passions, the free man as candidate for all the pleasures due to him, and so on."[58] In the following year, Benjamin attended a planning session, led by Bataille and Roger Caillois, to create a secret society and an "esoteric Leftist cult": the Collège de Sociologie and the Acéphale group.

Benjamin's participation in these intellectual circles has provoked speculation concerning the "parallels between the projects of Bataille and Benjamin."[59] According to Gary Smith, this "association ... deserves greater attention because of the natural affinity between these two early explorers of the then uncharted waters of fascist irrationality." As Jochen Hörisch has argued, moreover, Bataille's influence can be seen in Benjamin's works from the 1930s, which suggests that Acéphale may have informed Benjamin's peculiar version of Marxism.[60]

This view, however, is inconsistent with Benjamin's own account of his engagement with the Collège as well as with those of its members. Although Benjamin, as Klossowski points out, "was an assiduous auditor at the Collège de Sociologie," he "followed [its] ... goings-on with as much consternation as curiosity."[61] In spite of the fact that he "had understood Bataille well," "Benjamin disagreed with [him]."[62] For Benjamin, in fact, Bataille's idea of transgression, which would seem to resemble the radical eudemonia of his own Fourierism, was in fact a prelude to fascism: Benjamin "wanted to keep us from slipping; despite an appearance of absolute incompatibility [with fascism], we were taking the risk of playing into the hands of a 'prefascist aestheticism.' ... There was no possible agreement about this point of his analysis."[63] Although Bataille, then, admired "the great moral conscience of Benjamin," he would take "a disliking to him in the end," dismissing his views as those of "a child on whom one had stuck a moustache."[64]

As Paul Foss-Heimlich has suggested, the thrust of Benjamin's disagreement with the *Collège* can be appreciated in two groundbreaking essays that Klossowski completed in 1970: "The Phantasms of Perversion: Sade and Fourier" and *Living Currency*. The latter text was lauded by Michel Foucault as no less than "the greatest book of our time," a study whose brilliance makes "everything else recede ... and count ... only half as much anymore."[65] According to Gilles Deleuze, the significance of Klossowski's writings lies in the fact that they succeed in overcoming the gulf between political economy and analyses of the libidinal economy in psychoanalysis. Unlike earlier attempts to bridge the divide, Klossowski, by approaching the problem through Fourier, Nietzsche, and Sade, was able to "bypass … the sterile parallelism … between Freud and Marx."[66] In a letter to Klossowski, Deleuze praised *Living Currency* for introducing "desire into the infra-structure … I'm following you."[67] Klossowski's analysis of desire and labor was "enthusiastically appropriated" by other thinkers as well: "Lyotard's *Libidinal Economy* (1974) and Baudrillard's *Impossible Exchange* (1999) were are all direct responses, in one way or another, to the ideas developed in *Living Currency*."[68]

According to Daniel W. Smith, these ideas were originally formed during the period of Klossowski's collaboration on the work of art essay. *Living Currency* "looks back to 1936" in order to "look … forward to May '68," drawing on Benjamin's historical materialism in order to reconsider the relationship between desire and capitalism.[69] During their brief collaboration, Benjamin's "research … in regard to his treatment of Fourier's … themes … left a deep impression on the French philosopher."[70] After completing the translation of the work of art essay, Klossowski, as Adorno described in a letter to Benjamin, proposed to write an essay for the Institute of Social Research titled "*De Sade à Fourier*."[71] According to Foss-Heimlich, this project, which Klossowski would not complete until 1970, was already outlined in Benjamin's 1935 fragment, "A Different Utopian Will," which argues that "Sade and Fourier envision the direct realization of hedonistic life."[72] The historical materialism that Benjamin developed in the 1930s, therefore, would inform Klossowski's attempt to overcome the division of political economy and psychoanalysis, which exerted a significant influence on French philosophy in the '70s and after.

But if Benjamin's exile in Paris left an indelible mark on the work of postwar French thinkers, the effect of his work, contrary to Jeffrey Mehlman, cannot be identified with the concept of transgression. According to Mehlman, Bataille's account of transgression, as an act that "does not deny the taboo but transcends it and completes it,"[73] was derived from the Sabbatian notion of "redemption through sin," which Scholem developed in his writings. Benjamin purportedly relayed the idea to Bataille, and, in Bataille's formulation, it inspired the work of French post-structuralist thinkers. The concept of transgression, therefore, is "a neo-French gloss on the Hebrew concept … 'a commandment which is fulfilled by means of a transgression' … that Scholem labored … to rehabilitate."[74] Mehlman's argument, then, as Michael Weingrad describes, is that "Benjamin, in bequeathing his *Passagenwerk* notes and Klee painting to Bataille, also gave French theory the gift of Scholem's … Sabbatian" idea of transgression.[75] Given this intellectual genealogy, the "French school which culminates in Derrida, Deleuze and Foucault," according to Mehlman, can be considered "a late manifestation" of a radical Jewish tradition.[76]

As Weingrad points out, however, Bataille's seemingly Sabbatian view of transgression in fact appears in works written well before his encounter with Benjamin: "A quick review of Bataille's work will show that he was conversant with destructive forms of sacred experience years before he met Benjamin or could have been familiar with Scholem's studies."[77] And rather than being an intellectual gift that Benjamin bequeathed to Bataille, the idea of transgression (as an act that reenforces the law that it violates), which was central to Acéphale's ideology, was a source of consternation for Benjamin. Thus, at a meeting with Benjamin and Adorno, Klossowski explained that the aim of Bataille's organization was to "invent new taboos" so as to invite their transgression, to which Adorno replied, "Don't we already have enough taboos?" while "Benjamin nodded his head."[78]

In Klossowski's two essays, moreover, Fourier's utopianism, which was Benjamin's "most authentic depth," is repudiated precisely because of its failure to grasp the "seriousness" of transgression. If "Benjamin and Klossowski," then, were "united in thinking" the "great institutional experiment devised by Sade and Fourier," as Foss-Heimlich points out, "Benjamin's critical apparatus," nevertheless, also appears to have been Klossowski's "principal target": The "dialectical materialist argument is precisely what Klossowski set out to challenge in his Sade and Fourier project."[79]

The project, then, explores the same historical subject matter as the *Arcades* through a different theoretical framework. Like the *Arcades*, Klossowski's essays are a reflection on the new forms of industrial luxury that appeared in nineteenth-century France, new commodities created by "industrial intervention in the domain of fantastical representation." This period was marked by what Klossowski describes as "the industrial commodification of the voluptuous emotion under 'mass' relations of production," giving rise to an "industrial world, which ... exploit[s] every display, including displays of the perverse element."

According to Klossowski, a careful consideration of this period, and of the commodification of desire that constitutes its distinguishing characteristic, "obliges us to rethink the phalansterian utopia," a utopia for which Benjamin had "boundless admiration." Klossowski's project, therefore, will attempt to call into question a key component of the critical apparatus of the *Arcades*. In particular, Klossowski will propose a Acéphalean critique of Fourier's utopian socialism, and his notion of labor as impassioned play, in an account of perversion in the era of industrial capitalism, based on the writings of Sade, who expressed a utopian will different from Fourier's: "Sade's anti-utopian project, in what it reveals economically, insofar as perversion itself gives rise to value ... helps one understand more clearly the meaning of Fourier's playful freeness."[80]

Work and Desire in Sade

In *Living Currency*, Klossowski presents a Sadean account of the ethical subject, one that affirms the continual war between morality and desire, which Kant had failed to resolve in his natural teleology. From Sade's perspective, the subject is only an effect of this perpetual struggle. In the war between instinct and morality, desire continually threatens the subject's self-preservation, its ability to contain its impulses in order to satisfy need. The necessity or "seriousness" of work compels the subject to repress inclination and to "formulate [its] ... instinctual life by means of a set of suitable material and moral needs," forcing it to "defer voluptuous pleasure," enjoyed in the moment, for the sake of its future survival.[81]

As Klossowski describes, these material and moral needs constitute "*the economic form of repression that the existing institutions impose by and through the agent's consciousness on the imponderable forces of his psychic life."* Whereas Kant, then, identifies the autonomy of the subject with the suppression of natural instinct, for Sade, on the other hand, the subject is the effect of a repression which, imposed externally by economic constraints, is internalized as the self. The *"organic and psychic unity"* of the subject arises out of the *"battle waged by the instincts against the constraints that constituted that unity."*

The individual, then, is a "fiction" produced by the perpetual conflict between instinct and the economic and moral constraints that determine the unity of the subject: "For Sade … the individual is only ever the accidental meeting-place of different impulses which, unable to express themselves other than through an agent, only grant him an illusory identity." In constituting the individual's psychic and bodily unity, the clash between instinctual and institutional forces simultaneously engenders the individual as a subject of work and expenditure. The "battle among the instincts, which is waged … against the formation of … psychic and bodily unity … is where the first 'production' and 'consumption' schemes come into being."[82]

This description of the conflict between the subject and its natural instincts conforms to Bataille's account of the difference between "restricted" and "general economy," between "productive expenditure" and the "accursed share," which must be consumed unproductively. From the perspective of restricted economy, work—which can take the form of acquisition, preservation, and investment or productive consumption—is a calculated operation that aims either at utility or profit. In Klossowski's words, labor affirms itself by its "aptitude to possess goods external to [itself]; by preserving them, producing them."[83]

For Bataille, such actions, oriented toward utility, presuppose the denial of the impulse toward "exuberance through eating, death and sexual reproduction,"[84] the desire for extravagant and useless consumption, which Bataille referred to as "unproductive expenditure": "Now it is necessary to reserve the use of the word *expenditure* for the designation of these unproductive forms."[85] Such expenditures involve an exuberance that dissolves the unity of the subject: "measureless expenditures of energy [are] … a violation of the integrity of individual beings."[86] In order to preserve this integrity for the sake of subsistence, the "introduction of labor into the world replaced … the depth of desire and its free outbreaks, with rational progression." "[W]hat matters is no longer the truth of the present moment, but, rather, the subsequent results of operations."[87]

But just as the subject can never completely suppress its desires, so the impulse toward unproductive expenditure cannot be denied indefinitely. The wealth created by the rational progression of labor cannot be expanded forever. Surplus "cannot accumulate limitlessly in the productive forces; eventually, like a river into the sea, it is bound to escape us and be lost to us." Just as ethical development in Kant, therefore, results in a "retrogression in history," so, for Bataille, the rational progression of the history of production engenders a countervailing "movement of exudation," one that ensures that the surplus created by labor will eventually be consumed unproductively.[88]

In his 1933 essay, "Notion of Expenditure" (which Benjamin dismissed as "[m]ore gibbets … [and] gallows!"),[89] Bataille describes the bourgeoisie as a modern ruling class which, unlike earlier ones, refuses to recognize the necessity of unproductive expenditure: "The hatred of expenditure is the *raison d'être* of and the justification for the bourgeoisie."⁹⁰ As Bataille explains in the *Accursed Share*, the inability of bourgeois society to recognize that its surplus production can only be uselessly squandered would result in the unproductive expenditures of the First and Second World Wars. In these conflicts, the scale of destruction would be directly proportional to the superabundance of wealth created by a civilization based upon the denial of useless consumption: The "industrial plethora was at the origin of these recent wars ... this plethora that both wars exuded; its size was what gave them their extraordinary intensity."⁹¹

In *Living Currency*, Klossowski, drawing upon this theory, posits an inverse relationship between labor and the impulse for expenditure, between production or the "manufacturing of a useful object" and the "perverse elaboration of a fantasy":

> The two processes diverge, insofar as the fantasy, a product of instinctive impulse, signals a threat to the individual unit, while the manufactured object presupposes the stability of the individual: the fantasy tends to make itself a lasting one at the expense of the individual unit, while the manufactured object must serve that unit.⁹²

In the two 1970 texts, this inverse relation between the production of goods and the elaboration of fantasy will allow Klossowski to "overcome the duality between Marx and Freud," while avoiding what Deleuze called the "the sterile parallelism ... between Freud and Marx." By turning to Sade (via Bataille), Klossowski was able to recognize that "a purely analogical relationship ... between the 'economy' of emotions and the economy of needs ... would lead nowhere," since fantasy prevails only at the expense of production, and vice versa.⁹³ The relationship between political economy and the libidinal economy, then, is not a parallel, but an inversion: "The absurdity of an analogy like this shows the reversal that instinctive forces undergo in the realm of the economic expression of needs and of the manufactured objects corresponding to them."⁹⁴

Kant and de Sade on the Use of Persons and Property

As Klossowski argues, however, bourgeois society is not only characterized by the desire to indefinitely prolong the rational progression of work and productive consumption, denying useless expenditure. It is also defined by a rational mode of exchange that allows things to be purchased and sold, but which prohibits the sale of people as objects. Bourgeois society, in other words, is based upon an economy that proscribes "living currency," or the circulation of persons as objects to be used, which violates the imperative to treat them as ends-unto-themselves. The bourgeois subject of labor, then, affirms itself not only "by [its] ... aptitude to possess goods external to [itself]," but also by the "giving of [goods] for consumption by others, and by receiving them, as long as they are objects and not living units."⁹⁵ If production, therefore, in bourgeois civilization, denies unproductive expenditure, its mode of exchange prohibits the sale and circulation of "*the living objects of voluptuous desire.*"

The idea of living currency violates the fundamental distinction between persons and property underlying Kant's doctrine of right, which is based on the axiom that people should "use themselves as well as things without thereby degrading themselves into the things they use." This axiom informs the Neo-Kantian criticism of capitalism as a system that depends on the institution of selling the use of one's body for wages. For Kant, it is "self-contradictory" to treat someone like property, since that would amount to possessing a rational being whose free will is the condition of possession itself: A "person cannot be a property and so cannot be a thing which can be owned, for it is impossible to be a person and a thing, the proprietor and the property."[96]

This contradiction, however, is one that Kant himself will permit in his deduction of property, which suspends the axiom of right in a *lex permissiva* that restricts the freedom of others and subjugates things in order to save them from being practically annihilated for use. As Benjamin notes, moreover, in "Goethe's Elective Affinities," Kant permits a similar exception in his notorious deduction of marriage in *The Metaphysics of Morals*. As Kant explains in the text, the sexual act violates the axiom of right: "Sexual love makes of the loved person an object of appetite," and "as an object of appetite for another [the] person becomes a thing."[97]

In the marriage relation, however, the depravity of the sexual act is removed, according to Kant, by the reciprocal ownership by husband and wife of the other's "sexual properties." Because of the "reciprocal use made by one person of the sexual organs ... of another,"[98] marital intercourse, unlike all other forms of sexual commerce, does not degrade individuals through their treatment as things. Rather, it recognizes their moral freedom as persons. The reciprocity establishes an "equality of possession, equality ... in their possession of each other as persons."[99]

According to Benjamin, this deduction of marriage is Kant's "gravest mistake" as well as the "most sublime product of a *ratio* that ... penetrates ... deep[ly] into the facts of the matter." Although Kant grasps the "objective nature of marriage" in his account of the latter as the reciprocal ownership of another person's sexual properties, he makes a mistake in assuming that one can "deduce [the] ... moral necessity" of marriage from this definition: "From the objective nature of marriage," however, "one could obviously deduce only its depravity—and in Kant's case this is what it ... amounts to."[100]

For Benjamin, then, the morality of marriage cannot be derived from the axiom that persons should never be degraded as property. Rather, in its objective nature, the reciprocal ownership of another person's sexual properties is a mutual self-degradation that reduces the partners to the contradictory condition that Benjamin identifies with the prostitute, as "seller and sold in one."[101]

What this deduction of marriage, moreover, would seem to exclude is a sexual corollary to the original state of possessor-less things or *res nullius*, which is omitted in Kant's deduction of property (see Chapter 2). Just as the latter denies the right of things to remain without owners (despite being subject to anyone's use), so Kant's conception of marriage denies the fact of an original promiscuousness, in which persons can use one another as things, but no one can possess anyone else.

In the nineteenth century, as Benjamin notes, this paradisal condition, which was identified with European accounts of non-Western cultures, was one that thinkers like Fourier associated with the utopian possibility that technology could allow for a reorganization of desire and labor: "With the discovery of Tahiti, declares Fourier, with the example of an order in which 'large-scale industry' is compatible with erotic freedom, 'conjugal slavery' has become unendurable."[102]

For Fourier, then, the advent of machinery inspired wish images of a utopian future free from relations of property as well as from the reciprocal enslavement of sexual organs in bourgeois society. Like the primitive past, this future would be based on a common use of people and things. As Klossowski describes, Fourier's "'utopian socialism' decided to extend the '*communization*' *of all goods to the living objects of voluptuous desire*."[103] Liberated from bourgeois relations of property, industry and its superabundance could create the conditions for a utopia resembling an original state of permissiveness in which everyone has a claim upon everything and everyone else, but nothing and no one at all could ever be owned.

As Fourier argued, moreover, this primitive sexual communism cannot be conceived as an earlier stage in the development of bourgeois sexuality. Just as the French Revolution eternalized the "chimeras" of freedom and universal equality, which are ideals belonging to bourgeois civilization, so its "erotic Jacobinism" had forced "all sexual needs into the … harness of monogamy."[104] And just as the bourgeois economy, moreover, "constantly arrives at the very opposite to that which it wants to attain," creating poverty out of plenty, so marriage "seems to have been invented to reward perversity," promoting the very moral offenses that it is supposed to prevent: cuckoldry, adultery, and prostitution.[105] Fourier, therefore, proposed to abolish the bondage of persons in marriage along with the relations of property underlying bourgeois society, with the aim of "leading men and women alike to complete freedom and openness in affairs of love, and bringing the whole social body to sexual freedom."[106]

For Sade, similarly, the modern regime of marriage and property only serves to perpetuate the degradation of persons that it is supposed to suppress. The prohibition against the sale of persons and their sexual properties only guarantees prostitution. As Sade argued, therefore, the proscription against the sale of sexual commerce in the bourgeois economy is "criminal" since it engenders an "integral monstrosity" that is compelled to utilize the economy in order to violate this proscription in pursuit of its crimes. In *Juliette*, this monstrosity is represented by the members of "Society of the Friends of Crime," who seek to satisfy their "non-exchangeable" perversity precisely by purchasing it for its monetary equivalent. As Klossowski explains, "Sade's argument is … the following":

> institutions claim to preserve individual liberty by substituting for the exchange of bodies the exchange of goods by means of money … Under the pretext of circulating wealth, money only works to ensure the secret exchange of bodies in the name, and in the interest of, institutions. The disavowal of integral monstrosity by institutions returns, de facto, as a material and moral prostitution. The whole meaning of the secret societies imagined by Sade is to make this dilemma apparent: either communication through the exchange of bodies, or prostitution under the sign of money.[107]

In proscribing the use of persons as things, the money economy, then, creates a clandestine criminality that violates its rules of exchange.

Perversion and Money

As Klossowski emphasizes, however, Sade's secret society is not supposed to be an alternative to bourgeois civilization. Its crimes are not intended to overturn the moral proscriptions that they violate, including the prohibition against the sale of "the living objects of voluptuous desire." Sade had "no need to overthrow institutions."[108] In contrast to Fourier, who proposed to abolish bourgeois morality, Sade, in fact, affirmed the latter's repression as the very condition of the perversions that he wanted to practice. Because he recognized that the "fundamentally institutional structure of perversity" is in "perfect complicity with the means of repression,"[109] Sade "deliberately chained [the erotic force] to institutions ... condemning it to be destroyed along with them."

These institutions include the money economy, whose prohibition against the sale of persons as things arouses perversion while increasing the exchange value of the persons to which perversion attaches itself. Perversion, therefore, would require that "each person ... keep their moral propriety, which constituted the individual's value when on sale." Without moral propriety, the person who exchanges himself could not be degraded, depriving the act of prostitution of precisely what distinguishes it from the exchange of ordinary commodities: "[S]laves are not inert objects with no self-love, but living beings, reduced to objects whose attraction consists in their being humiliated or able to be humiliated (deliberately or otherwise), in their dignity, integrity, and aptitude to possess their own good, to possess themselves."[110]

In the economy of perversion, the loss of moral integrity is inversely related to the degree to which "voluptuous sensation is intensified," an intensification that is immediately tied to the amount of money it costs to acquire another person's debasement: The "'quality'" of a prostitute "comes from the bidding-up of the price that its subjects put on themselves in proportion to their moral degradation; the more they are 'corrupted,' the more their price goes up."[111]

In this way, money serves as *a symbol for both work and unproductive expenditure*, for the restricted as well as the general economy. As the "most general sign of equivalence," money, on the one hand, performs the "fantasy function" (or "fraudulent operation") of becoming the image of what it is not: it is a representation of labor, a "symbol of effort and struggle" that, in the "act of purchase or sale," establishes a "supposed compatibility between objects and needs." As a symbol of work, which denies the desire for useless consumption, money, then, can be exchanged for particular objects of utility, in spite of the fact that its equivalence with these objects is purely fictitious or fraudulent.[112]

As Klossowski argues, however, money is not only the "equivalent of rare riches," and of the rational effort required to appropriate, conserve, and increase material wealth. It also "must symbolize the [irrational] redirection of those riches to the benefit of ... perverse fantasy," which "demands an expenditure." Money, then, is a representation not only of labor, but also of its opposite, of what Bataille called the impulse toward "exuberance through eating, death and sexual reproduction," the desire to uselessly squander. In this capacity, "money, the equivalent of riches, thus signifies the destruction of those riches, *while retaining their value*." Money, then, is the sign of both production with unproductive expenditure. It is at once the symbol of work and "the representative mode of perversion." In this double role, money performs a *"mediating function,"* reenforcing both the "world of anomalies and the closed world of institutional norms."[113]

Impassioned Play and the Seriousness of Work and Desire

As Klossowski points out, this Sadean account of perversion provided the basis for Fourier's plan for a hedonistic utopia: the "prophecy of phalansterian felicity takes its point of departure in the tableau of perversions Sade provides."[114] In the phalansteries, as Benjamin explains in the *Arcades*, desires like sadism, which are regarded as perversions in bourgeois society, would be aligned with other passions so as the contribute to the happiness of the whole:

> The kinship between Fourier and Sade resides in the constructive moment that is proper to all sadism ... The experiences of the sadists, as presented in his *120 Jours de Sodome*, are, in their cruelty, exactly that extreme that is touched by the extreme idyllic of Fourier. *Les extremes se touchent*. The sadist, in his experiments, could chance on a partner who longs for just those punishments and humiliations which his tormentor inflicts. All at once, he could be standing in the midst of one of those harmonies sought after by the Fourierist utopia.[115]

Against Sade's perverse affirmation of bourgeois society, therefore, Fourier proposed what Klossowski described as affective *"exchanges between affinity groups."*[116] Whereas bourgeois "society fails to channel [the child's] passion for dirt toward any good and useful purpose,"[117] in the phalansteries, the mechanical arrangement of passions would *"ensure the balance and aptitude ... of all, like a vast ... recapitulation of the ... variations of instinctive life."*[118] In this way, the "erotic Jacobinism" of bourgeois society, forcing "all sexual needs into the ... harness of monogamy," would be replaced by a "phalansterian communization," harmonizing what Freud called the "polymorphous perverse," the diversity of "compounded passions."[119]

As Klossowski argues, however, Sade's account of perversion was not only the starting point of Fourier's idea of utopia. It was also the "preemptive refutation" of the Fourierist conception of communism, so central to the critical apparatus that Benjamin developed in the *Arcades*.[120] This refutation is based on the Sadean insight that the tableau of perversions, which Fourier wanted to harmonize in his utopia, was inextricably bound up with the bourgeois institutions he proposed to abolish. Because of this, Sade's account of perversion precluded the social harmonization of pleasure through play that defines Fourier's hedonistic utopia: "Fourier wants to restore in his project what implicitly exists in Sade, but what Sade relentlessly seems to destroy by virtue of his rational expression: voluptuous beatitude."[121] If both Sade and Fourier, then, according to Benjamin, envisioned the "direct realization of hedonistic life," the Sadean account of the latter, which identifies this realization with existing society, invalidates "Fourier's prophecy of future ... felicity": "Fourier bitterly resented Sade for having explored identical territory in such a way as to make his own project—the free play of the passions—unrealizable from the outset even though Sade's table of perversions had inspired it."[122]

Because "perversion," according to Sade, "is itself a game in relation to the indomitable power of norms," and because the "compound passions" are produced by the very morality that seeks to suppress them, perversion cannot be the principle of a future society.[123] But as such, Fourier's utopia would not be able to "promote the gratification of many desires that civilized society condemned as perversions," since those desires demand gratification precisely because they are denied in existing society. By detaching perversion from bourgeois morality, Fourier's plan would dissolve the very desire he intended to liberate. The free play of the passions, then, presupposes the very civilization that the propagation of phalansteries would completely abolish.

This Sadean refutation of Fourier recalls Foucault's critique of the "repressive hypothesis" in the *History of Sexuality*, which appeared six years after Klossowski overcame the "duality between Marx and Freud" in his two essays on Sade and Fourier. In his seminal text, Foucault argues that the "critical discourse that addresses itself to repression … is … in fact part of the same historical network as the thing it denounces (and doubtless misrepresents) by calling it 'repression.'"[124] The critical discourse that Foucault calls into question, in a manner recalling to Klossowski's refutation of Fourier, includes the "socialism … of the nineteenth century," which imagined the future "in terms borrowed from our society, from our civilization." In a "universalisation of the model of the bourgeois," this socialism "gave pride of place … to a sexuality of a bourgeois type," isolating it from the historical network that constituted its meaning and function and projecting it into a utopian future beyond bourgeois civilization.[125]

But if sexuality cannot be separated from the historical institutions that shape it by means of repression, neither can its energy be transposed onto labor so as to impassion it. Contrary to Fourier, desire cannot be bonded with labor in order to "suppress [the latter's] … punitive character," such that work could "take place in the euphoria of imagination, as the spontaneous and creative activity of man." Work cannot be carried out in accordance with "*passional* aspirations," rather than "industrially determined need," since the production of objects of utility and the elaboration of fantasy are inversely related. The one cannot be transformed into the other any more than a calculated action can be equated with an uncontrolled outburst of unproductive expenditure.[126]

A similar criticism of Fourier appears in Marx' writings. For Marx, Fourier's utopian vision of work transformed into passionate play is inconsistent with the serious nature of labor. Fourier was correct to assume that the abolition of the wage-relation would eliminate the opposition between "labour … as external forced labour" and "freedom, and happiness," transforming labor into "attractive work," aimed at "the individual's self-realization." But this attractive work would not be playful in character. Labor "in no way … becomes mere fun, mere amusement, as Fourier, with grisette-like naïveté, conceives it." "Labour cannot become play, as Fourier would like," since "[r]eally free working, e.g. composing, is at the same time precisely the most damned seriousness, the most intense exertion."[127] Liberated from the domination of capital, labor indeed would be free, but it would retain all of its seriousness, and would not resemble amusement.

In "Sade and Fourier," Klossowski combines a criticism similar to the one Marx makes of Fourier with a Freudian one. The transformation of work into passionate play would cancel the "seriousness" of both labor and fantasy, a seriousness that is essential to each. To impassion labor would be to invest it with the feeling of urgency that belongs to sexual fantasy. But this would deprive work of the seriousness that constitutes it precisely as such, turning it into a simulation of labor: "What is urgent (such as subsistence) must be taken seriously, and cannot be simulated in the same way as the urgency [of voluptuous emotion] is simulated."[128]

On the other hand, the transformation of work into a process that conforms to the elaboration of fantasy presupposes a "plasticity of the drives," "a malleability" that allows perversion to be mobilized for social production. The assumption, then, that underlies the entire design of the phalanstery is that it would be possible to *freely* create an "object compatible with perversion" by abolishing the institutions that seek to repress it.[129]

But this is "precisely what Sade does not propose." For Sade, "perversion is itself a game in relation to the indomitable power of norms." But unlike Fourier's conception of play, the Sadean game of perversion preserves the seriousness of the voluptuous emotion, which is defined by an "aggressive element, which demands and presupposes resistance."[130] It is the conflict or clash between the inevitability of norms and the seriousness of the voluptuous emotion that fixates the latter upon its specific "phantasms," with an urgency and intransigence that cannot be simulated in play. If the object of perversion is always "unappraisable, elusive, useless and arbitrary," this does not mean that it can be given an object at will.[131] The perverse, as both Sade and Fourier recognized, is polymorphous, but because of its seriousness, which arises "by reason of a perfect complicity with the means of repression," it is also immalleable.

As Klossowski describes, the seriousness of perversion, which makes its costly and compulsive pursuit appear as though free of burden, is directly opposed to the seriousness of subsistence or labor: "If there were no seriousness, there would be no real voluptuousness either since the latter can only be felt if it is taken seriously. Voluptuousness can be light and frivolous in comparison to the rest of existence only if it 'pays the price' of being taken seriously."[132] Just as the seriousness of subsistence represses the urgency of desire, so the seriousness of expenditure denies the urgency of production. By conflating these two forms of necessity, Fourier's program of passionate play would deprive work and desire of the seriousness that is specific to each: "[P]lay aims to capture and channel the expressions of the perverse depth that is implicit in every voluptuous emotion," but in attempting to do so, it "empties of its content that which it had intended to make blossom."[133]

Just as work transformed into play would be deprived of the seriousness that defines it precisely as work, so the reduction of perversion to play would eliminate the resistance that gives perversion its pleasure. The urgency that is specific to work cannot be simulated as fantasy any more than the seriousness of perversion can be adapted to the demands of subsistence. And as such, "the unsimulated reality of perversion," like the unsimulatable reality of work, "puts in question Fourier's enterprise."[134]

Thus, the concepts of play and passionate labor, underlying Fourier's utopian socialism, cannot reconcile the irreconcilable forms of seriousness that are specific to desire and work. The latter are exclusive forms of unsimulatable urgency that the subject must alternatively defer in order to preserve itself as a unity: "Impulsive fantasy" and "non-simulatable subsistence"[135] constitute "two circuits that merge in the individual unit, but which that unit can never break; all it can do is to perpetually defer the urgency of the one circuit or the other."[136]

Klossowski thus identifies the principal flaw of the phalansterian utopia with its very foundational principle: the concept of play and the ludic arrangement of passions, underlying Fourier's "cracking open of natural teleology ... in accordance with the plan of humor." Fourier's "whole invention consisted in wanting to satisfy ... voluptuous aggressiveness ... through a playful organization of passional situations which in themselves are not so playful."[137] The transformation of passion into play would only dissolve the erotic energy that Fourier wanted to harness in order to power his eudemonic machine: "[P]lay aims to capture and channel the expressions of the perverse depth that is implicit in every voluptuous emotion," but in attempting to do so, it "empties of its content that which it had intended to make blossom."[138]

The General Economy of the Arcades

In Fourier's work, then, the perversions created in bourgeois society are projected into a utopian future beyond this society where they can no longer exist. This criticism of Fourier appears to be a direct refutation of one of the central motifs of Benjamin's incomplete opus. Contrary to Benjamin, the development of new forms of industrial luxury in the mid-nineteenth century did not constitute a commodification of the utopian impulse for a better arrangement of desire and work. The reality was in fact the reverse: Fourier believed he could build his hedonistic utopia upon a tableau of perversions that cannot be detached from the organization of bourgeois production.

In Sade's work, on the other hand, the inextricable co-implication of perversion and the institutions of bourgeois society, including the exchange of commodities, is established with a sadistic rigor and clarity. As Klossowski points out, this is evident in the very style of Sade's writings, which is completely different from Fourier's in terms of how it represent the "mute" fact of pleasure.[139] "For Fourier, it is a question of reconstructing language according to a logic adapted to the passions, so as to render intelligible those very abnormalities made incommunicable by rational language." Because passion is denied by the language of moral rationality, Fourier assumed that "we must invent a new language based on the different idioms of the passions—something that Sade did not care for, and absolutely refused to do."[140]

Because "abnormality," from Sade's perspective, "always signifies" the "transgression of norms," to make it communicable would be precisely to normalize it.[141] For this reason, Sade's characters do not speak in an idiom of the passions. Instead, they use a rational language to communicate their irrational perversity: "Sade has them speak with a rigour of expression and argumentation which is perfectly rational, and does not himself invent some code language."[142]

In *120 Days of Sodom*, this use of language connects the members of the "Society of the Friends of Crime," a community or secret society that is bound by their incommunicable passions. Unlike Fourier's phalanstery, the Society has "no need to overthrow institutions," by propagating itself, for example, by means of explosion. Rather, just as its members can only convey their perversions by speaking a rational language that makes their communication impossible, so the crimes they commit against the norms of society reenforce the institutional repression that compels them to commit the crimes in the first place. In their crimes, then, the members "promote the fundamentally institutional structure of perversity … by reason of a perfect complicity with the means of repression."[143]

The Society, therefore, has no need to overthrow the institutions whose norms it criminally violates, since the institutions engender the very perversions for which the Society itself was created. Its members, then, "uphold these institutions," since, without them, "their perverse cravings would not take shape in their own eyes, or assume consistency." Whereas in Fourier's utopia, then, perversions are supposed to "create their own institutions,"[144] replacing those belonging to bourgeois civilization, in Sade, on the other hand, "the institutions 'structure' perversions" in existing society, and therefore would be "destroyed along with them."[145]

In Sade's secret society, the most important of these institutions is money, which, according to Klossowski, succeeds, where Fourier's utopia fails, in reconciling the seriousness of production and unproductive expenditure. Whereas impassioned labor or play would deprive both work and desire of their seriousness, money serves as both a representation of labor and a means of "symbolizing the unappraisable value of … fantasy."[146] It is a "symbol of effort and struggle" that is also "an integral part of the representative mode of perversion."[147]

In Klossowski's two essays, this refutation of Fourier, which would seem to be a response to Benjamin's criticism of Acéphale, provides the basis for what appears to be a retelling of the nineteenth-century history outlined in the *Arcades* from the perspective of general economy. During this period, the development of mass reproduction would allow "industry to *intervene in the genesis of individual phantasms in order to redirect them towards its own ends* … so as make them profitable."[148] To that end, the "*power of suggestion*" was employed in the "domains of marketing, advertising and film production," which became "*mechanized instruments of suggestion*." These technologies became the mechanical means with which to insinuate the phantasmatic objects of perversion to the masses, "standardizing suggestion at a low price."[149]

This production of fantasy for profit, however, did not simply subvert a utopian impulse to transform desire and work into play. On the contrary, it realized the synthesis of work and perversion that was already implicit in money, a synthesis which, as Sade had revealed in his writings, anticipated the "industrial commodification of the voluptuous emotion under 'mass' relations of production."[150] In the new products of industrial luxury, the two distinct functions of money are merged. Through the mass reproduction of the power of suggestion, industry endowed objects of labor, which had previously been valued by money as "the sign of toil and hardship,"[151] with the "*unappraisable*" aura of "perverted fantasy [which] is in itself … unexchangeable."[152]

The result was an integration of political economy and the "economy of voluptuous pleasure."[153] Overcoming its earlier "hatred of expenditure," the bourgeoisie, then, yoking its restricted economy to the general one, would reorient its society toward *the production of unproductive consumption.* Thus, the "sadist intuition," concerning the connection between the money economy and the economy of voluptuous emotion, "was to become the principle of our modern economy in its industrial form: the principle of excessive production, requiring excessive consumption."[154] In the modern economy, the price of an article of consumption is no longer determined solely by its utility or the "quantity of labor considered as a value standard."[155] Rather, invested with voluptuous emotion by the *"mechanized instruments of suggestion,"* price is also determined as a "result of a bargaining between phantasms and the individual who experiences them."

According to Klossowski, this development is "most pertinently raised within the Sadian outlook," an outlook that was preoccupied with the "question of the value of the incommunicable," of the exchange of money for the objects of perversion.[156] Sade's writings, in other words, address the question of how to define the "equivalent of the incommunicable phantasm": "Sade has the distinction of being the first modern thinker to recognize the intimate relationship between the phantasm and commercial exchange, and thus the role of currency as a sign of the incalculable value of the phantasm."[157]

By insisting upon this relationship, Sade provides a critique of Kant's famous answer to the question, "What is Enlightenment?" a critique that anticipates the one that Bataille presents in the "Notion of Expenditure." Contrary to Kant, enlightenment is not "the human being's emergence from his self-incurred minority," a tutelage that is overcome by means of a moral autonomy achieved through a continual struggle to suppress one's desires.[158] Rather, for Bataille, humanity remains immature so long as it refuses to recognize that its practical freedom, as well as its rational ability for work, can never subdue the impulse toward extravagant and useless consumption: "it is sad to say that *conscious humanity has remained a minor;* humanity recognizes the right to acquire, to conserve and to consume rationally, but it excludes in principle non-productive expenditure."[159]

As Sade had anticipated, these two kinds of necessity, work and expenditure, would be recognized in a modern economy based on the production of objects of unproductive consumption. For Fourier, this bourgeois economy was one in which the superabundance produced by technology reduces the value of goods, leading to crises of plethora. The ability of technology, then, to create products for free incites a rebellion by the mode of production against the mode of exchange. As Benjamin observes in the *Arcades*, such crises, however, could be overcome through the manufacture of "newness," which stimulated consumption by exciting perversion.

In *Living Currency*, Klossowski describes this development as one in which the mechanical means of mass suggestion are utilized in order to fix a value upon an experience of arousal that is valueless. The "world of industrial manufacturing" is defined by the "price put on what is naturally for free; a voluptuous emotion (non-communicated or incommunicable) … *has no value,* in the sense that *each person* can experience it freely."[160] By putting a price on a valueless pleasure, thereby creating an obstacle to its gratification, industry profits from what is naturally free, while stimulating the passions. As Benjamin explains in the *Arcades Project*, "this commodity appearance <*Warenschein*> of nature … is embodied in the whore. 'Money feeds sensuality."¹⁶¹ For Klossowski, this defining characteristic of the modern economy conforms to Stendhal's statement that *"Those who can't find a way to give themselves freely find a way to sell themselves."*¹⁶² In the modern bourgeois economy, then, an industrial mode of manufacturing, which can create products for free, is oriented toward the production of objects of unproductive consumption, the price of which is determined by the excitement of a voluptuous emotion that possesses no value.

The Price of Perversion and the Decline of Aura

But if Sade had anticipated the modern economy, based on unproductive expenditure, while providing a preemptive refutation of Fourier's conception of play, he did not, however, preclude the possibility of a future beyond bourgeois society. Perversion cannot become play in a future utopia free of the moral repression that produces perversion itself. Yet, as Klossowski contends, it is possible to create a more "rational" economy than the one that exists in the present, which fuses the restricted economy of calculative activity with useless expenditure. Such an economy, however, presupposes the dissolution of the subject, as the site of the perpetual struggle between the passions and the internalized institutional repression that "compound" them into perversions. Thus, Klossowski imagines a "day when human beings overcome, and thus subdue *external* perversion, i.e., the monstrous hypertrophy of 'needs,' and assent instead to their *internal* perversion, i.e., to the dissolution of their fictional unity."¹⁶³

This possibility, however, presupposes the creation of a society which, in accordance with Bataille's account of enlightenment, would recognize the necessity of irrational outbursts of desire, in all of their seriousness. For Klossowski, this seriousness demands that a price must be paid for a voluptuous emotion that is naturally free, an unappraisable passion that can only be gratified at the cost of resistance, and which therefore cannot be simulated in play. In this way, "a compatibility will form between desire and the production of its objects in an economy rationally organized around human instinctual impulse; and thus the *freeness of effort* will respond to the *price of the irrational*."¹⁶⁴

In *Living Currency*, Klossowski suggests that such an economy could potentially neutralize the endless cycle of transgression, underlying the modern economy, and create the conditions for another kind of society, which would unexpectedly verify Fourier's fantasies: "Sade's lesson will have demonstrated that Fourier's utopia conceals a profound reality. But until that reality appears, it is in the best interest of industry for Fourier's utopia to remain a utopia, and for Sade's perversion to remain the driving force behind the monstrousness of industry."¹⁶⁵

Toward the end of his essay, then, Klossowski, having presented a "preemptive refutation" of Fourier, points to what seems to be a potential refutation of Sade in Fourier's writings. In an unexpected turnaround in the text, Klossowski appears to leave open the possibility of a utopia beyond an existing society, in which perversion is inextricably bound to industrial capitalism and bourgeois morality. *Living Currency*, then, concludes by qualifying its otherwise relentless critique of the critical apparatus of the *Arcades*: Fourier's utopia could potentially be actualized, in the place of the

Sadean "monstrosity of industry," on the rational basis of an economy in which the "freeness" of an "incommunicable" voluptuous emotion would be in accord with the "price of the irrational."

The qualification, however, also appears to be a partial concession to Benjamin's critique of the Acéphale group. As Klossowski describes, Benjamin attributed the latter's "pre-fascist aestheticism" to "the metaphysical and poetic upward valuation of the incommunicable," which was "a function of the antinomies of industrial capitalist society."[166]

In the *Trauerspiel* book, Benjamin cites the philologist Georg Friedrich Creuze's definition of the mystical symbol as the paradoxical expression of the "inexpressible," which "ultimately burst[s] its earthly form."[167] As Benjamin suggests in the "Epistemo-Critical Prologue," however, the ineffable character of all forms of beauty lies in the fact that beauty does not exist in itself, but only as an appearance. For "the sake of its appearance," therefore, "beauty always flees ... the lover," fearing "an unveiling that destroys the mystery," disclosing the fact that there is nothing beneath the sensual form. Beauty, then, cannot be revealed by unveiling its content since it exists only in its appearance. But precisely as such, it is only in the disappearance of its sensual form that beauty reveals what it actually is. It is made "manifest ... in a process that can be described figuratively as the flaming up of the veil."[168]

In the work of art essay, this concept of beauty, as "beautiful semblance" or "the appearance of spirit in its immediate ... sensuous form," is identified with the notion of "aura." Thus, Benjamin quotes the following statement to show that "Goethe's work is still imbued with beautiful semblance as an auratic reality": "The beautiful is neither the veil nor the veiled object but rather the object in its veil."[169] As in the "Epistemo-Critical Prologue," therefore, beauty is defined in the work of art essay not as the unveiling of its object, but as the object as it appears under its veil.

In the artwork essay, however, Benjamin, in an argument that Adorno described as "disquieting," underlines the historical character of this conception of art: "The significance of beautiful semblance [*schöner Schein*] is rooted in the age of auratic perception that is now coming to an end."[170] What this would seem to suggest is that, for Benjamin, art loses its aura or ineffable beauty as a result of the rise of technological reproduction, which is characterized in the text as a form of "second technology." The "withering of semblance and ... decay of the aura" is attributed, then, to "the world-historical conflict between the first and second technologies. Semblance is the most abstract—but therefore the most ubiquitous—schema of all the magic procedures of the first technology."[171]

If second technology, then, in the sphere of production, increasingly makes labor irrelevant, in the realm of mimesis or representation, its technologies of mass reproduction threaten to undermine aura or semblance, which is characteristic of images created by first technology. As Benjamin goes on to explain, the fundamental procedure for creating auratic representations, which the artwork tries to preserve against the demands of second technology, first arises in magic: "As we know, the earliest artworks originated in the service of rituals—first magical, then religious. And it is highly significant that the artwork's auratic mode of existence is never entirely severed from its ritual function."[172] Like the "figures in the service of magic" from which it originates, art reproduces the "object as it appears under its veil." Since the veil must keep the object from view as a condition of its incommunicable beauty, artworks as well as magical figures remain distant, "however close [they] may be."[173]

> What is important for these figures is that they are present, not that they are seen. The elk depicted by Stone Age man on the walls of his cave is an instrument of magic, and is exhibited to others only coincidentally; what matters is that the spirits see it. Cult value as such even tends to keep the artwork out of sight: certain statues of gods are accessible only to the priest in the *cella*; certain images of the Madonna remain covered nearly all year round.[174]

Through the procedure of veiling an object, things acquire the "cult value" that constitutes objects as sacred, in the theological sense of the latter as that which is removed from common use, as opposed to the profane, which is "permissible for ordinary use" and "accessible to all."[175] In this way, an object that is useless or deprived of utility is endowed with inestimable value. In Klossowski's terms, a "price [is] put on what is naturally for free."

For Bataille, whom Benjamin criticized for his "upward valuation of the incommunicable," this experience of the sacred was increasingly lost in bourgeois society because its economy was restricted to the profane realm of production and profit.[176] This economy, then, was one that denied the necessity of sacrifice or unproductive expenditure, which "restores to the sacred world that which servile use has degraded, rendered profane."[177] For Bataille, the result of this restriction was a process of profanation that allowed for the creation of an immense "industrial plethora,"[178] a surplus production that, because it could not be consumed unproductively, caused the catastrophes of the First and Second World Wars: "the greatest orgies of wealth—and of human beings—that history has recorded."[179] As Bataille argues, therefore, such catastrophic "exudations" of "excess energy" can only be avoided by acknowledging the necessity of sacrifice and by "divert[ing] the surplus production ... into unproductive works that will dissipate in energy that cannot be accumulated in any case."[180]

The Sacred and the Profane in Benjamin and Bataille

In Bataille's "Acéphalean atheology," then, restoring the sacred entails the destruction of things without any regard for utility or profit: "Destruction is the best means of negating a utilitarian relation between man and the animal or plant."[181] If sacrifice, then, in "the etymological sense of the word ... is the production of sacred things," things become sacred only when they cease to exist. "[C]onstituted by an operation of loss," sacred things are destroyed by the very act that creates them.[182]

In the work of art essay, Benjamin identifies this procedure with first technology: "The achievements of the first technology might be said to culminate in human sacrifice."[183] Insofar as the semblance that constitutes objects as sacred is the "schema of all the magic procedures of the first technology," what the statement suggests is that, in sacrifice, people and things are destroyed for the sake of an image.[184] In that sense,

Bataille's notion of sacrifice literalizes the figure of beauty that Benjamin evokes in the *Trauerspiel* book: beauty is made "manifest … in a process that can be described figuratively as the flaming up of the veil."[185] In sacrifice, the worldly existence of people and things is destroyed for a semblance.

For Benjamin, this conception of sacrifice would have undoubtedly resembled the "*aestheticizing of politics, as practiced by fascism,*" which he denounced in the work of art essay.[186] And indeed, as Klossowski describes, one of the aims of the *Collège de Sociologie* was to research the Nazi deployment of myth. For Bataille, the fascist "sacralization of the political" needed to be carefully studied, not in order to gain immunity against it, but to discover a means of creating alternative political myths that could be used in order to fight it.[187] As Benjamin argued, however: "All efforts to render politics aesthetic culminate in one thing: war. … 'Fiat ars—pereat mundus,' says fascism, expecting … artistic gratification" from mechanical warfare.[188] For Benjamin, the notion of sacrifice as an assertion of sovereignty against a utilitarian world in which everything is rendered profane would have seemed like the expression of an "alienation [that] has reached the point where it can experience its own annihilation as a supreme aesthetic pleasure."[189] Thus, for Benjamin, as Klossowski recalled, Acéphale "risked playing the game of a pure and simple 'pre-fascist aestheticism.'"[190]

In the historical account of the origin of semblance presented in the work of art essay, Benjamin, moreover, affirms the process of profanation that Bataille identifies as the cause of the sacrificial destruction of people and things in the First and Second World Wars. As a result of the development of mass reproduction, the sacred aura of objects, created by semblance, is dissolved as "the opportunities for exhibiting … products increase."[191] Because of the "conflict between the first and second technologies" in the realm of mimesis or representation, "*exhibition value begins to drive back cult value on all fronts.*"[192]

As in the *Arcades Project*, moreover, Benjamin, in the work of art essay, defines "reactionary" movements in art in terms of their resistance to this tendency of technology toward desacralization: "For when, with the advent of the first truly revolutionary means of reproduction (namely photography, which emerges at the same time as socialism), art felt the approach of that crisis which a century later has become unmistakable, it reacted with the doctrine of *l'art pour l'art.*"[193] In the modern "secularized … cult of beauty," which culminates in art for art's sake, the fundamental magical procedure of veiling an image is preserved in a "negative theology" of semblance, devoid of any determinate "representational content," either religious or social.[194]

Because of this, the cult of beauty is directly opposed to what Benjamin describes as the revolutionary "desire of the present-day masses to 'get closer' to things, and their equally passionate concern for overcoming each thing's uniqueness by assimilating it as a reproduction." Since getting closer to things destroys the "unique apparition of a distance, however near it may be," an apparition which constitutes aura, the "urge … to get hold of an object at close range in an image" is the "social basis of the aura's present decay."[195]

This desire is stimulated by a second technology that, instead of veiling an object to create a sacred appearance, destroys the cult value of images by increasing the opportunities to exhibit and see them, thereby securing their common use for the masses. Just as second technology, then, created an industrial plethora that inspired the wish image of a state of permissiveness in which everyone has a claim on every possession, so, in representation, it results in an "anarchistic" propagation of images, depriving them of sacred authority.[196]

As Benjamin suggests in his discussion of Disney Cartoons as an example of Fourier's "cracking open of natural teleology ... in accordance with the plan of humor," this effect of second technology also applies to the "phantasms" to which perversion attaches itself. By "standardizing suggestion at a low price," and disseminating mass reproductions of "sadistic fantasies or masochistic delusions," technology decreases what Klossowski described as the *"price of the irrational,"* reducing the repression required to sustain the "seriousness" of perversion. In a sexual apocatastasis, the eternal conflict between instinct and morality (which, in Kant's teleology, postpones the final end of creation, and, in Sade's utopian will, sustains the passions, along with the institutions that serve to repress them) is defused by their consumption as comedy: "Collective laughter is ... [a] preemptive and healing outbreak of mass psychosis. The countless grotesque events consumed in films are a graphic indication of the dangers threatening mankind from the repressions implicit in civilization. ... Disney films trigger a therapeutic release of unconscious energies."[197] In its mass reproduction, the seriousness with which morality continually reproduces the "monstrous hypertrophy" of perverse desires becomes a source of collective amusement for the masses.

Such a humorous annihilation of Sade's tableau of perversion, then, would seem to point to the possibility of an eroticism that is no longer "tinged with the appeal of the commodity," nor tied to the bonds of bourgeois morality.[198] For Benjamin, this possibility is at once disavowed and expressed by the modern economy. In the fashion industry that emerged in the nineteenth century, the banalization of the objects of sexual fetishism became part of a perpetual cycle of novelty, the ever-recurring production of commodified forms of perversion and social distinction, which Sade had foreseen.

For Benjamin, this system is not only one that must constantly reproduce the urgency of desire through the mechanized means of suggestion or semblance. It must also preserve the seriousness of work, or what Benjamin calls the "inauthentic" appearance of labor as "mastery over nature," in an era when second technology has displaced labor itself from its primary role in the production of goods. It is precisely by preserving the fiction that "labor is the source of all wealth," despite the development of technology that "aims at liberating human beings from drudgery," that the system, paradoxically, perpetuates the exploitation of work while creating a superfluous population of workers.

Contrary to Bataille, then, the exudations of excess energy that characterized the First and Second World Wars were not the result of the catastrophic accumulation of the accursed share by a bourgeois society which, due to its "hatred of expenditure," denied the necessity of sacrifice. Rather, for Benjamin, the destruction was a consequence of the "antinomies of industrial capitalist society," a society that refused the revolutionary demand of technology to transform work into play. Impeded by a bourgeois property system, based on the fetishistic conception of labor as the source of all wealth (as opposed to a purely profane view of production), "the increase in technological means, in speed, in sources of energy will press toward an unnatural use ... found in war."[199] For Benjamin, then, war is a result of what Fourier described as a capitalist mode of production that is in rebellion against its own mode of exchange.

By preserving the "semblance of 'value,'" or the appearance that wealth is determined by labor alone, this mode of exchange creates crises of plethora, to which fascism responds by utilizing the superfluous labor and overproduction for war: "The most horrifying features of imperialist war are determined by the discrepancy between the enormous means of production and their inadequate use in the process of production (in other words, by unemployment and the lack of markets)."[200] Only "war makes it possible to mobilize all of today's technological resources while maintaining property relations."[201]

For Benjamin, this sacrificial destruction is not simply a consequence of the inherent profanity of the bourgeois economy, and of the irresistible demand to restore "to the sacred world that which servile use has degraded, rendered profane." On the contrary, it is a result of the refusal to accept the desacralizing tendency of second technology. Because capitalism, "according to its economic nature ... resolutely exclude[s] technology's right" to dissolves the semblance of value as well as that of the sacred, technology demands human sacrifice as the price for its inadequate utilization:[202] *"Imperialist war is an uprising on the part of technology, which demands repayment in 'human material' for the natural material society has denied it."*[203]

Expenditure in the Age of Mechanical Reproduction: Benjamin's Preemptive Refutation of Bataille

As Benjamin suggests in "Theories of German Fascism," in which he presents the analysis of German intellectual life that he will later apply to Acéphale, what fascism fails to perceive is the tragic comedy of restoring sacrifice and sacred experience in the age of mechanical warfare. Fascism:

> nowhere observe[s] that the new warfare of technology ... which appears to some of them as the highest revelation of existence, dispenses with all the wretched emblems of heroism ... [It] ... permanently displaces soldierly qualities by those of sports; all action will lose its military character and war will assume the countenance of record-setting.[204]

This profane view of modern warfare is directly opposed to Bataille's account of the two world wars as "the greatest orgies of wealth ... and ... human beings," created by the bourgeois economy in its attempt to accumulate an accursed share that could only be uselessly squandered. For Bataille, the sacred significance of these sacrificial events, though which "Man ... revealed and founded human truth,"[205] was proportional to the scale of the industrial plethora accumulated through the denial of the impulse toward unproductive expenditure, "abandoned by productive mankind."[206] For Benjamin, on the other hand, the mass death and destruction that modern warfare produces are deprived of significance to the same degree that modern warfare depends on technology. Just as crises of plethora destroy the semblance of value, so industrial warfare provides "a new means of abolishing aura": "Without approaching ... the economic causes of war, one may say that the harshest, most disastrous aspects of imperialist war are in part the result of the gaping discrepancy between the gigantic power of technology and the minuscule moral illumination it affords."[207]

The sacrifice, then, that technology demands in mechanical warfare, as retribution for its inadequate utilization in capitalism, does not afford the "highest revelation of existence." Rather, it extinguishes every semblance of meaning. Modern warfare, therefore, is a sacrifice that does not restore the experience of the sacred, but rather nullifies the sacred as such.

What this would appear to imply is that, contrary to Jürgen Habermas, the idea of divine violence in Benjamin only appears to be "separated by ... a hair's breadth from ... fascist power," which Habermas compares to "Bataille's conception of an immaculate sovereign power."[208] The difference between Benjamin and Bataille can be located perhaps in the expiatory effect of divine violence, an effect that Benjamin also appears to attribute to mechanical warfare. In contrast to both mythic violence and sacrifice, the latter produces destruction and death that yield no revelation.

As Agamben points out, this view of violence is one that Bataille will later acknowledge in his reading of Hegel, but without fully coming to terms with its profane implications: "Bataille ... discern[s] that sacrifice is insufficient and that it is, in the last analysis, a 'comedy.' ('In sacrifice, the one being sacrificed identifies with the animal struck with death. Thus he dies watching himself die, and even by his own will, at peace with the weapon of sacrifice. But this is a comedy!')" Bataille concludes, therefore, that "death, in fact, reveals nothing ... the revelation never takes place."[209]

Together with the work of art essay, the passage from "Theories of German Fascism," cited above, can be read, then, as a preemptive reply to Klossowski's refutation of Benjamin via Fourier. For Klossowski, Benjamin's "personal version of a 'phalansterial' renewal'" was based on a concept of play that is antithetical to the seriousness of both work and desire. The idea of an impassioned labor transformed into play is impossible because the seriousness of work can never be harmonized with the urgency of desire. Like Fourier's phalansteries, Benjamin's "erotic and artisanal" communism, therefore, "consisted in wanting to satisfy ... voluptuous aggressiveness ... through a playful organization of passional situations which in themselves are not so playful." In proposing to liberate perversion from the bonds of bourgeois civilization, this utopia hypostatizes desire as it exists in the present, projecting it as the principle of a future society where this desire, freed from the repression from which it arises, could no longer be mobilized.

The preemptive reply to this refutation, implicit in Benjamin's work, could be presented as follows: Acéphale's ideology is a pre-fascist aestheticism that espouses a trans-historical view of desire, labor, and sacrifice, one that accords with the viewpoint of first technology, which serves to perpetuate bourgeois society. It affirms the vulgar conception of labor as mastery over nature, rejects the revolutionary demand of technology to be absorbed as the second nature of humanity, and celebrates the outmoded mystery of human sacrifice in the era of mass reproduction and mechanical warfare. In an age when second technology, in its rebellion against the semblance of value or the bourgeois of mode of exchange, aims to liberate humans from labor, this view asserts the seriousness of work without any irony. Oblivious to the comedy of perversion at a time when its objects are mass produced and consumed—a time when Sade's intuition has become the basis of the modern economy itself—Klossowski can claim in all seriousness that the urgency of desire is an inviolable principle. And in an age when images everywhere are unveiled by mass reproduction, Acéphale's atheology expounded the seriousness of a sacred experience that is no more than a semblance.

This refutation of Acéphale is summed up in a 1938 letter to Horkheimer in which Benjamin writes that the "tortuous thinking" (*pensée tortueux*) of Roger Caillois, one of the founders of the secret society, is reminiscent of Joseph Goebbels' ideas. The "pathological cruelty" that Caillois displays in his writing was a product of the "praxis of monopoly capitalism," which "preferred to consecrate its resources to destruction rather than orienting them towards utility or happiness." The concept of expenditure without reserve, therefore, is a "metaphysically hypothesized" expression of "historically conditioned character traits of the present bourgeoisie" (*les traits de caractère historiquement conditionnes de l'actuel bourgeois*). It leads to a fascist apotheosis of war, one that eternalizes conditions of crisis specific to monopoly capitalism, transforming the latter into a metaphysical principle, purportedly underlying the "secret history of humanity."[210]

Finally, if the seriousness with which Acéphale understands work and perversion implies a greater degree of maturity than Kant's idea of Enlightenment, for Benjamin, it does so by simply affirming the incomplete character of Kant's teleology of the moral being of humanity. The Sadean subject maintains its moral autonomy as the price it must pay for its unappraisable perversion, for a happiness or voluptuous pleasure that is freely experienced. In this way, in contrast to Kant's teleology, it recognizes that the work of civilization is always accompanied by "retrogression in history."[211]

This recognition, however, simply replaces the perpetual war between instinct and morality in Kant with an interminable process of transgression that preserves both perversion and the institutions that seek to repress it. But as such, like the concept of eternal return in Blanqui and Nietzsche, this atheology capsizes the bourgeois conception of progress while transforming it into an inescapable fate. It is in this way as well that Sade, who "deliberately chained [the erotic force] to institutions, by condemning it to be destroyed along with them," sought to "defend the inevitable," or justify bourgeois society. From the standpoint of the historical materialism that Klossowski sought to refute, this perspective affirms the semblance of value, newness, and sacred experience, which block the emergence of a classless society, based on the liberation of work and desire.

In that regard, Sade's immoral justification for capitalism constitutes the dialectical complement to the neo-Kantian conception of socialism as an infinite ethical task. While the latter implicitly affirms capitalism's contradictions as a condition of progress toward the ideal of a socialism that conforms to the categorical imperative, Sade affirms the contradictory character of money and bourgeois morality as a condition for the endless pursuit of perversion. The infinite work of civilization is thereby replaced by its endless transgression.

These seemingly opposing positions, moreover, are rooted in the same historical situation that produced the arcades, that of a bourgeoisie who has renounced its revolutionary role within history. Thus, the neo-Kantian school represented "the withering of the bourgeoisie's oppositional resolve, and the withering of the historical ambition which had lived in that resolve," embracing the "ambiguity" of an infinite ethical task that can never be realized.[212] Likewise, Sade shared the sense of "impotence" with a "bourgeois class" that, around "the middle of the century ... ceases to be occupied with the future of the productive forces it had unleashed," affirming a historically transitory organization of desire and labor.[213]

Conclusion: The Angel of History, the Owl of Minerva, and the Eternal Return

Because Benjamin "hardly ever showed his cards,"[1] "steadfastly refusing in most cases to supply outright the meta-theoretical bases of his conceptual train," the interpretation of his writings inevitably seems to resemble an exercise of what he called the mimetic faculty. Benjamin's "intentionally a-systematic, fragmentary,"[2] and deliberately enigmatic work provokes the experience of a "perception of similarity," a revelation unveiling in "an instantaneous flash" a seemingly undeniable truth that dissolves upon closer inspection. To borrow Benjamin's account of astrology, the connections between disparate parts of his writings appear to offer themselves "to the eye as fleetingly and transitorily as a constellation of stars."[3] Or, to refer to one of the Borgesian labyrinths inspired by Blanqui's account of eternity, the interpreter of Benjamin's work is like the priest in "The God's Script," deciphering the meaningless patterns on the pelt of the jaguar pacing in the adjacent cell of his circular prison. As one reader recently concluded, therefore: "Anybody foolhardy enough to attempt a philosophical digest of [Benjamin's] themes and methods will quickly find themselves turning about in [a] … labyrinth."[4]

But if the attempt to broadly interpret Benjamin's work is an imprudent endeavor, it is also an unavoidable one, given the unmistakable impression of a coherent and expansive philosophical system that is so clearly discernable across his episodic production. As Giorgio Agamben observed, the "more one analyzes Benjamin's thought, the more it appears … to be animated by a rigorously systematic intention … as Benjamin once wrote of another philosopher usually thought to be fragmentary, Friedrich Schlegel."[5]

As Agamben suggests, then, Benjamin's characterization of Schlegel's fragmentary reflections can be applied to his own. These reflections do "not count … as proving anything against [Schlegel's] systematic intentions. Nietzsche … wrote aphoristically … yet he thought through his philosophy in a comprehensive and unitary manner in keeping with his guiding ideas."[6] According to Benjamin, the mystical fragments that Schlegel used in his writings were intended to excite the mimetic faculty, allowing them to convey his systematic ideas in a flash in which everything is revealed instantaneously. These fragments, therefore, serve as a means of "combining the maximum systematic range of thought with the most extreme truncation of discursive thinking."[7] Like

Schlegel's writing, therefore, Benjamin's work was "systematically oriented" without being "systematically developed."[8]

Furthermore, a reading of Benjamin's work that refuses to give an account of its systematic intention risks lapsing into the sort of aesthetic and historical nominalism that Benjamin tried to correct in his concept of the constellation as a paradoxical unity of irreducibly singular objects. Applied to Benjamin's own writings, the twofold imperative to "think the 'idea' as a configuration of singular extremes"[9] would have to entail the attempt (which Benjamin never succeeded in making) to "express the contradictory and mobile whole that my convictions represent in their multiplicity."[10] Without a philosophical digest of its methods and themes, Benjamin's writings become a collection of disparate objects of historical interests, the study of which would consist in their enumeration and detailed description. By "clinging to the particular," however, such an approach, to use Benjamin's critique of nominalism, would "forfeit ... the essential."[11] The result would be a "proliferation of à la carte Walter Benjamins: the Marxist literary critic, the theologian, the surrealist, the philosopher of language, the philosopher of history, the born again romantic, the melancholic," and so on.[12] The "ascetic discipline," however, to which Benjamin subjected himself "in omitting all the crucial theoretical answers" would not have been necessary if there were no theoretical answers to withhold for aesthetic or methodological reasons.

The systematic intention in Benjamin's writings can be appreciated perhaps in the dialectical, but decidedly non-Hegelian manner in which his criticism of other thinkers, including Hegel and Nietzsche, often appears as a more consistent version of their own rigorous systems. Rather than simply repudiating another's position, Benjamin asserted his own original style of thought by taking the philosophy developed by others to the extreme.

This aspect of Benjamin's writing, however, has not always been recognized even by well-informed readers. Thus, as Adorno asserted (in a critique of the "undialectical positivity" that purportedly defines Benjamin's work as a whole), the theory of the dialectical image demonstrates an insufficient understanding of dialectics. The theory is undialectical insofar as it eliminates the principle of becoming that defines the dialectic itself.[13] Moreover, what "Benjamin would later call 'dialectics at a standstill'" was a procedure that Hegel (whose writings Benjamin "hardly would have known") had already applied.[14] In Hegel's philosophy, however, the standstill or stasis, as Adorno describes, is only a moment in the dialectical process, in the perpetual "restlessness ... which Hegel calls Becoming."[15] "Thus intertwined, the system's static and dynamic characters keep clashing." Stasis must serve to sustain the system's never-ending dynamic since a complete suspension of movement would create a "closed system," one which could "tolerate nothing outside its domain, it will become a positive infinity – in other words, finite and static ... bring[ing] it to a standstill. Bluntly put, closed systems are bound to be finished."[16]

The imperative, however, in Hegel's philosophy, to preserve the openness of the system by ensuring its constant becoming comes into conflict with the idea of absolute knowledge. Like the doctrine of eternal return, the dialectic requires humanity to continue a history that, as absolute knowledge asserts, has already ended. Thus, in Hegel's account of the French Revolution, the attempt to achieve "absolute freedom" produces the Terror. In a dialectical reversal, the struggle to actualize the ideals of the French Revolution results in senseless destruction: "The sole work and deed of universal freedom is thus *death*, the most meaningless death of all."[17]

For Hegel, therefore, what the progress of history demonstrates is that the ethical principles which define its ultimate ends cannot be used to create a morally perfect future society. What *is* cannot be opposed to what *ought to be* since, with regard to the "desire to teach the world what it ought to be ... philosophy at least always comes too late."[18] Because every individual "is a son of his time," all moral ideals are products of the society from which they originate. In that sense, the future can only be a projection of the present. As such, it is "foolish to fancy that any philosophy can transcend its present world." Theory cannot "transgress ... its [own] time, and build ... up a world as it ought to be."[19] Progress, therefore, only reveals that its end is an unrealizable ethical principle belonging to the very society that it was supposed to transcend: "History thus corroborates ... that only in the maturity of reality does the ideal appear as counterpart to the real."[20] History, then, reveals that the real is the (morally) rational, and that our representation of a more rational future is only a product of our incurably irrational world.

What history teaches, therefore, is that the role of philosophy is only to recognize, retrospectively, that reality necessarily contradicts its ideals, and therefore cannot be fundamentally changed for the better. But in order for Hegel to avoid a closed system, history has to continue even after the failure of the French Revolution. After the end of history, the state must continue to embody a bourgeois conception of freedom that history has already shown can never be actualized.[21] For the owl of Minerva, therefore, progress, which drives the angel of history "irresistibly into the future," can never be brought to a standstill, even though philosophy already knows that the future is only an ideal representation of society as it exists in the present.[22] In Hegel's philosophy, then, the movement of history remains open to an ending that is a foregone conclusion. But as such, it does not remain open at all.

It is precisely this feature of Hegel's conception of history that distinguishes it from what would seem to be a messianic misreading of the owl of Minerva that appears in the essay "Unpacking My Library": "But, as Hegel put it, only when it is dark does the owl of Minerva begin its flight. Only in extinction is the collector comprehended."[23] For Benjamin, then, the owl represents an end rather than an unreachable goal. For Hegel, however, philosophy does not explain a reality that no longer exists, but rationalizes an outmoded state of affairs, a "form of life [that] has become old."

From the perspective of Benjamin's theory of the dialectical image, the "restlessness" of Hegel's philosophy, its refusal to come to a standstill implies that *its knowledge is not absolute*. Unable to grasp the progress of history in the completed and completely static image of a "constellation saturated with tensions ... between dialectical opposites," the Hegelian dialectic demands that humanity continue to look to the future of an existing society that is already outmoded.[24] After the end of history, philosophy can only interpret the world, but it can no longer change it: "When philosophy paints its grey in grey, one form of life has become old, and by means of grey it cannot be rejuvenated, but only known."[25]

This justification for progress, however, oddly resembles the nihilistic refutation of progress proposed by Blanqui, in the "resignation without hope" that was the "last word of the great revolutionary." "Everything new [that humanity] could hope for turns out to be a reality that has always been present; and this newness will be ... [in]capable of rejuvenating society."[26] But in that sense, the perspective of the owl of Minerva is identical to that of the eternity of the stars: The "eternal return appears precisely as that 'shallow rationalism' which the belief in progress is accused of being."[27]

On the other hand, in the ideology of Acéphale, Hegel's conception of history is inverted: in spite of the fact that it can never accomplish its end, the progress of bourgeois morality is affirmed as an infinite task for the sake of prolonging perversion. Like morality, perversion is a product of existing society. As such, contrary to Fourier, it cannot serve as the principle for a new social order. If philosophy always comes too late to teach the world what it ought to be, perversion comes too late to teach society how to free itself from repression.

But just as the notion of absolute knowledge, from the perspective of Benjamin's theory, is not absolute, so the thought of eternal recurrence, as the *Arcades Project* implies, is not nihilistic enough. In particular, it retreats from the meaninglessness of mechanical time as well as from the "*thèse pessimiste du temps circulaire*," an infinite circle from which nothing new can ever arise.[28] Although Blanqui, then, asserted that "All that's done is done, and will be done,"[29] he continued, nevertheless, to believe that the future "will bring its new bifurcation," new events which have not yet occurred in the past, despite its eternity.[30] Blanqui did not "exclude all hope or expectation," even though this faith in the future violates the conclusions he derived from his own mechanical view of the universe.[31] Progress remains possible in spite of the fact that it can only repeat what has already happened. Unlike Benjamin, therefore, who rejected any "view of history that puts its faith in the infinite extent of time," Blanqui was a thinker who "recognize[d] no theatre appropriate to progress but the infinite. Only the plurality of existences in the infinite expanse of time and space measures up to the demands of ... progress."[32]

For Nietzsche, on the other hand, the concept of eternal return "is not simply a mechanistic conception; for if it were that, it would not condition in infinite recurrence of identical cases but a final state."[33] In such a final state, the process of becoming, which Nietzsche, like Hegel, wished to affirm, would be brought to a standstill. To keep time from becoming immobilized, the cycle must be repeated forever, even though the result is always the same: the future will only reveal what has already happened. In Nietzsche's doctrine, therefore, progress, in search of the new, must continue *ad infinitum*, even though the future is only the eternal return of the primordial past.

But in that case, the doctrine of eternal recurrence is not equal perhaps to the mythological image that Nietzsche evokes to define it. The "great thought as Medusa's head: all features of the cosmos become immobile, a frozen death struggle."[34] To borrow Benjamin's description of the shield of Medusa, Nietzsche's thought is not that of a "petrified unrest," but of a process that cannot be suspended even though its outcome is known in advance. The great thought of an infinite cosmos eternally repeating itself, therefore, is opposed to a dialectical thinking that grasps the immobile image of an unlimited "constellation saturated with tensions."

From that perspective, from the perspective of Benjamin's "Medusan glance,"[35] the doctrine of eternal return appears as an imperfect nihilism, one that differs, however, from the "incomplete nihilism" that Nietzsche describes in Will to Power. The nihilism that defines the thought of eternal return is imperfect not because it tries to "escape nihilism without revaluating our values."[36] On the contrary, it is incomplete because it continues to put faith in the future, one that it knows will never reveal anything new, continuing to hope for a world that will one day be revalued.

It is this incomplete nihilism that distinguishes the thought of eternal return, for which Nietzsche proposed the image of the Medusa's head, from the allegorical mode of perception, which grasps the "*facies hippocratica* of history as petrified primal landscape ... inscribed ... in a death's head."[37] Against this primordial landscape—which embodies the infinite duration of time, a reified time of things, shorn of human significance—what exists in the present already appears as a ruin, the traces of vain human endeavors forgotten by the passage of empty, homogeneous time.

During the seventeenth century, this representation of nature emerged as a result of the "general 'mechanization of the world view' of that time."[38] History was subject to a "total secularization of the historical in the state of creation," as time became spatialized due to the "same metaphysical tendency ... in the exact sciences [in which] ... temporal process is caught up and analyzed in a spatial image."[39]

This spatialization of time resulted in a "collapse of all eschatology." For the seventeenth century, history was no longer conceived as either a cyclical movement or a linear one in which humanity seeks to transcend the creaturely plane of spatialized time. In a "reversion to the bare creaturely condition,"[40] a pure immanence without transcendence, history, freed from all eschatology, became a "headlong flight into a nature without grace," or "a graceless Creation."[41]

This profane conception of nature is excluded in the thought of eternal return, which attempts to find meaning in a mechanical world whose infinite repetition only confirms its utter meaninglessness. The infernal vision of the universe as eternal recurrence, therefore, excludes the Baroque conception of nature, which "looms before [all] ... as eternal transience," as the infinite extension of mechanical time, encompassing a cosmos "deprived of all value."[42] Whereas Nietzsche, therefore, proposed to complete his nihilistic philosophy through a revaluation of the world that would save it from its meaningless transience, Benjamin defines this state of creation, devoid of human significance, as an "immanent state of perfection."[43]

As Stéphane Mosès has argued, therefore, "negating the idea of progress" did not lead Benjamin to a "pessimistic conception of history," or to the "collapse of all his hopes for communism." The "end of belief in a meaning of history did not involve abolishing the idea of hope." Contrary to Mosès, however, this does not mean that, for Benjamin:

> ... Utopia, which can no longer be thought as belief in the necessary advent of the ideal at the mythical end of history, reemerges through the category of *Redemption* – as the modality of its *possible* advent at each moment of time. In this model of a random time, open at any moment to the unpredictable eruption of the new, the imminent realization of the ideal becomes conceivable again, as one of the possibilities offered by the unfathomable complexity of historical processes.[44]

This concept of redemption, as the possible rather than inevitable actualization of an ideal, excludes Benjamin's own messianic "definition of politics" as the "fulfillment of an unimproved humanity," in which the progress of history would make it *unnecessary* to achieve its objective. In this profane idea of fulfillment, hope lies neither in the necessity nor in the possibility of the new, but in the impossibility of progress itself. Only such a conception of history would be adequate to a "historical materialism which has annihilated within itself the idea of progress."

Contrary to Michael Löwy, therefore, Benjamin does not reconcile his unwavering "commitment to ... the oppressed" with his essentially "pessimistic" view of history, based on the "fear of an eternal return of defeats," by conceiving of revolution as "a wager, in the Pascalian sense." Revolution, in Benjamin's writings, is not understood as a gamble that preserves "optimism" or hope in the "possibility of a struggle for emancipation," the outcome of which can no longer be assumed to be a necessary consequence of history. On the contrary, Benjamin's philosophy of history was characterized by a refusal to accept the concept of progress even in the negative theological form of a leap of faith, or in the belief in the possibility that its unachievable ends will somehow be realized in the future.[45]

In his later historical materialism, Benjamin will consider the "connection ... between the secularization of time in space" (which, "as becomes clear in Blanqui's last writing ... is hidden in the 'worldview of the natural sciences' of the second half of the [nineteenth] century") and the "allegorical mode of perception."[46] As Benjamin explains elsewhere in the *Arcades*, the transition from the seventeenth to the nineteenth century was marked by the rise of a new mode of production, based on the exchange of commodities. "In the Baroque age, the fetish character of the commodity was still relatively undeveloped. And the commodity had not yet so deeply engraved its stigma – the proletarianization of the producers – on the process of production. Allegorical perception could thus constitute a style in the seventeenth century, in a way that it no longer could in the nineteenth."[47]

In the phantasmagoria that Benjamin identifies with modernity, the secular conception of history, resulting from the spatialization of time (as the object of allegorical representation), becomes part of a modern theology. The allegorical perception of nature as an empty eternity is replaced by a fetishism that identifies bourgeois society with the meaninglessness of the mechanical universe. In *Eternity by the Stars*, capitalism is portrayed as a mythical fate, imposed by "mechanistic natural science." The infinity of the mechanical universe, then, which "looms before [all] ... as eternal transience," serves to conceal the transitory character of bourgeois society. In that way, the doctrine of eternal recurrence eternalizes a particular mode of production, based on what Marx had described as the "continual movement of growth in productive forces, of destruction in social relations ... the only immutable thing is the abstraction of movement – *mors immortalis*."[48]

As this book has argued, Benjamin's analysis of this phantasmagoria implies a critique of the generalizing interpretation of the concept of commodity fetishism, underlying Lukács' theory of reification, which identifies capitalism with the mechanical notion of time. "Thus time sheds its qualitative, variable, flowing nature; it freezes into an exactly delimited, quantifiable continuum filled with quantifiable 'things.'"[49] If Blanqui, in his "unconditional surrender" to capitalism, portrays bourgeois society as an eternal reality that is demonstrated by science, the theory of reification identifies capitalism with measurable time, a phenomenon that exists in all forms of society. "Thus, economy of time," according to Marx, and "planned distribution of labour time among the various branches of production, remains the first economic law on the basis of communal production. ... However, this is essentially different from a measurement of exchange values (labour or products) by labour time."[50] Like commodity fetishism, therefore, the theory of reification confuses a "super-sensible" property (exchange value, measured according to socially necessary labor time) for a natural one, measurable time.

The analysis of such phantasmagorias as the defining feature of modernity is a distinguishing characteristic of the historical materialism that Benjamin began to develop in the late stage of his work. The primary thesis that this book has tried to establish is that this materialism was not a departure from Benjamin's "romantic-metaphysical period," vulgar-Marxist or otherwise.[51] Rather, it is a synthesis of his early "coming philosophy," based on a theory of time, "directed toward both the timeless validity of knowledge" and immediate "temporal experience," and the Marxian critique of capitalism as a transitory form of society that assumes an eternal appearance. In a "transposition into Marxist perspectives of [his earlier] metaphysical and even theological ideas,"[52] Benjamin developed a critique of capitalist modernity as a condition in which an historically determinate mode of production projects its image across all of eternity.

Notes

Prelims

1. Benjamin, Walter. 2016. *One-Way Street*. ed. Michael W. Jennings and trans. Edmund Jephcott. Cambridge and London: The Belknap Press of Harvard University Press, 65–6.
2. Agamben, Giorgio. 2008. *Means without Ends: Notes on Politics*. Minneapolis, Minnesota University Press, 86–7.
3. Benjamin, Walter. 2005. "Theories of German Fascism: On the Collection of Essays War and Warrior." *Walter Benjamin: Selected Writings, Volume 2: Part 1 1927–1930*. ed. Michael W. Jennings and Howard Eiland. Cambridge and London: Belknap, 313.
4. Benjamin, Walter. 2003. *The Arcades Project*. Cambridge, MA: Belknap Press, 114.
5. Benjamin, Walter. *Origin of the German Trauerspiel*. Cambridge: Harvard University Press, 2019, 174.
6. Agamben, Giorgio. 1998. *Homo Sacer: Sovereign Power and Bare Life*. Stanford: Stanford University Press, 73.
7. Gordon, Peter E. 2021. *Migrants in the Profane: Critical Theory and the Question of Secularization*. New Haven: Yale University Press, 40.
8. Gordon. *Migrants in the Profane*, 53.
9. Ibid., 34.
10. Wolin. *Aesthetic of Redemption*, 214.
11. See Benjamin. "Coming Philosophy," 106.
12. Benjamin, Walter. "World and Time." *Walter Benjamin: Selected Writings, 1: 1913–1926*. Cambridge: Belknap, 2004, 226.
13. qtd. Poma, Andrea. 2006. *Yearning for Form and Other Essays on Hermann Cohen's Thought*. Dordrecht: Springer, 55.
14. Cohen, Hermann. 1972. *Religion of Reason: Out of the Sources of Judaism*. trans. Simon Kaplan. New York: Frederick Unger, 21.
15. Benjamin, Walter. 1996. "Critique of Violence." *Selected Writings, vol. 1, 1913–1926*. Cambridge: Belknap Press of Harvard University Press, 247.
16. Benjamin, Walter. 2005. "Surrealism: The Last Snapshot of the European Intelligentsia." *Walter Benjamin: Selected Writings, Volume 2: Part 1 1927–1930*. ed. Michael W. Jennings and Howard Eiland. Cambridge and London: Belknap, 210.
17. Klossowski, Pierre. 2014. "Between Marx and Fourier," *Anthropology & Materialism* [Online], 2, Online since April 15, 2014, connection on May 22, 2021. URL: http://journals.openedition.org/am/356; DOI: https://doi.org/10.4000/am.356.
18. Derrida, Jacques. 2016. "Force of Law: The 'Mystical Foundation of Authority.'" *Deconstruction and the Possibility of Justice*. ed. Drucilla Cornell, Michel Rosenfeld, and David Carlson. London: Routledge, 64, ft. 3.
19. Derrida. "Force of Law," 42.
20. Benjamin. "World and Time," 226.
21. Benjamin. "Theories of German Fascism," 313.

22 Benjamin. "Surrealism," 210.
23 Benjamin. "Theories of German Fascism," 312.
24 Benjamin, Walter. 1996. "Capitalism as Religion." *Selected Writings, vol. 1, 1913–1926*. ed. Marcus Bullock and Michael W. Jennings. Cambridge: Belknap Press of Harvard University Press, 288.
25 Benjamin, Walter. 2006. "On the Concept of History." *Walter Benjamin: Selected Writings, 4: 1938–1940*. ed. Michael W. Jennings and Howard Eiland. Cambridge and London: Belknap Press of Harvard University Press, 393.
26 Marx, Karl. 1977. *Capital: A Critique of Political Economy*. Volume I. trans. Ben Fowkes. New York: Vintage, 127.
27 Benjamin. *Arcades Project*, x.
28 Ibid., 112.
29 Benjamin. "Paralipomena," 401.

Introduction

1 Benjamin, Walter. 1994. "Benjamin to Horkheimer, January 6, 1938." Benjamin, Walter, Gershom Scholem, and Theodor W. Adorno. 1994. *The Correspondence of Walter Benjamin, 1910–1940*. Chicago: University of Chicago Press, 549.
2 Benjamin, Walter. 2003. *The Arcades Project*. Cambridge, MA: Belknap Press, x.
3 Benjamin, Walter, and Theodor Adorno. 1999. "Exchange with Theodor W. Adorno on the Essay 'Paris, the Capital of the Nineteenth Century.'" *Selected Writings Volume 3: 1935–1938*. ed. Howard Eiland and Michael W. Jennings. trans. Edmund Jephcott and Harry Zohn. Cambridge, MA: Harvard University Press, 51.
4 Adorno, Theodor. "Exchange with Theodor W. Adorno on 'The Paris of the Second Empire in Baudelaire.'" 129.
5 Benjamin and Adorno. "Exchange with Theodor W. Adorno." 107.
6 "Benjamin to Horkheimer, January 6, 1938." *Correspondence of Walter Benjamin*, 549.
7 qtd. in Spitzer, Alan B. 1957. *The Revolutionary Theories of Louis Auguste Blanqui*. New York: Columbia University Press, 17.
8 Ibid.
9 Benjamin. *Arcades Project*, 667.
10 Benjamin to Horkheimer, January 6, 1938. *Correspondence of Walter Benjamin*, 549.
11 Benjamin, Walter. 1996. "Blanqui." *Walter Benjamin: Selected Writings, 4: 1938–1940*. ed. Howard Eiland and Michael W. Jennings. Cambridge, MA: Belknap Press, 93.
12 Benjamin to Adorno, May 31,1935. *Correspondence of Walter Benjamin*, 490.
13 Chouraqui, Frank. 2013. "Introduction." *Eternity by the Stars: An Astronomical Hypothesis* by Louis-Auguste Blanqui. New York: Contra Mundum Press, 30.
14 Chouraqui. "Introduction." *Eternity by the Stars*. 6.
15 Ibid., 30.
16 Ibid., 58.
17 Benjamin. *Arcades Project*, 15.
18 Blanqui. *Eternity by the Stars*, 147.
19 qtd. in Benjamin. *Arcades Project*, 112.
20 Ibid., 119.
21 Ibid., 12–13.
22 qtd. in Benjamin. *Arcades Project*, 115.

23 Benjamin, Walter. 2008. "Eduard Fuchs: Collector and Historian." *The Work of Art in the Age of Its Technological Reproducibility, and Other Writings on Media.* ed. Michael W. Jennings, Brigid Doherty, and Thomas Y. Levin. London: The Belknap Press of Harvard University Press, 123.
24 Benjamin. *Arcades Project*, 119.
25 Marx, Karl and Friedrich Engels. 1955. *The Communist Manifesto, with Selections from the Eighteenth Brumaire of Louis Bonaparte and Capital by Karl Marx.* New York: Appleton-Century Crofts, 15.
26 qtd. in Hahn, Roger. 2005. *Pierre Simon Laplace, 1749-1827: A Determined Scientist.* Cambridge, MA: Harvard University Press, 185.
27 Benjamin, Walter. 2006. "Review of Hönigswald's *Philosophie und Sprache*." *Walter Benjamin: Selected Writings, 4: 1938-1940*. ed. Howard Eiland and Michael W. Jennings. Cambridge and London: Belknap Press of Harvard University Press, 139.
28 Chouraqui. "Introduction" *Eternity by The Stars*, 15.
29 Benjamin, Walter. 2006. "On the Concept of History." *Walter Benjamin: Selected Writings, 4: 1938-1940*. ed. Howard Eiland and Michael W. Jennings. Cambridge and London: Belknap Press of Harvard University Press, 393.
30 Benjamin. "Review of Hönigswald's *Philosophie und Sprache*," 139.
31 qtd. in Mosès, Stéphane. 1996. "Benjamin, Nietzsche, et l'idée de l'éternel retour." *Europe, revue littéraire mensuelle* 74, no. 804.
32 Nietzsche, Friedrich. 2001. *The Gay Science.* ed. Bernard Williams, trans. Josefine Nauckhoff. Cambridge: Cambridge University Press, 239.
33 Benjamin, Walter. 2004. "*Trauerspiel* and Tragedy." *Walter Benjamin: Selected Writings*, 1: 1913-1926. Cambridge: Belknap, 55.
34 Benjamin. "Coming Philosophy," 101.
35 Ibid., 100.
36 Benjamin, Walter. "Paralipomena to 'On the Concept of History.'" *Walter Benjamin: Selected Writings, 4: 1938-1940*, 401.
37 Mosès. "Benjamin, Nietzsche, et l'idée de l'éternel retour," 144.
38 Ibid., 143.
39 Ibid.
40 Ibid.
41 Ibid.
42 Benjamin, Walter. 2005. "On the Image of Proust." *Selected Writings Volume 2: Part 1 1927-1930*. ed. Michael W. Jennings and Howard Eiland. Cambridge and London: Belknap, 244.
43 Benjamin, Walter. 2008. *The Work of Art in the Age of Its Technological Reproducibility, and Other Writings on Media.* London: The Belknap Press of Harvard Univ. Press, 254.
44 Benjamin, Walter. "Central Park." *Selected Writings 4*, 166.
45 Benjamin. *Arcades Project*, 557.
46 Ibid.
47 Löwy, Michael. 1995. *Fire Alarm: Reading Walter Benjamin's "On the Concept of History."* trans. Chris Turner, London: Verso, 102.
48 Benjamin. "Coming Philosophy," 100-1.
49 Benjamin. *Arcades Project*, 472.
50 Hallward, Peter. 2014. "Blanqui's bifurcations Dossier." *Radical Philosophy* 185 (May/Jun), 38.
51 Mosès. "Benjamin, Nietzsche, et l'idée de l'éternel retour," 152.

52 "Benjamin to Horkheimer, January 6, 1938." *Correspondence of Walter Benjamin*, 549.
53 Mosès. "Benjamin, Nietzsche, et l'idée de l'éternel retour," 151–2.
54 qtd. in Richard Wolin. 1982. *Walter Benjamin: An Aesthetic of Redemption*. New York: Columbia University Press, xlix.
55 Benjamin. *Arcades Project*, 26.
56 Benjamin. "Eduard Fuchs," 123.
57 Korsch, Karl. 2015. *Karl Marx*. Leiden: Koninklijke Brill NV, 96.
58 Marx. *Capital*, 127.
59 Ibid., 175.
60 Ibid., 575.
61 Korsch. *Karl Marx*, 62.
62 Marx. *Capital*, ft. 174, 34.
63 Ibid., 152.
64 Marx, Karl. 1974. *Grundrisse: Foundations of the Critique of Political Economy*. trans. Martin Nicolaus. Harmondsworth: Penguin Books, 248.
65 Marx. *Capital*, 178, ft. 2.
66 Korsch. *Karl Marx*, 100.
67 Marx, Karl and Friedrich Engels. 1955. *The Communist Manifesto, with Selections from the Eighteenth Brumaire of Louis Bonaparte and Capital by Karl Marx*. New York: Appleton-Century Crofts, 15.
68 Blanqui, Louis Auguste. 2018. "Thought, Ideas, Morality." *The Blanqui Reader: Political Writings, 1830–1880*. ed. Philippe Le Goff and Peter Hallward. London; Brooklyn, NY: Verso, 129.
69 Blanqui, Louis Auguste. 2018. "Communism, the Future of Society." *The Blanqui Reader: Political Writings, 1830–1880*, 244.
70 Proudhon, Pierre-Joseph. 2007. *The Philosophy of Misery*. New York: Cosimo, 161.
71 *Arcades*, 113.
72 Blanqui. "Communism, the Future of Society," 244.
73 qtd. in Buse, Peter. 2006. *Benjamin's Arcades: An Unguided Tour*. Manchester: Manchester University Press, 86.
74 Benjamin, Walter. 1996. "Critique of Violence." *Selected Writings, vol. 1*, 236.
75 Benjamin, Walter. 2006. "Germans of 1789." *Walter Benjamin: Selected Writings, 4: 1938–1940*. Jennings, Michael W. and Howard Eiland. Cambridge and London: Belknap Press of Harvard University Press, 286.
76 Sorel, Georges. 1999. *Reflections on Violence*. United Kingdom: Cambridge University Press, 162.
77 Benjamin. "Critique of Violence." *Selected Writings, vol. 1*, 236–7.
78 Robespierre, Maximilien. 1974. "Robespierre: December 3, 1792." *Regicide and Revolution. Speeches at the Trial of Louis XVI*. ed. Michael Walzer. Cambridge: University Press, 132.
79 Blanqui. "Social Wealth Must Belong to Those Who Created It." *The Blanqui Reader: Political Writings, 1830–1880*, 53.
80 Bruguière, Marie-Bernadette (ed.). 2002. *Prendre le pouvoir: force et légitimité*. New edition [online]. Toulouse: Presses de l'Université Toulouse 1 Capitole (generated 10 août 2021). Available on the Internet: http://books.openedition.org/putc/12619. ISBN: 9782379280993. DOI: https://doi.org/10.4000/books.putc.12619.
81 Greene, Doug Enaa. 2017. "Blanqui and the Communist Enlightenment." *Left Voice*. December 28. https://www.leftvoice.org/blanqui-and-the-communist-enlightenment/.

82 Marx, Karl. 2008. *Critique of the Gotha Program*. Rockville, MD: Wildside Press, 27.
83 Benjamin, Walter. "Germans of 1789." *Selected Writings 4*, 286.
84 Marx. *Grundrisse*, 249.
85 Marx, Karl. 1895. *The Class Struggles in France (1848–50)*. London: Martin Lawrence, 126.
86 Korsch. *Karl Marx*, 114.
87 Benjamin. *Arcades Project*, 361.
88 Ibid., 26.
89 "Benjamin to Horkheimer, January 6, 1938." *The Correspondence of Walter Benjamin, 1910–1940*, 549.
90 Benjamin, Walter. 2004. "Life of Students." *Walter Benjamin: Selected Writings, 1: 1913–1926*. ed. Michael W Jennings and Marcus Paul Bullock. Cambridge: Belknap, 37.
91 Benjamin. *Arcades Project*, 119.
92 qtd. in Löwy. *Fire Alarm*, 2.
93 Arendt, Hannah. 1968. "Introduction." *Illuminations*. edited and with an introduction by Hannah Arendt; preface by Leon Wieseltier; translated by Harry Zohn. New York: Harcourt, Brace & World, 11.
94 Benjamin. "The Work of Art in the Age of Its Technological Reproducibility," 254.
95 Foss-Heimlich, Paul. 2017. "Sade and Fourier and Klossowski and Benjamin." Klossowski, Pierre, Vernon W. Cisney, Nicolae Morar, and Daniel W. Smith. *Living Currency*.
96 *Arcades*, 361.
97 Lukács, Georg. 1978. "On Walter Benjamin." *New Left Review*, I/110 July–August.
98 Korsch. *Karl Marx*, 122.
99 Löwy. *Fire Alarm*, 109.
100 Benjamin. *Arcades Project*, 119.
101 Ibid., 462
102 Benjamin. "Karl Kraus," 448.
103 "Benjamin to Scholem, October 22, 1917." *The Correspondence of Walter Benjamin, 1910–1940*, 98.
104 Benjamin, Walter. 2004. "World and Time." *Walter Benjamin: Selected Writings, 1: 1913–1926*. Cambridge: Belknap, 226.
105 Benjamin. *Arcades Project*, 460.
106 Benjamin, Walter. "Paralipomena to 'On the Concept of History,'" 402.
107 Benjamin. *Arcades Project*, 474.
108 Scott, David. 1997. "Leibniz and the Two Clocks." *Journal of the History of Ideas*, vol. 58, no. 3, 445.
109 *Arcades*, 112.
110 Scholem, Gershom. 2003. *Walter Benjamin: The Story of a Friendship*. New York: New York Review, 233.
111 Jacobson, Eric. 2003. *Metaphysics of the Profane: The Political Theology of Walter Benjamin and Gershom Scholem*. New York: Columbia University Press, 3.
112 Benjamin, Walter. 1996. "On the Program of the Coming Philosophy," *Selected Writings 1, 1913–1926*. ed. Marcus Bullock and Michael W. Jennings. Cambridge, MA: Belknap Press of Harvard University Press, 100.
113 See Fenves, Peter. 2010. *The Messianic Reduction: Walter Benjamin and the Shape of Time*. Stanford, CA: Stanford University Press, 49.
114 Benjamin, Walter. "Critique of Violence." *Selected Writings, vol. 1*, 236.

115 Benjamin. "Critique of Violence." *Selected Writings*, vol. 1, 251.
116 Benjamin. *Arcades Project*, 483.
117 Korsch. *Karl Marx*, 12.
118 Wolin. *An Aesthetic of Redemption*, xi.
119 Fourier, Charles. 1996. *Theory of the Four Movements*. Cambridge: Cambridge University Press, 3.
120 Benjamin. *Arcades Project*, 112.

Chapter 1

1   qtd. Fenves. *The Messianic Reduction*, 1.
2   *A Critical Life*, 60.
3   Staiti, Andrea. 2014. *Husserl's Transcendental Phenomenology: Nature, Spirit, and Life*. Cambridge: Cambridge University Press, 111.
4   Benjamin. "Some Motifs in Baudelaire," 314.
5   qtd. in Tagliacozzo, Tamara. 2018. *Experience and Infinite Task: Knowledge, Language, and Messianism in the Philosophy of Walter Benjamin*, 19.
6   Benjamin. "Coming Philosophy," 105.
7   Ibid., 100, 103.
8   Ibid., 101.
9   Ibid.
10 Benjamin. 1996. "On Perception." *Selected Writings 1, 1913–1926*. ed. Marcus Bullock and Michael W. Jennings. Cambridge, MA: Belknap Press of Harvard University Press, 95.
11 Benjamin. "Coming Philosophy," 101.
12 qtd. in Metaphysics of the Profane, 69.
13 Benjamin. "Poverty and Experience," *Selected Writings Volume 2*, 731.
14 Benjamin. "Coming Philosophy," 101.
15 *A Critical Life*, 618.
16 Kant, Immanuel. 1998. *Critique of Pure Reason*. ed. and trans. Paul Guyer and Allen W. Wood. Cambridge: Cambridge University Press, 99.
17 Benjamin. "On Perception," 94.
18 Kant. *Critique of Pure Reason*, 129.
19 Caygill, Howard. 1998. *Walter Benjamin: The Colour of Experience*. London: Routledge, 1.
20 Kant. *Critique of Pure Reason*, 99.
21 Benjamin. "On Perception," 93.
22 Benjamin. "Coming Philosophy," 101, 105.
23 Wolin. *Aesthetic of Redemption*, 32.
24 Benjamin. "*Trauerspiel* and Tragedy," 55.
25 Benjamin. "On Perception," 95. According to Annika Thiem, "it is probable that both Cohen and Rickert are the foils for Benjamin's criticism of the neo-Kantian treatment of experience" in the "Coming Philosophy." In Cohen's writings, the "scientificity of philosophical knowledge is won at the expense of either ignoring … the singular, unrepeatable material transience (*Vergänglichkeit*) of experience as affecting philosophical knowledge." (Thiem, Annika. 2016. "Benjamin's Messianic Metaphysics of Transience." *Walter Benjamin and Theology*. ed. Colby Dickinson and Stéphane Symons. New York: Fordham University Press, 25–8). As Lydia Patton

points out, Hermann Cohen will use Kant's epistemology as the "basis for applying pure laws of thought to real phenomena," "the paradigm case of which is the conceptual reasoning behind Newton's laws of nature." *Hermann Cohen's History and Philosophy of Science*, PhD Thesis, McGill University, 2004, 75.

26 Benjamin. "Coming Philosophy," 106.
27 Benjamin. "On Perception," 94; Benjamin, "Coming Philosophy," 106.
28 Ibid., 95–6.
29 Ibid.
30 Ferber, Ilit. 2013. *Philosophy and Melancholy: Benjamin's Early Reflections on Theater and Language*. Stanford, CA: Stanford University Press, 45.
31 Benjamin. "Coming Philosophy," 101.
32 Ibid., 100.
33 Benjamin, Walter. "World and Time." *Walter Benjamin: Selected Writings 1: 1913–1926*, 226.
34 *A Critical Life*, 33.
35 qtd. in Moran, 169.
36 Ibid., 170.
37 Benjamin. "Coming Philosophy," 101.
38 Benjamin, Walter. 1913–1926. "Theses on the Problem of Identity." *Walter Benjamin: Selected Writings*, vol. 1, 76.
39 Benjamin, Walter. "The Paradox of the Cretan." *Walter Benjamin: Selected Writings 1: 1913–1926*, 210.
40 Benjamin. "The Paradox of the Cretan," 211.
41 Ibid., 210.
42 Ibid.
43 Ibid., 211.
44 Charles, Matthew. 2009. *Speculative Experience and History: Walter Benjamin's Goethean Kantianism*. Speculative Experience and History: Walter Benjamin's Goethean Kantianism. PhD thesis, Middlesex University, 2.
45 Benjamin. "On Perception," 93.
46 Ibid.
47 Ibid.
48 Ibid.
49 Charles. *Speculative Experience and History*, 3.
50 Benjamin. "On Perception," 94.
51 Ibid., 96.
52 Benjamin. "Coming Philosophy," 101.
53 Caygill. *Colour of Experience*, 1.
54 Wolin. *Aesthetic of Redemption*, 17.
55 Scholem. *Story of a Friendship*, 73.
56 Ng, Julia. 2012. "Walter Benjamin's and Gershom Scholem's Reading Group around Hermann Cohen's *Kants Theorie Der Erfahrung* in 1918: An Introduction." *MLN*, vol. 127, no. 3, 437.
57 Ibid.
58 Arendt, Hannah. 1968. "Introduction." Benjamin, Walter. *Illuminations: Essays and Reflections*. ed. Hannah Arendt. trans. Harry Zohn. New York: Schocken Books, 11.
59 Wolin. *Aesthetic of Redemption*, 35.
60 Ibid., 132.
61 Benjamin. "On Language as Such," 62.

62 Ibarlucía, Ricardo. 2017. "The Organization of Pessimism: Profane Illumination and Anthropological Materialism in Walter Benjamin." *Aisthesis. Pratiche, Linguaggi E Saperi dell'estetico*, vol. 10, no. 1, 139–60. https://doi.org/10.13128/Aisthesis-20914
63 Benjamin. *Origin of the German Trauerspiel*, 70–1.
64 Wolin. *Aesthetic of Redemption*, 205.
65 Ibid., 214.
66 Ibid., 249.
67 Benjamin. "On Perception," 96.
68 Benjamin. "Theory of Knowledge," 276.
69 Benjamin. "Coming Philosophy," 101.
70 Kant. *Critique of Pure Reason*, 93–4.
71 Ibid., 129.
72 Benjamin. "On Perception," 94.
73 "Benjamin to Scholem, ca. December 23, 1917." *The Correspondence of Walter Benjamin*, 1910–1940, 105.
74 Benjamin. "On Perception," 93.
75 Benjamin, Walter. 1918. "Fragment 30: Zweideutigkeit des Begriffs der 'unendlichen Aufgabe' in der kantischen Schule." *Gesammelte Schriften VI*. Frankfurt am Main: Suhrkamp, 1996, 51–3.
76 "Benjamin to Scholem, ca. December 23, 1917." *The Correspondence of Walter Benjamin*, 1910–1940, 106.
77 Benjamin. "Coming Philosophy," 106.
78 "Benjamin to Scholem, ca. December 23, 1917." *The Correspondence of Walter Benjamin*, 1910–1940, 106.
79 Benjamin. "Coming Philosophy," 100.
80 Ibid.
81 Adorno, Theodor. 1977. "The Actuality of Philosophy." *Telos* 31, Spring, 121.
82 Benjamin, Walter. "Curriculum Vitae (VI): Dr. Walter Benjamin." *Selected Writings 4*, 381. See also, Agamben, Giorgio. 1997. "Cronologia della opera di Walter Benjamin," *Walter Benjamin, Metafisica della gioventù: Scritti 1910–1918*. ed. Giorgio Agamben. Torino: Einaudi, xix–xx.
83 Fenves. *Messianic Reduction*, 9.
84 Husserl. Edmund. 2001. *Logical Investigations*. London: Routledge & Kegan Paul, 318.
85 Husserl. *Logical Investigations*, 15.
86 Husserl. Edmund. 2014. *Ideas Pertaining to a Pure Phenomenology and to a Phenomenological Philosophy, Book 3: Phenomenology and the Foundation of the Sciences*. trans. Ted E. Klein and William E. Pohl. The Hague, Boston, London: Martinus Nijhoff Publishers, 22.
87 Husserl. *Ideas Pertaining to a Pure Phenomenology*, 139–40.
88 Trần Đức Thảo. 1986. *Phenomenology and Dialectical Materialism*. Dordrecht: D. Reidel, 17.
89 qtd. in Thảo. *Phenomenology and Dialectical Materialism*, 21.
90 qtd. Fenves. *Messianic Reduction*, 75.
91 Thảo. *Phenomenology and Dialectical Materialism*, 21.
92 See ibid., 25.
93 Benjamin, Walter. "The Concept of Criticism in German Romanticism." *Selected Writings* I, 127.
94 Husserl, Edmund. 1993. *Ideas: General Introduction to Pure Phenomenology*. London: George Allen & Unwin, 108.

95 Ibid., 109.
96 Descartes, René. 1971. *Descartes: Philosophical Writings*. ed. G. E. M. Anscombe, Alexandre Koyré, and P. T. Geach. Indianapolis: Bobbs-Merrill Company, 63.
97 Derrida, Jacques. 1978. *Edmund Husserl's Origin of Geometry, an Introduction*. Stony Brook, NY: N. Hays, 45, ft. 37.
98 Descartes, René. 1901. *The Method, Meditations and Philosophy of Descartes*. Washington, DC: M.W. Dunne, 224.
99 Thảo. *Phenomenology and Dialectical Materialism*, 26.
100 "The position of the world, which is a 'contingent' position, is opposed to that of my egological life, which is a 'necessary' position that is absolutely indubitable. Every given thing 'it-self' ('in person') also can not be; any lived given 'it-self' ('in person') cannot not be." On the topic of certainty in Husserl and Descartes, see Ronald H. Brady. 1998. "The Idea in Nature: Rereading Goethe's Organics." *Goethe's Way of Science*. ed. David Seamon. New York: State University of New York Press, 86.
101 Husserl. *Ideas: General Introduction to Pure Phenomenology*, 107.
102 Ibid., 98.
103 Benjamin. "Coming Philosophy," 101.
104 Fenves. *Messianic Reduction*, 48.
105 Ibid.
106 qtd. ibid.
107 Benjamin. "Imagination." *Selected Writings* I, 281.
108 Benjamin. "Coming Philosophy," 101.
109 Benjamin. "On Language as Such and on the Language of Man," *Selected Writings* I, 72.
110 Ibid., 65.
111 "Benjamin to Scholem, ca. December 23, 1917." *The Correspondence of Walter Benjamin, 1910-1940*, 106.
112 Benjamin. "On Language as Such and on the Language of Man," 63.
113 Benjamin. "The Concept of Criticism in German Romanticism," 144.
114 Benjamin. "On Language as Such and on the Language of Man," 63.
115 Benjamin. "The Concept of Criticism in German Romanticism," 143.
116 Benjamin. "Coming Philosophy," 107.
117 Benjamin. "Theory of Knowledge," *Selected Writings* I, 144.
118 Benjamin. "Coming Philosophy," 106.
119 Caygill. *Colour of Experience*, 9.
120 Husserl. *Ideas: General Introduction to Pure Phenomenology*, 208.
121 Thảo. *Phenomenology and Dialectical Materialism*, 4.
122 Husserl. *Logical Investigations Volume 1*, 69.
123 Eiland. *A Critical Life*, 33.
124 qtd. in Staiti, Andrea S. 2014. *Husserl's Transcendental Phenomenology: Nature, Spirit, and Life*. Cambridge; New York: Cambridge University Press, 111.
125 qtd. in ibid.
126 Staiti. *Husserl's Transcendental Phenomenology: Nature, Spirit, and Life*, 113.
127 Benjamin. *Origin of the German Trauerspiel*, 11.
128 Husserl. *Logical Investigations*, 69.
129 Benjamin. *Origin of the German Trauerspiel*, 11-2.
130 qtd. in Fenves. *Messianic Reduction*, 53.
131 Adorno, Theodor W. 1982. *Prisms*. Cambridge, MA: MIT Press, 231.
132 Wolin. *Aesthetic of Redemption*, 32.

Chapter 2

1. Steiner, Uwe, and Colin Sample. 2001. "The True Politician: Walter Benjamin's Concept of the Political." *New German Critique*, vol. 83, no. 83, 46.
2. Fenves, Peter. 2010. *The Messianic Reduction: Walter Benjamin and the Shape of Time*. Stanford: Stanford University Press, 208. See also Tomba, Massimiliano. 2009. "Another Kind of *Gewalt*: Beyond Law Re-Reading Walter Benjamin," in *Historical Materialism* 17, 127 and Deuber-Mankowsky, Astrid. January 2002. "Walter Benjamin's Theological-Political Fragment as a Response to Ernst Bloch's Spirit of Utopia." *The Leo Baeck Institute Year Book*, vol. 47, no. 1, 10.
3. Benjamin. "Coming Philosophy," 100.
4. Benjamin, Walter. "Introductory Remarks on a Series for *L'Humanité*." *Selected Writings Volume 2*, 20. During the period preceding his ambiguous turn to Marxism, Benjamin was "driven by a desire to define his own political convictions" (*A Critical Life*, 128), renouncing his earlier "rejection of every contemporary political trend," while seeming oddly disinterested in the dramatic political events of the period. He dismissed the Hungarian Soviet Republic as a "childish aberration." Similarly, the "Munich soviet republic of April 1919 came into his purview only because Felix Noeggerath, whom he highly esteemed as a philosopher, was arrested for participating in it—something that greatly excited Benjamin" (Scholem, *Story of a Friendship*, 96).
5. "Benjamin to Scholem, ca. December 23, 1917." *The Correspondence of Walter Benjamin, 1910–40*, 105.
6. Fenves. *Messianic Reduction*, 191.
7. Kant, Immanuel, Pauline Kleingeld, Jeremy Waldron, Michael W. Doyle, and Allen W. Wood. 2006. *Toward Perpetual Peace and Other Writings on Politics, Peace, and History*. New Haven: Yale University Press, 104.
8. Fenves. *Messianic Reduction*, 190.
9. Ibid., 190.
10. qtd. in ibid., 191.
11. qtd. in ibid.
12. Kant, Immanuel. 1996. *Practical Philosophy*. Cambridge: Cambridge University Press, 404–5. This assumption would appear to be inconsistent with Kant's own distinction between empirical and intelligible possession.
13. Kant. *Practical Philosophy*, 405.
14. qtd. in Fenves. *Messianic Reduction*, 192.
15. Kant. *Practical Philosophy*, 420.
16. Ibid.
17. Skees, Murray. 2009. "The *Lex Permissiva* and the Source of Natural Right in Kant's *Metaphysics of Morals* and Fichte's *Foundations of Natural Right*." *International Philosophical Quarterly*, 9 3, 377.
18. Kant. *Practical Philosophy*, 406.
19. Skees. "The *Lex Permissiva*," 383.
20. Kant. *Practical Philosophy*, 404–5.
21. Benjamin. "Category of Justice," 257.
22. Fenves. *Messianic Reduction*, 196.
23. See Bartoloni, Paolo. 2015. "Suchness and the Threshold between Possession and Violence." ed. B. Moran and C. Salzani. *Towards the Critique of Violence: Walter Benjamin and Giorgio Agamben*. London: Bloomsbury Academic, 160.
24. Benjamin. "Category of Justice," 257.

25 Benjamin. *Origin of the German Trauerspiel*, 200.
26 Benjamin. "Category of Justice," 257.
27 Ibid.
28 Ibid.
29 Fenves. *Messianic Reduction*, 196.
30 Ibid.
31 Ibid.
32 Ibid., 166.
33 Ibid., 196.
34 Ibid., 193.
35 Ibid., 196.
36 Khatib, Sami. 2011. "Towards a Politics of 'Pure Means': Walter Benjamin and the Question of Violence." Anthropological Materialism, August 28. anthropologicalmaterialism.hypotheses.org/1040.
37 Benjamin. "Critique of Violence." *Selected Writings, vol. 1*, 238.
38 Ibid.
39 Ibid.
40 Ibid., 241.
41 Ibid., 237.
42 Ibid., 236.
43 Ibid., 238.
44 Fenves. *Messianic Reduction*, 196.
45 qtd. in ibid., 218.
46 Ibid., 194.
47 Benjamin. "Critique of Violence." *Selected Writings, vol. 1*, 237.
48 Ibid.
49 Ibid., 236.
50 Ibid.
51 Benjamin, Walter. 2021. *Toward the Critique of Violence: A Critical Edition*. Stanford: Stanford University Press, 41.
52 Benjamin, "Critique of Violence." *Selected Writings, vol. 1*, 238.
53 Ibid.
54 Ibid., 252.
55 Ibid., 242.
56 qtd. in Kambas Chryssoula. 1984. "Walter Benjamin lecteur des Réflexions sur la violence." In: *Cahiers Georges Sorel*, n°2, 82.
57 Benjamin. "Critique of Violence." *Selected Writings, vol. 1*, 249.
58 Ibid., 241.
59 Ibid., 249.
60 Ibid., 237.
61 Ibid., *vol. 1*, 238.
62 Benjamin. "Coming Philosophy," 100.
63 Benjamin. "Critique of Violence." *Selected Writings, vol. 1*, 241.
64 Benjamin. "Coming Philosophy," 101.
65 Fenves. *Messianic Reduction*, 214.
66 Benjamin. "Critique of Violence." *Selected Writings, vol. 1*, 249.
67 Ibid., 240.
68 Ibid.
69 Ibid., 242.

70 Ibid., 249.
71 Ibid., 248.
72 Ibid., 243.
73 Ibid., 244.
74 Ibid., 243.
75 Ibid., 251.
76 Ibid., 237.
77 Ibid.
78 Ibid.
79 Ibid., 247.
80 Ibid., 249.
81 Ibid., 245.
82 Ibid., 247.
83 Ibid.
84 Ibid.
85 Ibid., 247–8.
86 Benjamin. "The Paradox of the Cretan," 211.
87 Benjamin. "Category of Justice," 257.
88 Ibid.
89 Benjamin. "Critique of Violence." *Selected Writings, vol. 1*, 240.
90 Ibid., 239.
91 Ibid., 240.
92 Ibid., 246.
93 Sorel. *Reflections on Violence*, 162.
94 Benjamin. "Critique of Violence." *Selected Writings, vol. 1*, 244.
95 Sorel. *Reflections on Violence*, 245.
96 Benjamin. "On the Concept of History," 393.
97 Sorel. *Reflections on Violence*, 279.
98 Ibid., 18.
99 Ibid.
100 Ibid., 17.
101 Sorel. *L'avenir socialiste des syndicats*, 2
102 Marx, Karl. 1900. *The Civil War in France*. New York: International Library Publishing, 48.
103 Lenin, V. I. 2014. *State and Revolution*. Chicago: Haymarket Books, 18.
104 Sorel. *Reflections on Violence*, 293.
105 Ibid., xviii.
106 Ibid., 286.
107 Sorel, Georges. 1901. *L'avenir socialiste des syndicats* (Nouvelle édition, considérablement augmentee). Paris: Librairie G. Jacques & cie., 2.
108 Horrox, James. "Landauer Biography." Anarchist Archives: An Online Research Center on the History and Theory of Anarchism, dwardmac.pitzer.edu/Anarchist_Archives/bright/landauer/landauerbioHorrox.html.
109 Benjamin. "Capitalism as Religion," 290. See also *Walter Benjamin: The Story of a Friendship*, 11.
110 Horrox. "Landauer Biography."
111 Benjamin. "Critique of Violence." *Selected Writings, vol. 1*, 246.
112 Horrox. "Landauer Biography."
113 Benjamin. "Critique of Violence." *Selected Writings, vol. 1*, 239.

114 Ibid., 246.
115 qtd. in ibid., 246.
116 Ibid.
117 Ibid., 257.
118 Ibid., 246.
119 Ibid., 248.
120 Ibid., 252.
121 Ibid., 248.
122 Ibid., 252.
123 Fenves, Peter. 2021. "Introduction." *Toward the Critique of Violence: A Critical Edition*. ed. Peter Fenves and Julia Ng. Stanford: Stanford University Press, 1.
124 Toscano, Alberto. 2021. "Georges Sorel, *Reflections on Violence* Translator's Preface." *Toward the Critique of Violence: A Critical Edition*. ed. Peter Fenves and Julia Ng. Stanford: Stanford University Press, 1.
125 Benjamin. "Critique of Violence." *Selected Writings, vol. 1*, 58.
126 Hiller, Kurt. 2021. "Anti-Cain: A Postscript to Rudolf Leonhard's 'Our Final Battle against Weapons.'" *Toward the Critique of Violence: A Critical Edition*. ed. Peter Fenves and Julia Ng. Stanford: Stanford University Press, 182.
127 Ibid., 189.
128 Ibid., 186–7.
129 Ibid., 185.
130 Benjamin. "Critique of Violence." *Selected Writings, vol. 1*, 45.
131 Benjamin. "The Author as Producer." *Selected Writings Volume 2, Part 2*, 773.
132 Fenves, Peter. "Introduction." *Toward the Critique of Violence*, 36.
133 Landauer, Gustave. 2010. "To Martin Buber Krumbach (Swabia), November 15, 1918." *Revolution and Other Writings: A Political Reader*. ed. and trans. Gabriel Kuhn. Oakland, CA: PM Press, 317.
134 Radnóti, Sándor. "Benjamin's Politics," *Telos*, September 21, 1978 vol. 1978 no. 37, 66.
135 Schmitt, Carl. 1988. *The Crisis of Parliamentary Democracy*. Cambridge, MA: MIT Press, 69.
136 Kambas Chryssoula. 1984. "Walter Benjamin lecteur des *Réflexions sur la violence*." *Cahiers Georges Sorel*, no. 2, 83.
137 Toscano. "Georges Sorel, *Reflections on Violence* Translator's Preface," 197.
138 Benjamin. "Capitalism as Religion," 290.
139 Sorel. *Reflections on Violence*, 169.
140 Ibid., 168–9.
141 Ibid., 172.
142 Ibid., 168.
143 Ibid., 169.
144 Ibid.

Chapter 3

1 Benjamin, Walter. 2005. "Curriculum Vitae (III)." *Walter Benjamin: Selected Writings*. ed. Michael W. Jennings, Howard Eiland, and Gary Smith. Cambridge, MA: Belknap, 78.

2   Ginev, Dimitri. 2019. "Disclosing Authentic Lifeforms." *Scientific Conceptualization and Ontological Difference*. Berlin: Boston De Gruyter, 170.
3   Benjamin. *Origin of the German Trauerspiel*, 49.
4   Ibid., 202.
5   qtd. in Bredekamp, Horst, et al. 1999. "From Walter Benjamin to Carl Schmitt, via Thomas Hobbes." *Critical Inquiry*, vol. 25, no. 2, 249–50.
6   qtd. in "From Walter Benjamin to Carl Schmitt," 249.
7   Newman, Jane. 2011. *Benjamin's Library: Modernity, Nation, and the Baroque*. Ithaca, NY: Cornell University Press, 28.
8   Benjamin. *Origin of the German Trauerspiel*, 20.
9   qtd. in Fenves. *Messianic Reduction*, 20.
10 Moritz, Geiger. 1986. *The Significance of Art: A Phenomenological Approach to Aesthetics*. Washington, DC: Center for Advanced Research in Phenomenology & University Press of America, 3.
11 Ibid., 7.
12 Ibid., 190.
13 Ibid., 189.
14 Ibid., 7–8.
15 Ibid., 8–9.
16 Ibid., xxii.
17 Ibid., 9.
18 Trần Đức Thảo. 1986. *Phenomenology and Dialectical Materialism*. Dordrecht: Reidel, 4.
19 On eidetic intuition as consciousness of an impossibility, see Trần Đức Thảo. *Phenomenology and Dialectical Materialism*, 4–5.
20 qtd. in Fenves. *Messianic Reduction*, 48.
21 Geiger. *The Significance of Art*, 8.
22 Fenves. *Messianic Reduction*, 272, fn. 2.
23 Benjamin. "Curriculum Vitae (III)," 78
24 Benjamin. *Origin of the German Trauerspiel*, 11.
25 Husserl, Edmund. 2001. *Logical Investigations Volume 1*. London: Routledge, 69.
26 Benjamin. *Origin of the German Trauerspiel*, 11.
27 Fenves. *Messianic Reduction*, 2.
28 Benjamin. *Origin of the German Trauerspiel*, 2.
29 Benjamin. Walter. 2004. "Language and Logic." *Walter Benjamin: Selected Writings, 1: 1913–1926*. Cambridge: Belknap, 272–3.
30 Ibid.
31 Benjamin. "Language and Logic," 173.
32 Weber, Samuel. 1992. "Taking Exception to Decision: Walter Benjamin and Carl Schmitt." *Diacritics*, vol. 22, no. 3/4, 6.
33 Benjamin. *Origin of the German Trauerspiel*, 11.
34 Ibid.
35 Ibid.
36 Weber. "Taking Exception to Decision," 7.
37 Benjamin. *Origin of the German Trauerspiel*, 10–11. See the discussion of the constellation and the extreme in Friedlander, Eli. 2012. *Walter Benjamin: A Philosophical Portrait*. Cambridge, MA: Harvard University Press, 41.
38 Benjamin. *Origin of the German Trauerspiel*, 21.
39 Ibid., 21–2.
40 Ibid., 18–9.

41 Ibid., 15.
42 Ibid., 21.
43 Ibid., 18.
44 Ibid., 22.
45 Ibid., 18–19.
46 Ibid.
47 Ibid.
48 Ibid., 40.
49 Ibid., 40–1.
50 Ibid., 120.
51 Ibid., 188.
52 Ibid., 193.
53 Ibid., 40–1.
54 Wolin. *Aesthetic of Redemption*, 84.
55 Benjamin. *Origin of the German Trauerspiel*, 41.
56 Ibid., 41.
57 Ibid., 43.
58 Ibid.
59 Ibid.
60 Ibid., 15.
61 Ibid.
62 Ibid.
63 Ibid., 167.
64 "Benjamin to Scholem, July 21, 1925." *The Correspondence of Walter Benjamin, 1910–1940*, 276.
65 qtd. in Newman. *Benjamin's Library: Modernity, Nation, and the Baroque*, 35.
66 qtd. Newman. "Periodization, Modernity, Nation: Benjamin between Renaissance and Baroque," 9.
67 "Benjamin to Scholem, September 16, 1924." *The Correspondence of Walter Benjamin, 1910–1940*, 247.
68 Benjamin. *Origin of the German Trauerspiel*, 164.
69 Weber. "Taking Exception to Decision," 8.
70 Benjamin. *Origin of the German Trauerspiel*, 44.
71 Ibid., 54.
72 Bürger, Peter. 1986. "Carl Schmitt oder die Fundierung der Politik auf Ästhetik." *Zerstorung: Rettung des Mythos durch Licht*. ed. Christa Burger. Frankfurt: Suhrkamp Verlag, 174.
73 Kant, Immanuel. 2007. *Critique of Judgement*. Oxford: Oxford University Press, 136.
74 Bürger. "Carl Schmitt oder die Fundierung der Politik auf Ästhetik," 174.
75 Kant. *Critique of judgement*, 100.
76 Ibid., 71.
77 Kahn, Victoria. 2003. "Hamlet or Hecuba: Carl Schmitt's Decision." *Representations*, vol. 83, no. 1, 68–9.
78 Benjamin. *The Work of Art in the Age of Its Technological Reproducibility*, 20.
79 Benjamin. "On the Concept of History," 392.
80 Benjamin. "Coming Philosophy," 103.
81 Benjamin. *Origin of the German Trauerspiel*, 72.
82 Ibid., 29.
83 Ibid., 155.

84 Ibid., 60.
85 Ibid., 131.
86 Ibid., 45.
87 Ibid., 44.
88 Ibid., 129.
89 Ibid., 45.
90 Ibid., 58.
91 Ibid., 57.
92 Ibid., 137.
93 qtd. in ibid.
94 Ibid.
95 Ibid., 46.
96 Ibid.
97 Ibid., 128.
98 Ibid., 77–8.
99 Ibid., 59.
100 Ibid., 56.
101 qtd. in "From Walter Benjamin to Carl Schmitt, via Thomas Hobbes," 249–50.
102 Benjamin. *Origin of the German Trauerspiel*, 49.
103 Schmitt, Carl. *Political Theology: Four Chapters on the Concept of Sovereignty*. Chicago and London: University of Chicago Press, 2005, 14.
104 Ibid., 9.
105 Ibid.
106 Ibid., 46.
107 Ibid., 49.
108 Ibid., 14.
109 Ibid., 37.
110 Ibid., 36.
111 Strong. "Foreword." Ibid., xxv.
112 Benjamin. *Origin of the German Trauerspiel*, 69.
113 For an account of this period, see Cassirer, Ernst. 1961. *The Myth of the State*. New Haven: Yale University Press, 166–70, and Oestreich, Gerhard. 1981. *Neostoicism and the Early Modern State*. Cambridge: Cambridge University Press, 8, 17.
114 Benjamin. *Origin of the German Trauerspiel*, 49.
115 Schmitt. *Political Theology*, 9.
116 Benjamin. *Origin of the German Trauerspiel*, 49.
117 Ibid.
118 Benjamin. *Origin of the German Trauerspiel*, 59.
119 Ibid., 50.
120 Ibid.
121 Agamben, Giorgio. *State of Exception*. trans. Kevin Attell. Chicago: University of Chicago Press, 2005, 56.
122 Schmitt. *Political Theology*, 41.
123 Benjamin. *Origin of the German Trauerspiel*, 68.
124 Ibid., 51.
125 Ibid., 68.
126 Ibid., 167.
127 Ibid., 65.
128 Gordon. *Migrants in the Profane*, 39.

129 Ibid.
130 Benjamin. *Origin of the German Trauerspiel*, 67.
131 Ibid., 68.
132 Weber. "Taking Exception to Decision," 12.
133 Ibid.
134 Benjamin. *Origin of the German Trauerspiel*, 50.
135 Ibid.
136 Wolin. *Aesthetic of Redemption*, 61.
137 Benjamin. *Origin of the German Trauerspiel*, 174.
138 Ibid., 157.
139 Ibid.
140 Kant, Immanuel. 2008. *Practical Philosophy*. Cambridge: Cambridge University Press, 392.
141 Kant, Immanuel. 2010. *Kant: Political Writings*. Cambridge and New York: Cambridge University Press, 81–2.
142 "The state suspends the law in the exception on the basis of its right of self-preservation." Schmitt, *Political Theology*, 12.
143 Kant. *Practical Philosophy*, 392.
144 Ibid.
145 Fenves. *Messianic Reduction*, 196.
146 Agamben. *Homo Sacer*, 73.
147 Giorgio, Agamben. 2003. *State of Exception*. Chicago and London: University of Chicago Press, 52–3.
148 Benjamin. *Origin of the German Trauerspiel*, 50.
149 Taubes, Jacob. 2015. *To Carl Schmitt: Letters and Reflections*. New York: Columbia University Press, 16.
150 Agamben. "Gigantomachy Concerning a Void," 55.
151 Schmitt. *Political Theology*, 36.
152 Ibid., 42.
153 Ibid., 43.
154 Ibid.
155 Ibid.
156 Ibid.
157 Ibid., 47.
158 Ibid., 45–6.
159 Ibid., 46–7.
160 Ibid., 37.
161 Ibid., 37.
162 Ibid., 41.
163 qtd. in Salter, Michael. 2012. *Carl Schmitt: Law as Politics, Ideology and Strategic Myth*. Abingdon, Oxon: Routledge, 53.
164 Benjamin. *Origin of the German Trauerspiel*, 62.
165 Ibid., 165.
166 Ibid., 166.
167 Ibid.
168 Ibid., 78.
169 Ibid., 79–80.
170 Ibid., 79.
171 qtd. in Atger, Frédéric. 1906. *Essai Sur L'histoire Des Doctrines Du Contrat Social*. Paris: F. Alcan, 153.

172 Benjamin. *Origin of the German Trauerspiel*, 76.
173 Schmitt. *Political Theology*, 46–7.
174 *A Critical Life*, 685.
175 Bergson, Henri. 1913. *Time and Free Will: An Essay on the Immediate Data of Consciousness*. London: G. Allen & Co, 208.
176 On Meyerson, see Telkes-Klein, Eva. "Emile Meyerson: A Great Forgotten Figure." *Iyyun: The Jerusalem Philosophical Quarterly*, vol. 52, 235–44.
177 Meyerson, Émile. 1991. *Explanation in the Sciences*. Dordrecht: Kluwer Academic Publishers, 117.
178 Benjamin. "Theses on the Problem of Identity," 76.
179 Benjamin. "The Paradox of the Cretan," 211.
180 qtd. in Gorham, Geoffrey. 2008. "Descartes on God's Relation to Time." *Religious Studies*, vol. 44, no. 4, 416.
181 qtd. in Khafiz Kerimov. "Descartes, Bergson, and Continuous Creation," *Methodos* [En ligne], 18 | 2018, mis en ligne le 15 février 2018, consulté le 23 mai 2021. URL: http://journals.openedition.org/methodos/5083; DOI: https://doi.org/10.4000/methodos.5083
182 Bergson. *Time and Free Will*, 208.
183 Benjamin, Walter. "On Perception." trans. Rodney Livingstone. *Walter Benjamin: Selected Writings*, Volume 1, 102.
184 Descartes. *The Philosophical Writings of Descartes*, 201.
185 Nadler, Steven. 1999. "Knowledge, Volitional Agency and Causation in Malebranche and Geulincx." *British Journal for the History of Philosophy*, vol. 7, no. 2, 270.
186 Windelband, W. 1898. *A History of Philosophy with Especial Reference to the Formation and Development of Its Problems and Conceptions*. New York: Macmillan and Co, 415–16.
187 Nadler. "Knowledge, Volitional Agency and Causation," 263.
188 Garber, Daniel. 1992. *Descartes' Metaphysical Physics*. Chicago: University of Chicago Press, 264.
189 Benjamin. *Origin of the German Trauerspiel*, 76.
190 Ibid.
191 qtd. in Kerimov. "Descartes, Bergson, and Continuous Creation."
192 Benjamin. *Origin of the German Trauerspiel*, 134.
193 qtd. in Gorham. "Descartes on God's Relation to Time," 415.
194 Benjamin. *Origin of the German Trauerspiel*, 87.
195 Scott, David. 1997. "Leibniz and the Two Clocks." *Journal of the History of Ideas*, vol. 58, no. 3, 445.
196 Benjamin. *Origin of the German Trauerspiel*, 86.
197 Kant. *Critique of Pure Reason*, 180.
198 Husserl, Edmund. 1965. *Phenomenology and the Crisis of Philosophy: Philosophy as Rigorous Science and Philosophy and the Crisis of European Man*. trans. with Notes and an Introduction by Quentin Lauer. New York: Harper & Row, 46.
199 Ibid., 180.
200 Ibid., 178.
201 Benjamin, Walter. 1996. "Two Poems by Friedrich Hölderlin." *Selected Writings 1, 1913–1926*. ed. Marcus Bullock and Michael W. Jennings. Cambridge, MA: Belknap Press of Harvard University Press, 32.
202 Bergson. *Time and Free Will*, xxiii.
203 Ibid., xxiv.

204 Ibid., 237.
205 Benjamin. *Origin of the German Trauerspiel*, 87.
206 qtd. in Gorham, "Descartes on God's Relation to Time," 415.
207 *Political Theology*, 46.
208 Benjamin. *Origin of the German Trauerspiel*, 236.
209 Ibid., 86–7.
210 Windelband. *A History of Philosophy*, fn. 1, 416.
211 qtd. in Moorjani, Angela B. 2012. *Early Modern Beckett*. Amsterdam: Rodopi, 297.
212 Benjamin. *Origin of the German Trauerspiel*, 87.
213 Ibid., 46.
214 Ibid., 87.
215 Schmitt. *Political Theology*, 36.
216 See Gorham. "Descartes on God's Relation to Time," 423.
217 Bergson, Henri-Louis. 1913. *Matiere et mémoire: essai sur la relation du corps a l'esprit*. Paris: Félix Alcan, 185.
218 Gordon. *Migrants in the Profane*, 61.
219 qtd. in ibid.
220 Ibid., 61.
221 Ibid., 33.
222 Ibid., 24.
223 Ibid., 34.
224 Ibid., 35–6.
225 Scott, David. 1997. "Leibniz and the Two Clocks." *Journal of the History of Ideas*, vol. 58, no. 3, 445.
226 qtd. in Moorjani, Angela B. 2012. *Early Modern Beckett*. Amsterdam: Rodopi, 297.
227 Gordon. *Migrants in the Profane*, 53.
228 Ng. "Walter Benjamin's and Gershom Scholem's Reading Group," 437.
229 Benjamin. "On Perception," 96.
230 Ibid., 102.
231 Benjamin. *Origin of the German Trauerspiel*, 81.
232 Benjamin. "Capitalism as Religion," 289.
233 Benjamin. *Arcades Project*, 391.
234 Gordon. *Migrants in the Profane*, 57.
235 Benjamin, Walter. 2005. "Karl Kraus." *Walter Benjamin: Selected Writings Volume 2, Part 2, 1931–1934*. ed. Michael W. Jennings, Howard Eiland, and Gary Smith. Cambridge: Belknap Press, 437.
236 Gordon. *Migrants in the Profane*, 42.
237 Marx. *Capital*, 165.
238 Benjamin. *Arcades Project*, 26.
239 Ibid., 391.
240 Gordon. *Migrants in the Profane*, 40.
241 Löwy. *Fire Alarm*, 12.
242 Lukács. *History and Class Consciousness*, 88.
243 Marx. *Capital*, 255.
244 Ibid., 532.
245 Benjamin. *Origin of the German Trauerspiel*, 86.
246 Ibid., 76.
247 Ibid., 84.
248 Ibid., 44.

249 Ibid., 77.
250 Ibid., 68.
251 Ibid., 8.
252 Ibid., 81.
253 Ibid., 82.
254 Ibid., 85.
255 Ibid., 72.
256 Benjamin, Walter. "Two poems by Hölderlin." *Selected Writings Volume 1*, 26.
257 Benjamin. *Origin of the German Trauerspiel*, 67.
258 Ibid.
259 Ibid., 87.
260 Ibid., 82–3.
261 Ibid., 71.
262 Ibid., 135.
263 Ibid., 61.
264 Ibid., 135.
265 Ibid., 166.
266 Urbich, Jan. 2015. *Benjamin and Hegel, a Constellation in Metaphysics: Walter Benjamin-Lectures at the Càtedra Walter Benjamin*. Girona: Càtedra Walter Benjamin.
267 "Benjamin to Scholem, September 16, 1924." *The Correspondence of Walter Benjamin, 1910–1940*, 248
268 Fehér, Ferenc. 1985. "Lukács and Benjamin: Parallels and Contrasts." *New German Critique*, no. 34, 126–7.
269 "Benjamin to Scholem, September 16, 1924." *The Correspondence of Walter Benjamin, 1910–1940*, 248.
270 Lukács, Georg. 1971. *History and Class Consciousness: Studies in Marxist Dialectics*. London: Merlin Press, 90.
271 Benjamin. *Origin of the German Trauerspiel*, 82.
272 Agamben, Giorgio. 2005. *State of Exception*. Chicago: University of Chicago Press, 52.
273 Lukács, Georg. "On Walter Benjamin." *New Left Review*, I/110 July–August 1978.
274 Wolin, Richard. 1990. "Carl Schmitt, Political Existentialism, and the Total State." *Theory and Society*, vol. 19, no. 4, 389–416. On Lukács's "vitalism," see Stedman Jones, G. 1977. "The Marxism of the Early Lukács." *Western Marxism: A Critical Reader*. ed. Stedman Jones et al. London: New Left Review, 11–60.
275 Lukács. *History and Class Consciousness*, 144.
276 qtd. in *Gustav Landauer: Anarchist and Jew*, 90.
277 While "all revolutionary movements," according to Lukács "begin with the romanticism of illegality," this illegality is ultimately to be justified on the basis of its "utility" in relation to the aims of the Revolution and the "legitimacy of its [eventual] rule." The "hypostatisation of 'illegality,'" and the performance of actions "against the *law qua law*," actions which attempt to "break the law with a grand gesture," merely preserve the legality of the existing order in "an inverted form," "endow[ing] the existing state with a certain legal validity." Lukács, "Legality and Illegality," in *History and Class Consciousness*, 226.
278 Lukács, György. 1974. "Metaphysics of Tragedy." *Soul and Form*. ed. John Sanders. Cambridge: MIT Press, 179.
279 Benjamin. *Origin of the German Trauerspiel*, 169.
280 Ibid., 172.

281 Ibid., 166.
282 Ibid., 166.
283 Ibid., 168.
284 Ibid.
285 Ibid.
286 Ibid., 187.
287 Ibid., 169.
288 Ibid., 172.
289 Ibid., 169.
290 Ibid., 173.
291 Ibid., 172-3.
292 "Benjamin to Florens Christian Rang December 9, 1923." *The Correspondence of Walter Benjamin, 1910-1940*, 224.
293 Benjamin, Walter. "Some Motifs in Baudelaire." *Walter Benjamin: Selected Writings, 4: 1938-1940*, 315.
294 Benjamin. "Two Poems by Friedrich Hölderlin," 30.
295 Ibid., 26.
296 Benjamin. *Origin of the German Trauerspiel*, 209.
297 Ibid., 61.
298 Lukács. "Metaphysics of Tragedy," 181-2.
299 Ibid., 197.
300 Benjamin. *Origin of the German Trauerspiel*, 173.
301 Ibid., 167.
302 Lukács. "Metaphysics of Tragedy," 182.
303 Benjamin. *Origin of the German Trauerspiel*, 173.
304 Ibid., 174.
305 Lukács. "Metaphysics of Tragedy," 181.
306 Ibid., 182.
307 Fenves. *The Messianic Reduction*, 12.
308 Benjamin. *Origin of the German Trauerspiel*, 61.
309 De Man, Paul. 1969. "Rhetoric of Temporality." *Interpretation: Theory and Practice.* ed. Charles S. Singleton. Baltimore: Johns Hopkins University Press, 190.
310 Benjamin. *Origin of the German Trauerspiel*, 187.
311 Ibid., 174.
312 qtd. Adorno, Theodor. 2012. "The Idea of Natural-History." *Things beyond Resemblance: Collected Essays on Theodor W. Adorno.* ed. Robert Hullot-Kentor with Preface by Lydia Goehr. New York: Columbia University Press, 261-2.
313 Adorno. "The Idea of Natural-History," 262.
314 Wolin. *Aesthetic of Redemption*, 72.
315 Ibid.
316 Ibid.
317 As Ágnes Heller has argued, however, this verdict is acknowledged in the "The Foundering of Form against Life," in which Lukács concedes that "the shaping of life proves to be a futile, shipwrecked endeavour." (Heller, Agnes. 1983. "Georg Lukács and Irma Seidler." *Lukács Reappraised.* ed. Heller Agnes. New York: Columbia University Press, 29.
318 Benjamin. *Origin of the German Trauerspiel*, 81.
319 Ibid., 50.
320 Ibid., 81.

321 Wolin. *Aesthetic of Redemption*, xi.
322 Benjamin. *Origin of the German Trauerspiel*, 134.
323 Weigel, Sigrid. "Between Creation and Last Judgement, the Creaturely and the Holy." *Paragraph*, vol. 32, no. 3, 359–381, Passage-work: Walter Benjamin between the Disciplines (November 2009), 367.
324 Benjamin. *Origin of the German Trauerspiel*, 67.
325 Benjamin. "Theological-Political Fragment." *Walter Benjamin: Selected Writings Volume 3: 1935–1938*, 306.
326 Benjamin. "Life of Students," 37.
327 Benjamin. "Theologico-Political Fragment," 305.
328 Benjamin. *Origin of the German Trauerspiel*, 243.
329 Ibid., 91.

Chapter 4

1   "Benjamin to Scholem, October 22, 1917." *The Correspondence of Walter Benjamin, 1910–1940*, 98.
2   Benjamin. "Life of Students," 37.
3   Ibid.
4   Homburg, Peter. 2018. *Walter Benjamin and the Post-Kantian Tradition*. Lanham: Rowman & Littlefield International, 89.
5   qtd. Löwy. *Fire Alarm*, 92.
6   Benjamin. "Eduard Fuchs," 267.
7   Benjamin. "World and Time," 226.
8   Benjamin. "Coming Philosophy," 106.
9   Benjamin. *Origin of the German Trauerspiel*, 179.
10 Ibid.
11 Löwy. *Fire Alarm*, 67.
12 Agamben, Giorgio. 2007. *Potentialities: Collected Essays in Philosophy*. Stanford: Stanford University Press, 148.
13 Wolin. *Aesthetic of Redemption*, 31.
14 Ibid., 39.
15 Benjamin. *One-Way Street*, 55.
16 See Löwy. *Fire Alarm*, 67.
17 Wolin. *Aesthetic of Redemption*, xxxix.
18 Benjamin. "Paralipomena to 'On the Concept of History,'" 402.
19 Ibid., 401.
20 Ibid., 402.
21 Benjamin. "Theologico-Political Fragment," 312.
22 Benjamin. "Diary from August 7, 1931, to the Day of My Death," in *Walter Benjamin: Selected Writings volume 2, part 2, 1931–1934*, 502.
23 Benjamin. "On the Concept of History," 402.
24 Ibid., 395.
25 Benjamin. *Arcades Project*, 463.
26 Benjamin. "On the Concept of History," 396.
27 "Life of Students," 32.
28 Benjamin. "Theory of Knowledge," 276.

29 "Life of Students," 37.
30 Löwy, Michael. 1985. "Revolution Against 'Progress': Walter Benjamin's Romantic Anarchism." *New Left Review*, vol. 152, 43.
31 Benjamin. "On the Concept of History," 397.
32 *A Critical Life*, 42.
33 Ibid., 39.
34 Eiland, Howard. 2011. "Translator's Introduction." *Early Writings: 1910–1917*. Cambridge: The Belknap Press of Harvard University Press, 12.
35 Tagliacozzo. *Experience and Infinite Task*, 110.
36 Benjamin. *Arcades Project*, 119.
37 Benjamin. *Origin of the German Trauerspiel*, 82.
38 Ibid., 81.
39 Agamben, Giorgio. 2010. *The Time That Remains: A Commentary on the Letter to the Romans*. Stanford: Stanford University Press 143.
40 Schopenhauer, Arthur. 1897. "The Emptiness of Existence." *Essays of Schopenhauer*. ed. Rudolph Dircks. London: W. Scott, 58.
41 qtd. Agamben. *Time That Remains*, 143.
42 Schopenhauer. "The Emptiness of Existence," 58.
43 Heidegger, Martin. 2010. *Being and Time*. Albany: State University of New York Press, 302.
44 qtd. Agamben. *Time That Remains*, 143.
45 Heidegger. *Being and Time*, 311.
46 Ibid., 302.
47 Heidegger. *Being and Time*, 391.
48 Ibid., 352.
49 Ibid.
50 Agamben. *Time That Remains*, 143.
51 Benjamin. "On Perception," 96.
52 Benjamin. "On the Concept of History," 396.
53 Ibid., 397.
54 Ibid., 389.
55 Ibid., 394.
56 Ibid., 394–5.
57 Benjamin. "Paralipomena to 'On the Concept of History,'" 401.
58 Benjamin. "On the Concept of History," 397.
59 Benjamin. "Paralipomena to 'On the Concept of History,'" 407.
60 Benjamin. "On the Concept of History," 397.
61 Benjamin. *Arcades Project*, 471.
62 Benjamin. "On the Concept of History," 395.
63 Benjamin. "On the Image of Proust," 244.
64 Benjamin. "On the Concept of History," 391.
65 Žižek, Slavoj. 1999. *The Ticklish Subject: The Absent Centre of Political Ontology*. London: Verso, 20.
66 Theodor W. Adorno. Spring 1977. "The Actuality of Philosophy," *Telos*, vol. 31, 123.
67 Benjamin. *Origin of the German Trauerspiel*, 134.
68 Ng, Julia. 2012. "Walter Benjamin's and Gershom Scholem's Reading Group Around Hermann Cohen's *Kants Theorie Der Erfahrung* in 1918: An Introduction." *MLN*, vol. 127, no. 3, 437.
69 *Correspondence of Walter Benjamin*, 82.

70 See Kisiel, Theodore and Thomas Sheehan. 2007. *Becoming Heidegger: On the Trail of His Early Occasional Writings, 1910-1927*. Evanston: Northwestern University Press, xxxviii.
71 Heidegger. *Being and Time*, 306.
72 Massey, Heath. 2016. *The Origin of Time: Heidegger and Bergson*. Albany, NY: State University of New York Press, 20.
73 Benjamin. *Origin of the German Trauerspiel*, 87.
74 Heidegger, Martin. 2002. "The Concept of Time in the Science of History." *Supplements: From the Earliest Essays to Being and Time and Beyond*. ed. John Van Buren. Albany: State University of New York Press, 55.
75 Heidegger. "The Concept of Time in the Science of History," 53.
76 Massey. *The Origin of Time*, 20.
77 "Benjamin to Scholem, January 31, 1918." *Correspondence of Walter Benjamin*, 112.
78 Benjamin, Walter. "Metaphysics of Youth." *Selected Writings Volume 1*, 13.
79 See Blattner. William D. 2005. *Heidegger's Temporal Idealism*. ed. John van Buren. Cambridge: Cambridge University Press.
80 Ibid.
81 Benjamin, Walter. "Two poems by Hölderlin." *Selected Writings Volume 1*, 27.
82 Benjamin, "Two poems by Hölderlin," 34.
83 Benjamin. *Origin of the German Trauerspiel*, 82.
84 Bergson. *Time and Free Will*, 237
85 Benjamin. "Two poems by Hölderlin," 26.
86 Ibid., 27.
87 Benjamin, Walter. "A Berlin Chronicle." *Selected Writings, Volume 2*, 596.
88 Gelley, Alexander. 1993. *City Texts: Kracauer and Benjamin*. Berkeley, CA: Center for German and European Studies, University of California, 14.
89 Benjamin. "A Berlin Chronicle," 612.
90 Gelley. *Benjamin's Passages*, 35.
91 Benjamin. *Arcades Project*, 476.
92 Benjamin. *Origin of the German Trauerspiel*, 71.
93 Benjamin. *Arcades Project*, 545.
94 "Benjamin to Scholem, April 25, 1930." *Correspondence of Walter Benjamin*, 365.
95 "Benjamin to Scholem, January 20, 1930." *Correspondence of Walter Benjamin*, 359-60.
96 Benjamin. *Arcades Project*, 462-3.
97 Ibid., 473.
98 Benjamin. *Arcades Project*, 475.
99 Benjamin. "On the Concept of History," 395.
100 Agamben. *Potentialities*, 153.
101 Benjamin. "On the Concept of History," 406.
102 Benjamin. "On the Concept of History," 392.
103 Benjamin. *Arcades Project*, 475.
104 Ibid., 476.
105 Benjamin. "The Work of Art in the Age of Its Technological Reproducibility," 22.
106 Ibid., 24.
107 Benjamin. "On the Concept of History," 395.
108 Benjamin. *Arcades Project*, 470.
109 Benjamin. "On the Concept of History," 397.
110 Adorno. "Actuality of Philosophy," 123.

111 Benjamin. "On the Concept of History," 396-7.
112 Benjamin. "Paralipomena to 'On the Concept of History,'" 407.
113 Benjamin. "Theological-Political Fragment," 306.
114 Montanelli, Marina. Dec. 2018. "Walter Benjamin and the Principle of Repetition." *Aisthesis: Pratiche, linguaggi e saperi dell'estetico*, vol. 11, no. 2, 261+. Gale Academic OneFile, link.gale.com/apps/doc/A573094793/AONE?u=gmilcs_amherst&sid=googleScholar&xid=47999810. Accessed September 28, 2021.
115 Ng. "Walter Benjamin's and Gershom Scholem's Reading Group," 437.
116 Benjamin. "On Language as Such," 62.
117 Benjamin. *Arcades Project*, 112.
118 Westerman, Richard. 2019. *Lukács's Phenomenology of Capitalism: Reification Revalued*. Cham, Switzerland: Palgrave Macmillan, 8.
119 Benjamin. "Coming Philosophy," 105.
120 Ibid., 105.
121 Benjamin. "The Concept of Criticism in German Romanticism," 168.
122 Agamben. *State of Exception*, 56.
123 Benjamin. "Capitalism as Religion," 289.

Chapter 5

1 Beiser, Frederick C. 2017. *The Genesis of Neo-Kantianism, 1796-1880*. Oxford: Oxford University Press, 3.
2 Benjamin. "On the Concept of History," 402.
3 Beiser. *Genesis of Neo-Kantianism*, 269.
4 Ibid., 6.
5 Engels, Friedrich. 1987. "Engels to Friedrich Albert Lange in Duisburg, Manchester, March 29, 1865, 7 Southgate." Marx, Karl, and Friedrich Engels. 1987. *Karl Marx, Frederick Engels: Collected Works*. Moscow: Progress Publishers, 138.
6 "Benjamin to Scholem, January 31, 1918." *The Correspondence of Walter Benjamin, 1910-40*, 113.
7 Scholem. *Walter Benjamin: The Story of a Friendship*, 39.
8 Beiser. *Genesis of Neo-Kantianism*, 6.
9 Ernst Cassirer. 1932. "Kant, Immanuel." in Seligman and Johnson. *Encyclopedia of the Social Sciences*. Macmillan, volume 8, 541.
10 Moran, Philip Donald. 1981. *The Neo-Kantian Critiques of Karl Marx's Philosophy of History*. Dissertation, State University of New York at Buffalo, 210.
11 Keck, Timothy Raymond. 1975. *Kant and Socialism: The Marburg School in Wilhelmian Germany*. Madison: University of Wisconsin, 159-60.
12 qtd. Moran. *The Neo-Kantian Critiques of Karl Marx*, 6-7.
13 Ibid., 67. See also Gay, P., 1970. *The Dilemma of Democratic Socialism: Eduard Bernstein's Challenge to Marx*, New York: Columbia University Press.
14 Patton. *Hermann Cohen's History and Philosophy of Science*, 370.
15 qtd. Nettl, J. P. 2019. *Rosa Luxemburg*. London: Verso, 21.
16 Benjamin. "Eduard Fuchs," 270.
17 Keck. *Kant and Socialism*, 275.
18 Benjamin. "Review of Hönigswald's *Philosophie und Sprache*," 139.

19 qtd. Schwartz, Peter. "One Hundred Years since the Death of Franz Mehring." *World Socialist Web Site* 6.2.2019.
20 qtd. in Keck. *Kant and Socialism*, 274.
21 Moran. *The Neo-Kantian Critiques of Karl Marx*, 2–3.
22 Ibid., 8.
23 Lenin, V. I. "Once again about the Duma Cabinet." *Collected Works, Volume 11*. Moscow: Progress Publishers, 1978, 71.
24 Beiser. *Genesis of Neo-Kantianism*, 366.
25 qtd. in Moran. *The Neo-Kantian Critiques of Karl Marx*, 366.
26 Benjamin. "On the Concept of History," 390.
27 qtd. in Beiser, Frederick C. 2018. *Hermann Cohen: An Intellectual Biography*. Oxford: Oxford University Press, 87.
28 Beiser. *The Genesis of Neo-Kantianism*, 428.
29 Beiser. *Hermann Cohen*, 87.
30 Benjamin. "Eduard Fuchs," 273
31 Ibid., 296, fn. 48.
32 Marx. *Capital*, 296.
33 Beiser. *Hermann Cohen*, 87.
34 Moran. *The Neo-Kantian Critiques of Karl Marx*, 131–2.
35 Marx, Karl. "Postface to the Second Edition." *Capital: A Critique of Political Economy*. Volume I. trans. Ben Fowkes. New York: Vintage, 1977, 102.
36 Marx. "Postface to the Second Edition," 102.
37 Keck. *Kant and Socialism*, 237.
38 Lukács. *History and Class Consciousness*, xliv.
39 Lange, Friedrich Albert. 1894. *Die Arbeiterfrage in ihrer Bedeutung für Gegenwart und Zukunft*. Duisburg: W. Falk & Volmer, 248.
40 Marx, Karl. "Marx to Ludwig Kugelmann in Hanover, London, June 27, 1870." Marx, Karl, and Friedrich Engels. *Karl Marx and Frederick Engels: Selected Works*. Volume 43. Moscow: Progress Publishers, 1988, 295.
41 Marx. "Marx to Ludwig Kugelmann in Hanover, London, June 27, 1870," 295.
42 Korsch. *Karl Marx*, 122.
43 Benjamin. *Arcades Project*, 483.
44 Marx. "Marx to Ludwig Kugelmann in Hanover, London, June 27, 1870," 294.
45 Engels, Frederick. "Engels to Friedrich Albert Lange in Duisburg." *Karl Marx, Frederick Engels: Collected Works*. Volume 42. London: International Publishers, 1987, 137.
46 Malthus, Thomas Robert. 1959. *Population: The First Essay*. Ann Arbor, MI: University of Michigan Press, 5.
47 Ibid.
48 Marx. *Grundrisse*, 609.
49 Ibid., 608.
50 Marx, Karl and Friedrich Engels. *The Communist Manifesto, with Selections from the Eighteenth Brumaire of Louis Bonaparte and Capital by Karl Marx*. New York: Appleton-Century Crofts, 1955, 15.
51 Engels. "Engels to Friedrich Albert Lange in Duisburg," 137.
52 Ibid.
53 Ibid.
54 qtd. in Benjamin. "Eduard Fuchs," 261.

55 Marx, Karl. 1989. "Critique of the Gotha Programme." *Karl Marx, Frederick Engels: Collected Works, Volume 24.* ed. Jack Cohen et al. London: Lawrence & Wishart, 91.
56 "Benjamin to Scholem, June 13, 1924. *Correspondence of Walter Benjamin*, 244.
57 Bloch, Ernst. 1923. "Actuality and Utopia: On Lukacs' *History and Class Consciousness*." in Moir, C. 2020. "The Archimedean Point: Consciousness, Praxis, and the Present in Lukács and Bloch." *Thesis Eleven*, vol. 157, no. 1, 14–15.
58 Bloch. "Actuality and Utopia," 17.
59 Lukács. *History and Class Consciousness*, 160–1. This Kantian duality, however, is repeated in Lukács's theory of reification, in the opposition between history and reified time (see Chapter 6).
60 Beiser. *The Genesis of Neo-Kantianism*, 429.
61 Moran. *The Neo-Kantian Critiques of Karl Marx*, 131–2.
62 Kant, Immanuel. 1980. *The Foundations of the Metaphysics of Morals*. trans. Lewis White Beck. Indianapolis: Bobbs-Merrill, 53.
63 Dodson, Kevin E. 1991. *Kant's Theory of the Social Contract*. Dissertation. University of Massachusetts at Amherst, 206.
64 Dodson. *Kant's Theory of the Social Contract*, 208.
65 Ibid.
66 Moran. *The Neo-Kantian Critiques of Karl Marx*, 133.
67 Ibid., 125.
68 Ibid., 126–7.
69 Ibid., 135.
70 Ibid., 127.
71 Beiser. *Hermann Cohen*, 246.
72 Ibid.
73 Keck. *Kant and Socialism*, 290.
74 *The Correspondence of Walter Benjamin, 1910–40*, 106.
75 Lukács. *History and Class Consciousness*, 161.
76 Bloch. "Actuality and Utopia," 19.
77 qtd. Moran. *The Neo-Kantian Critiques of Karl Marx*, 136.
78 Ibid., 131.
79 Ibid., 133.
80 Ibid., 82.
81 Ibid., 73.
82 Plekhanov, Georgi. 1974. "On Mr Heinrich Rickert's Book." *Selected Philosophical Works: Volume I*. Moscow: Progress Publishers, 481.
83 "Benjamin to Scholem, ca. December 23, 1917." *The Correspondence of Walter Benjamin, 1910–40*, 106.
84 Simmel, Georg. 1977. *The Problems of the Philosophy of History: An Epistemological Essay*. New York: Free Press, 185.
85 Vorländer, Karl. 1900. *Kant und der Sozialismus*. Berlin: Verlag von Reuther & Reichard, 31.
86 qtd. Keck. *Kant and Socialism*, 218.
87 qtd. ibid., 219.
88 Benjamin. "Eduard Fuchs," 277.
89 Vorländer. *Kant und der Sozialismus*, 60.
90 Ibid., 5–6.

91 Marx. *Capital*, 174.
92 Engels. "Engels to Friedrich Albert Lange in Duisburg," 137.
93 Marx. *Capital*, 175.
94 Marx. *Grundrisse*, 243.
95 Marx. *Capital*, 178.
96 Ibid., 271.
97 Marx. *Grundrisse*, 244.
98 Bloch, Ernst. 2018. *On Karl Marx*. New York: Verso, 22.
99 Keck. *Kant and Socialism*, 219.
100 Korsch. *Karl Marx*, 100.
101 Marx. *Capital*, 167–8.
102 Moran, *The Neo-Kantian Critiques of Karl Marx*, 133.
103 Marx. *Grundrisse*, 164.
104 Karatani, Kōjin. 2005. *Transcritique: On Kant and Marx*. Cambridge: MIT, vii.
105 Schwarzschild, Steven S. 2018. *The Tragedy of Optimism: Writings on Hermann Cohen*. Albany: State University of New York Press, 5.
106 Hegel, Georg W. F., and S. W. Dyde. 2012. *Philosophy of Right*. New York: Dover Publications, xx.
107 Schwarzschild. *The Tragedy of Optimism*, 5.
108 Marx. *Capital*, 178 fn. 2.
109 Marx. "Critique of the Gotha Programme," 86.
110 Marx. *Grundrisse*, 248.
111 Ibid., 248.
112 Benjamin. *Arcades Project*, 634.
113 Ibid., 478.
114 Ibid., 479.
115 Ibid., 478.
116 Wolin. *Aesthetics of Redemption*, 115.
117 Ibid., 117.
118 Radnóti, Sándor. September 21, 1978. "Benjamin's Politics," *Telos*, vol. 1978, no. 37, 73.
119 Adorno. "Exchange with Theodor W. Adorno on 'The Paris of the Second Empire in Baudelaire.'" 129.
120 Benjamin. *Arcades Project*, 4.
121 Ibid., 893.
122 Ibid.
123 Zamora, Lois Parkinson and Monika Kaup. 2010. "Editor's Note to *The Origin of German Tragic Drama*, Excerpts, by Walter Benjamin." *Baroque New Worlds: Representation, Transculturation, Counterconquest*. ed. Lois Parkinson Zamora and Monika Kaup. Durham; London: Duke University Press, 56.
124 Benjamin. *Arcades Project*, 4.
125 Ibid., 462.
126 Wolin. *Aesthetic of Redemption*, 180.
127 For a discussion of the influence of Klages's work on the dream theory in the *Arcades Project*, see Lebovic, Nitzan. "The Beauty and Terror of 'Lebensphilosophie': Ludwig Klages, Walter Benjamin, and Alfred Baeumler." *South Central Review*, vol. 23, no. 1. South Central Modern Language Association, Johns Hopkins University Press, 2006, 29.
128 Benjamin. "Johann Jakob Bachofen," *Selected Writings Volume 3*, 12.
129 *A Critical Life*, 465. See also Michael Löwy's discussion of the role of "idealized past" in Benjamin's "romantic protest" against capitalism in *Fire Alarm*, 12–13.

130 Korsch. *Karl Marx*, 33.
131 Ibid., 31.
132 Marx. *Capital*, 175.
133 "Exchange with Theodor W. Adorno," 55.
134 Korsch. *Karl Marx*, 43.
135 Benjamin. *Arcades Project*, 474.
136 Buck-Morss, Susan. 1999. *The Dialectics of Seeing: Walter Benjamin and the Arcades Project*. Cambridge, MA: MIT Press, 49.
137 Kellner, Douglas. 1977. "Korsch's Road to Marxian Socialism." *Karl Korsch: Revolutionary Theory*. ed. Douglas Kellner. Austin: University of Texas Press, 14.
138 *A Critical Life*, 63.
139 Kellner. "Korsch's Road to Marxian Socialism," 14.
140 *A Critical Life*, 465.
141 Kellner. "Korsch's Road to Marxian Socialism," 15.
142 Buck-Morss, Susan. 1979. *The Origin of Negative Dialectics: Theodor W. Adorno, Walter Benjamin, and the Frankfurt Institute*. New York: The Free Press, 207.
143 Adorno, Theodor W. and Walter Benjamin. 1999. *The Complete Correspondence, 1928-1940*. Cambridge: Harvard University Press, 7.
144 "Benjamin to Scholem, January 20, 1930." *The Correspondence of Walter Benjamin, 1910-40*, 359.
145 *A Critical Life*, 323.
146 Levitt, Cyril. 1982. "Karl Korsch: A Review Essay." *Labour / Le Travail*, vol. 10, 178-9.
147 Levitt. "Karl Korsch," 179-80.
148 Korsch. *Karl Marx*, 89.
149 Engels. "Engels to Friedrich Albert Lange in Duisburg," 137.
150 Korsch. *Karl Marx*, 47.
151 Benjamin. *Arcades Project*, 939. For Benjamin, then, as Irving Wohlfarth has argued: "Phantasmagoria is thus not merely the false consciousness of ideological discourse. It is materialized in space, objects, and practices. To 'interiorize' it by confining it to some disembodied realm of ideas is thus itself a phantasmagoric operation." (Wohlfarth, Irving. 1996. "Smashing the Kaleidoscope: Walter Benjamin's Critique of Cultural History." *Walter Benjamin and the Demands of History*. ed. Michael P. Steinberg. Ithaca: London: Cornell University Press, 199.
152 Korsch. *Karl Marx*, 29.
153 Ibid., 40.
154 Ibid., 9.
155 Ibid., 22.
156 Ibid., 122.
157 Ibid., 121.
158 qtd. in Levitt. "Karl Korsch," 179-80.
159 Korsch. *Karl Marx*, 122.
160 Benjamin. *Arcades Project*, 484-5.
161 Benjamin. "Johann Jakob Bachofen," *Selected Writings Volume 3*, 17.
162 Jay, Martin. 1992. *Marxism and Totality: The Adventures of a Concept form Lukács to Habermas*. Berkeley: University of California Press, 17.
163 "Benjamin to Scholem, May 20, 1935." *The Correspondence of Walter Benjamin, 1910-40*, 482.
164 As Kojève acknowledged in his correspondence to the Vietnamese philosopher Trần Đức Thảo, his lectures had deliberately exaggerated the importance of the

Notes

master-slave dialectic in order present Hegel's philosophy as a "phenomeneological anthropology." "[J]'ai fait un cours [sur Hegel] ... [mais] ... il m'importait relativement peu de savoir ce que Hegel lui-même a voulu dire dans son livre." Je "ne disant que ce que je considérais être la verité ... D'autre part, mon cours était essentiellement une œuvre de propagande destinée à frapper les esprits. C'est pourquoi j'ai consciemment renforcé le rôle de la dialectique du Maître et de l'Esclave et, d'une manière générale, schématisé le contenu de la phénoménologie." (Jarczyk, Gwendoline, Pierre-Jean Labarrière, A. Kojève, and Thao. 1990. " Alexandre Kojève et Tran-Duc-Thao: correspondance inédite." Genèses, no. 2, 134.).

165 Derrida, Jacques. 1972. "The Ends of Man." *Margins of Philosophy*. trans. Alan Bass. Chicago, IL: University of Chicago press, 117.
166 Hollier, Denis, ed. 1988. *The College of Sociology (1937–39)*. trans. Betsy Wing. Minneapolis: University of Minnesota Press, 86.
167 qtd. in Weingrad, Michael. 2001. "The College of Sociology and the Institute of Social Research." *New German Critique*, no. 84, 141.
168 Walter, Benjamin. 1977. "Walter Benjamin: Conversations with Brecht." *Aesthetics and Politics*, ed. Ernst Bloch et al. London: Verso, 96.
169 Eiland and Jennings. *A Critical Life*, 640.
170 Korsch. *Karl Marx*, 157.
171 Ibid., 97.
172 qtd. in *Arcades*, 667.
173 Schnadelbach, Herbert. 1984. *Philosophy in Germany 1831–1933*. trans. Eric Matthews. Cambridge: Cambridge University Press, 161.
174 Benjamin. "Literary History and the Study of Literature." *Selected Writings Volume 2*, 460.
175 Rose, Gillian. 1978. *The Melancholy Science: An Introduction to the Thought of Theodor W. Adorno*. London: Macmillan, 33.
176 Rose. *The Melancholy Science*, 32.
177 qtd. in Frisby, David. "Introduction to the Translation." Simmel, Georg. 2013. *Philosophy of Money*. trans. Tom Bottomore and David Frisby. London: Routledge, 22.
178 Benjamin. *Arcades Project*, 660.
179 Simmel. *Philosophy of Money*, 429–30.
180 Ibid., 430.
181 Ibid., 430–1.
182 Simmel. *Philosophy of Money*, 431.
183 Benjamin. *Arcades Project*, 660.
184 Ibid., 661.
185 Ibid., 664.
186 Simmel. *Philosophy of Money*, 430.
187 Benjamin. *Arcades Project*, 664.
188 Marx. *Capital*, 167.
189 Turner, Jonathan H., Leonard Beeghley, and Charles H. Powers. 2012. *The Emergence of Sociological Theory*, Thousand Oaks: Pine Forge Press, 205.
190 qtd. in Frisby, "Introduction to the Translation," 28.
191 Rose. *Melancholy Science*.
192 Benjamin. *Arcades Project*, 664.
193 Ibid., 664.
194 Benjamin. *Arcades Project*, 665.
195 Simmel. *Philosophy of Money*, 430.

196 Benjamin. *Arcades Project*, 657.
197 Korsch. *Karl Marx*, 62.
198 Ibid., 32.
199 Wolin. *Aesthetic of Redemption*, 180.

Chapter 6

1 Korsch. *Karl Marx*, 44.
2 Pinloche, A. 1933. *Fourier Et Le Socialisme*. Paris: F. Alcan, 49.
3 Ibid.
4 qtd. in Pinloche. *Fourier Et Le Socialisme*, 50.
5 qtd. in ibid., 52.
6 Ibid.
7 Korsch. *Karl Marx*, 12.
8 Ibid., 44.
9 Ibid.
10 Benjamin. *Arcades Project*, 44.
11 Löwy. *Fire Alarm*, 76.
12 Benjamin. *Arcades Project*, 5.
13 qtd. in ibid., 628.
14 qtd. in Bataille, Georges. 1970. *Œuvres complètes I: Premiers écrits 1922–1940*. Paris: Gallimard, 391.
15 Pierre Klossowski. "Between Marx and Fourier."
16 Agamben. *Potentialities*, 139.
17 Benjamin, Walter. "Préface à la version allemande des *Quatre Mouvements* de Charles Fourier." *Cahiers Charles Fourier*, 2010 / n° 21, en ligne: http://www.charlesfourier.fr/spip.php?article806 (consulté le 2 avril 2021).
18 Klossowski. "Between Marx and Fourier."
19 Ibid.
20 Benjamin. *Arcades Project*, 5.
21 Ibid., 4.
22 Benjamin, Walter. "'The Regression of Poetry,' by C. G. Jochmann." *Selected Writings Volume 3*, 363.
23 qtd. in Benjamin. *Arcades Project*, 343.
24 qtd. in Florent, Perrier. "Présences de Charles Fourier dans Paris, Capitale du XIXe siècle de Walter Benjamin," *Cahiers Charles Fourier*, 2010 / n° 21, en ligne: http://www.charlesfourier.fr/spip.php?article795 (consulté le 24 mai 2021).
25 Benjamin. *Arcades Project*, 4.
26 Ibid.
27 Ibid., 361.
28 Benjamin, Walter. "On Scheerbart." *Walter Benjamin: Selected Writings, 4: 1938–1940*, 387.
29 Fourier, Charles. 1996. *Theory of the Four Movements*. Cambridge: Cambridge University Press, 159.
30 Barthes, Roland. 1977. *Sade, Fourier, Loyola*. trans. Richard Miller. London: Jonathan Cape, 81.
31 Fourier. *Theory of the Four Movements*, 293.

32 Engels, Frederick. 1989. "Socialism: Utopian and Scientific." *Karl Marx, Frederick Engels: Collected Works*, Volume 24. London: Lawrence & Wishart, 293.
33 See Stedman Jones, Gareth. "Introduction." *Theory of the Four Movements*, xxiii.
34 Pinloche. *Fourier Et Le Socialisme*, 21.
35 Ibid., 92.
36 Fourier. *Theory of the Four Movements*, 269.
37 Engels, Friedrich. 1989. *Anti-Dühring*. *Karl Marx, Frederick Engels: Collected Works*, Volume 24. London: Lawrence & Wishart, 316.
38 Marx and Engels. *The Communist Manifesto*, 15.
39 Engels. *Anti-Dühring*, 317.
40 Marx, Karl and Friedrich Engels. 1947. *The German Ideology*. New York: International Publishers, 183.
41 Benjamin. "Eduard Fuchs," 267.
42 "Exchange with Theodor W. Adorno," 54.
43 Benjamin. *Arcades Project*, 475.
44 Benjamin. *Origin of the German Trauerspiel*, 132.
45 Ibid., 133.
46 Lukács, György. 2005, "On Walter Benjamin." Osborne, Peter. *Walter Benjamin: Critical Evaluations in Cultural Theory*. London: Routledge, 4–5.
47 Ibid.
48 Lukács. "On Walter Benjamin," 4.
49 Ibid., 1.
50 Lukács. "On Walter Benjamin," 4.
51 Marx. *Capital*, 165.
52 Feher, Ferenc. 1985. "Lukács and Benjamin: Parallels and Contrasts." *New German Critique*, no. 34, 126–7.
53 "Exchange with Theodor W. Adorno on the Essay 'Paris, the Capital of the Nineteenth Century.'" *Selected Writings Volume 3*, 55.
54 Benjamin, Walter. "Problems in the Sociology of Language," *Selected Writings Volume 3*, 72.
55 Korsch. *Karl Marx*, 93.
56 Benjamin. *Origin of the German Trauerspiel*, 168.
57 Urbich. *Benjamin and Hegel, a Constellation in Metaphysics*.
58 Benjamin. *Origin of the German Trauerspiel*, 174.
59 Lukács. *History and Class Consciousness*, 84.
60 *A Critical Life*, 10.
61 Korsch. *Karl Marx*, 122.
62 Benjamin. *Arcades Project*, 664.
63 Lukács. *History and Class Consciousness*, ix.
64 Rose, Gillian. 1981. *Hegel Contra Sociology*. London: Humanities Press, 27. On the influence of the Baden School of Neo-Kantianism on Lukács, see Kavoulakos, Kōstas. 2018. *Georg Lukács's Philosophy of Praxis: From Neo-Kantianism to Marxism*. London: Bloomsbury Press.
65 See Jay, Martin. 1984. *Marxism and Totality: The Adventures of a Concept from Lukács to Habermas*. Berkeley: University of California Press, 268–70, and 1996. *The Dialectical Imagination: A History of the Frankfurt School and the Institute of Social Research, 1923–1950*, London: Heinemann, 152.
66 "Adorno to Benjamin, 2 August 1935." *Aesthetics and Politics*, 113.
67 Adorno. Theodor W. 2015. *Negative Dialectics*. London: Routledge, 11.

68 Benjamin. *Arcades Project*, 665.
69 Adorno. *Negative Dialectics*, 146.
70 Ibid.
71 Benjamin. *Arcades Project*, 657.
72 Lukács. "On Walter Benjamin," 4.
73 Marx. *Capital*, 165.
74 Benjamin. *Arcades Project*, 669.
75 Adorno. "Exchange with Theodor W. Adorno," 58.
76 Löwy. *Fire Alarm*, 11-12.
77 Feher. "Lukács and Benjamin: Parallels and Contrasts," 133.
78 "Adorno to Benjamin, August 2, 1935." *Aesthetics and Politics*, 116.
79 Benjamin. "Theories of German Fascism," 120.
80 Benjamin. "The Work of Art," 42.
81 Ibid.
82 Simmel. *Philosophy of Money*, 489.
83 Wolin, Richard. 2008. "Walter Benjamin Meets the Cosmics: A Forgotten Weimar Moment." Keynote address at the conference "The Weimar Moment: Liberalism, Political Theology and Law," University of Wisconsin-Madison, October 25. www.law.wisc.edu/m/ndkzz/wolin_revised_10-13_benjamin_meets_the_cosmics.doc.
84 Klages, Ludwig. 1929. *The Science of Character*. trans. by Johnston, Walter Henry. London: Allen and Unwin, 70.
85 qtd. in McCole, John Joseph. 1993. *Walter Benjamin and the Antinomies of Tradition*. Ithaca, NY: Cornell University Press, 238.
86 qtd. in Bishop, Paul. 2012. *The Archaic: The Past in the Present*. London: Routledge, 29-30.
87 Benjamin. *Arcades Project*, 15.
88 Wolin. "Walter Benjamin Meets the Cosmics," 22.
89 Benjamin. *Arcades Project*, 390.
90 Ibarlucia, Ricardo. "The Organization of Pessimism: Profane Illumination and Anthropological Materialism in Walter Benjamin." Aisthesis: Pratiche, linguaggi e saperi dell'estetico, vol. 10, no. 1, June 2017, pp. 139+. Gale Academic OneFile, link.gale.com/apps/doc/A533409553/AONE?u=gmilcs_amherst&sid=googleScholar&xid=104c0260. Accessed September 30, 2021.
91 Naville, P. 1975: *La Revolution et les intellectuels*. rev. and augmented ed. Gallimard/NRF, Paris.
92 Löwy. *Fire Alarm*, 11-12.
93 Wohlfarth, Irving, 2002. "Walter Benjamin and the Idea of a Technological Eros. A Tentative Reading of *Zum Planetarium*." Benjamin Studies/Studien 1, 74-5.
94 Kavoulakos, Kōstas. 2018. *Georg Lukács's Philosophy of Praxis from Neo-Kantianism to Marxism*. London: Bloomsbury, 120.
95 Marx. *Grundrisse*, 173.
96 Benjamin. *Arcades Project*, 654.
97 Ibid., 656.
98 Marx. *Capital*, 127.
99 Ibid., 174-5.
100 Ibid., 136-7.
101 Ibid., 174-5.
102 Benjamin. "The Author as Producer." *Selected Writings Volume 2, Part 2*, 779.

103 Benjamin. *Arcades Project*, 360–1.
104 Benjamin. "The Work of Art," 26–7.
105 Benjamin. *Arcades Project*, 360–1.
106 Benjamin. *Art in the Age of Its Technological Reproduction*, 31.
107 Walter, Benjamin. "Language in *Trauerspiel* and Tragedy." *Selected Writings Volume 1*, 61.
108 Walter, Benjamin. "Calderon and Hebbel." *Selected Writings Volume 1*, 381.
109 Benjamin. "Calderon and Hebbel." *Selected Writings Volume 1*, 379.
110 Benjamin. *Origin of the German Trauerspiel*, 70.
111 Walter, Benjamin. "Toys and Play." *Selected Writings Volume 2*, 120.
112 Benjamin, Walter. "Some Motifs in Baudelaire." *Selected Writings 4*, 329.
113 Montanelli, Marina. "Walter Benjamin and the Principle of Repetition." *Aisthesis: Pratiche, linguaggi e saperi dell'estetico*, vol. 11, no. 2, Dec. 2018, pp. 261+. Gale Academic OneFile, link.gale.com/apps/doc/A573094793/AONE?u=gmilcs_amherst&sid=googleScholar&xid=47999810. Accessed September 28, 2021.
114 Benjamin. "Toys and Play," 120.
115 Freud, Sigmund. 2011. *Beyond the Pleasure Principle*. Peterborough, Ont: Broadview Press, 59.
116 Powers, Michael. 2018. "The Smallest Remainder: Benjamin and Freud on Play." *MLN*, vol. 133 no. 3, 735.
117 Benjamin. "Toys and Play," 120.
118 Powers. "The Smallest Remainder," 729.
119 Benjamin. "Toys and Play," 120.
120 Powers. "The Smallest Remainder," 721.
121 Benjamin. "Toys and Play," 118.
122 Ibid., 120.
123 Ibid., 118.
124 Montanelli.
125 Benjamin, Walter. "Old Forgotten Children's Books." *Selected Writings: 1913–1926, Volume 1*, 408.
126 Benjamin, Walter. "Old Toys." *Selected Writings: 1927–1934, Volume 2*, 101.
127 Marx, Karl, Friedrich Engels. *The German Ideology*, 42.
128 Benjamin. "Toys and Play," 119.
129 Benjamin. "Art in the Age of Its Technological Reproduction," 48, fn. 23.
130 Benjamin. "Experience and Poverty." *Selected Writings Volume 2*, 733.
131 Benjamin. *Arcades Project*, 340.
132 Benjamin. "Experience and Poverty," 732.
133 Benjamin. "Theories of German Fascism," 313.
134 Benjamin. *Arcades Project*, 653.
135 Benjamin. "Some Motifs in Baudelaire," 329.
136 qtd. Benjamin. *Arcades Project*, 79.
137 Benjamin. "Art in the Age of Its Mechanical Reproducibility," 45, fn. 11.
138 Benjamin. "On the Concept of History," 393.
139 Benjamin. *Arcades Project*, 361.
140 Ibid., 459.
141 Benjamin. "Art in the Age of Its Technological Reproducibility," 32.
142 Ibid., 26.
143 Benjamin. *Arcades Project*, 390.

144 Ibid., 392.
145 qtd. in Cooper, David. E. 1998. "Reactionary Modernism and Self-Conscious Myth." *Myth and the Making of Modernity: The Problem of Grounding in Early Twentieth-Century Literature.* ed. Michael Bell and Peter Poellner. Amsterdam and Atlanta: Rodophi, 102.
146 Benjamin. *Arcades Project*, 393.
147 Ibid., 431.
148 Benjamin. "Art in the Age of Its Mechanical Reproducibility," 22.
149 Benjamin. Walter. "Blanqui." *Selected Writings 4*, 93.
150 Benjamin. *Arcades Project*, 342.
151 Benjamin. "Eduard Fuchs," 266.
152 Benjamin. *One-Way Street*, 94–5.
153 Benjamin. "Art in the Age of Its Mechanical Reproducibility," 42.
154 Ibid., 41.
155 Ibid., 42.
156 Benjamin. *Arcades Project*, 361.
157 Agamben. *State of Exception*, 53.
158 Benjamin, Walter and Gershom Scholem. 1992. *The Correspondence of Walter Benjamin and Gershom Scholem 1932-1940.* Cambridge: Harvard University Press, 100.
159 Benjamin. *Origin of the German Trauerspiel*, 72.
160 Benjamin. "Category of Justice," 257.
161 Löwy. *Fire Alarm*, 11–12.
162 Benjamin, Walter. 2006. "A Different Utopian Will." *Walter Benjamin: Selected Writings, Volume 3.* ed. Walter Benjamin, Howard Eiland, and Michael W. Jennings. Cambridge, MA: Belknap, 135.
163 Benjamin. *Arcades Project*, 9.
164 Ibid., 15.
165 Ibid., 5.
166 Ibid., 16.
167 Benjamin. "The Work of Art," 20.
168 Ibid., 42.
169 "Adorno to Benjamin, March 18, 1936." *Politics and Aesthetics*, 121.
170 Buck, Susan. *The Origin of Negative Dialectics*, 148.
171 "Adorno to Benjamin, March 18, 1936." *Aesthetics and Politics*, 122.
172 Hullot-Kentor, Robert. "Translator's Introduction." *Aesthetic Theory.* London: Continuum, 1997, xvi.
173 Adorno. *Aesthetic Theory*, 227.
174 Ibid., 106.
175 Ibid., 227.
176 Ibid., 226.
177 Ibid., 58.
178 Benjamin, Water. "Little History of Photography." *Selected Writings Volume 2, Part 2*, 526.
179 Debord, Guy. 1995. *Society of the Spectacle.* Brooklyn: Zone Books, 136.
180 Adorno. *Aesthetic Theory*, 45.
181 Benjamin. "Letter from Paris (2) Painting and Photography," *Selected Writings Volume 3*, 240.
182 Benjamin. "Art in the Age of Its Mechanical Reproducibility," 24.

Notes

183 Sieber, Jan. "Walter Benjamin's Concept of Technique." *Anthropology & Materialism* [En ligne], 4 | 2019, mis en ligne le 13 octobre 2019, consulté le 24 mai 2021. URL: http://journals.openedition.org/am/944; DOI: https://doi.org/10.4000/am.944.
184 Benjamin. "On the Concept of History," 393–4.
185 Ibid., 394.
186 Marx. "Critique of the Gotha Programme," 81.
187 Benjamin. "The Work of Art," 42.
188 Ibid., 45, fn. 11.
189 Ibid.
190 Ibid., 41.
191 Benjamin. "The Work of Art," 45, fn. 11.
192 Benjamin. *Arcades Project*, 17.
193 Pinloche. Fourier et le socialisme, 23,
194 Benjamin, Walter. "Theories of German Fascism," 312.
195 Benjamin. *Arcades Project*, 361.
196 Pinloche. Fourier et le socialisme, 34.
197 Benjamin, Walter. "A Chronicle of Germany's Unemployed." *Selected Writings 4*, 130.
198 Benjamin, Walter. "'The Regression of Poetry,' by C. G. Jochmann," 369.
199 "Walter Benjamin and the Idea of a Technological Eros: A Tentative Reading of *Zum Planetarium*." *Benjamin Studien/Studies*. ed. Helga Geyer-Ryan et al. Amsterdam, New York: Rodopi, 2002, 73.
200 Benjamin. *Arcades Project*, 5.
201 Ibid., 15.
202 Ibid., 5.
203 Ibid., 342.
204 Korsch. *Karl Marx*, 35.
205 Ibid., 342.
206 Ibid.
207 Similarly, Marx distinguished utopian socialists like Fourier and Robert Owen from the "vulgar socialists" who followed them. In the work of "philistine Utopian[s]," like Pierre-Joseph Proudhon, "the Utopias of … Fourier, Owen, etc., [which] contain the presentiment and visionary expression of a new world," becomes "corrupted." ("Marx To Ludwig Kugelmann, London, October 9, 1866." Marx, Karl and Friedrich Engels. 1987. *Karl Marx, Friedrich Engels: Collected Works*. New York: International Publishers, 326).
208 Benjamin. *Arcades Project*, 342.
209 Balzac, Honoré de. 1869. *Œuvres complètes* (Complete Works), vol. 20. Paris: Michel Lévy Frères, 461–2.
210 qtd. in Benjamin. *Arcades Project*, 74.
211 qtd. in ibid., 77.
212 Ibid., 345.
213 Ibid., 894.
214 qtd. in *Arcades*, 79.
215 Ibid., 345.
216 Adorno. "Exchange with Adorno on 'Paris of the Second Empire,'" 111.
217 Benjamin. *Arcades Project*, 339.
218 Benjamin. "Karl Kraus," in Selected Writings Volume 2, Part 2, 1931–1934, p. 446.
219 qtd. Benjamin. *Arcades Project*, 79.
220 Ibid., 22.

221 Benjamin. *Arcades Project*, 77.
222 qtd. in ibid.
223 qtd. in ibid., 75.
224 Marx. *Capital*, 137.
225 Ibid., 147–8.
226 Benjamin. *Arcades Project*, 3.
227 Marx. *Capital*, 531.
228 Benjamin. *The Arcades Project*, 395.
229 Marx. *Capital*, 532.
230 Ibid., 609.
231 Ibid., 609, fn. 12.
232 Fourier. *Theory of the Four Movements*, 256.
233 Benjamin. *The Arcades Project*, 345.
234 Ibid., 361.
235 Ibid., 896.
236 Ibid., 125.
237 qtd. in Benjamin, *The Arcades Project*, 75.
238 Fourier, Charles. 1901. "Of Luxury and Saving." *Selections from the Works of Fourier*. ed. Charles Gide, trans. Julia Franklin. London: Swan Sonnenschein & Co., 196.
239 Benjamin. *The Arcades Project*, 141.
240 Beecher, Jonathan. 1986. *Charles Fourier: The Visionary and His World*. Berkeley, CA: University of California Press, 303.
241 Patterson, Ian and Gareth Stedman Jones, "Introduction," Fourier, Charles, *The Theory of the Four Movements*, xviii.
242 Fourier. *Theory of the Four Movements*, 3.
243 Benjamin. *The Arcades Project*, 623.
244 Klossowski, Pierre. 2017. *Living Currency*. London: Bloomsbury Academic, 52.
245 Benjamin. *The Arcades Project*, 11.
246 Ibid., 345.
247 Ibid., 572.
248 Benjamin. "The Author as Producer," 2, 776.
249 Benjamin. *The Arcades Project*, 342.
250 Ibid., 896.
251 Ibid.
252 Ibid.
253 Marx and Engels. *Communist Manifesto*, 13.
254 Benjamin. *Arcades Project*, 341.
255 Ibid.
256 Ibid., 118.
257 Nietzsche, Friedrich. 1910. *The Complete Works of Friedrich Nietzsche Vol. X. The Gay Science*. ed. Dr. Oscar Levy. Edinburgh: T.N. Foulis, 277.
258 Benjamin. *Arcades Project*, 113.
259 Ibid., 112.
260 qtd. in ibid., 112.
261 Ibid., 111.
262 Engels, Friedrich. 1962. "Letter from Engels to Franz Mehring in Berlin, London, July 14, 1893." *Karl Marx and Frederick Engels Selected Works Volume II*. Moscow: Foreign Languages Publishing House, 498.

263 Benjamin. *The Arcades Project*, 111.
264 Ibid., 116.
265 qtd. in ibid., 113.
266 Ibid., 912.
267 Ibid., 302.
268 Ibid., 111.
269 Ibid., 113.
270 qtd. in ibid.
271 qtd. in ibid., 118.
272 Benjamin. *Origin of the German Trauerspiel*, 82.
273 Ibid., 76.
274 Ibid., 174.
275 qtd. in Benjamin. *Arcades Project*, 113.
276 qtd. in ibid., 114.
277 Benjamin. *Origin of the German Trauerspiel*, 174.
278 qtd. in Benjamin. *Arcades Project*, 114.
279 qtd. in ibid., 115.
280 qtd. in ibid.
281 Ibid., 116.
282 Ibid., 112.
283 qtd. ibid., 114.
284 qtd. ibid.
285 Ibid., 25.
286 qtd. ibid., 114.
287 Ibid., 116.
288 Ibid., 119.
289 Ibid., 117.
290 Benjamin. *Origin of the German Trauerspiel*, 46.
291 Benjamin. *Arcades Project*, 458.
292 Benjamin. *Origin of the German Trauerspiel*, 59.
293 Benjamin. *Arcades Project*, 118.
294 Benjamin. "Capitalism as Religion," 289.
295 Ibid.
296 Löwy. *Fire Alarm*, 47.
297 Benjamin. *The Arcades Project*, 26.
298 Ibid., 463. Emphasis added.
299 Ibid., 119.
300 Benjamin. "Paralipomena," 401.
301 Ibid., 402.
302 Ibid., 401.
303 Benjamin, "Eduard Fuchs," 267.
304 Benjamin. "Paralipomena," 407.
305 Benjamin. *Arcades Project*, 119.
306 Benjamin. "Paralipomena," 403.
307 Benjamin. *Arcades Project*, 113.
308 Ibid., 26.
309 Ibid., 15.
310 Adorno, Theodor W. 1982. *Prisms*. Cambridge, MA: MIT Press, 238.

Chapter 7

1. Benjamin. *Arcades Project*, 631.
2. Ibid., 625.
3. Ferrari, Giuseppe. 1845. "Des idées et de l'école de fourier depuis 1830." *Revue des Deux Mondes*, période initiale, tome 11, 398.
4. Fenves. *Messianic Reduction*, 208.
5. See Beatrice Hanssen, "On the Politics of Pure Means: Benjamin, Arendt, Foucault," in *Violence, Identity, and Self-Determination*, ed. Hent de Vries and Samuel Weber. 1997. Stanford, CA: Stanford University Press, 236–52.
6. qtd. in *Messianic Reduction*, 218.
7. Ibid., 208.
8. Windelband. *A History of Philosophy*, 556.
9. Ibid., 554.
10. Ibid.
11. Ibid., 555.
12. Ibid.
13. Ibid., 559.
14. Benjamin. "Coming Philosophy," 106.
15. qtd. in Benjamin, Walter. 2021. *Toward the Critique of Violence: A Critical Edition*. Stanford: Stanford University Press, 20.
16. Kant, Immanuel. 1987. *Critique of Judgment*. Indianapolis: Hackett Pub. Co, 331.
17. Ibid.
18. Kant. *Critique of Judgment*, 332.
19. Ibid.
20. Windelband. *A History of Philosophy*, 555.
21. Benjamin. *The Arcades Project*, 631.
22. Benjamin. "Karl Kraus," 452.
23. Pinloche. *Fourier et le socialisme*, 56.
24. Fourier, Charles. "Of the Role of the Passions." *Selections from the Works of Fourier*. ed. Charles Gide, trans. Julia Franklin, 55.
25. qtd. in Marx, Karl and Frederick Engels. 1975. *Karl Marx, Frederick Engels: Collected Works, Volume 4*. Moscow: International Publishers, 133.
26. Benjamin. *The Arcades Project*, 5.
27. Fourier. "Of the Role of the Passions," 55.
28. Benjamin. *The Arcades Project*, 16.
29. *Dictionary of Political Economy*. Vol. 2. ed. Palgrave, Robert H. I. London: Macmillan, 1923, 124–5.
30. Benjamin. *The Arcades Project*, 16.
31. Ibid., 621.
32. "Benjamin to Scholem, ca. December 1, 1920." *Correspondence of Walter Benjamin*, 168.
33. Benjamin, Walter. "On Scheerbart." *Selected Writings 4*. ed. Howard Eiland and Michael W. Jennings, 286.
34. Benjamin. "On Scheerbart," 287.
35. Ibid.
36. Benjamin. "On the Concept of History," 394.
37. Benjamin. "On Scheerbart," 286.

38 Benjamin. "On the Concept of History," 394.
39 Benjamin. "On Scheerbart," 286.
40 Benjamin. "A Different Utopian Will," 135.
41 Ibid., 134.
42 Ibid., 135.
43 Ibid., 134.
44 Benjamin, "Addendum to the Brecht Commentary: The Threepenny Opera," *Selected Writings Volume 3*, 258.
45 Ibid.
46 Marx. *Capital*, 131.
47 Benjamin, Walter. 2005. "Mickey Mouse." *Walter Benjamin: Selected Writings. Vol 2 Part 2*. ed. Walter Benjamin, Michael W. Jennings, Howard Eiland, and Gary Smith. Cambridge, MA: Belknap, 545.
48 Ibid.
49 Benjamin. *The Arcades Project*, 635.
50 Benjamin, Walter. "Brecht's Threepenny Novel," *Selected Writings Volume 3*, 9.
51 Benjamin. "The Work of Art," 41.
52 Benjamin. *The Work of Art in the Age of Its Technological Reproducibility*, 137.
53 Benjamin. "The Work of Art," 38.
54 Surya, Michel. 2010. *Georges Bataille: An Intellectual Biography*. London: Verso, 266.
55 Gershom Scholem. 1988. "Walter Benjamin and His Angel." *On Walter Benjamin: Critical Essays and Recollections*. ed. Gary Smith. Cambridge: MIT Press, 62, 65.
56 "De Walter Benjamin à Max Horkheimer, le 3 août 1938." "Walter Benjamin et le Collège de sociologie." *Critique* 2013/1-2 (n° 788–789), 100.
57 *A Critical Life*, 519.
58 qtd. ibid., 520.
59 Stoekl, Allan. 1985. "Introduction." Bataille, George. *Visions of Excess: Selected Writing, 1927–1939*. Minneapolis: University of Minnesota Press, xxv.
60 Hörisch, Jochen. 1986. "Benjamin entre Bataille et Sohn-Rethel. Theorie de la depense et depese de la theorie." *Walter Benjamin et Paris*. ed. Heinz Wismann. Cerf, 347.
61 Klossowski, Pierre. "Letter on Walter Benjamin." *Parrhesia* 19 (2014), preveo Christian Hite. Dostupno na: http://www.parrhesiajournal.org/parrhesia19/parrhesia19_klossowski.pdf (pristupljeno 4. 3. 2016.).
62 Monnoyer, Jean-Maurice. 1985. *Le peintre et son demon: entretiens avec Pierre Klossowski*. Paris: Flammarion, 185–6.
63 qtd. in Hollier. *The College of Sociology*, 389.
64 Monnoyer. *Le peintre et son demon*, 186.
65 qtd. *Living Currency*, 41.
66 Deleuze, Gilles, and Félix Guattari. 1983. *Capitalism and Schizophrenia*. Minneapolis: University of Minnesota Press, 63.
67 qtd. in Wilson, Sarah. 2006. *Pierre Klossowski*. Ostfildern: Hatje Cantz, 24.
68 Smith, Daniel. 2017. "From Theatrical Theology to Counter Utopia." *Living Currency*. ed. Pierre Klossowski. London: Bloomsbury, 2.
69 Foss-Heimlich, Paul. 2017. "Sade and Fourier and Klossowski and Benjamin." *Living Currency*. ed. Pierre Klossowski. London: Bloomsbury, 111.
70 Foss-Heimlich, "Sade and Fourier and Klossowski and Benjamin," 105.
71 Perrier, Florent. "Présences de Charles Fourier dans Paris, Capitale du XIXe siècle de Walter Benjamin."

72 Foss-Heimlich. "Sade and Fourier and Klossowski and Benjamin," 107.
73 Bataille, Georges. 1986. *Erotism: Death and Sensuality.* trans. Mary Dalwood. San Francisco: City Lights, 63
74 Mehlman, Jeffrey. 1983. *Legacies of Anti-Semitism in France.* Minneapolis: University of Minnesota Press, 90.
75 Weingrad, Michael. 1999. *Benjamin or Bataille: Transgression, Redemption, and the Origins of Postmodern Thought.* Dissertation, University of Washington, 92.
76 Weingrad. *Benjamin or Bataille*, 92.
77 Ibid., 93.
78 Monnoyer. *Le peintre et son demon*, 187.
79 Foss-Heimlich. "Sade and Fourier and Klossowski and Benjamin," 113.
80 Klossowski. *Living Currency*, 54.
81 Ibid., 65.
82 Ibid., 48.
83 Ibid.
84 Bataille, Georges. 1988. *The Accursed Share: 1.* New York: Zone Books, 13.
85 Bataille, George. 1985. "The Notion of Expenditure." *Visions of Excess, Selected Writings, 1927–1939.* ed. Allan Stoekl. Minnesota: University of Minnesota Press, 169.
86 Bataille. *Accrused Share*, 71.
87 Ibid., 57.
88 Ibid., 23.
89 qtd. in Monnoyer, Jean-Maurice. 1985. *Le peintre et son demon: entretiens avec Pierre Klossowski.* Paris: Flammarion, 188.
90 Bataille. "Notion of Expenditure," 176.
91 Bataille. *Accrused Share*, 25.
92 Klossowski. *Living Currency*, 60.
93 Ibid., 51.
94 Ibid., 58.
95 Ibid., 48.
96 Kant, Immanuel. 2008. *Lectures on Ethics.* Cambridge: Cambridge University Press, 165.
97 Kant. *Lectures on Ethics*, 163.
98 qtd. in Lukács. *History and Class Consciousness*, 100.
99 Kant, Immanuel. 2017. *The Metaphysics of Morals.* Cambridge: Cambridge University Press, 68.
100 Benjamin, Walter. 1996. "Goethe's Elective Affinities." *Selected Writings 1, 1913–1926.* ed. Marcus Bullock and Michael W. Jennings. Cambridge, MA: Belknap Press of Harvard University Press, 299.
101 Benjamin. *The Arcades Project*, 10.
102 Ibid., 511.
103 Klossowski. *Living Currency*, 52.
104 qtd. in Beecher. *Charles Fourier*, 303.
105 Fourier. *Theory of the Four Movements*, 111.
106 Ibid., 91.
107 Ibid., 70.
108 Ibid., 83.
109 Ibid., 83.
110 Ibid., 55.
111 Ibid.

112 Ibid., 68.
113 Ibid., 69.
114 Ibid., 82.
115 Benjamin. *The Arcades Project*, 638–9.
116 Klossowski. *Living Currency*, 52.
117 Benjamin, Walter. 2006. "Commentary on Poems by Brecht." *Selected Writings* 4, 241.
118 Klossowski. *Living Currency*, 52.
119 Ibid., 80.
120 Ibid., 80.
121 Ibid., 80.
122 Ibid., 82.
123 Ibid., 53.
124 Foucault, Michel. 1990. *The History of Sexuality: An Introduction*. New York: Vintage, 10.
125 Noam Chomsky and Michel Foucault. 1974. "Noam Chomsky and Michel Foucault. Human Nature: Justice versus Power." *Reflexive Water: The Basic Concerns of Mankind*. ed. Fons Elders. London: Souvenir, 174.
126 Klossowski. *Living Currency*, 52.
127 Marx. *Grundrisse*, 611.
128 Klossowski. *Living Currency*, 65.
129 Ibid., 53.
130 Ibid., 53.
131 Ibid., 70.
132 Ibid., 54.
133 Ibid., 53.
134 Ibid., 86.
135 Ibid., 65.
136 Ibid., 40.
137 Ibid., 66.
138 Ibid., 53.
139 Ibid., 95.
140 Ibid., 83.
141 Ibid., 69.
142 Ibid., 83.
143 Ibid.
144 Ibid., 84.
145 Ibid., 82.
146 Ibid., 57.
147 Ibid., 89.
148 Ibid., 50.
149 Ibid., 49–50.
150 Ibid.
151 Ibid., 89.
152 Ibid., 69.
153 Ibid., 49.
154 Ibid., 59.
155 Ibid., 75.
156 Ibid., 91.
157 Ibid., 89.

158 Kant, Immanuel. 1996. "What Is Enlightenment." *Practical Philosophy*. ed. Mary J. Gregor. Cambridge: Cambridge University Press, 17.
159 Bataille. "Notion of Expenditure," 168.
160 Klossowski. *Living Currency*, 67.
161 Benjamin. *The Arcades Project*, 345.
162 qtd. in Klossowski. *Living Currency*, 27.
163 Klossowski. *Living Currency*, 66.
164 Ibid.
165 Ibid.
166 Klossowski. "Between Marx and Fourier."
167 Benjamin. *Origins of the German Trauerspiel*, 171.
168 Ibid., 7.
169 Benjamin. "The Work of Art," 48, fn. 23.
170 Ibid.
171 Ibid.
172 Ibid., 24.
173 Benjamin, "The Work of Art," 23.
174 Ibid., 25.
175 Catholic University of America. 2003. *New Catholic Encyclopedia, Volume* 12. Detroit, MI: Gale Group in association with the Catholic University of America, 489.
176 Klossowski. "Letter on Walter Benjamin."
177 Bataille. *Accrused Share*, 55.
178 Ibid., 25.
179 Bataille. *Accrused Share*, 37.
180 Ibid., 25.
181 Ibid., 56.
182 Bataille. "Notion of Expenditure," 170.
183 Benjamin. "The Work of Art," 26.
184 Ibid., 48, fn. 23.
185 Benjamin. *Origin of the German Trauerspiel*, 7.
186 Benjamin. "The Work of Art," 42.
187 Klossowski, Pierre. 1947. *Sade, mon prochain*. Editions du Seuil, 165. See also Habermas' discussion of Bataille's relation to fascism in Habermas, Jurgen. 1992. *The Philosophical Discourse of Modernity: Twelve Lectures*. trans. Frederick Lawrence. Cambridge, MA: MIT, 221.
188 Benjamin. "The Work of Art," 42.
189 Ibid.
190 Klossowski. "Between Marx and Fourier."
191 Benjamin. "The Work of Art," 25.
192 Ibid., 27.
193 Ibid., 24.
194 Ibid.
195 Ibid., 23.
196 "Letter, Adorno to Benjamin, March 18, 1936," *Aesthetics and Politics*, 123.
197 Benjamin. "The Work of Art," 38.
198 Benjamin. *The Arcades Project*, 345.
199 Benjamin. "The Work of Art," 42.
200 Ibid.
201 Ibid., 41.

202 Benjamin. "Theories of German Fascism," 120.
203 Benjamin. "The Work of Art," 42.
204 Benjamin. "Theories of German Fascism," 313.
205 Bataille. 1990. "Hegel, Death and Sacrifice." *Yale French Studies*. trans. Jonathan Strauss, 78: On Bataille, ed- Allan Stoekl. 18.
206 Bataille, Georges. 1992. *Theory of Religion*. trans. Robert Hurley. New York: Zone, 92.
207 Benjamin. "Theories of German Fascism," 313.
208 Habermas. *The Philosophical Discourse of Modernity*, 220.
209 Agamben, Giorgio. 2017. *The Omnibus Homo Sacer*. Stanford, CA: Stanford University Press, 95.
210 "De Walter Benjamin à Max Horkheimer, le 3 août 1938," 100.
211 *History of Philosophy*, 559.
212 Walter Benjamin, Fragment 30, "Zweideutigkeit des Begriffs der 'unendlichen Aufgabe' in der kantischen Schule" (1918) in *Gesammelte Schriften VI*, Frankfurt: Suhrkamp, 51–3.
213 Benjamin. *The Arcades Project*, 342.

Conclusion

1 qtd. in *A Critical Life*, 4.
2 Wolin. *Aesthetic of Redemption*, xi.
3 Benjamin, Walter. Spring 1979. "Doctrine of the Similar." *New German Critique*, no. 17, Special Walter Benjamin Issue, 66.
4 Walton, Stuart. "What We Call Progress." *Review*, vol. 31. http://review31.co.uk/article/view/743/what-we-call-progress.
5 Agamben. "Potentialities,"155–6.
6 Benjamin. "The Concept of Criticism in German Romanticism," 136.
7 Ibid., 139.
8 Osborne, Peter. 1994. "Small-scale Victories, Large-scale Defeats: Walter Benjamin's Politics of Time." *Walter Benjamin: Destruction and Experience*. ed. Andrew E. Benjamin and Peter Osborne. London: Routledge, 61.
9 Weber. "Taking Exception to Decision," 7.
10 "Benjamin to Scholem, unmailed draft of the beginning of the letter of May 6, 1934." *The Correspondence of Walter Benjamin and Gershom Scholem*, 108–9.
11 Benjamin. *Origin of the German Trauerspiel*, 21.
12 Caygill. *Colour of Experience*, viii.
13 Adorno. *Negative Dialectics*, 19.
14 Adorno. *Prisms*, 236.
15 Adorno. *Negative Dialectics*, 157.
16 Ibid., 27.
17 Hegel, Georg W. F. 2013. *Phenomenology of Spirit*. Oxford: Oxford University Press, 360.
18 Hegel, Georg W. F. 2001. *Philosophy of Right*. Kitchener, Ontario: Batoche, 20.
19 Hegel. *Philosophy of Right*, 19.
20 Ibid., 20.
21 See Nguyen, Duy Lap. 2015. "On the Suspension of Law and the Total Transformation of Labour: Reflections on the Philosophy of History in Walter Benjamin's 'Critique of Violence.'" *Thesis Eleven*, vol. 130, no. 1, 9.

22 Benjamin. "On the Concept of History," 392.
23 Benjamin. "Unpacking My Library." *Selected Writings Volume 2*, 492.
24 Benjamin. *The Arcades Project*, 475.
25 Hegel. *Philosophy of Right*, 20.
26 qtd. in Benjamin. *The Arcades Project*, 15.
27 Ibid., 15.
28 Mosès. "Benjamin, Nietzsche, et l'idée de l'éternel retour," 146.
29 qtd. Hallward. "Blanqui's Bifurcations Dossier," 38.
30 Blanqui. *Eternity by the Stars*, 125.
31 Rancière, Jacques. May-June 2014. "The Radical Gap." preface to Auguste Blanqui, *L'Eternité par les astres. Radical Philosophy*, 185, 24.
32 Ibid.
33 qtd. Benjamin. *The Arcades Project*, 116.
34 qtd. ibid., 115.
35 Adorno, *Prisms*.
36 Nietzsche, Friedrich. 1968. *The Will to Power*. New York: Vintage Books, 19.
37 Benjamin. *Origin of the German Trauerspiel*, 174.
38 Scott, David. 1997. "Leibniz and the Two Clocks." *Journal of the History of Ideas*, vol. 58, no. 3, 445.
39 Benjamin. *Origin of the German Trauerspiel*, 82.
40 Ibid., 68.
41 Ibid., 67.
42 Ibid., 190.
43 Benjamin. "Life of Students," 37.
44 Mosès, Stéphane. 2009. *The Angel of History: Rosenzweig, Benjamin, Scholem*. Stanford: Stanford University Press, 12–13.
45 Löwy. *Fire Alarm*, 11.
46 Benjamin. *The Arcades Project*, 472.
47 Ibid., 669.
48 Marx, Karl. 1963. *Poverty of Philosophy*. New York: International Publishers, 114.
49 Lukács. *History and Class Consciousness*, 90.
50 Marx. *Grundrisse*, 173.
51 Steiner, George. 1998. "Introduction." *The Origin of German Tragic Drama*. ed. Walter Benjamin. London: Verso, 15.
52 Scholem, Gershom. 2003. *Walter Benjamin: The Story of a Friendship*. New York: New York Review, 233.

Selected Bibliography

Adorno, Theodor W. "The Actuality of Philosophy," *Telos* 31 (Spring 1977), 120–33.
Adorno, Theodor W. 2012. "The Idea of Natural-History." *Things beyond Resemblance: Collected Essays on Theodor W. Adorno*, ed. Robert Hullot-Kentor. New York: Columbia University Press, 252–70.
Agamben, Giorgio. 2007. *Potentialities: Collected Essays in Philosophy*. Stanford: Stanford University Press, 148.
Agamben, Giorgio. 2010. *The Time That Remains: A Commentary on the Letter to the Romans*. Stanford: University Press.
Atger, Frédéric. 1906. *Essai Sur L'histoire Des Doctrines Du Contrat Social*. Paris: F. Alcan.
Arendt, Hannah. 1968. "Introduction." *Illuminations*. New York: Harcourt, Brace & World, 1–58.
Bataille, Georges. 1988. *The Accursed Share: 1*. New York: Zone Books.
Benjamin, Walter. 2003. *The Arcades Project*. Cambridge, MA: Belknap Press.
Benjamin, Walter. 1996. "Fragment 31: Zweideutigkeit des Begriffs der 'unendlichen Aufgabe' in der kantischen Schule" (Ambiguity of the Concept of the 'Infinite Task' in the Kantian school). Gesammelte Schriften VI. Frankfurt am Main: Suhrkamp, 51–3.
Benjamin, Walter. 2019. *Origin of the German Trauerspiel*. Cambridge: Harvard University Press.
Benjamin, Walter. "Préface à la version allemande des *Quatre Mouvements* de Charles Fourier." *Cahiers Charles Fourier*, 2010/n° 21, en ligne: http://www.charlesfourier.fr/spip.php?article806 (consulté le 2 avril 2021).
Benjamin, Walter. 2004. *Walter Benjamin: Selected Writings, 1: 1913–1926*. Cambridge: Belknap.
Benjamin, Walter. 2005. *Walter Benjamin: Selected Writings, Volume 2: Part 1 1927–1930*. ed. Jennings, Michael W. and Howard Eiland. Cambridge and London: Belknap.
Benjamin, Walter. 2006. *Walter Benjamin: Selected Writings Volume 3: 1935–1938*. ed. Howard Eiland and Michael W. Jennings. trans. Edmund Jephcott and Harry Zohn. Cambridge, MA: Harvard University Press.
Benjamin, Walter. 2006. *Walter Benjamin: Selected Writings, 4: 1938–1940*. ed. Michael W. Jennings and Howard Eiland. Cambridge and London: Belknap Press of Harvard University Press.
Buck-Morss, Susan. 1999. *The Dialectics of Seeing: Walter Benjamin and the Arcades Project*. Cambridge, MA: MIT Press.
Blanqui, Louis Auguste. 2018. *The Blanqui Reader: Political Writings, 1830–1880*. London; Brooklyn, NY: Verso.
Bergson, Henri-Louis. 1913. *Matiere et mémoire: essai sur la relation du corps a l'esprit*. Paris: Félix Alcan.
Bergson, Henri-Louis. 1913. *Time and Free Will: An Essay on the Immediate Data of Consciousness*. London: G. Allen & Co.
Caygill, Howard. 1998. *Walter Benjamin: The Colour of Experience*. London: Routledge.

Charles, Matthew. 2009. *Speculative Experience and History: Walter Benjamin's Goethean Kantianism*. Speculative experience and history: Walter Benjamin's Goethean Kantianism. PhD thesis, Middlesex University.

Cohen, Hermann. 1972. *Religion of Reason: Out of the Sources of Judaism*. trans. Simon Kaplan. New York: Frederick Unger.

Derrida, Jacques. 2016. "Force of Law: The 'Mystical Foundation of Authority.'" *Deconstruction and the Possibility of Justice*, ed. Drucilla Cornell, Michel Rosenfeld, and David Carlson. London: Routledge, 3–67.

Descartes, René. 1901. *The Method, Meditations and Philosophy of Descartes*. Washington, DC: M.W. Dunne.

Fenves, Peter. 2010. *The Messianic Reduction: Walter Benjamin and the Shape of Time*. Stanford, CA: Stanford University Press.

Fourier, Charles. 1901. *Selections from the Works of Fourier*. London: Swan Sonnenschein & Co.

Fourier, Charles. 1996. *Theory of the Four Movements*. Cambridge: Cambridge University Press.

Hegel, Georg W. F. 2013. *Phenomenology of Spirit*. Oxford: Oxford University Press.

Heidegger, Martin. 2010. *Being and Time*. Albany: State University of New York Press.

Hollier, Denis, ed. 1988. *The College of Sociology* (1937–39). trans. Betsy Wing. Minneapolis: University of Minnesota Press.

Husserl, Edmund. 1993. *Ideas: General Introduction to Pure Phenomenology*. London: George Allen & Unwin.

Ibarlucía, Ricardo. "The Organization of Pessimism: Profane Illumination and Anthropological Materialism in Walter Benjamin," *Aisthesis. Pratiche, Linguaggi E Saperi dell'estetico* 10 (1) (2017), 139–60. https://doi.org/10.13128/Aisthesis-20914

Jacobson, Eric. 2003. *Metaphysics of the Profane: The Political Theology of Walter Benjamin and Gershom Scholem*. New York: Columbia University Press.

Jay, Martin. 1996. *The Dialectical Imagination: A History of the Frankfurt School and the Institute of Social Research, 1923–1950*. London: Heinemann.

Kant, Immanuel. 2007. *Critique of Judgement*. Oxford: Oxford University Press.

Kant, Immanuel. 1998. *Critique of Pure Reason*. ed. and trans. Paul Guyer and Allen W. Wood. Cambridge: Cambridge University Press.

Kant, Immanuel. 2017. *The Metaphysics of Morals*. Cambridge: Cambridge University Press.

Kant, Immanuel. 2006. *Toward Perpetual Peace and Other Writings on Politics, Peace, and History*. trans. David Colclasure. New Haven: Yale University Press.

Keck, Timothy Raymond. 1975. *Kant and Socialism: The Marburg School in Wilhelmian Germany*. Madison: University of Wisconsin.

Klossowski, Pierre. "Letter on Walter Benjamin." *Parrhesia* 19 (2014), preveo Christian Hite. Dostupno na: http://www.parrhesiajournal.org/parrhesia19/parrhesia19_klossowski.pdf

Klossowski, Pierre. 2017. *Living Currency*. London: Bloomsbury Academic.

Korsch, Karl. 2015. *Karl Marx*. Leiden: Koninklijke Brill NV.

Löwy, Michael. 1995. *Fire Alarm: Reading Walter Benjamin's "On the Concept of History."* trans. Chris Turner. London: Verso.

Lukács, Georg. 1974. *Soul and Form*. Cambridge: MIT Press, 176–98.

Marx, Karl. 1977. *Capital: A Critique of Political Economy*. Volume I. trans. Ben Fowkes. New York: Vintage.

Marx, Karl. 2008. *Critique of the Gotha Program*. Cabin John, MD: Wildside Press.
Marx, Karl. 1974. *Grundrisse: Foundations of the Critique of Political Economy*. trans. Martin Nicolaus. Harmondsworth: Penguin Books.
Monnoyer, Jean-Maurice. 1985. *Le peintre et son demon: entretiens avec Pierre Klossowski*. Paris: Flammarion.
Moran, Philip Donald. 1981. *The Neo-Kantian Critiques of Karl Marx's Philosophy of History*. Dissertation, State University of New York at Buffalo.
Moritz, Geiger. 1986. *The Significance of Art: A Phenomenological Approach to Aesthetics*. Washington, DC: Center for Advanced Research in Phenomenology & University Press of America.
Mosès, Stéphane. 2009. *The Angel of History: Rosenzweig, Benjamin, Scholem*. Stanford: Stanford University Press.
Meyerson, Émile. 1991. *Explanation in the Sciences*. Dordrecht: Kluwer Academic Publishers.
Naville, P. 1975. *La Revolution et les intellectuels*. rev. and augmented ed. Paris: Gallimard/NRF.
Nietzsche, Friedrich. 2001. *The Gay Science*. ed. Bernard Williams, trans. Josefine Nauckhoff. Cambridge: Cambridge University Press.
Pinloche, A. 1933. *Fourier Et Le Socialisme*. Paris: F. Alcan.
Proudhon, Pierre-Joseph. 2007. *The Philosophy of Misery*. New York: Cosimo.
Schmitt, Carl. 2005. *Political Theology: Four Chapters on the Concept of Sovereignty*. Chicago and London: University of Chicago Press.
Scholem, Gershom. 2003. *Walter Benjamin: The Story of a Friendship*. New York: New York Review.
Simmel, Georg. 2013. *Philosophy of Money*. trans. Tom Bottomore and David Frisby. London: Routledge.
Sorel, Georges. 1901. *L'avenir socialiste des syndicats* (Nouvelle édition, considérablement augmentee). Paris: Librairie G. Jacques & cie.
Taubes, Jacob. 2015. *To Carl Schmitt: Letters and Reflections*. New York: Columbia University Press.
Windelband, W. 1898. *A History of Philosophy with Especial Reference to the Formation and Development of Its Problems and Conceptions*. New York: Macmillan and Co.

Index

abstract labor (see Marx, Karl)
Accursed Share (see Bataille, Georges)
Acéphale 20, 146, 153, 200–1, 202–3, 213, 216, 218, 220–2, 228
atheology 217, 222
Bataille, Georges 20, 146, 153, 200–5, 208, 214–15, 217–22
　Accursed Share 204–5, 219
　Collège de Sociologie 218, 153, 201
　expenditure 20, 204–5, 208, 210–11, 213–15, 217, 219–20, 222
　general economy 20, 204, 208, 213
　sacred, the x, 79, 105, 174, 176, 202, 217–22
　transgression 20, 201–3, 212, 215, 222
Caillois, Roger 146, 201, 222
Klossowski, Pierre 20, 153, 201–3, 205, 207–16, 218–19, 221–2
　Living Currency 201, 202–3, 204–5, 214, 215
　seriousness of work and desire 168, 199, 203, 209–11, 215, 219–22
perversion xi, 20, 181–2, 185, 200–1, 203, 207–15
Adorno, Theodor (see Institute of Social Research)
Agamben, Giorgio 8, 10, 79, 111, 117, 153, 173, 221, 225
allegory (see language)
analogy (see language)
anarchy xi, 8, 11–15, 17–19, 22, 24, 41, 43, 45, 47, 56, 58, 60, 79, 105, 132, 193
　Landauer, Gustav 15, 56, 59–60
　metaphysical anarchism (see Scholem, Gershom)
　Sorel, Georges 8, 50, 55–7, 61
　　on Blanqui 8
　　critique of parliamentary socialism 55–6
　　demythologization 61–2

　Reflections on Violence 8, 55, 61
angel of history (see Benjamin, Walter)
apocatastasis (see Benjamin, Walter)
Arcades Project (see Benjamin, Walter)
Aristotle 72, 94
　on classical drama 72
　on technology 94
Atger, Frédéric 82–3
Aufhebung (see Hegel, Georg Wilhelm Friedrich)
Augenblick (see Heidegger, Martin)
aura (see Benjamin, Walter)

Bachofen, Johann Jacob (see vitalism)
Balzac, Honoré de (see fashion)
bare life (see life)
Baroque, the (see *Trauerspiel*)
Bataille, Georges (see Acéphale)
Baudelaire, Charles 6, 21, 100, 166, 169
beauty (see also aura) 69, 71, 185, 216–18
Being and Time (See Heidegger, Martin)
Beiser, Frederick C. 123, 125–6, 131
Benjamin, Walter
　aesthetic extreme 15, 63, 65–75, 80, 82
　angel of history viii, 104, 109, 227
　and owl of Minerva 227–8
　　Klee, Paul 201
　apocatastasis 77, 171, 219
　Arcades Project xi–xii, 1–3, 5–6, 9, 11–12, 18–20, 25, 93, 97, 116, 118, 120–121, 128, 139, 141, 143–6, 152–5, 157, 159–66, 169–71, 173–5, 177, 184–5, 187, 189, 192–3, 196–7, 201, 203, 209, 212–15, 218
　　Convolute N 116–18, 141, 144, 146, 171
　　Convolute X 143, 147–50, 164
　　exposés for *The Arcades Project* 3, 6, 142, 150, 152, 158–9, 161, 182, 191
　art for art's sake 174–7, 218

Index

"Art in the Age of its Technological Reproducibility" 71, 12, 19–20, 161, 169, 171, 174–5, 177–8, 198, 200–2, 216–18, 221
  aura 161, 168, 175–6, 215–16;
    decline of 215–16, 218, 221
  cult value 118, 176–7, 217–18
  exhibition value 176, 218
"The Author as Producer" 60, 165
"Capitalism as Religion" 56, 61, 92, 121, 190
"Concept of Criticism in German Romanticism" 35
"On the Concept of History" 4, 17, 31, 55, 84, 90, 109, 113, 118–19, 123, 138, 141, 146, 153, 177, 191
constellation 15, 66–8, 71, 96, 106, 109–10, 116–17, 142, 226–8
"Critique of Violence" (see also general strike and violence) 8, 14–15, 41–2, 45, 48–61
  absoluteness of ends and contingency of means 14, 49, 51–2
  missing criterion of violence 14, 48
dialectical image 116–17, 119, 156, 158, 226–7
"A Different Utopian Will" 198–202
empty, homogenous time (see time) 99–100, 106, 110–15, 118–20, 140, 168, 191, 229
"Epistemo-Critical Prologue" 15, 63, 66, 216
experience
  empty Enlightenment concept of experience 13, 22, 23–7, 29–30, 37, 39–40, 91
  ephemeral experience/"experience itself and unto itself" 4–5, 13, 24, 26–7, 29, 31–4, 38–40, 51, 54, 84, 91, 163
  impoverishment of experience (see also bare life) 22, 24, 162, 166, 169–72
  lived-experience (*Erlebnis*) 21, 37–8, 98, 187
  mechanical experience 22–8, 31–4, 39, 119, 120
Fall, the xi, 35, 108

fate 2, 5–7, 11, 14, 19–20, 29, 51–3, 62, 72–3, 95–6, 112, 116–18, 147, 166, 168, 188, 190–2, 222, 230
first and second nature 20, 171–2, 198–9
general strike 54–9, 61–2, 79, 98
  versus political strike 54–8
  as pure means 54–5, 57–8, 79
  as total withdrawal from capitalism and state power 15, 56–7, 61
"good-right of the good" 14, 18–19, 45, 47, 54, 161, 173–4, 177
happiness 105, 112, 153–4, 168, 188, 193–7, 209–10, 222
historiography 68, 118, 134
history of philosophy x, 12, 86
Jetztzeit 17, 111–19
justice xi, 7–9, 14, 18, 42, 44–8, 53–4, 58–60, 108, 132, 138, 155, 160, 173–4
messianism ix, x, xi, xiii, 11, 17, 47, 90–3, 105, 107–12, 117–20, 132, 140–1, 153–4, 163, 166, 170–2, 191, 227, 230
  and happiness 105, 112, 153–4, 168, 188
  profane messianism 17
  weak messianism 117
metaphysical-theological and materialist stages of Benjamin's work x, xii, 4, 11–12, 15, 17–19, 29, 93, 94, 97, 110–12, 114, 142, 163, 166, 197, 231
Mickey Mouse 199
modernity x–xii, 1, 5–6, 10–12, 19, 24, 27, 29, 90, 92–3, 112, 120–1, 157, 161, 164, 182, 186, 190–2, 230–1
newness xi, 2, 6, 19, 170, 182–6, 189, 191, 214, 219, 222, 228
  newness versus use and exchange value 184–7
"Notes toward a Work on the Category of Justice" 14, 41–2, 44–7, 54, 108, 173
"Now of knowability" 30, 32, 110
origin x, xi, 2, 24, 35, 37, 38, 66–7, 102, 109, 141, 154
"paradox of the Cretan" 25–6, 54

phantasmagoria xii, 3, 6, 10–11, 93, 120, 144, 189, 191–2, 230–1
"politics," treatise on 41, 51, 193–4, 196–7
"primacy of the thingly" 45, 47, 156–7, 160, 173, 177
primal history (see also origin) 141, 152, 172, 186–90
principle of non-contradiction 25–6, 31
profane, the x, xi, xiii, 17, 24, 28–9, 34, 76–7, 80, 91, 97, 102, 104–5, 107–9, 111–12, 115, 118–21, 142, 163, 166, 168, 171, 174, 217–18, 220–1, 229, 230
profane illumination 28–9, 91, 163
profane redemption (see also creaturely life and eternal transience) xi, xiii, 17, 76, 102, 104–5, 107–9, 111–12, 115, 118–21, 142, 166, 171, 230
profane theology 15, 28–30, 75–6, 79–80, 90–1
"Program of the Coming Philosophy" 5, 12–15, 17, 22, 24–5, 27–33, 36, 39–41, 45–6, 51, 72, 91, 108, 114, 119–20, 163, 194, 231
semblance 10, 165, 170–1, 184, 216–22
"semblance of value" 10, 165, 170–1, 184, 220–2
beautiful semblance 216–20
technology
"bungled reception" of 6, 172–3
first technology 170, 178, 198, 216–17, 221
inadequate utilization in capitalism 161–2, 172, 179, 197–8, 220–1
right of technology 18, 161, 163, 165, 173–4, 177, 181, 184, 191, 193
second technology 10, 19, 25, 166, 170–2, 178–80, 198–9, 216, 218–20, 222
"slave revolt of technology" xii, 160–6, 177, 179
teleology without final purpose 194, 196, 199
"Theological-Political Fragment" 14, 41–2, 105, 109, 119, 153

"Theories of German Fascism" 161, 179, 220–1
tradition 17, 19, 111–13, 116–19, 124–5, 167–2, 182–3, 186, 189
transience (see time)
Trauerspiel
Baroque, the 16–17, 20, 47, 63, 66–70, 72, 74–80, 82, 86, 88–90, 92, 94–7, 99, 102, 104–5, 107–9, 111, 115, 120, 141–2, 157, 160, 166, 187, 191, 229, 230; Baroque eschatology (see also Profane Redemption); Baroque sovereign 63, 70, 72, 74–80, 88; and the psycho-physical parallelism 15–16, 87–9, 94
Calderón de la Barca, Pedro 95
Cysarz, Herbert 70
classicist misinterpretation of 63, 69, 75, 142
Lohenstein, Daniel Casper von 166
Shakespeare, William 64, 73
versus tragedy 16–17, 69–70, 72–3, 94–6, 101, 104, 116, 142–3, 166, 189
virtual history of 15, 68–70, 80, 98
"unimproved humanity" x–xi, 11, 24, 46, 107–9, 171, 230
violence (see also "Critique of Violence") viii, 8–9, 14–15, 41–2, 44–5, 47–62, 69, 79, 96, 98, 108, 173, 194, 197, 221
extortionate violence (see general strike)
law-making 14–15, 44, 47–61, 96
law-preserving 9, 15, 52–4, 58, 60, 96
police 52, 56
pure violence 59, 61
terrorism viii, 8, 56, 59–61, 174
wish image 152–4, 162, 219
Bergson, Henri (see vitalism)
Bernstein, Eduard (see Social Democracy)
Blanqui, Louis Auguste ix, xii, 1–3, 5–10, 19, 93, 120, 182, 187–92, 222, 225, 227–8, 230
Eternity by the Stars xii, 1, 2–6, 10, 187–8, 192, 225, 230
revolutionary conspiracy 8

Bloch, Ernst 56, 130, 133, 136
Borges, Jorge Luis 2, 225
Brecht, Bertolt 143, 146, 174–5, 200
Burdach, Konrad 67
Bürger, Peter 71

Caillois, Roger (see Acéphale)
Calderón de la Barca, Pedro
    (see *Trauerspiel*)
Capital (see Marx, Karl)
Capitalism viii, xi–xiii, 1, 3, 6–12, 15,
    18–20, 55–8, 61–2, 92–4, 97,
    116, 120–1, 125–32, 135–9,
    142–66, 169–206, 210, 215–16,
    219–22, 230–1
    as religion (see Benjamin, Walter)
Cartesian conception of God (see
    Descartes, René)
Cassirer, Ernst 124
Categorical Imperative (see Kant,
    Immanuel)
Caygill, Howard 27, 36
Charles, Matthew 27
Christianity (see religion)
class struggle (see Marxism)
clock metaphor (see Geulincx and
    Occasionalism)
Cohen, Hermann (see Neo-Kantianism)
Collège de Sociologie (see Acéphale)
comedy 29, 219, 221
commodity fetishism (see Marx, Karl)
communism (see Marxism) 9, 10, 97
"Communist Manifesto" (see Marx, Karl)
"On the Concept of History"
    (see Benjamin, Walter)
constellation (see Benjamin, Walter)
contradictory movement of capital (see
    Marx, Karl)
creaturely life (see Benjamin, Walter)
Critique of Judgment (see Kant, Immanuel)
critique of political economy (see Marx)
Critique of Pure Reason (see Kant,
    Immanuel)
"cracking open of natural teleology"
    (see Kant)
"Crises of Plethora" (see Fourier, Charles)
"Critique of Violence"
    (see Benjamin, Walter)
Croce, Benedetto 67

cult value (see Benjamin, Walter)
Cysarz, Herbert (see *Traurspiel*)

Debord, Guy (see Marxism)
decision (see sovereignty)
Deleuze, Gilles 201–202, 205
Derrida, Jacques xi, 33, 202
Descartes, René 15, 26, 31–4, 83–6, 88–9,
    91, 111
    Cartesian conception of God 15–16,
        81–3, 88–9, 91
    Cogito 32–3
    demon 26, 33, 84
    Meditations 26, 32–4, 84, 91
    method of doubt 13, 32, 34
    mind/body dualism 33, 88
    Occasionalism 86, 89, 91
        Arnold Geulincx' clock metaphor
        (see also psychophysical
        parallelism) 15, 86–91
dialectical image (see Benjamin, Walter)
dialectics (see also Hegel, Georg Wilhelm
    Friedrich)
"Different Utopian Will" (see Benjamin,
    Walter)
Dilthey, Wilhelm 21
doctrine of Right (see Kant, Immanuel)
drilling (see Marx, Karl)
durée (see Bergson)

eidetic intuition (see Phenomenology)
Eiland, Howard viii, 110, 146, 159, 201
Eisner, Kurt (see German Revolution)
empty, homogenous time (see time)
end of history (see Hegel, Georg Wilhelm
    Friedrich)
Engels, Friedrich (see Marxism)
Enlightenment xi, 2–3, 10, 12, 22–4, 27,
    29, 30, 33–4, 39–40, 47, 74–5,
    78, 107–8, 121, 155, 214–15, 222
"Epistemo-Critical Prologue" (see
    Benjamin, Walter)
epistemology (See theory of knowledge)
equality 1, 7–9, 25, 126–7, 136, 138–40,
    147, 150, 155, 181, 192, 206–7
    and commodity fetishism (see Marx,
        Karl)
eternal return (see Nietzsche)
eternal transience (see time)

eternalization of Capitalism (see Marx, Karl)
Eternity by the Stars (see Blanqui)
exhibition value (see Benjamin, Walter)
expenditure (see Bataille, Georges)
exposés for *The Arcades Project* (see Benjamin, Walter)
extreme, the (see Schmitt)

Fall, the (see Benjamin, Walter)
fascism xi–xii, 21, 61, 71, 161, 172–4, 176–7, 179, 200–1, 218, 220–1
fashion (see also newness) 19, 170, 180–6, 189, 191, 219
    crinoline 182, 189
fate (see Benjamin, Walter)
Fehér, Ferenc 97, 102, 157, 161
Fenves, Peter 34, 42–3, 48–9, 59, 65
Fichte, Johann Gottlieb (see German Idealism)
first and second nature (see Benjamin, Walter)
first technology (see Benjamin, Walter)
Foucault, Michel 20, 201–2, 210
Fourier, Charles (see utopian socialism)
Frankfurt School (see Institute of Social Research)
French Revolution (see Revolution)
Freud, Sigmund 167–8, 202, 205, 209–11
Friedlander, Eli 245
Friedrich, Hölderlin (see Romanticism)
Fuchs, Eduard (see Marxism)

Geiger, Moritz (see Phenomenology)
general economy (see Acéphale)
general strike (see Benjamin, Walter)
German Idealism
    Fichte, Johann Gottlieb 33, 123
    Hegel, Georg Wilhelm Friedrich 36, 73, 96–7, 116, 123–5, 127–8, 137–8, 143–6, 154, 156, 159, 161, 171, 176, 221, 226–8
    Aufhebung 150, 171
    end of history 140–1, 154, 227
    Hegel's dialectics 96–7, 127–8, 143–6, 154, 156, 171, 226–7
    Marx's use of the dialectical method (see Marx, Karl)
    owl of Minerva 227–8

Philosophy of Right 176
speculative deduction of science 123–6, 128
German Ideology (see Marx, Karl)
Geulincx, Arnold (see Descartes, René)
Goethe, Johann Wolfgang von 108, 153, 206, 216
"Good-right of the good" (see Benjamin, Walter)
Grün, Carl (see Marxism)

Habermas, Jürgen 17, 109, 221
happiness (see Benjamin, Walter)
hedonism (see Fourier, Charles)
Hegel, Georg Wilhelm Friedrich (see German Idealism)
Heidegger, Martin 11, 17, 37, 112, 119, 177
    Augenblick 17, 112–13, 116, 119
    intratemporality 114
    heritage 17, 112–13, 117–18, 175–7
    Historicity 11, 112–13, 116–18, 128, 145
Hiller, Kurt (see Revolution)
historical materialism (see Marxism)
historicity (see Heidegger)
historiography (see Benjamin, Walter)
History and Class Consciousness (See Lukács, György)
history of philosophy (see Benjamin, Walter)
Hobbes, Thomas 83
Horkheimer, Max (see Institute of Social Research)
Hornburg Letter (see Adorno, Theodor)
Horrox, James 56
Husserl, Edmund (see phenomenology)

identity principle (see mechanism)
infancy (see play)
infinite task (see Neo-Kantianism)
Institute of Social Research 39, 201–2
    Adorno, Theodor 10, 18, 31, 39, 102, 114, 118, 120, 141–3, 147, 156–61, 174–7, 182, 192, 200, 202–3, 216, 226
    Aesthetic Theory 175
    generalization of commodity fetishism (see Marx, Karl)
    Hornburg Letter 141, 159, 161, 182

Negative Dialectics 159
  and neo-Kantianism 159
Horkheimer, Max 1, 9, 146, 177, 200, 222
instrumental rationality 39, 120, 177–8
intratemporality (see Heidegger, Martin)

Jetztzeit (see Benjamin, Walter)
Jochman, Carl Gustav 179
Juliette (Sade, Marquis de)
justice (see Benjamin, Walter)

Kant, Immanuel
  biology 194–5
  categorical imperative 14, 19, 42, 43–4, 48–51, 53–4, 58, 124, 126–7, 130–1, 135–7, 140, 152, 222
  conflation of experience itself with mechanical experience (see also mechanism) 23, 27–8, 32, 38, 92, 119
  "cracking open of natural teleology" 25, 193, 196, 199–200, 212, 219
  Critique of Judgment 72
  Critique of Pure Reason 12–13, 23–5, 27–8, 30, 32–3, 38–9, 51, 72, 87, 119, 124, 194
  distinction between persons and property 42–8, 54, 58, 131, 135–7, 161, 173–4, 205–8
  doctrine of right xi, 14, 42–6, 47–51, 53, 58–9, 78–9, 108, 173, 194, 205–6
  genius, concept of 70–2, 78, 89, 174
    and sovereignty 70–2
  final purpose of creation 108, 194–7, 199
  lex permissiva 44, 47, 50, 79, 174, 206
  marriage 186, 206–7
  morality x, 8, 19–20, 25, 41–4, 46–51, 53–4, 61, 94, 108, 127, 132–3, 135, 137, 152–4, 179, 185, 193–200, 203, 206, 208, 210, 215, 219, 222, 228
    dualism of nature and morality 127, 130, 133, 194–7
    is and the ought 2, 130, 132–4, 137–8, 148, 227–8

Notrecht (see state of exception)
organism (see Kant, Immanuel, biology)
rational theology 78
res nullius xi, 43, 45, 47, 174, 206
risk of speculative rationalism 23, 26–7, 30, 36, 39
sublime 108
"true politics" 42, 44, 51, 193–4
Karatani, Kōjin 137
Karl Marx (see Korsch, Karl)
Klages, Ludwig (see vitalism)
Klee, Paul (See Benjamin, Walter)
Klossowski, Pierre (see Acéphale)
Kojève, Alexandre 146
Korsch, Karl (see Marxism)
Kraus, Karl 182, 196

labor (see Marx, Karl)
labor theory of value (see Marx, Karl)
Landauer, Gustav (see Anarchism)
Lange, Friedrich Albert (see Social Democracy)
language 35–6, 46, 65–6, 101, 212–13
  allegory 16, 69, 70, 97–104, 106, 141, 156, 157–9, 187
    as negative of the symbol 98–9
    and time 16, 99–104
  analogy 15–16, 82–91, 94–5, 100, 103, 168, 205
    of politics to natural science 16, 82, 84, 94
    of politics to theology 15–16, 82–3, 88–9
    systematic analogy 82–3, 88, 91
    of time to space (see also psychophysical parallelism) 15–16, 82, 86–9
  bourgeois conception of language 35
  language as such 35, 46
  personification 43–4, 46, 156–7, 160, 173, 177–8
  symbol 16, 82, 98–104, 141, 158, 163, 167, 172, 187, 190, 216
    money as symbol 208, 213
Laplace, Pierre-Simon 3
law of value (See Marx, Karl)
Lebensphilosophie (see vitalism)
Lenin, Vladimir (see Marxism)

Lesabéndio (see Scheerbart, Paul Karl Wilhelm)
lex permissiva (see Kant, Immanuel)
Liebknecht, Karl (see German Revolution)
life (see also first nature) x, 4, 13, 17, 20–1, 24–5, 27, 29, 31, 37, 59, 60, 72–3, 76–8, 88, 93, 95, 100, 104–5, 108–9, 111, 114–16, 118–19, 156, 162–9, 171, 195, 199–200, 202, 209
  bare life x, 13, 21, 25, 27, 29, 37, 60, 73, 109
  "creaturely life" x, 17, 24, 95, 104–5, 108–9, 111, 195, 199
  "historical life" 73, 75–7, 100, 111, 134
  and spatialization of time 17, 113, 115–16, 119
lived-experience (see experience)
Living Currency (see Klossowski, Pierre)
Locke, John 43, 177
Löwith, Karl 189
Löwy, Michael 5, 93, 110, 152, 161, 174, 230
Lukács, György 10, 16, 46, 93–4, 96–104, 120–1, 127, 130, 133, 143, 156–61, 163, 177, 190, 230–1
  critique of the *Trauerspiel* book 10, 46, 97, 102, 156–9
  History and Class Consciousness 16, 96, 98, 127, 130, 133, 143
  "Metaphysics of Tragedy" 16, 97, 98, 100, 103, 104, 190
  reification xi, 10, 16, 94, 97–8, 120–1, 157–8, 160–1, 163, 230–1
Luxemburg, Rosa (see German Revolution)
Lyotard, Jean-François 202

Malthus, Thomas (see also Social Darwinism) 126, 128–30
Marburg School (see Neo-Kantianism)
Marx, Karl xii, 3, 7, 9, 55–6, 127–30, 133–42, 144–56, 159, 200
  Capital xii, 6–7, 10, 18–19, 55, 93, 116, 127–8, 135–6, 143–50, 156, 158–60, 164, 182–4, 186
    Benjamin's study of 143–5
    commodity fetishism
      and equality 7–9, 25, 136, 138–40, 148, 150
    generalization of 18, 121, 150, 159–60, 165, 230
  "Communist Manifesto" 3, 93, 155, 186
  contradictory movement of capital viii, 156, 164–6, 183, 194, 199
  critique of Blanqui 9–10
  "Critique of the Gotha Program" 130, 138–9, 177–8
  critique of Lange (see also Lange, Friedrich Albert) 127–30
  critique of political economy xi–xii, 7–8, 12, 18, 61, 93, 121, 128, 135–7, 140, 143–8, 158, 199
  eternalization of capitalism in political economy 94, 121, 126, 146
  principal of historical specification 18, 143, 151
  dialectical method, Marx's use of 128, 144
  drilling 169–70
  exchange value 7, 139, 150, 156, 159–60, 164, 182–5, 208, 231
  German Ideology 152, 169
  Grundrisse 138
  inverse relation between value and technology (see also contradictory movement of capital)
  labor 164
    abstract labor 12, 20, 164
    labor theory of value 147–50, 173
    law of value 7, 146, 149
    vulgar Marxist notion of labor 165, 177–8, 219
  on the Paris Commune 55
  primitive communism 142
  principle of historical specification 18, 143, 151
  use value 136, 148–50, 159, 160, 164, 177, 184–5
  young Marx 136, 144
Marxism
  communism 9, 10, 97
    primitive communism 142, 151–2, 186
  class struggle viii, x, 29, 109, 180–1
  Debord, Guy 176

Engels, Friedrich 3, 9–10, 123, 125, 127–30, 133, 145, 152, 154–6, 160, 186, 188
Fuchs, Eduard 134, 156, 181, 183
historical materialism 18, 130
   neo-Kantian view of (see neo-Kantianism) 130, 133–5, 137, 140, 159
   Korsch, Karl 6–10, 18, 128, 136, 142–6, 148–52, 159, 180
      influence on Benjamin 6, 143–5
      Karl Marx 6, 142–9
      Marxism and Philosophy 143–4
   Lenin, Vladimir 125, 133, 143
   orthodox Marxism 10, 18, 145–6, 161
      Grün, Carl 142, 152, 154, 156, 185
      Plekhanov, Georgi 18, 134, 146
Marxism and Philosophy (see Korsch)
Massey, Heath 114–15
Matiere et memoire (see vitalism)
mechanical reason (see Mechanism)
mechanical reproduction (see Mechanism)
mechanical warfare (see war)
mechanism 4, 62, 86, 90–3, 114, 120, 125–6, 130, 196–7
   identity principle 25–6, 31, 33, 35, 45, 84, 86, 89
      "fixing of the concept of identity" 34–6
   mechanical experience (see experience)
   mechanical reason x–xii, 4–6, 12–13, 20, 22, 24–31, 36, 38–40, 54, 71, 85, 91–2, 114, 119, 121, 142, 163–4
      "extreme extension" of mechanical reason in neo-Kantianism 22, 39
   mechanical time (see time)
   "natural-historical troping" 83, 86
   natural science xii, 3–7, 12–13, 15–16, 20, 24–8, 30, 32, 39–40, 82–9, 91–5, 111, 114–15, 119, 123–4, 126–7, 134, 149, 156, 162–3, 177, 189, 194, 230
   Newtonian physics 4, 23, 28, 31, 40
   principle of non-contradiction 25–6, 31, 118
Mehlman, Jeffrey 202

Mehring, Franz (see Social Democracy)
messianism (see Benjamin, Walter)
metaphysics 23, 26, 30, 39, 123, 125–6
   metaphysical anarchism (see Scholem, Gershom)
   "Metaphysics of Tragedy" (see Lukács, György)
Meyerson, Émile 84
Mickey Mouse (see Benjamin, Walter)
modernity (see Benjamin, Walter)
morality (see Kant, Immanuel)
Mosès, Stéphane
mythology

natural science (see Mechanism)
nature
   first and second nature (see Benjamin, Walter)
Nietzsche, Friedrich (see vitalism)
neo-Kantianism 4, 12–13, 17–18, 21, 23, 25, 39, 119–220, 123–5, 133–5, 191
   Baden School 12, 21, 25, 120
   Cohen, Hermann xi, 22, 61, 99, 103, 107, 120, 124–7, 131–40
      concept of allegory as ambiguity 99, 103
      concept of messianism xi
   Marburg School 4, 12–13, 21–3, 25, 31, 107, 119, 123–5, 130–4, 140, 168
   "extreme extension" of mechanical reason in Neo-Kantianism (see mechanism)
   infinite task xi, 10, 13, 15, 18, 20, 30–1, 36, 52, 107, 110, 119, 123–4, 131–3, 140, 148, 191, 199, 228
   Rickert, Heinrich 21, 25, 37–8, 84, 107, 114, 134, 147
      seminar on Bergson 37, 84, 114
   Riehl, Alois 84
   view of historical materialism 18, 130, 133–4, 137
   Windelband, Wilhelm 86, 147, 194–5
      and the concept of value 147
newness (see Benjamin, Walter)
Newtonian physics (see natural science)
Ng, Julia 27
Nietzsche, Friedrich (see vitalism)

nihilism ix, 22, 76, 91, 97–8, 105, 153, 157–8
  and allegory 157–8
  Benjamin's nihilism versus Nietzsche's 97–8, 228–9
  "incomplete nihilism" 76
  and messianism 91, 105, 153
  method of ix
  revolutionary nihilism 163
  Russian nihilists 22
nominalism 15, 25, 67–8, 226
"Notes Toward a Work on the Category of Justice" (see Benjamin, Walter)
Novalis (Romanticism)
novelty (see newness)
"now of knowability" (see Benjamin, Walter)

Occasionalism (see Descartes, René)
ought, the (see Morality)
owl of Minerva (see Hegel, Georg Wilhelm Friedrich)

"paradox of the Cretan" (see Benjamin, Walter)
Paris Commune (see Revolution)
personification (see language)
perversion (see Acéphale)
phalanstery (see Fourier)
phantasmagoria (see Benjamin, Walter)
phenomenological reduction (see Phenomenology)
phenomenology xii, 13, 15, 21, 31, 34–9, 51, 64–5, 91, 114, 146
  Geiger, Moritz 31, 64–5
  Husserl, Edmund 5, 12–13, 15, 21, 31–9, 64–5, 87, 91, 95, 114
    eidetic Intuition 31–4, 37–9, 64–5
philosophy of history x–xi, 11–12, 30, 81, 107–8, 119, 134, 136, 153, 230
  "conservative-revolutionary" conception of history (see Habermas, Jürgen)
Philosophy of Money (see Simmel)
Pinloche, Auguste 151, 153, 179, 196
Plato 21, 23
play 10, 19–20, 29, 154, 166–73, 179–80, 188, 193, 198, 200–1, 203, 209–13, 215, 218–19, 221–2

  and infancy 168, 171
  and *praxis* 167
  and repetition 167–70
  and *Spielraum* 168, 170–2
  and toys 168–9
  and tradition 167–72
Plekhanov, Georgi (see Marxism)
police (see violence)
Political Theology (see Schmitt, Carl)
politics, treatise on (see Benjamin, Walter)
"pre-fascist aestheticism" (see Bataille)
"primacy of the thingly" (see Benjamin, Walter)
primal history (see Benjamin, Walter)
primitive communism (see Marx, Karl)
principle of historical specification (see Marx, Karl)
principle of non-contradiction (see mechanical reason)
profane illumination (see Benjamin, Walter)
profane messianism (see Benjamin, Walter)
profane redemption (see Benjamin, Walter)
profane, the (see Benjamin, Walter)
profane theology (see Benjamin, Walter)
"Program of the Coming Philosophy" (see Benjamin, Walter)
progress (see Enlightenment)
property xi–xii, 7, 12, 14, 18–20, 42–8, 50, 58, 79, 131, 135–6, 144, 161–2, 168, 172–4, 176–81, 200, 205–7, 219, 220
  Kantian distinction between persons and property (see Kant, Immanuel)
  private and collective ownership 45
Proudhon, Pierre 138–40, 142
Proust, Marcel 4–5, 113, 116
psychoanalysis 20, 202
psychophysical parallelism (see time)

Quaini, Carolina viii

Rang, Florens Christian 100
Reflections on Violence (see Anarchism)
reification (see Lukács, György)

religion 3, 5, 27–9, 56, 61–3, 75, 90–3,
    119–221, 134, 136, 141–2, 155,
    158, 176, 189, 190
  "Capitalism as Religion" (see
    Benjamin, Walter)
  Christianity 17, 72, 92, 100, 121, 142
  messianism (see Benjamin, Walter)
  theology x, 5–6, 12–16, 23–4, 27–9, 74,
    78–85, 89–93, 97–8, 102, 104–5,
    119, 121, 126, 155, 175–7,
    191–2, 195, 217–18, 230–1
  atheology (see Acéphale)
  negative theology 77, 176, 218
  political theology 15, 73–5, 78–83,
    89, 90, 98
  profane theology (see Benjamin,
    Walter)
  rational theology (see Kant,
    Immanuel)
repetition (see play)
res nullius (see Kant, Immanuel)
revolution xii, 1–3, 6–9, 11, 17, 19, 41,
    55–7, 59–61, 98, 110, 113, 124,
    139, 154–5, 170–1, 178–81, 183,
    193, 196–9, 207, 226–7, 230
  French Revolution 1–3, 7–9, 55, 60,
    110, 113, 139, 155, 181, 199,
    107, 226–7
    Robespierre, Maximilien 8–9, 113
    Paris Commune 1, 55, 188
    Terror, the 8, 60, 174, 227
  German Revolution 41, 57, 59–61
    Hiller, Kurt 59–61
    Munich Soviet Republic 41, 59, 241
    Spartacist Uprising 41, 59–60;
      Eisner, Kurt 124; Liebknecht,
      Karl 59; Luxemburg, Rosa 124
  as innervation of the collective 178,
    193, 196–7
  July Revolution 1
  Paris Commune 1, 55, 188
  Russian Revolution 41, 56, 59
Rickert, Heinrich (see Neo-Kantianism)
Riegl, Alois 63, 84
Riehl, Alois (see Neo-Kantianism)
Robespierre, Maximilien (see French
    Revolution)
Romanticism 33
  Hölderlin, Friedrich 87, 95, 100–1, 115

Novalis 35
Schlegel, Friedrich 35, 225
Rose, Gillian 159

sabbatianism (see Scholem, Gershom)
sacred, the (see Bataille)
sacrifice xii, 217–21
Sade, Marquis de 199, 201–5, 207–16, 219,
    222–3
  Juliette 207
  on money 207–9, 213–14, 222
  120 Days of Sodom 209, 212
Scheerbart, Paul Karl Wilhelm 197–8
  Lesabéndio 197
Schlegel, Friedrich (see Romanticism)
Schmitt, Carl x, 14–16, 61, 63–7, 71–5,
    77–8, 80–3, 89–90, 92–3, 96–8,
    120, 173, 177
  Crisis of Parliamentary Democracy 61
  decision 16, 52, 71–5, 78–9, 89, 94, 98,
    173, 179
  extreme, the 15, 63, 65–72, 74–6, 80,
    82, 106, 173, 179, 226
    aesthetic extreme (see Walter,
      Benjamin)
  Political Theology 15, 74–5, 78, 80–1,
    90
  sociology of sovereignty 81–2
  sovereignty 16, 63, 66–7, 70–6, 78–83,
    156, 179, 218
  state of exception (see Benjamin,
    Walter)
  systematic analogy 88, 91
Scholem, Gershom 12, 22, 30–1, 34, 38,
    41, 56, 60, 65, 70, 96–7, 107–9,
    114, 116, 123, 143, 145, 193–4,
    201–2
  metaphysical anarchism 11, 12, 15,
    17, 110
  sabbatianism 202
Schopenhauer, Arthur (see vitalism)
second nature (see reification)
second technology (see Benjamin, Walter)
secularization x, xii, 5, 12, 29, 79, 80, 82–3,
    89–97, 100, 104–5, 111, 120,
    175–6, 229, 230
  and secularization of history and
    spatialization of time 94–6
Weber, Max 90, 92, 121, 177

semblance (see Benjamin, Walter)
"seriousness of work and desire
    (see Klossowski)
seventeenth century (see Baroque)
sexual fetishism 19
Shakespeare, William (see *Trauerspiel*)
Simmel, Georg 18, 37, 125, 134, 147–50,
    159–60, 162, 164–5, 183
  critique of Marx 147–50
  "petty-bourgeois-idealist theory of
    labor" 149, 159
  Philosophy and Culture 183
  Philosophy of Money 18, 147–50, 162
"slave revolt of technology" (see Benjamin,
    Walter)
Social Democracy 18, 41, 55–6, 59, 112,
    123–4, 126, 138, 140, 150, 165,
    170, 177–9, 181
  Bernstein, Eduard 18, 124, 126, 130
  Lange, Friedrich Albert 93, 123–31,
    137, 149
    *The History of Materialism and
    Critique of its Contemporary
    Significance* 123, 126
    and Social Darwinism 127
  Mehring, Franz 124–5, 130
  Stadler, August 124, 147
  Vorländer, Karl 124, 137, 134–5, 137
Social Darwinism (see Social Democracy)
Sorel, Georges (see Anarchism)
sovereignty (see Schmitt, Carl)
Spartacist Uprising (see German
    Revolution)
spatialization of time (see time)
Spielraum (see play)
state of exception (see sovereignty)
Stifter, Adalbert 92
Surrealism 28–9, 163
  Naville, Pierre 163
symbol (see Language)

Tagliacozzo, Tamara 111
Taubes, Jacob 80
technology (see Benjamin, Walter)
teleology without final purpose (see
    Benjamin, Walter)
Terror, the (see French Revolution)
theology (see Religion)

"Theological-Political Fragment"
    (see Benjamin, Walter)
theory of knowledge 12–13, 15, 22–32,
    36, 39–41, 45, 51, 54, 67, 91, 97,
    116, 119–20, 124, 139, 141, 163
time
  empty, homogenous time 2, 4, 15–17,
    84, 87, 89, 95 99–100, 106,
    110–15, 118–20, 140, 168, 191,
    229
  mechanical time 4–5, 17, 20, 23, 85, 91,
    107, 111–19, 162–4, 191, 228–9
  mechanical time versus value 12,
    20, 164, 230–1
  spatialization of time 15–17, 87–9,
    95–101, 105, 109, 111, 113–16,
    119–21, 188, 191, 229–30
  psychophysical parallelism 15–16,
    87–9, 94, 101
  transience ix–x, 4, 16–17, 77, 103–6,
    111, 118–20, 191, 229
  eternal transience ix, 104–5, 111,
    118, 120, 191, 229, 230
toys (see play)
tradition (see Benjamin, Walter)
tragedy (see *Trauerspiel*)
Trần Đức Thảo 245, 260
Transcritique (see Karatani, Kojin)
transgression (see Bataille, Georges)
transience (see time)
Trauerspiel (see Benjamin, Walter)

Urbich, Jan 96, 158
use value (see Marx)
utopian socialism xii, 10, 12, 151, 153, 155,
    180, 181, 186, 191, 193, 196–7,
    203, 207, 210–13, 267
  Bellamy, Edward 180
  Campanella, Tommaso 180
  Fourier, Charles xi, xii, 8, 10, 12, 18–
    20, 142, 151–7, 159–63, 165–7,
    169, 171, 173, 175, 178–81, 183
    "colossal conception of man" 152,
      155, 197
    "cracking open of natural teleology"
      (see Kant, Immanuel)
    crises of plethora 19, 155, 161, 166,
      179, 183–4, 199, 214, 220–1

hedonism xi, 19–20, 25, 152–3,
    196–7, 199–200, 202, 209, 212
  "humorous annihilation" of
    capitalism 154, 165, 179, 191,
    199, 219
  influence on Marx xii, 18, 151–2,
    155
  phalanstery 10, 151–5, 165, 180,
    185–6, 193, 196–7, 203, 209–13,
    221
  rebellion of the mode of
    production against mode of
    exchange xi, xii, 18, 156, 161,
    162, 165, 176, 184, 193, 214,
    220, 222
  transformation of work into play
    10, 19–20, 166, 171–3, 179, 193,
    198, 213, 219
More, Thomas 180

Valéry, Paul 182
value (see Marx, Karl)
violence (see Benjamin, Walter)
vitalism 5, 12–13, 19, 21, 31, 37, 39, 93–4,
    111, 114, 124, 162–3, 191
  Bergson, Henri (see also spatialization
    of time) 5, 12, 21, 37, 81–9, 95,
    99–101, 113–15, 163
  durée 87, 95, 100–1, 114–15
  *Essai Sur Les Données Immédiates
    De La Conscience* 114
  Matière et mémoire 21
  seminar on (see Rickert, Heinrich)

Klages, Ludwig 5, 21, 141, 162–3,
    171–2
Nietzsche, Friedrich 3–4, 12, 19, 21, 39,
    76, 93, 111, 162, 186–91, 202,
    222, 225–9
  eternal return 2–6, 10–11, 19–20,
    111, 120, 130, 144, 162–3,
    186–91, 222, 226, 228–31
Schopenhauer, Arthur 112
Vorländer, Karl (see Social Democracy)
vulgar Marxist notion of labor (see Marx,
    Karl)

war xii, 41, 50, 155, 161–2, 166, 169,
    172–3, 178–80, 194, 196, 198–9,
    203, 218, 220–2
  mechanical warfare xii, 22, 169, 179,
    203, 218, 220–1
  World War I 205, 217–20
  World War II 205, 217–20
Weber, Max (see secularization)
Weber, Samuel 66–7, 70, 77, 109
Windelband, Wilhelm (see Neo-
    Kantianism)
wish image (see Benjamin, Walter)
Wohlfarth, Irving 163, 179
Wolin, Richard 18, 23, 28–9, 38, 77, 102,
    104–5, 108–9, 140, 150, 162
Wyneken, Gustav 143

Young Marx (see Marx, Karl)
"unimproved humanity" (see Benjamin,
    Walter)

www.ingramcontent.com/pod-product-compliance
Lightning Source LLC
Chambersburg PA
CBHW052153300426
44115CB00011B/1645